CLASSICAL SĀṂKHYA AND YOGA

Sāṃkhya and Yoga are among the oldest and most influential systems of classical Indian thought and religious practice. In their classical forms they constitute two of the six major systems of Hindu philosophy, and their influence has been pervasive throughout Indian culture. Despite this, much in the core texts of Sāṃkhya and Yoga, the *Sāṃkhyakārikā* and *Yogasūtra*, remains poorly understood. This book provides a thorough examination of Sāṃkhya and Yoga. Placing particular emphasis on the metaphysical schema which underlies both systems, the author adeptly develops a new interpretation of these systems and exposes the weaknesses of standard views. He shows how Sāṃkhya–Yoga metaphysics can be most coherently understood when regarded as an analysis of experience. Drawing upon existing sources and using insights from both Eastern and Western philosophy and religious practice, this comprehensive interpretation is respectful to the underlying spiritual purpose of the Indian systems, whilst illuminating the relation between the theoretical and practical dimensions of Sāṃkhya and Yoga. The book fills a gap in current scholarship and will be of interest to those concerned with Indology, especially Indian philosophies and their similarities and differences with other traditions.

Mikel Burley received his PhD in Indian philosophy from the University of Bristol, and currently teaches in the School of Philosophy at the University of Leeds. His previous publications include *Haṭha-Yoga: Its Context, Theory and Practice* and numerous articles on both Western and Indian philosophy.

ROUTLEDGE HINDU STUDIES SERIES
Series Editor: Gavin Flood, *University of Stirling*
Former Series Editor: Francis X. Clooney, SJ, *Harvard University*

The *Routledge Hindu Studies Series*, in association with the Oxford Centre for Hindu Studies, intends the publication of constructive Hindu theological, philosophical and ethical projects aimed at bringing Hindu traditions into dialogue with contemporary trends in scholarship and contemporary society. The series invites original, high quality, research level work on religion, culture and society of Hindus living in India and abroad. Proposals for annotated translations of important primary sources and studies in the history of the Hindu religious traditions will also be considered.

EPISTEMOLOGIES AND THE LIMITATIONS OF PHILOSOPHICAL INQUIRY
Doctrine in Mādhva Vedānta
Deepak Sarma

A HINDU CRITIQUE OF BUDDHIST EPISTEMOLOGY
Kumārila on perception
The 'determination of perception' chapter of Kumārilabhaṭṭa's *Ślokavārttika* – Translation and commentary
John Taber

ŚAṂKARA'S ADVAITA VEDĀNTA
A way of teaching
Jacqueline Hirst

ATTENDING KṚṢṆA'S IMAGE
Caitanya Vaiṣṇava mūrti-sevā as devotional truth
Kenneth Russell Valpey

ADVAITA VEDĀNTA AND VAIṢṆAVISM
The philosophy of Madhusūdana Sarasvatī
Sanjukta Gupta

CLASSICAL SĀṂKHYA AND YOGA
An Indian metaphysics of experience
Mikel Burley

CLASSICAL SĀṂKHYA AND YOGA

An Indian metaphysics of experience

Mikel Burley

Routledge
Taylor & Francis Group
LONDON AND NEW YORK

First published 2007
by Routledge
2 Park Square, Milton Park, Abingdon, Oxon OX14 4RN

Simultaneously published in the USA and Canada
by Routledge
711 Third Avenue, New York, NY 10017

Routledge is an imprint of the Taylor & Francis Group, an informa business

First issued in paperback 2012

Typeset in Times New Roman by
Newgen Imaging Systems (P) Ltd, Chennai, India

British Library Cataloguing in Publication Data
A catalogue record for this book is available from the British Library

Library of Congress Cataloging in Publication Data
A catalog record for this book has been requested

ISBN13: 978–0–415–39448–2 hardback
ISBN13: 978–0-415-64887-5 paperback

CONTENTS

SERIES EDITOR'S PREFACE

The Routledge Hindu Studies Series, published in collaboration with the Oxford Centre for Hindu Studies, intends primarily the publication of constructive Hindu theological, philosophical and ethical projects. The focus is on issues and concerns of relevance to readers interested in Hindu traditions in particular, yet also in the context of a wider range of related religious concerns that matter in today's world. The Series seeks to promote excellent scholarship and, in relation to it, an open and critical conversation among scholars and the wider audience of interested readers. Though contemporary in its purpose, the Series recognizes the importance of retrieving the classic texts and ideas, beliefs and practices, of Hindu traditions, so that the great intellectuals of these traditions may as it were become conversation partners in the conversations of today.

The Indian philosophical tradition known as Sāṃkhya has attracted less attention from scholars than other systems of thought, particularly Vedānta. Yet Sāṃkhya is an extremely important tradition. Although the developed system itself is probably quite late (not predating the Buddha who died around 400 BCE), Sāṃkhya could arguably be said to lie at the root of Indian philosophical traditions both in the sense that Sāṃkhya-like speculation can be traced to the very earliest developments, and in the sense that Sāṃkhya categories are assumed and used by the later systems. The prototypical Indian philosophy is often taken in the West to be some kind of monism, yet Sāṃkhya is an uncompromisingly dualist system that upholds an ontological distinction between self and 'matter' or 'nature'. Furthermore, it is one of the earliest traditions to offer a description of human experience; how contact with the world through the senses occurs, and how this contact is processed through our mental apparatus.

Mikel Burley's lucidly clear book is the first for a number of years to offer a historical and systematic study of Sāṃkhya. Not only does the book present Sāṃkhya as a system of historical interest or curiosity, it takes the tradition seriously as philosophy and engages with it in terms of philosophical debates in the West over realism and non-realism, offering a more nuanced interpretation. The book also offers a convincing account of the relationship between Sāṃkhya and Yoga showing how they share a dualist metaphysics. One of the original features of the book is the way it deals with the problem of the fundamental categories or *tattvas*, having both a cosmological and psychological designation. On the one hand they seem to be presented as an account of how the universe unfolds in a causal sequence in which fundamental matter is transformed into multiple forms, on the other they are presented as an account of how human experience arises. The problem can be resolved, argues Burley, if we abandon a realistic and diachronic interpretation in favour of a reading that takes the *tattvas* as a synchronic analysis of experience. Burley shows how the *tattvas* can be understood in terms of transcendental conditionality rather than as direct causality and offers an original account of the elements as the forms that must accompany sensory content rather than as material entities that are themselves transformations of more subtle entities. What makes this an important book is its philosophically sophisticated readings of the Sāṃkhya and Yoga texts based on an accurate exegesis that offers corrections of previous readings. The power or Burley's philosophical reading is that it is firmly grounded in close, textual study. Rather than an inchoate account of entities beyond direct perceptual grasp, Sāṃkhya is a systematic account of cognition and the senses, a phenomenology of human experience akin to accounts developed by Kant and later philosophers. With this book we have a return of Sāṃkhya and Yoga as philosophical accounts of human being in the world which need to be taken seriously by all engaged with Indian and comparative philosophy.

Gavin Flood
Series Editor

PREFACE

I began thinking hard about the meaning of metaphysics in classical Sāṃkhya and Yoga in 1996, when I undertook a research MA on this subject at the University of Nottingham. At that time I was quite attracted to the view that the soteric aspirations of Sāṃkhya and Yoga involve merely a dissociation of one's sense of identity from the panoply of spatiotemporal objects and events that arise and subside in the world around us. On this view, the process of attaining 'aloneness' (*kaivalya*) or 'release' (*mokṣa*) is one of steadily reducing and eventually eradicating one's false identification with worldly phenomena – including supposedly 'internal' phenomena such as thoughts and sensations – but it need not have any ontological consequences for the phenomena themselves. Of course, if one engages in a disciplined programme of yogic meditation then, inevitably, the sorts of thoughts and feelings that arise in one's consciousness will be modified thereby (although not in a way that is necessarily predictable). But the thoughts and feelings, and other mental activities (*vṛtti*s) will still exist, and so will the entities one experiences 'out there in the world'. This might be called the 'reformist' view of Sāṃkhya and Yoga: it sees the goal of these systems as consisting in a shift of self-identity accompanied by a 'purification' of one's experience at the levels of emotional responsiveness, perceptual acuity, and general epistemic performance: we come, through the sustained implementation of yogic techniques, to know ourselves and the world more thoroughly – we see things as they 'truly are'.

After completing my MA at Nottingham in 1997, I moved my focus of attention to Tantric traditions of Yoga, especially *haṭha-yoga*, and explored this fascinating area both theoretically and practically. This research involved some intensive training in India and Nepal, and resulted in my first book, *Haṭha-Yoga: Its Context, Theory and Practice* (2000). *Haṭha-yoga* tends to be saturated with elaborate symbolism, as does Tantrism more generally. The theory underlying the practice is so overlaid with imagery – relating to tutelary deities, energy channels (*nāḍī*s) and plexuses (*cakra*s), mythological creatures and the coiled serpent-power (*kuṇḍalinī-śakti*) – that the pithy mnemonic statements of classical Yoga's *Yogasūtra* appear arid by comparison. This imagery creates a rich and colourful mythic environment within which Tantric practice occurs. It is an environment that can, however, be worrying for those such as myself who have a persistent intellectual urge to ask: What does this all *mean*?

Thus I have repeatedly been drawn back to the classical *darśana*s ('viewpoints', 'systems') – to the apothegmatic 'threads' of the *Yogasūtra* and the dense poetry of the *Sāṃkhyakārikā*. And it was in these two religio-philosophical systems that I immersed myself from 2001, when I began working in earnest on the project that resulted in my PhD at the University of Bristol (2005), and, after some substantial revisions of my doctoral dissertation, in the book that you are now reading.

As my study of the traditional texts deepened, the 'reformist' reading became increasingly less plausible to me. I began to see that what Sāṃkhya and Yoga advocate is more than a process of bringing our experience progressively into closer conformity with the true nature of empirical reality. Instead, they seem to be proposing something more radical, namely that we should come to recognize that empirical reality is purely contingent. It is not a collection of entities that exists independently of its being encountered by conscious subjects, but is, rather, generated as a consequence of (something approximating) that very encounter. The encounter in question is between two principles, one of them being what Sāṃkhya generally calls the 'self' (*puruṣa*) and Yoga calls the 'seer' (*draṣṭṛ*), and the other being what Sāṃkhya generally calls *prakṛti* and Yoga calls the 'seeable' (*dṛśya*). Of these terms, I find *prakṛti* the hardest to translate by a single English term. Etymologically, it is very close to the words 'procreate' and 'procreatrix', the latter of which has the sense of a feminine creative source or 'mother'. These implications of creativity and femininity are perfectly apt for *prakṛti*; however, 'procreatrix' is too unfamiliar a word to serve as a workable translation, and 'procreate' is not nounal enough.

Prakṛti has typically been translated as 'matter' (or as 'primordial matter' and similar expressions), which is a highly problematic translation because it is so likely to be interpreted in a narrowly realist sense. By this I mean that it is liable to be construed as referring primarily to the sort of stuff that common sense and most contemporary science tell us composes the physical universe that we inhabit and roam around in. On the whole, people assume that this universe, though affected by our physical actions, is not touched by our mere experience of it. I think the confusions that arise from assuming that prakṛti is 'matter' in *that* sense are littered throughout the secondary literature on Sāṃkhya and Yoga. My view now is that prakṛti is 'matter' only in the sense that it is that which makes up *the matter of experience*. It is, very roughly speaking, the content of experience, but is also its own formal container. Puruṣa, meanwhile, is the bare witness, to whom container and content are displayed. This metaphor is too crude to take us very far, but it gets us started. The crucial point is that, if prakṛti is the matter of experience, then it makes no sense to think of prakṛti and its manifestations as 'real' in a sense that implies mind-independence. According to Sāṃkhya and Yoga, the mind–world (or empirical-self–world) distinction is something that occurs *within* experience, rather than experience being something that happens within the mind. Thus, for these systems, there is no sense in which experience and one's conception of selfhood can be transformed without, at the same time, the empirical world being transformed.

Ultimately the goal of Sāṃkhya and Yoga is to reach a self-sufficient state, in which all empirical factors have been disidentified with and experience possesses no further purpose. At that point, experience ceases, and hence the world ceases too. This might be called the 'abolitionist' interpretation of Sāṃkhya and Yoga, since it takes it to be the view of these systems that the liberated state is not one in which experience has been emotionally and epistemically purified or reformed; rather, experience, and the world that featured in it, have been abolished. This interpretation tends to produce in us more discomfort than the 'reformist' one, for understandable reasons. We are, after all, very attached to the idea that experience is something worth having, and worth having in itself, not merely because it is a means to some higher spiritual end. Sāṃkhya and Yoga do not promise us an afterlife in heaven. They do speak of heavenly realms, but these are merely temporary stations that offer less distressing modes of experience from that which we endure in the present life; they are not the final destination. That final destination is not merely beyond words, but beyond experience, and hence nothing intelligible can be said about it.

I do, at various places, and in Chapter 7 in particular, try to say *something* intelligible about the liberated state. But for the most part, the reader will be glad to hear, I try to stick to matters about which intelligible things can be said, notably the metaphysical schema that forms the contribution to philosophical theory for which Sāṃkhya in particular is most immediately recognized. Whether what I have said about it succeeds in being intelligible is a matter that readers will have to judge for themselves.

There are many people whose assistance has enabled me in one way or another to bring this project to its current state. Looking back to my years as an undergraduate at the University of Essex (1990–1993), I'd like to thank Jay Bernstein (now at The New School for Social Research, New York) for his inspiring lectures and seminars on Kant's critical philosophy and on phenomenology. Little did I (or he) know at the time how these strands of modern Western thought would inform my thinking about classical Indian philosophy. It was also at Essex that I first met Nick Bunnin (now Director of the Institute for Chinese Studies, University of Oxford), whose dual commitment to Western and Chinese philosophy has spurred me to persevere with my own peculiar menagerie of interests.

My teachers at the University of Nottingham were Jonardon Ganeri (now at the University of Liverpool) and Brian Carr (now at the University of Exeter). I am grateful to both of them, and also to Ian Whicher (now at the University of Manitoba), who I first met in Cambridge at that time and with whom I have since had some interesting correspondence. Our views on Yoga have diverged increasingly over the years, and he will not agree with the interpretation presented herein; but disagreement is not unfruitful in philosophy.

The doctoral research that forms the more immediate background of this book was supervised by John Peacock at the University of Bristol. I wish to thank him, and other members of the Department of Theology and Religious Studies, notably Paul Williams and Rupert Gethin. Staff at Bristol's Arts and Social Sciences Library also deserve thanks for their efficiency in obtaining the many out-of-print obscurities that I requested.

At Routledge, Dorothea Schaefter and Tom Bates have guided the book towards publication. I extend my thanks to them, and to two anonymous reviewers who provided helpful comments on an early draft; and also to Gavin Flood (Universities of Oxford and Stirling) who, as editor of the Hindu Studies Series, has been immensely supportive from the outset.

Parts of Chapter 7 formed the basis of an article, ' "Aloneness" and the Problem of Realism in Classical Sāṃkhya and Yoga', which was published in *Asian Philosophy*, vol. 14, no. 3 (November 2004). I am grateful to the editors of that journal, Indira Mahalingam and Brian Carr, and to Carfax Publishing (http://www.tandf.co.uk/journals/carfax/09552367.html) for permission to re-use the material in this book.

On a more personal note, I wish to thank my parents, Stephanie and Roger, who have not only tolerated but actively encouraged my idiosyncratic pursuits; and Sue Richardson, without whom I don't know where I would be.

Mikel Burley
University of Leeds
December 2005

NOTE ON THE USE OF ITALICS AND UNDERLINING

In the literature on Indian philosophy there is no universal standard of practice concerning the italicization of Sanskrit terms. Some scholars invariably italicize them, while others do so very sparingly. Although I do not claim to be entirely consistent in my use of italics, I generally employ them in the following cases: (*a*) when a Sanskrit term is being used for the first time in the work as a whole; (*b*) when the term (or phrase, etc.) appears in parentheses to indicate what an English term is intended to stand for; (*c*) when it is the word itself, or the concept, that is being indicated, as distinct from the referrent of the word; (*d*) in footnotes, when the original version of a sentence or verse that has been quoted in the main text is given.

In several places, when quoting from the works of other scholars, I have made use of underlining as a means of emphasizing certain terms or statements. This is to avoid confusion when the original passage already contains one or more italicized words. In those cases where the original passage contains no italics, I have myself used italics for the purpose of supplying emphasis. I have acknowledged all cases where emphasis has been added.

ABBREVIATIONS

Ahir.	*Ahirbudhnya-saṃhitā*
BhG/Gītā	*Bhagavadgītā*
Bṛhad.	*Bṛhadāraṇyaka-upaniṣad*
BSBh	*Brahmasūtrabhāṣya* (of Śaṅkarācārya)
CPR/Critique	Kant's *Critique of Pure Reason* [I have followed the standard practice of indicating its first and second editions by the letters 'A' and 'B' respectively]
EIP	*Encyclopedia of Indian Philosophies* (general editor, Karl Potter)
*EIP*4	*Encyclopedia of Indian Philosophies*, vol. 4, entitled: *Sāṃkhya: A Dualist Tradition in Indian Philosophy*, edited by Larson and Bhattacharya
GBh	*Gauḍapādabhāṣya* (of Gauḍapāda)
Maitr.	*Maitrāyaṇīya-/Maitrī-upaniṣad*
MBh	*Mahābhārata*
MW	Monier–Williams' *Sanskrit–English Dictionary*
Prol.	Kant's *Prolegomena to Any Future Metaphysics*
SK/Kārikā	*Sāṃkhyakārikā* (of Īśvarakṛṣṇa)
SPBh	*Sāṃkhyapravacanabhāṣya* (of Vijñānabhikṣu)
SS	*Sāṃkhyasūtra* (attributed to Kapila)
SSV	*Sāṃkhyasūtravṛtti* (of Aniruddha)
STV	*Sāṃkhyataruvasanta* (of Muḍumba Narasiṃhasvāmin)
Śvet.	*Śvetāśvatara-upaniṣad*
TK	*Tattvakaumudī* (of Vācaspatimiśra)
TV	*Tattvavaiśāradī* (of Vācaspatimiśra)
up.	*Upaniṣad*
Webster's	*Webster's Third New International Dictionary of the English Language* (unabridged), 16th edn, 3 vols (paginated consecutively)
YBh/Bhāṣya	*Yogabhāṣya* (attributed to Vyāsa)
YD	*Yuktidīpikā*
YS	*Yogasūtra* (attributed to Patañjali)
YV	*Yogavārttika* (of Vijñānabhikṣu)

INTRODUCTION

The present work is the result of a detailed inquiry into the classical systems of Indian philosophy known as Sāṃkhya and Yoga. My aim has been to develop an interpretation that takes seriously the claim of these systems to provide a comprehensive strategy for the overcoming of suffering and discontent by means of spiritual awakening.

Many previous attempts have been made by scholars to present the philosophies of Sāṃkhya and Yoga in an intelligible fashion, and some of these have made extremely valuable contributions to a general understanding of the subject. I am not, however, convinced that any previous interpretation has adequately explained the relation between, on the one hand, the schema of metaphysical principles or categories set forth systematically in the *Sāṃkhyakārikā* and alluded to in the *Yogasūtra*, and, on the other hand, the professed salvific goal of establishing the 'self' (*puruṣa*) or 'seer' (*draṣṭṛ*) in a state of immaculate disassociation from empirical existence. I do not claim to have unravelled all the intricate mysteries of Sāṃkhya and Yoga; indeed, it would not be feasible to try to cover every aspect of these systems within a single study. I do, however, feel confident that the aspects I have focused upon have been dealt with here in a way that represents a significant advance on much of the existing interpretive literature.

What are classical Sāṃkhya and Yoga?

I have already referred to Sāṃkhya and Yoga as systems of Indian philosophy. When I use the term 'systems' in this way, the Sanskrit term that I have chiefly in mind is *darśana*. A *darśana* is literally a 'vision', an event of 'seeing'; but, more figuratively, it has traditionally been used to mean a worldview or systematic attempt to represent how reality is. Thus a *darśana* can be said to be a philosophy, or a philosophical viewpoint or system.

As is to be expected from a highly evolved culture, or collection of cultures, with a history as long and colourful as that of the Indian subcontinent, the number of darśanas that could be listed is very large indeed. In order to classify them in a manageable way, the standard method has been to distinguish them according to broad religious affiliations. Thus, in most textbooks on Indian philosophy, we find the darśanas divided into those which are 'orthodox' (*āstika*) and those which are 'non-orthodox' or 'heterodox' (*nāstika*). *Āstika* is an affirmative expression, translatable as 'it is' or 'there is', which, in the present context, is taken to imply acceptance of the divinely inspired and infallible nature of the Vedas. *Nāstika* (*na-āstika*) – 'it is not', 'there is not' – meanwhile implies denial of Vedic authority. Typically, into the latter ('heterodox') category are placed Buddhism (*bauddha-darśana*) and Jainism (*jaina-darśana*), along with the Cārvāka darśana, which is generally characterized as metaphysically materialist and highly sceptical about religious claims. The 'orthodox' category is standardly divided into six main darśanas, each of which has its own classical formulation – that is, a central text, tersely constructed – which subsequently came to be interpreted and commented upon in ways that were not always consistent, thereby giving rise to various minor schools and lineages under the rubric of the classical system concerned.

The categorization of Indian philosophies in terms of their 'orthodoxy' and 'heterodoxy' in relation to Vedic doctrine is, on the whole, unhelpful in my view. This is because such categorization (a) falsely suggests a uniformity concerning the importance that was placed by classical Indian philosophers upon one's attitude to Vedic authority, and (b) serves to mask the diversity of philosophical positions within each of the broad religious categories. In short, the lines of philosophical agreement and disagreement do not map neatly onto those of religion. Since Indian philosophies *have* tended to be categorized in these ways, however, it is worth mentioning where Sāṃkhya and Yoga sit in relation to this schematic demarcation.

Sāṃkhya and Yoga are commonly regarded as two of the six 'orthodox' darśanas of classical Indian philosophy, the other four being Nyāya, Vaiśeṣika, Pūrva-mīmāṃsa, and Vedānta. Of the six, it is the last two (Pūrva-mīmāṃsa and Vedānta) whose status as orthodox is least problematic, as these two darśanas (which, of course, have their own sub-schools and hermeneutic diremptions) are chiefly concerned with the interpretation and systematization of Vedic teachings. Each of the other four, however, has a contentious association with Vedic orthodoxy. I will say nothing about Nyāya and Vaiśeṣika here beyond the fact that, like Sāṃkhya and Yoga, their relationship with one another is usually viewed as that of philosophical comrades rather than dogged opponents.

The relation between Sāṃkhya and Yoga is sometimes characterized in terms of their being two expressions of the same system, while at other times they are said to differ on matters such as theology and soteric methodology. I shall say more about their relation in Chapter 2. Their 'orthodoxy' is questionable on the grounds that their connection with Vedic doctrine is by no means clearly definable. Several of the texts known as Upaniṣads – which have been appended to, and incorporated into, the Vedic canon – give expression to concepts and themes distinctive of Sāṃkhya and Yoga; but where these concepts and themes seem most in step with classical Sāṃkhya and Yoga, they seem least accordant with what is commonly perceived as the Upaniṣads' strong emphasis upon the identity of absolute Being (*brahman*) and the essential self (*ātman*).

Where Sāṃkhya and Yoga come more to the fore is in the great Indian epic known as the *Mahābhārata* (especially in the portions known as the *Bhagavadgītā* and *Mokṣadharma*), and also in the mythological narratives of several of the Purāṇas, and in parts of the early legal compendiums such as the *Manusmṛti*. But, again, in each of these cases the version of Sāṃkhya and Yoga that we get is noticeably 'brahmanized' in the sense that the dualistic opposition between the 'seer' and the 'seeable' that is so notoriously characteristic of classical Sāṃkhya and Yoga is typically subordinated to the unifying absolute principle, *brahman*. This is a recurrent feature in the history of Sāṃkhya and Yoga: what we have come to call their 'classical' forms are in fact untypical of the general trend, which is towards bringing the ostensibly dualist metaphysics of these systems into conformity with the monistic aspirations of leading religious theoreticians. It has thus become standard practice to distinguish between classical Sāṃkhya and Yoga, on the one hand, and pre- and post-classical versions of these systems, on the other. A family resemblance between the different versions warrants our referring to them by a generic name, but it would be unwise to try to stipulate a precise set of dogmatic criteria, exclusive accordance with which qualifies a philosophical viewpoint as belonging to that family.

This study deals with Sāṃkhya and Yoga in their respective classical forms. I shall make reference to non-classical versions of these systems in Chapter 1, and occasionally elsewhere, but for the majority of the time there will be quite enough to concentrate on just in the classical material. When I say 'the classical material', what I am referring to is the central texts of classical Sāṃkhya and Yoga, namely the *Sāṃkhyakārikā* and *Yogasūtra* respectively. Although it is common for scholars to mean by 'classical' not only these central texts but also the commentaries upon them that were composed over subsequent centuries, I have broken from this practice slightly. I have opted to restrict my use of the term 'classical' to the *Sāṃkhyakārikā* and *Yogasūtra* alone, and to use other phrases – such as 'the Sanskrit commentaries' (where appropriate) and 'traditional commentaries' – to denote the relatively early Indian (and, more rarely, non-Indian) works that are primarily concerned with explicating and discussing them. In my view the standard practice of lumping the commentaries in with the primary texts under the heading 'classical' leads to confusion when one wishes to discuss what the classical view is on a certain matter. Since there is no general agreement on which commentaries count as 'classical' and which do not, and since the commentaries frequently conflict with one another on substantial interpretive issues, we would – if we were to adopt too liberal an application of 'classical' – never be quite sure what we were meaning by it. (For the sake of brevity, I shall of course often use the terms 'Sāṃkhya' and 'Yoga' without any adjectival qualifier. In each instance it should be clear from the context whether it is the classical or some other version of these systems that is being referred to.)

I won't say much at this point about how classical Sāṃkhya and Yoga are situated within the history of Indian philosophy, as this topic will be addressed (to some extent at least) in Chapter 1. If it is precise historical dates that one is seeking, then, as with so much other Indian material, one is unlikely to find them. These days the *Yogasūtra* is generally estimated to date from the third or fourth century CE, and the *Sāṃkhyakārikā* from around the middle of the fifth century, but the evidence for these dates is far from secure. They are both evidently composed with an eye on concision, and would undoubtedly have been transmitted by means of oral recitation prior to, or at any rate alongside, their transcription.[1] I shall continue to refer to them, for the sake of convenience, as *texts*, although I intend this term to be taken in the broad sense of a verbal composition, whether written or spoken.

As their titles suggest, the *Yogasūtra* is composed in the *sūtra* form and the *Sāṃkhyakārikā* in the *kārikā* form. A *sūtra* is a single statement, comprising only a small number of words and in some texts (though not in the *Yogasūtra*) only one word. A *kārikā*, meanwhile, is a distich; that is, a unit of verse consisting of two lines which together usually constitute a sense unit. It is therefore longer than most *sūtra*s, but both *sūtra*s and *kārikā*s can be semantically dense and are frequently open to varying interpretations.

The prevailing orientation of the *Yogasūtra* and *Sāṃkhyakārikā* is soteriological, by which I mean that in each case what the text is chiefly concerned with is the inculcation of a set of teachings that will aid hearers and readers in their quest for salvation, a final deliverance from sin, pain and ignorance. The texts are therefore not straightforwardly philosophical in the way that this term is applied in the modern academic world; that is, they do not consist in tightly argued expositions, in which a named author endeavours to advance or defend a specific thesis and to criticize and undermine rival positions. Such a disputatious style of philosophical discourse did exist in ancient India, but it is frequently intermixed with concerns that would be better described as philological or hermeneutic, that is, concerns about the proper interpretation of authoritative (often *religiously* authoritative) texts.

Neither the *Yogasūtra* nor the *Sāṃkhyakārikā* is disputatious, whether in a philosophical or a philological way, although both texts certainly make claims that are philosophical in content. One of the major difficulties that the modern reader faces in trying to understand these ancient works derives from the fact that the process by means of which a particular philosophical position was arrived at is frequently left unexplicated in the original text. This lack of explication can result in considerable ambiguity surrounding the status of an ostensibly philosophical claim in relation to rational standards; and this ambiguity has repercussions for the claim's persuasive force and also our comprehension of its semantic content (the meanings of philosophical statements often remain opaque unless we are aware of the theoretical milieu out of which those statements arose). Rational arguments do occur in the two classical texts that we are concerned with – albeit far more noticeably in the *Sāṃkhyakārikā* than in the *Yogasūtra* – but these are invariably highly abbreviated.

Owing to the difficulties to which I have just alluded, a large part of the task of any would-be interpreter of classical Sāṃkhya and Yoga consists in trying to establish at least an approximate idea of what is going on in the texts: what the points being made are, and how they cohere with other points in their vicinity and with the overall soteriological programme of the system. These are the sorts of issues that have been at the front of my mind throughout the detailed textual examination contained herein.

The interpretation of Sāṃkhya and Yoga given in this study

My purpose in this study of classical Sāṃkhya and Yoga is, then, primarily exegetical. It is to address the question of what the central texts of these Indian systems mean. In order to explore this question I have concentrated mainly upon the metaphysics that constitutes the systems' theoretical core. In practical terms, this means that, although the material contained in this book inevitably ranges over the whole of the *Sāṃkhyakārikā* and *Yogasūtra*, its principal focus is the first half of the former of these two texts, for it is there (in, roughly speaking, *SK* 1–38) that we find the basic metaphysical structure presented in its most systematic way.

My subtitle for this work – 'An Indian Metaphysics of Experience' – is intentionally Kantian in flavour,[2] but the Kantian resonance ought not to be extended too far. My main thesis is that there exist some serious problems in the ways that Sāṃkhya and Yoga have commonly been interpreted, and that these problems derive primarily from what I regard as a false assumption, namely that, in presenting their metaphysical doctrines, the Indian systems are concerned with giving an account of how the universe is – that is, what it comprises and how it is constructed – independently of anyone's experiencing it. In short, the assumption is that Sāṃkhya and Yoga are offering a realist account of the world or universe. Closely connected with this assumption of realism (or, more fully, 'external realism') is the view that the major part of the metaphysics – namely, the schema of twenty-three principles or ontological categories, which are held to emerge from an unmanifest source – constitutes a cosmogony or creation myth, that is a narrative reconstruction of the chronological order in which a set of cosmological entities came into existence.

The two most important of the problems that the above interpretive assumptions give rise to are the following. First there is the problem of explaining why, if the ontological categories presented in the *Sāṃkhyakārikā* are cosmological in nature, most of them are described in ways that link them explicitly with psychological capacities and processes. One response to this problem – indeed, perhaps the only response in the literature that amounts to more than a mere brushing aside of the incongruity – is to argue that the Sāṃkhya categories are *both* cosmological *and* psychological; or, rather, that the unitary (or univocal) definitions and descriptions given in the *Sāṃkhyakārikā* are only *apparently* unitary, and this apparent unitariness disguises the fact that each description operates on two levels. That is, each description simultaneously relates to a cosmological entity that exists in itself without reference to any individual's experience, and to a psychological capacity or process that constitutes part of a living organism's (and, more specifically, a *human* organism's) mental architecture. Such an interpretation amounts to an exceedingly unparsimonious treatment of the textual material, for it requires that, for each of the twenty-three ontological categories, we read its description in a way that attributes that description to two entirely distinct kinds of entity, when at no point in the text itself is such bivalence even hinted at.

The second important problem arising from what I will call the 'realist–cosmological' interpretation of Sāṃkhya metaphysics is that of determining how – if the ontological categories are partially, or perhaps exclusively, cosmological in nature – our improved understanding of them is supposed to assist us in overcoming suffering and dissatisfaction and ascending to the spiritual goal of self-abiding pure consciousness. In short, it is the problem of how, in Sāṃkhya and Yoga, metaphysics relates to soteriology. No interpreter of Sāṃkhya and Yoga would deny that the soteriological approach of these systems involves a translocation of one's sense of identity, away from the mutable structures of experience (which are always morally and epistemically compromised) and towards the immutable and essential self. In order to see any purpose in the amount of time and effort that Sāṃkhya expends on presenting its metaphysical schema, it is therefore necessary to understand the schema as relating to the structure of experience – for it is this that Sāṃkhya and Yoga are evidently most interested in. This means that, when it comes to discussing the relation between metaphysics and soteriology, interpreters of Sāṃkhya and Yoga often conveniently leave to one side the cosmological reading of the metaphysical schema (which they are otherwise committed to) and dwell exclusively upon the psychological reading. But even then they typically fail to grasp why the ontological categories – which have now become psychological ones – are presented in precisely the order that they are in the *Sāṃkhyakārikā*; and hence such interpreters are liable to conclude that the sequence of emergence (or 'evolution') of the categories has, as Larson puts it, 'very little to do with the problem of salvation' and is, as Radhakrishnan remarks, merely the result of 'historical accidents'.[3]

I do not wish to claim that I have entirely resolved these problems. I think the precise relation between the metaphysical schema and the soteriological practice remains unclear, and I can see no way of fully clarifying it. To do so would require having insight into the philosophical and mystical methodologies of the originators of the Sāṃkhya and Yoga systems, and these insights are simply not available to us. What I do wish to claim, however, is that the interpretation put forward in this book eradicates the first of the problems outlined above, namely that of how to explain the incongruity of a cosmogonic narrative whose components seem in the main to be psychological in nature. At first glance, my solution is very simple: it is, in essence, to abandon the cosmological reading from the outset, and to stick with the psychological one. Upon closer inspection, however, it is both more complicated and more radical than this. The psychological reading of Sāṃkhya metaphysics has generally taken the categories to be, as I have suggested already, psychological processes and capacities (faculties, powers). Now, I do not want to say that this is an altogether misguided way of seeing the matter. What I do want to say, however, is that a shift of emphasis needs to be made, away from a psychological analysis in terms of capacities or faculties and towards an analysis of *experience*. A large proportion of the present work is an attempt to think through the implications of this suggestion, but I shall endeavour to say something briefly about it here.

The problem with the psychological reading of Sāṃkhya metaphysics as it is typically formulated is that, while it manages to avoid the incongruity that ineradicably plagues the cosmogonic or cosmological reading, it holds onto the assumption that what is being provided is a realist account of the chronological order in which a set of entities comes into being. Although most of these entities are now construed as psychological or psychosensory, the conviction is frequently maintained among interpreters that at least some of them must be physical, most notably the five known as 'elements' or 'gross elements' (*bhūta*s or *mahābhūta*s). The standard psychological reading therefore gives rise to two problems. One is that of explaining how a set of psychological faculties can be said to come into existence sequentially, when ordinarily we take a mind to be an integrated unit whose components would have great difficulty existing independently of the integrated whole. And the second problem is that of explaining how physical entities can be said to emerge or evolve from psychological ones. These two problems can be resolved, in my view, only if we jettison the assumption that the schema of twenty-three categories is to be understood realistically and diachronically. If instead we understand it as a synchronic analysis of experience – that is, as an account of the constituents that make up experience at any one time – then, I believe, we stand a chance of comprehending the meaning of Sāṃkhya metaphysics in a way that significantly ameliorates the incongruities with which multiple generations of interpreters have saddled it.

Just as, in the 1780s, Kant sought to engender a 'Copernican revolution' in our thinking about the relation between the world and our cognition of it, so this study, in its own much more modest way, represents my attempt to bring about a revolution in the way the metaphysics of Sāṃkhya and Yoga is construed. Like Kant, and like certain phenomenological philosophers of more recent times, Sāṃkhya and Yoga did not, I think, begin with fanciful speculations about the sorts of entities that exist beyond the reaches of our experience. Rather, they began with a careful and systematic analysis of experience itself. The system they devised from this analysis is far from being identical to that of Kant or anyone else; and yet it is, when viewed in the proper light, surprisingly astute and both psychologically and philosophically insightful. My interpretation is not entirely original. It builds upon a smattering of suggestions from earlier interpreters. It does, however, go against the grain of the standard way of interpreting Sāṃkhya and Yoga; and it carries a certain exegetical line – what might be called a phenomenological reading – of Sāṃkhya and Yoga metaphysics further than any previous treatment that I know of.

Methodological considerations

W. V. O. Quine once remarked that 'The more absurd the doctrine attributed to someone, *ceteris paribus*, the less the likelihood that we have well construed his words' (1969: 304). In some ways this could be taken as the guiding methodological statement of the present study. That is, in approaching the task of interpreting the textual material of Sāṃkhya and Yoga, one of my key considerations has been: Does the interpretation I am offering make sense? By this I do not primarily mean to ask whether the system, as interpreted, 'makes sense' to us in the light of our own philosophical predilections (although, inevitably, such factors do encroach upon one's exegetical judgement). Rather, what I mean is: Does it have a high degree of internal consistency; and, more specifically, does the way that I am understanding the Sāṃkhya and Yoga metaphysics cohere with (and seem plausible in view of) the overall soteriological enterprise of these systems?

In approaching a system of philosophy, one must not rule out in advance the possibility that the system could turn out to be internally inconsistent. Indeed, it is to be expected (due to the prodigious difficulties associated with philosophical construction) that any system will contain ingredients that are in tension with one another. However, with this in view, I still consider it to be incumbent upon the diligent scholar, where there is a choice of interpretations, to opt for the one that harbours the fewest inconsistencies and nonsensical elements – *ceteris paribus* (as Quine wisely notes). This last qualification – the need for all other factors to be equal – is crucial; since of course, if the weight of evidence tips the scales towards an interpretation that happens not to be the most coherent of those available, then we would be obliged to relinquish coherence in favour of exegetical fidelity. It should go without saying that one must be guided first by the evidence and only second, where alternative readings are possible, by the coherence criterion.

As it happens, however, in the present case I think both the textual evidence and the coherence criterion point in the same direction. It was the *in*coherence of standard interpretations of Sāṃkhya and Yoga that alerted me to the need to look again at the textual sources, but having embarked upon this reappraisal I started to see that the most coherent reading was also the most parsimonious in the sense that it required, on the whole, the least tortuous treatment of the primary texts (although this is not to say that the reading it requires is always the most literal).

Now, in practical terms my method of gathering together the relevant data, and of assessing it in such a way as to arrive at what seems to me the most plausible interpretation, can be broken down into four main constituents, which I shall outline below.

(1) First and foremost has been a close and thorough reading and analysis of the primary texts, namely the *Sāṃkhyakārikā* and *Yogasūtra*, traditionally ascribed to Īśvarakṛṣṇa and Patañjali respectively.[4] It is rare indeed that a scholar finds an existing translation of a text satisfactory in every respect; and, while retaining great admiration for those translators that have gone before me, it gradually dawned upon me over the course of my inquiry that a whole new translation of the *Sāṃkhyakārikā* would be required. This is included as Appendix A. I did not go to the trouble of also translating the entire *Yogasūtra*, as I am doubtful that I could bring anything to this task that has not already been covered in the

abundance of translated editions that are currently available. However, unless otherwise stated, all quotations from Sanskrit texts – whether from the *Sāṃkhyakārikā*, the *Yogasūtra*, or anything else – may be assumed to be my own. (And, incidentally, it should not be assumed that my translations of passages from the *Sāṃkhyakārikā* in the main body of the book are in every case identical to those in Appendix A. There are invariably multiple options as to how a text may be translated, and not one of these is definitive.)

It should be noted that, at the same time as enhancing one's appreciation of the semantic and syntactic nuances of a text, a greater familiarity with it in its original language can serve to dampen the exaggerated awe with which a highly esteemed work of philosophy is often approached. Having heard, for instance, that a text is the work of a single author, and that it expresses the condensed wisdom gleaned from that author's flashes of gnostic inspiration, it can come as a sobering disappointment to discern signs of, for example, multiple authorship and a somewhat cut-and-paste style of composition. Such signs are especially prevalent in the *Yogasūtra*, in comparison with which the *Sāṃkhyakārikā* comes across as being a relatively strongly cohesive work. I should point out, however, that I do not see it as part of the purpose of this study to enter into these compositional issues in any depth. They are probably impossible to resolve, and for the most part both of the classical texts I am dealing with are sufficiently cohesive to warrant their being treated as integral wholes rather than as more or less baggy collections of disparate fragments.

(2) The second component of my approach has been a broad-ranging consideration of secondary sources, within which category I include: (a) traditional (almost exclusively Sanskrit) commentaries, (b) pre- and post-classical versions of Sāṃkhya and Yoga, and (c) more recent interpretive works by scholars, mainly from India, Europe and the USA. In the use that I have made of each of these types of text I have, of necessity, needed to be selective, since a fully comprehensive discussion of them would have made the book unmanageably bloated. I have endeavoured to draw upon them fairly and representatively in order to exemplify particular views upon issues raised by the primary sources.

The traditional commentaries that I have consulted are all included in the Bibliography (under 'Primary Sources A', since they are invariably published alongside the primary texts). Of these, the ones I have found most useful, and which I most frequently cite, are (on the *Sāṃkhyakārikā*) Gauḍapāda's *Bhāṣya* and Vācaspatimiśra's *Tattvakaumudī*, and (on the *Yogasūtra*) Vyāsa's *Yogabhāṣya* and Vācaspatimiśra's *Tattvavaiśāradī* (which is, strictly speaking, a sub-commentary upon the *Yogabhāṣya*). A good deal of excitement has been expressed in recent decades concerning an extensive commentary on the *Sāṃkhyakārikā* entitled the *Yuktidīpikā*. This commentary is thought to date from somewhere between the sixth and tenth centuries, but was rediscovered by scholars of Sāṃkhya only in the 1930s. Although its rediscovery has been heralded by some as being of such great significance as to render all previous scholarship 'outdated',[5] my own view is that such claims are exaggerated. The *Yuktidīpikā*'s significance derives mostly from the information it provides about disputes between proponents of Sāṃkhya and those of rival Indian systems, especially Buddhism. What it does not do, in my opinion, is shed any new light upon the meaning of the classical text itself. While I have, then, consulted the available editions, I have not treated the *Yuktidīpikā* as any more or less authoritative than the other traditional commentaries.

An unfortunate characteristic of a lot of modern-day exegetical work on Sāṃkhya and Yoga is that, while it does an admirable job of informing us what some commentators say about a particular passage and how other commentators differ from them, it takes us very little distance towards a deepened understanding of the philosophical content of the original text. The solution to this problem is not to ignore the traditional commentaries; for they do in many places have vital contributions to make. Rather, it is to treat them discerningly, and to refrain from believing that knowing what each of the commentaries says on a certain matter is equivalent to fully explicating the matter in question.

With regard to pre- and post-classical formulations of Sāṃkhya and Yoga – that is, those works which put forward what is recognizably a version of the same system but is not merely a commentary upon the classical text – I make relatively few references to these anywhere other than in Chapter 1. This is because my intention has been to provide a close and detailed study of the classical material and not a comprehensive (and therefore relatively thinly spread) treatment of the gamut of Sāṃkhyas and Yogas. At certain places I find it useful to mention passages from one particular post-classical work on Sāṃkhya, namely the *Sāṃkhyasūtra* (which is generally agreed to be several centuries later than the *Sāṃkhyakārikā*) along with a couple of commentaries upon it (most notably in the section on the 'strands' (*guṇa*s) in Chapter 5); but in the main I limit the discussion to the classical works.

As a background to the inquiry, I have familiarized myself with the scholarly literature on Sāṃkhya and Yoga that has been written in or translated into English, from Henry Colebrooke and Horace Wilson (1837) through to the present day; and selective references to this literature will be found throughout this study. The existing interpretations that have been of particular value to me during the course of my research are those presented by Dasgupta (1922, 1924), Davies (1894), Eliade (1969), Feuerstein (1980, 1989a), Ghosh (1977), Larson (1979, 1987), Radhakrishnan (1927, II) and Whicher (1998). Although my view is that none of these interpretive efforts is completely satisfactory – and this view is reflected in a number of critical comments upon them – each of them (among others) has in some way or other not only made my task easier, but made it possible; for, as any scholar knows, it is on the back of, and in response to, previous scholarship that one's own work evolves.

Of the scholars just mentioned, Jajneswar Ghosh is the one whose understanding of Sāṃkhya and Yoga comes closest to my own, although even in his case much of his published work on the subject remains within strictures dictated by the realist–cosmological assumption that I find objectionable. It is principally in the introductory chapter that he wrote for a book by his guru, Swāmī Hariharānanda

Āraṇya (first published in 1936, and reissued in 1977), that Ghosh begins to develop a more thoughtful and sophisticated articulation of Sāṃkhya philosophy. He stresses the phenomenological character of the metaphysical schema, noting that Sāṃkhya's world is 'the world of experience, as it [i.e. Sāṃkhya] knows nothing of any world or system of objects and events existing in independence of consciousness' (1977: 3). He describes Sāṃkhya's methodology as one of 'analytic reflection' which 'is brought to bear primarily on the contents of consciousness' and which involves 'no great leap from thought to things in themselves'; that is, no commitment to the existence of empirical objects independently of experience itself (p. 4). This is a refreshingly different perspective from the standard line about Sāṃkhya's being 'realist' with regard to physical entities, and I think it is essentially on the right track. Due to the necessary brevity of an introductory essay, however, Ghosh is unable adequately to flesh out the pertinent insights that he exhibits, and he seems nowhere to have given a fuller exposition of this viewpoint. Furthermore, the essay has been passed over in silence by most subsequent scholars, who have for the most part gravitated back to a simplistically realist interpretive paradigm.

The plausibility of a phenomenological reading of Sāṃkhya and Yoga metaphysics was also spotted by Braj Sinha, who, in a comparative study of Sāṃkhya–Yoga and Abhidharma Buddhism, refers to that metaphysics as 'primarily an attempt at a transcendental analysis of the facts of human experience' (1983: 17). The use of the expression 'transcendental analysis' is more Husserlian than Kantian here; while it is not inappropriate, it requires a good deal of clarification if it is to help us understand the Sāṃkhya and Yoga position. Sinha, however, limits the scope of his study to the concept of temporality and does not fully work out his initial intuition concerning the metaphysical schema as a whole.

Larson, too, hinted at the possibility of an interpretation of Sāṃkhya along phenomenological lines when, in an early article, he compared it with the phenomenological ontology of Jean-Paul Sartre (Larson 1969). In his subsequent publications, however, Larson has moved away from this approach and adopted a version of the cosmological-cum-psychological interpretive model instead. This has led him to question whether Sāṃkhya's metaphysics bears any relation to its professed soteriological aim (see Chapter 6). My view is that the metaphysics and soteriology are intimately connected, but that the nature of the connection will be seen only if we stick with, and follow through as far as we can, the phenomenological interpretation, which Larson once saw the potential of but never worked out in any detail.

(3) The third component of my approach relates to my training and experience in western philosophy. While taking care not to try to force uniquely Indian doctrines and models into the conceptual molds of a foreign tradition, I have at several places found certain terms and concepts derived from western thought to be particularly helpful for drawing out the meanings of the Sāṃkhya and Yoga material. Since I am writing in English for a largely Anglophone readership, and since I cannot extract myself from my European cultural heritage, there is a

degree of inevitability attached to my using western philosophical tools; but such inevitability does not extend to the particular way in which I interpret the Indian systems. This is shown by the fact that among the targets of my criticisms of several existing interpretations is what I regard as their misapplication of western concepts to Sāṃkhya and Yoga, including especially such concepts as realism and materiality.

As will have become evident to the reader already, the two areas of western philosophy that I draw most heavily upon are Kant's so-called 'critical philosophy' (which he also dubbed 'transcendental philosophy') and the phenomenological approach to philosophy most closely associated with the likes of Franz Brentano and Edmund Husserl.[6] My point is decidedly not to try to make out that the Indian systems I am discussing are straightforwardly prototypes of either Kantian or phenomenological philosophy. The situation is far more complicated than that. For a start, whole industries of scholarship have grown up around the tasks of interpreting Kant and Husserl (along with other phenomenologists) and the relations between their respective philosophies. Therefore anyone who wishes to cite the work of these philosophers for the purposes of comparison is obliged to be aware that many questions of how to interpret that work are yet to be settled (and will probably always remain contentious). Since I did not wish the present book to turn into yet another exercise in Kantian, Brentanian, or Husserlian exegesis, any comparisons that I make between the ideas of these philosophers and those of Sāṃkhya and Yoga must necessarily have a degree of tentativeness and conditionality about them.

A further reason for this tentativeness is the fact that, insofar as the Sāṃkhya and Yoga texts do not lend themselves to definitive explication, any declaration to the effect that these texts are putting forward views that precisely match those of Kant or anyone else would be out of place. Of course I do, in a sense, want to argue that there are proto-Kantian and proto-phenomenological elements in Sāṃkhya and Yoga. If I did not think this were so, there would be little point in my making the comparisons that I do. But this 'proto-' should not be assumed to commit me to anything approximating a simple equation of what are patently very different philosophical systems.

With all these qualifications in view, the reader could be excused for wondering why I ever bothered to bring Kant and phenomenology into the discussion in the first place. The answer is that I do think that, in their respective ways and notwithstanding their less than limpid expository styles, Kant, Brentano and Husserl brought about a radical reorientation, not only of much philosophical theory, but of the very way in which those who have intensively investigated their philosophies view reality and the self–world relation. Kant in particular has made an impact on world philosophy, the repercussions of which are likely to go on being felt for many generations to come. The reorientation that I have in mind here is that which takes place when one ceases to conceive of empirical reality – that is, the world as we experience it – as something that exists outside and independently of our consciousness, and instead conceives of consciousness as being, in some sense, the field or domain within which empirical reality exists. It is this reorientation that constitutes the first step towards idealism and away from metaphysical realism; and while it is a step that is by no means unique to Kant or phenomenology, I think each of these two approaches exemplifies an extraordinarily interesting way of trying to think through its implications. What makes this reorientation so pertinent to Sāṃkhya and Yoga is that, on my understanding, these Indian systems were also involved in formulating a conception of empirical reality in which that reality is exclusively contained within the bounds of consciousness. Again, like Kant and phenomenology, they were not unique in this endeavour; indeed it is likely that some version of this idealist manoeuvre is common to most of the eastern contemplative traditions. But in the case of Sāṃkhya and Yoga the fact that they are performing such a manoeuvre has been so abysmally overlooked by the majority of interpreters, that a rectification is urgently required.

Although, for the sake of brevity, I have been referring, and will continue to refer, to my interpretation of Sāṃkhya and Yoga as a *phenomenological* interpretation, this expression does not tell the whole story. These Indian systems are concerned not merely with the analysis of phenomena, in the sense of observing and categorizing the various constituents that make up the content of experience. They are also concerned with postulating metaphysical principles that must be in place if experience of any kind is to be possible. To this extent, then, Sāṃkhya and Yoga are engaged in both phenomenological analysis – that is, the analysis of experiential content – *and* transcendental analysis in a roughly Kantian sense – that is, the analysis of the necessary conditions of any possible experience. These latter conditions are structurally prior to experience and hence are themselves unexperienceable, although (to make use of Kantian language once again) they are knowable *a priori*. It is for these reasons that I consider it useful to bring in comparisons with Kant, who unquestionably pioneered the use of transcendental reflection as a means of excavating the universal and necessary conditions of experience. Of course, the distinction between what is phenomenological and what is transcendental, in the senses of these terms that I have just outlined, is rarely as clear as we would like it to be. We must wait until Chapter 3 for further examination of these points.

(4) The fourth of my methodological components could be called 'intrapsychic fieldwork'. By this I mean practical training in the techniques of yoga[7] – including a comprehensive range of postural, breathing and meditative procedures – designed to engender the kinds of sharpened states of awareness alluded to in Sāṃkhya and Yoga texts. Although teachers of yoga disagree over the precise methods that are best suited to achieving the desired results, there is little disagreement about the fact that, for most students, significant results are not easily obtained. 'Practice (*abhyāsa*) is the effort [required to gain] stability,' says the *Yogasūtra* (1.13). 'It becomes firmly embedded [or consolidated (*bhūmi*)] when cultivated diligently for an extended period without interruption' (1.14). It would be insipient, therefore, for one such as myself to claim to be anything more than a novice when it comes to accomplishment in the discipline of yoga. The training

I have undergone with a number of teachers, in India and Nepal as well as Europe and Australia, has however given me a better understanding of what yoga *sādhana* (roughly: 'spiritual practice') comprises – and of the psychological and physiological effects it can initiate – than I would otherwise have had. Moreover, while I would certainly not make any claim to possess superior access to the underlying truths of Sāṃkhya and Yoga by means of contemplative insight, I do regard my experience of yoga as having enhanced my appreciation of the ways in which the theory and practice of the two systems cohere and interrelate.

That completes this summary of the four main elements in my methodological approach. There remains just one more element that could be mentioned, although it is perhaps more like the glue that binds the other elements together. This is imagination. I have, to some extent, followed the advice that K. C. Bhattacharyya offers in the Preface to his 'Studies in Sāṃkhya Philosophy', which is that the interpretation of Sāṃkhya (and presumably of Yoga as well) 'demands imaginative–introspective effort at every stage on the part of the interpreter' (1956, I: 127). As I understand it, this demand does not give the exegete a licence to attribute all manner of fantastic doctrines to the classical darśanas; rather, it recognizes the necessary contribution that imaginative reconstruction must make to an interpretive project if that project is not to be unduly constrained by, but is to venture beyond, the limits of existing interpretations.

1

AN HISTORICAL OVERVIEW OF SĀṂKHYA AND YOGA

Time is commonly depicted in Indian mythology as the great producer and the great destroyer. It devours everything that it has previously emitted. This analogy is very apt when it comes to the historical investigation of pre-modern India, and with regard to philosophical traditions such as Sāṃkhya and Yoga, time has certainly eaten up the source materials that would be required to arrive at anything even remotely resembling a clear picture of their historical development. Yet, despite the paucity of information, there is no option of ignoring the historical dimension completely, for an appreciation of the meaning of any tradition of Indian philosophy demands at least some attempt to view it within its broader context. The present chapter constitutes such an attempt.

Several studies exist on the histories of Sāṃkhya and Yoga, some of which are portions of works that set out to cover Indian philosophy in its entirety,[1] and others of which attend more singularly to either Sāṃkhya or Yoga, or to both of these together.[2] The reader interested in a more comprehensive treatment of the subject than that which can be given here is referred to these works and to others mentioned in the notes. What I shall provide is, for the most part, a summary of existing data, and, on points of contention, a brief assessment of competing arguments. Since it is principally philosophical history that we are concerned with, I shall follow the standard approach of focussing upon textual sources without venturing far into other cultural domains.

Early sources

Sāṃkhya is often said to be the oldest of the major systems of Indian philosophy.[3] It is not always clear, however, what this claim amounts to. Very few scholars would deny that what has come to be known as classical Sāṃkhya – that is, the version of the system given expression in the *Sāṃkhyakārikā* – is by no means the system's earliest or original formulation. It was preceded by, and probably existed contemporaneously with, several other formulations, all of which bore a discernible resemblance without adhering to a monolithic doctrinal catechism.

When the claim to unrivalled antiquity is made, therefore, it is rarely meant that *classical* Sāṃkhya is the oldest system of Indian philosophy.[4] It is, rather, something much vaguer than that. What is usually meant, I suspect, is that the genealogical ragbag of Sāṃkhyan-esque or proto-Sāṃkhyan (and Yogic) themes and ideas can be traced further back in the ancient textual record – and most particularly in the category of text known as major Upaniṣads – than can any of the other systems of Indian philosophy. The claim, in its usual form, is therefore highly dubious, for there is no firm evidence that a cohesive Sāṃkhya *system* existed earlier than other systems. Indeed, there is no definitive data to show that such a system pre-existed the founding of Buddhism sometime during the fourth or fifth century BCE, or that of Jainism around the same time. And Vedāntins, irrespective of which particular sub-school they belong to, would argue that the Upaniṣads themselves present a coherent body of teachings, which, while containing Sāṃkhya elements in places, subsumes and eclipses Sāṃkhya as a philosophical system.

The story of the formation of Sāṃkhya and Yoga is sometimes presented using a metaphor of gestation or ontogeny, according to which the two systems – or, at least, some embryonic forms of them – were conceived alongside a range of competing ideas and speculations sometime around the time when the earliest Upaniṣads were composed. If a date is to be put on this period, then it is usually estimated at *c.* 900–600 BCE, although such estimates are not undisputed.[5] The Upaniṣads are sacred texts consisting largely of myths and sermons, attributed to renowned sages and prompted by the pertinent questions of disciples. Dozens of them have been appended to one or other of the four Vedas, although there is a core set of thirteen or fourteen which are customarily regarded as the major Upaniṣads. Among these, the gestation model has it that a number of themes and ideas characteristic of Sāṃkhya and Yoga are evident in early prose Upaniṣads – such as the *Chāndogya*, *Bṛhadāraṇyaka*, *Aitareya* and *Kauṣītaki* – and that these ideas continued to develop until, in the metrical Upaniṣads, most notably the *Kaṭha* and *Śvetāśvatara* (both *c.* 500–200 BCE according to standard estimates), they 'emerged from the womb' as an identifiable philosophical viewpoint.[6]

Typical examples of 'proto-Sāṃkhyan' ideas to be found in the earliest Upaniṣads include the following. *Chāndogya* VI.4.1–7 speak of fire, sun, moon and lightning each being composed of three forms (*rūpa*s), these being: 'light' or 'heat' (*tejas*), which is identified with the colour red; 'water' (*ap*), identified with whiteness; and 'earth' or 'food' (*anna*), identified with blackness or the 'dark' (*kṛṣṇa*). These three forms and their corresponding colours, which are also mentioned at *Śvetāśvatara* 4.5, are evocative of the three 'strands' (*guṇa*s) that, in Sāṃkhya, constitute the creative source known as *prakṛti* or *pradhāna*.

It is also in the *Chāndogya* (VII.25.1) that we find the earliest textual appearance of the term *ahaṃkāra*. The verse is of considerable interest, suggesting, as it does, a conformity between the empirical world and the personal ego: 'So now the doctrine of the *ahaṃkāra*: "I, indeed, am below; I am above; I am to the west; I am to the east; I am to the south; I am to the north; I am, indeed, all this."' In relation to this passage, and to Chapter VI of the same work, van Buitenen has plausibly postulated a continuity between the act of creation depicted in the *Chāndogya* (and also at *Bṛhadāraṇyaka* I.2.1 and I.4.1–3) and the concept of *ahaṃkāra* as it occurs in classical Sāṃkhya: in both cases there is an affirmation – or 'formulation', as van Buitenen puts it – of oneself as 'I' (*aham*), which affirmation is the very moment of the world's coming into manifestation.[7]

Moving on now to the metrical Upaniṣads: One of many precursors of later Sāṃkhya and Yoga in the *Kaṭha* is its account of the stages through which one passes on the way to the 'highest goal':

> Beyond the sense-capacities (*indriya*s) are their objects (*artha*s), and beyond these objects is mentation (*manas*); beyond mentation is discernment (*buddhi*), and beyond discernment is the great self (*ātmāmahat*). Beyond the great self is the unmanifest (*avyakta*); beyond the unmanifest is self (*puruṣa*). Beyond self there is nothing. That is the destination; that is the highest goal (*parāgati*).
>
> (*Kaṭha* I.3.10–11)

Although neither the schema of categories presented in these verses, nor the slightly variant one that that appears later in the same Upaniṣad (*Kaṭha* II.3.7–8), is identical with that of classical Sāṃkhya, the similarities between them can hardly be ignored. The passages appear to portray a progressive refinement of attention, leading ultimately to the disclosure of the true self (*puruṣa*), which is the declared goal of Sāṃkhya and Yoga. That the means of achieving this self-revelation are those of sustained meditation is indicated at other places in the text. *Kaṭha* I.3.13, for example, speaks of restraining speech (*vāc*), mentation (*manas*), and other capacities 'in the tranquil self (*śānta-ātman*)', while at II.3.10–11 the 'highest state' (*paramāṃ gati*) is said to be instantiated upon the cessation of sensory and intellectual activity; and the 'steady holding of the capacities' (*sthirām indriya-dhāraṇām*) is explicitly referred to as *yoga*.[8]

The first known mention of *sāṃkhya* and *yoga* together occurs at *Śvetāśvatara* 6.13. They are there described as mutually important factors for 'knowing the divine (*deva*)' and thereby gaining 'release from all fetters', although they are not explicitly defined. It is likely that the use of the terms here is similar to that in the third chapter of the *Bhagavadgītā*, where *sāṃkhya* is identified with revelatory knowledge (*jñāna*) and renunciation (*saṃnyāsa*), and *yoga* is identified with disciplined action (*karman*). The optimum method, as presented at *BhG* 3.3–8, is to combine the two factors by performing dutiful actions while at the same time maintaining an attitude of non-attachment to the fruits of those actions.

Whatever might be the precise meanings of *sāṃkhya* and *yoga* in the *Śvetāśvatara*, the end to which they are directed is knowledge of the 'lord' (*īśa*, *hara*) or the 'divine' (*deva*). In certain places the descriptions of this supreme being anticipate those of the self (*puruṣa*) in classical Sāṃkhya, such as when he is said to be 'a witness (*sākṣin*), consciousness (*cetas*), solitary (*kevala*), and without strands (*nirguṇa* [i.e. devoid of any features characteristic of empirical reality])' (*Śvet.* 6.11). Elsewhere, however, the impression is given of the lord's performing a more active and controlling role in relation to the world: his 'magic power' (*māyā*) is the world's creative source (*prakṛti*) (4.10); it is due to the lord's greatness that the 'wheel of generation (*brahman*)' turns (6.1);[9] and it is he who, 'like a spider, covers himself with threads from the primordial source (*pradhāna*)' (6.10). Throughout the *Śvetāśvatara*, the lord is treated more as a focus for reverence and devotion than is *puruṣa* in classical Sāṃkhya, and in this respect the concept is closer to that of *īśvara* in classical Yoga.[10]

Of the later prose Upaniṣads (*c.* 400–200 BCE), the *Praśna* (4.8) contains a comprehensive list of existent principles, which tallies very closely with that of the manifestations of prakṛti in classical Sāṃkhya. But it is the *Maitrāyaṇīya* (or *Maitrī*) that, of all the major Upaniṣads, displays the strongest affinity with both classical Sāṃkhya and Yoga. Although it relies heavily upon quotations from earlier Upaniṣadic and other sources, and appears to lack a consistent approach of its own, when the *Maitrāyaṇīya* gets round to discussing metaphysical and methodological matters its similarity with the two classical systems is often very striking. The self (*puruṣa*) is identified with consciousness (*cetas*),[11] and is described as the 'enjoyer of food [supplied by] prakṛti' (*Maitr.* 6.10).[12] Prakṛti is said to comprise the 'three strands' (*triguṇa*) and to exist in both a manifest and an unmanifest state (ibid.).

The *Maitrāyaṇīya*'s instructions on yoga practice, and its descriptions of extraordinary experiences engendered thereby, are among the most explicit in the whole of Indian literature. In certain respects they foreshadow elements of classical Yoga; for example, the 'six-limbed' (*ṣaḍaṅga*) system of practice introduced at *Maitrāyaṇīya* 6.18 resembles the last five limbs of the classical 'eight-limbed' (*aṣṭāṅga*) regimen (*YS* 2.29 ff.).[13] In other ways, the *Maitrāyaṇīya* is more like a Tantric treatise on haṭha-yoga, especially in passages such as 6.21–22, where the technique of concentrating 'vital breath' (*prāṇa*) in the 'gracious channel' (*suṣumnā-nāḍī*) is described along with the various sounds that are heard internally as the 'breath' ascends through that channel.[14]

In addition to the Upaniṣads, textual sources that anticipate themes and concepts of classical Sāṃkhya and Yoga include portions of India's immense wealth of epic and mythological literature, most notably the *Mokṣadharma* and *Bhagavadgītā* sections of the *Mahābhārata*, but also passages in several Purāṇas.[15] These works, which are often encyclopaedic in scope, tend to be philosophically promiscuous in the sense that, as Arthur Keith notes with regard to the *Mahābhārata*, they frequently present diverse and incompatible ideas 'in immediate proximity to one another without any apparent sense of their incongruity' (1949: 36). The relevant passages in these works are too numerous to receive full attention here, and thus I shall restrict my comments to one fairly general observation, and a couple of more specific ones.[16]

The general observation is that, within the epic (or *itihāsa*, literally 'thus it was') and Purāṇic literature – as also in the case of the Upaniṣads – there seems not to be a clear and consistent distinction between Sāṃkhyan (or 'proto-Sāṃkhyan') doctrines on the one hand, and what are these days loosely referred to as Vedāntic doctrines on the other. There is in particular a considerable degree of ambiguity attached to the important term *brahman*; which ambiguity is, again, not unique to the epic–Purāṇic branch of Indian verbal composition, but is especially noticeable therein. *Brahman* is conspicuous by its absence in the *Sāṃkhyakārikā* and *Yogasūtra*, although it does occur in several commentaries (among the synonyms of *prakṛti*, for example, but also in other contexts).[17] In the pre-classical versions of Sāṃkhya and Yoga, however, *brahman* figures prominently as a term for the supreme metaphysical principle.[18] This might spur us to question whether they can be counted as versions of Sāṃkhya and Yoga at all; or contrariwise, we might wonder (as at least one provocative writer has done) whether it is not these ostensibly earlier texts that represent the authentic teaching, and the so-called classical systems that are eccentric.[19] In my view, rather than accept either of these extreme positions, we would do better to recognize that there is a range of more or less systematic doctrinal collections that are sufficiently similar to one another to warrant their being called Sāṃkhyan or Yogic. We are concerned here more with relations of resemblance than with either strict identity or 'authentic' versus 'inauthentic' expressions of a viewpoint. It thus remains legitimate to speak of 'epic Sāṃkhyas and Yogas' and 'Purāṇic Sāṃkhyas and Yogas', just as it does of classical Sāṃkhya and Yoga. The term 'classical' does, of course, lend a certain prestige to these latter systems, but such prestige should not be confused with an exclusive entitlement to the names 'Sāṃkhya' and 'Yoga'.

The more specific points I want to make relate to the use of the terms *sāṃkhya* and *yoga* in the epic and Purāṇic material; for although these two terms do occur together at several places (thereby indicating a close association between them), it appears that their meanings bear only an oblique relation to the systems of philosophy with which I am chiefly concerned. One instance of this from the *Bhagavadgītā* has been mentioned already in the discussion of the *Śvetāśvatara-upaniṣad* above, and it may be instructive to consider another of the *Gītā*'s statements on the theme. In Chapter 5 the 'blessed lord' (*śrī bhagavān*) says to Arjuna:

> Fools (*bālāḥ*) proclaim that sāṃkhya and yoga are separate, not the learned (*paṇḍitāḥ*).
> Diligently abiding in one of them alone, the fruit of both is won.
> The station reached by adherents of sāṃkhya is also reached by adherents of yoga.
> He who sees that sāṃkhya and yoga are one, he [truly] sees.
>
> (*BhG* 5.4–5)[20]

As in the earlier passage (3.3 f.), it seems that *sāṃkhya* and *yoga* are being used here to mean 'renunciation' and 'disciplined activity' respectively. This is further suggested by the succeeding verse (5.6), which reads: 'But, without yoga, [only] distress (*duḥkha*) is achieved by means of renunciation (*saṃnyāsa*) [. . .]. Fixed in yoga (*yoga-yukta*), the sage goes to brahman in no time.' If *sāṃkhya* is synonymous with *saṃnyāsa* – as is implied in these verses – then we are faced with two incompatible statements: on the one hand both sāṃkhya and yoga are declared to be equally successful (and self-sufficient) means of attaining the sought-after goal, whereas on the other hand it is said that sāṃkhya can generate only distress in the absence of yoga. We need not dwell upon such incongruities here, however, for my immediate purpose is merely to highlight the distinctly non-classical employment of the terms *sāṃkhya* and *yoga* that is exemplified in the *Gītā*.

A qualification needs to be added to the point I have just made. This is that, although it is evident that *sāṃkhya* does not in the *Gītā* denote any particular metaphysical system, and is in this respect applied in a way that seems to differ from classical usage, we should not leave this discussion without noting the strong probability that the sense of 'renunciation' did not fall away entirely from the term in the classical period. The *Sāṃkhyakārikā* is not a work that sets out to vindicate the value of worldly activity (as the *Gītā*, at least in part, tries to do); it starts from the premise that such activity is inherently dissatisfying (*SK* 1, cf. *SK* 55), and concludes with an account of the utter relinquishment of experience and of the embodied personality that is its pre-condition (*SK* 68). It is, in short, a treatise whose guiding principle is the necessity of renunciation. And thus the sense of renunciation is relevant to the term *sāṃkhya* both as it occurs in the *Gītā* and as it applies to the classical system presented in the *Sāṃkhyakārikā*. What is different is that, in the systematic expressions of the Sāṃkhya philosophy, the term *sāṃkhya* implies, in addition to a renunciant orientation, an approach to metaphysics that involves the exposition of principles in enumerated sets.[21]

Before leaving the *Bhagavadgītā*, I would like to suggest that, in the sāṃkhya-and-yoga duad that we find there, we have a forerunner (or coeval variant, depending on one's view of the chronology of the texts concerned) of the two-pronged methodology that is central to both Sāṃkhya and Yoga in their classical forms. The two prongs are *vairāgya* and *abhyāsa* (*YS* 1.12–16) or (at *SK* 45) *vairāgya* and *aiśvarya*. The first of these, *vairāgya* (desirelessness), involves letting go of the 'thirst' (*tṛṣṇa*) for worldly enjoyment (*YS* 1.15), and hence shares much in common with the *Gītā*'s notion of *sāṃkhya* as renunciation. *Abhyāsa*, meanwhile, is the assiduous practice required to achieve the transformation of mind that Yoga demands; and *aiśvarya* (mastery, lordliness) is the power, self-control and composure necessary to eradicate obstacles; both terms having, therefore, an affinity with the broad sense of *yoga* as 'disciplined action'.

Among other textual sites of pre-classical Sāṃkhya, the following deserve to be mentioned: ancient collections of doctrines and laws such as the *Mānavadharmaśāstra*, also known as the *Manusmṛti* (*c*. 200 BCE–200 CE); treatises on Indian medical science (*āyurveda*), notably the *Suśrutasaṃhitā* and *Carakasaṃhitā*; and a section in an early (*c*. 100 CE) account of the life of the Buddha known as the *Buddhacarita* of Aśvaghoṣa. A further text, Kauṭilya's *Arthaśāstra (c.* fourth century BCE–first century CE), famously names only three philosophical approaches (*ānvīkṣikī*) in its second verse, these being Sāṃkhya, Yoga and Lokāyata. Once again, we cannot assume that *sāṃkhya* and *yoga* denote here anything even approximating the systems associated with Īśvarakṛṣṇa and Patañjali, and nor can we say exactly what is meant by *lokāyata*. The latter term is often associated with the philosophy of Cārvāka, which in turn is taken to be a kind of materialism.[22] As Debiprasad Chattopadhyaya has pointed out, however, *lokāyata* can also be understood to mean 'prevalent among the people' and, consequently, 'the philosophy of the people' (1968: 1);[23] and, if it is taken in this way, then *sāṃkhya* and *yoga* may, by contrast, stand for those approaches to philosophy or life more generally that are *not* so prevalent, but are adhered to by select groups of initiates. On this interpretation we need not be surprised that other philosophical sects or schools go unmentioned by Kauṭilya, for the sense of *sāṃkhya* (and to a lesser extent of *yoga*) could be sufficiently wide here to cover a range of such schools.

One further contribution to the somewhat perplexing picture of pre-classical Sāṃkhya and Yoga is provided by a treatise belonging to the Pāñcarātra sect of Vaiṣṇavism entitled the *Ahirbudhnya-saṃhitā* ('Compendium of the serpent-from-the-depths'). The Pāñcarātra, or Bhāgavata, sect is generally held to be at least as old as Buddhism (i.e. *c.* fourth century BCE), although the textual sources associated with it are likely to be considerably later. The *Ahirbudhnya*, essentially a work of Tantric Vaiṣṇavism, comprises material that was probably composed over a span of several centuries during the first millennium of the Common Era. The reason for mentioning it here is that in its twelfth chapter are included summaries of two earlier works, or bodies of doctrine (*tantra*s), which deal with Sāṃkhya and Yoga respectively. The first of these two summaries (*Ahir.* 12.18–30) is of the so-called *Ṣaṣṭitantra* ('sixty doctrines'), which itself comprises two parts, one of thirty-two topics and the other of twenty-eight. The expression *ṣaṣṭitantra* also occurs at *SK* 72, where the claim is made that the seventy verses which constitute the text's main part cover the topics of the ṣaṣṭitantra but forgo the illustrative examples and objections of opponents. The list of topics given in the *Ahirbudhnya*'s summary of the *Ṣaṣṭitantra* indicates, however, some important differences between this latter work and that of Īśvarakṛṣṇa, and it is therefore likely that the *Ahirbudhnya*'s version is not the only ṣaṣṭitantra but is perhaps one of several, which may or may not have shared a common source.

The theory that more than one version of the ṣaṣṭitantra existed is supported by Vācaspatimiśra's commentary on *SK* 72, in which he refers to an alternative version that is outlined in a now unavailable text called the *Rājavārtika*.[24] This latter version of the ṣaṣṭitantra is remarkably – indeed, one might say suspiciously – compatible with Īśvarakṛṣṇa's text, whereas that summarized in the *Ahirbudhnya* seems closer to the types of Sāṃkhya presented in certain of the Purāṇas and in some passages of the *Mahābhārata*. By this I mean, for example, that it includes *brahman* as the ultimate principle, refers to *śakti* ('power') apparently as a synonym of *prakṛti*, and gives a prominent place to time (*kāla*) among the major principles.[25]

The other noteworthy summary in the *Ahirbudhnya* is of a work on yoga attributed to Hiraṇyagarbha (*Ahir.* 12.31–38). In the *Śvetāśvatara-upaniṣad*, Hiraṇyagarbha appears to be identified with Kapila (the legendary founder of Sāṃkhya),[26] and although no such identification is made explicitly in the

Ahirbudhnya, the name nevertheless retains an important symbolic resonance. As with the *Ṣaṣṭitantra*, the summary amounts to little more than a list of contents, divided into two main parts. The first part comprises twelve sections, on the 'yoga of cessation' (*nirodha-yoga*) and the second comprises four sections, on the 'yoga of action' (*karma-yoga*). Chakravarti (1975: 70 f.) attributes considerable significance to the fact that the treatise is referred to as *yogānuśāsana* ('exposition of yoga'), which expression also occurs in the opening line of the *Yogasūtra* (*atha yogānuśāsanam*: 'now, an exposition of yoga'). He also draws attention to the use of the term *nirodha* in the *Yogasūtra*'s first chapter (1.2, 12, 51), and to a number of other apparently common features,[27] none of which in my view vindicate Chakravarti's assertion that the *Yogasūtra* exhibits a 'remarkable dependence' upon the Hiraṇyagarbha text and that this dependence 'tends to suggest that Patañjali was an adherent of the Hiraṇyagarbha school of Yoga' (1975: 72).

Notwithstanding the wilder speculations of the likes of Chakravarti, the available evidence is insufficient even to confirm that the yoga treatise summarized in the *Ahirbudhnya* antedates the *Yogasūtra*, let alone whether the *Yogasūtra*'s compiler borrowed material from it. Indeed, just as was the case with the relation between the *Sāṃkhyakārikā* and the *Ṣaṣṭitantra*, it is possible that no direct borrowing occurred at all, and that the two 'expositions of yoga' (i.e. those of 'Hiraṇyagarbha' and 'Patañjali' respectively) are instead based upon still earlier sources, which have, like much else, succumbed to the ravages of time.

The classical Sāṃkhya and Yoga texts and their commentaries

The patchy nature of the available evidence precludes the reaching of any definitive judgement on the level of sophistication and coherence achieved by the pre-classical forms of Sāṃkhya and Yoga, and hence it is the classical systems themselves that are generally held up as representating the fully mature stage of these systems' development. The high status that the *Sāṃkhyakārikā* and *Yogasūtra* acquired within the Indian philosophical milieu is attested to by the relatively large number of commentaries that have been composed upon them, and which have survived through to the present day, and also by both the polemical and complimentary references made to the classical systems in the works of other schools and traditions.

Eight early commentaries on the *Sāṃkhyakārikā* are known to have survived. There is some uncertainty about the chronological order of these, but one of the first, and perhaps the earliest of all, is a Chinese translation of the text with an accompanying Chinese commentary. It is agreed that the translation – known by the Sanskrit name *Suvarṇasaptati* ('Golden seventy') – was made by the Buddhist sage, Paramārtha, around 557–569 CE, although there is no consensus of opinion on whether the commentary was authored by the translator or taken from an existing Sanskrit source.[28] Whatever the facts of the matter may be, knowledge of the approximate date of Paramārtha's translation has helped to set a temporal limit to the composition of the *Sāṃkhyakārikā* itself. Having now raised this issue of the latter text's date, I shall pursue it a little further before returning to the commentaries as a whole.

Owing to the existence of Paramārtha's Chinese translation, the *Sāṃkhyakārikā* (whether communicated orally or by written means) must have been composed prior to 569 CE. Indeed, it would probably need to have been put together at least a century before this date in order to have acquired the prestigious status deserving of translation into a foreign language such as Chinese. An *early* limit to the *Sāṃkhyakārikā*'s composition is not so forthcoming, however, despite 350 CE having been settled upon by most recent researchers.[29] Much of the research has been based on references to two prominent Sāṃkhya teachers that are said to have lived close to the time of Īśvarakṛṣṇa, named respectively Vārṣagaṇya (or Vṛṣagaṇa) and Vindhyavāsa (or Vindhyavāsin). The former of these two is first mentioned in the *Mokṣadharma* (*MBh* XII.306.57), although this is merely as a name in a list of Sāṃkhya teachers. Both individuals are mentioned in Paramārtha's biography of the Buddhist teacher, Vasubandhu, with Vindhyavāsa being represented as a disciple of Vārṣagaṇya. A slightly later Chinese source complicates matters by speaking of Vārṣagaṇya not as a particular person but as the name of a group of followers of Kapila headed by a man named Varṣa ('rain'), so called due to his having been born during the rainy season.[30] This account carries less authority, however, than a Sanskrit commentary on the *Sāṃkhyakārikā* called the *Yuktidīpikā*, which clearly portrays Vārṣagaṇya, Vindhyavāsin, and Īśvarakṛṣṇa as three separate individuals, each of whom has a slightly different perspective on Sāṃkhya.[31]

Added to the above pieces of evidence regarding the *Sāṃkhyakārikā*'s period of composition is a reference in the work of the Buddhist logician, Dignāga (*c*. 480–540 CE), to the Sāṃkhya advocate Mādhava as a 'destroyer of Sāṃkhya' (*sāṃkhya-nāśaka*), that is, as one whose views are at such variance to a standard Sāṃkhya position that they tend to undermine it. This has been taken to suggest the presence by Dignāga's time of a standard Sāṃkhya viewpoint, which is to be distinguished from renegade positions such as Mādhava's; and the most likely candidate for this standard is the classical system of Īśvarakṛṣṇa.

To my mind, the case for the *Sāṃkhyakārikā*'s having been composed no earlier than 350 CE seems extremely weak. The references to Vārṣagaṇya and Vindhyavāsin in the *Yuktidīpikā* give no indication of the respective dates of these individuals, and the same is true of the references to Īśvarakṛṣṇa himself. Paramārtha's biography of Vasubandhu does at least state that Vindhyavāsa lived nine hundred years after the death of the Buddha (the Buddha having died, according to recent estimates, around 400 BCE), and that this same Vindhyavāsa studied under Vṛṣagaṇa's (i.e. Vārṣagaṇya's) tutelage, thereby implying that the two men were contemporaries. But it would be foolhardy to assume that Paramārtha's principal concern was historical accuracy. Indeed, it is a common practice in accounts of the lives of renowned individuals, composed by a disciple or admirer, for the subject of the work to be associated with other eminent figures, whether as friend or opponent, in order to enhance the reputation of that subject.

Needless to say, it is immensely difficult to determine the intentions and historiographical credibility of an author some fourteen centuries after his work was composed. With regard to the time-frame of the *Sāṃkhyakārikā*'s composition, then, while concurring that sometime between 350 and 450 CE is the best estimate we can currently make, I would wish to emphasize the tenuousness of the evidence for the earlier of these two limits.

It would be appropriate at this point to make a few remarks concerning the textual integrity of the *Sāṃkhyakārikā*. In comparison with the controversies that surround many texts of similar antiquity, the issue of what does and what does not belong in it is relatively untroublesome. What appear in most editions as the final two verses, numbered 72 and 73, are not mentioned by all commentators, which suggests that these two are later additions. This is highly likely since they merely laud the text as a whole (*SK* 73) and assert its status as a concise exposition of the ṣaṣṭitantra (*SK* 72).

The only other verse that has been queried is the sixty-third, which happens to be absent from Paramārtha's Chinese version. Due to there being no other known commentaries from which it is missing, my inclination would be to regard this as a quirk of the Paramārtha text and not as evidence that what has come to be numbered as kārikā 63 is an interpolation by someone other than Īśvarakṛṣṇa. Suryanarayana Sastri has taken the opposite view on the grounds that *SK* 63 is philosophically redundant, merely reasserting what has already been stated at *SK* 44 and 45;[32] and some other scholars – among them, apparently, Potter and Larson (*EIP*4: 151) – have taken this suggestion seriously. If *SK* 63 is interpreted in a particular way then there is indeed an overlap with *SK* 44. But the emphasis of the two kārikās remains very different, the earlier of the two being far more matter-of-fact in its account of the 'predispositions' or 'personal characteristics' (*bhāvas*), whereas *SK* 63 is part of a veritable crescendo of verses, building up to the description of the final separation between puruṣa and prakṛti that occurs at *SK* 68. Moreover, it is not even clear to me that the 'forms' (*rūpas*) mentioned at *SK* 63 are 'predispositions' at all. The 'seven forms' by which prakṛti is there said to bind herself may in fact be the seven major categories of her manifest aspect, these being:

1 mahat/buddhi,
2 ahaṃkāra,
3 manas,
4 buddhīndriyas,
5 karmendriyas,
6 tanmātras and
7 bhūtas.

And, correspondingly, the 'one form' by which 'she releases herself for the sake of each puruṣa' may be prakṛti's unmanifest aspect, which is really the absence of any form at all. Whatever the case may be, there is no reason to regard *SK* 63 as dispensable.

In addition to the *Suvarṇasaptati*, three commentaries are generally placed in the period from 500–600 CE. One of these, the *Sāṃkhyavṛtti*, remains anonymous; and in the case of another, the *Sāṃkhyasaptativṛtti*, because of damage to the one existing palm leaf manuscript we know only that the author's name began with the syllable *Ma*. Esther Solomon (1974; *EIP*4: 179) has speculated that the *Sāṃkhyavṛtti* may be an autocommentary (*svopajñavṛtti*) by Īśvarakṛṣṇa himself, but there is no particular reason for supposing this to be true. The *Sāṃkhyasaptativṛtti* closely resembles a commentary eponymously titled the *Māṭharavṛtti*, which is usually thought to be a few centuries later (post-800 CE). The latter text is likely to be an expanded and slightly modified version of the former.[33]

The fourth of the commentaries held to date from the sixth century is that referred to as the *Sāṃkhyakārikābhāṣya*, or as the *Gauḍapādabhāṣya* after the name of its author, Gauḍapāda, about whom nothing further is known. His name is shared by the author of a well-known series of kārikās that take the *Māṇḍūkya-upaniṣad* as their starting-point, but there are no significant textual or philosophical similarities that might indicate a common authorship. Indeed, the *Māṇḍūkyakārikā* (or *Gauḍapādīyakārikā*) is usually taken to be a statement of non-dualist (*advaita*) Vedānta, which harbours no sympathy for the dualist position of classical Sāṃkhya.

What, since its first publication in the 1930s, has come to be widely regarded as the most important of all the commentaries on the *Sāṃkhyakārikā*, is the *Yuktidīpikā*. Larson's enthusiasm is obvious: 'No other text compares with it in terms of its detailed treatment of Sāṃkhya arguments and its apparent thorough familiarity with the various teachers and schools that preceded Īśvarakṛṣṇa, and it is no exaggeration to assert, therefore, that it is the *only* commentary on the *Kārikā* that appears to understand the full scope and details of classical Sāṃkhya philosophy' (*EIP*4: 227). Such comments are, however, somewhat over-flattering, and Larson admits elsewhere (1979: 281) that the value of the *Yuktidīpikā* is due more to its historical than its philosophical significance. Neither the author nor the date of the commentary are known, but since it quotes Dignāga and Bhartṛhari, and makes no reference to Vācaspatimiśra, it has been placed between the early sixth century and the end of the tenth century (*EIP*4: 228, citing Pandeya 1967: xv). Early speculations that Vācaspatimiśra might himself have authored the *Yuktidīpikā* have now been abandoned.

The two commentaries on the *Sāṃkhyakārikā* that remain to be mentioned here are the *Jayamaṅgalā* (not to be confused with a well-known commentary on the *Kāmasūtra* with the same title) and the *Tattvakaumudī*. The author of the first of these is not known, although he has been assumed to be a Buddhist due to the inclusion of a benedictory verse to the sage (*muni*) of the *loka-uttara-vādin*s (which is the name of a Buddhist sect) (Chakravarti 1975: 165; cf. Kaviraj 1926). Whether he was, or was not, a Buddhist, there is nothing in the commentary itself to suggest that he was writing from a Buddhist standpoint. Indeed, the *Jayamaṅgalā* diverges little from the interpretive line taken by the four earliest commentaries (i.e. those within the 500–600 CE period discussed above). Certain indications that it relies on the *Yuktidīpikā*, however, combined with Chakravarti's observation that Vācaspatimiśra denies (at *TK* 51) a viewpoint that appears only in the *Jayamangalā*, has set the date of the latter text between the sixth and tenth centuries (Chakravarti 1975: 166–68).[34]

This brings us to the *Tattvakaumudī* itself, which, as Larson has noted, 'is by far the best-known text of Sāṃkhya all over India' (*EIP*4: 302). It has survived in at least ninety manuscripts, and these were utilized to produce a critical edition in 1967 (edited by Srinivasan). Vācaspatimiśra (or simply Vācaspati) composed works on several schools of Indian philosophy, and there is nothing in the *Tattvakaumudī* or anywhere else to show that he was especially committed to the Sāṃkhya system. His style is, however, highly accessible, and he provides some helpful interpretive suggestions on a number of points. There is an ambiguity pertaining to his dates, for the reason that, in his *Nyāyasūcīnibandha*, he notes that the work was composed in 898, but it is unclear whether this date accords with the Vikrama era (which begun in 58 BCE) or with the Śaka era (78 CE onwards). The dispute as to whether Vācaspati flourished in the mid-ninth or the mid-to-late-tenth century still continues.

Turning now to classical Yoga, it may not come as a great surprise to hear that there is a considerable amount of mystery associated with its origins and founder. The Yoga tradition attributes the *Yogasūtra* to a sage named Patañjali, who is lauded as an incarnation of the thousand-headed serpent *Ananta* ('unending', 'infinite') or *Ādiśeṣa* ('initial trace', 'primordial residue').[35] At least since the time of Bhojarāja's commentary (tenth or eleventh century CE), the author of the *Yogasūtra* has been identified with the Patañjali who composed the famous 'great commentary' (*Mahābhāṣya* or *Vyākaraṇamahābhāṣya*) on Pāṇini's grammatical work, *Aṣṭādhyāyī*, and also with a redactor of Caraka's compendium on Āyurveda. Bhoja (or a later interpolator) included in the introduction to his *Rājamārtaṇḍa* a stanza in which Bhoja himself is compared with Patañjali on the grounds that both men are responsible for purifying speech, mind, and body by composing works on grammar, yoga, and medicine. A commentary by Cakrapāṇi on the *Carakasaṃhitā*, dating from around 1060 CE, also praises Patañjali for these three achievements and explicitly attributes to him the *Mahābhāṣya* and a revised version of Caraka's text (*caraka-pratisaṃskṛta*) (cf. Dasgupta 1922: 230 ff.). Similar benedictory verses have been included in manuscripts and published editions of both the *Mahābhāṣya* and the *Yogasūtra* up to the present day, and the identity of the three Patañjalis is widely taken for granted by Indian practitioners of yoga who are unfamiliar with academic debates. The matter has still not been resolved by scholars, although the prevalent tendency is to reject the identity thesis.

The view that the *Yogasūtra*'s author also edited and revised the *Carakasaṃhitā* has been criticized by Dasgupta (ibid.), and I am not aware of any subsequent defence of the view. The identification of the 'Yoga Patañjali' with his grammarian namesake, however, constitutes a more persistent controversy. James Woods firmly denounces the thesis in the introduction to his 1914 translation of the *Yogasūtra*, partly as the result of a comparison between the philosophical content of this text and that of the *Mahābhāṣya*, but also because he accepts the claim made in Vācaspati's *Tattvavaiśāradī* that certain sūtras contain an attack on the 'idealist' school of Buddhism known as *vijñānavāda* ('consciousness[-only] view'). Taken together, this evidence leads Woods to propose a time-period of 300–500 CE for the *Yogasūtra*, considerably later than the second century BCE, which is the period generally agreed upon for the *Mahābhāṣya*.[36]

Pace Woods, Dasgupta (1922: 231 f.) carries out his own comparison of the *Yogasūtra* and *Mahābhāṣya* and concludes that there is nothing in them to indicate a difference of opinion on any significant issue. Furthermore, he cites a number of passages in the *Mahābhāṣya* that illustrate an acquaintance with 'most of the important points of the Sāṃkhya–Yoga metaphysics' on the part of its author (p. 232). Dasgupta addresses the matter of Yoga's supposedly anti-idealist critique, not by reinterpreting the salient sūtras, but by proposing that the *Yogasūtra*'s fourth chapter (*Kaivalyapāda*), in which those sūtras appear, is a later appendage to the work by someone other than Patañjali. As Dasgupta points out (p. 230), the third chapter ends with the expression *iti*, which is roughly equivalent to the Latin *finis*, denoting the end of a work. It is also notable that the fourth chapter displays certain features that distinguish it from other portions of the *Yogasūtra*; it is, for example, substantially shorter than any of the other three chapters, and yet on the whole it is more philosophically engaging. I would add to this the observation that the fourth chapter employs a number of important terms that either do not occur at all or are used very sparingly in other parts of the text.[37]

It would not be especially surprising if the Kaivalyapāda did turn out to be later than other parts of the *Yogasūtra*, since it is a view not uncommon among scholars that the *Yogasūtra* is a compilation of passages from diverse sources rather than the unified expression of a single mind.[38] A consequence of taking this view of the *Yogasūtra* is that the type of comparative textual analysis performed by both Woods and Dasgupta becomes redundant as a method of determining the relation between the composer of this text and that of the *Mahābhāṣya*; for in the one case we would be concerned with an editor or compiler and in the other case with a sole author.

It should be noted that neither the *Mahābhāṣya* nor the *Yogasūtra* claims originality, but rather begins by declaring itself to be an 'exposition' (*anuśāsana*) of a pre-existing body of teaching. The *Mahābhāṣya* sets out to explicate Pāṇini's work on *śabda* ('word', 'language', hence 'grammar'), whereas in the *Yogasūtra* the source of Yoga's teachings is said to be *īśvara* (the 'lord'), 'the guru of even the earliest [yogins]' (*YS* 1.26). The occurrence of the expression '*atha* . . . *ānuśāsanam*' in the opening line of both works is noteworthy but not exceptional. *Atha* is considered to be an auspicious invocatory term, somewhat analogous to *oṃ*, and as such often appears at the beginning of treatises, especially those composed in the sūtra form.[39] It is most often, and most concisely, translated as 'now', but should be understood in the sense of 'And so commences . . . '. The *Ahirbudhnya-saṃhitā*'s inclusion of the phrases 'great exposition of yoga' (*mahad yogānuśāsanam*, 12.31) and 'treatise on the exposition of yoga' (*yogānuśāsanaṃ śāstram*, 12.38) shows that there has been at least one other text, probably pre-dating the *Yogasūtra*, that has presented itself as an exposition of yoga. As has been noted above, this does not constitute a clear indication that the *Yogasūtra* borrowed significantly from the 'Hiraṇyagarbha' text that the *Ahirbudhnya* summarizes, but it should be enough to make us question whether the *Yogasūtra*'s opening line gives us any good reason to identify its author with that of the *Mahābhāṣya*.[40]

Before moving on from the issue of who might be responsible for the *Yogasūtra*, I should mention what Dasgupta takes to be the clinching piece of evidence for the identity thesis I have been discussing. 'The most important point in favour of this identification', he states, 'seems to be that both the Patañjalis as against other Indian systems admitted the doctrine of *sphoṭa* which was denied even by Sāṃkhya' (1922: 238 n. 1; cf. Dasgupta 1920: App. 1). Very briefly, the term *sphoṭa* translates literally as 'bursting forth' or 'erupting' (cf. 'spurt', 'spout', etc.), and, in Indian semantics, may be taken to express the theory that the meanings of certain sounds and symbols are already present in the minds of the members of a linguistic community prior to the instantiation of interpersonal communicative episodes. Such episodes merely allow, or provide the occasion for, the appropriate meanings to 'burst forth' in the sense of being revealed or manifested in the mind of the 'receiving' communicant rather than their being conveyed *to* that mind (cf. *Sphoṭaváda* of Nágeśabhaṭṭa, in Krishnamacharya 1956: 5). Some version of the sphoṭa theory was undoubtedly maintained by the author of the *Mahābhāṣya*, and it would indeed be a matter of some interest to find signs of it in the *Yogasūtra* (although it is difficult to see how such signs could, on their own, win the argument for the identity thesis). But as far as I can see, there is no reference to sphoṭa in the *Yogasūtra*; there is merely one sūtra (3.17) that traditional commentators have typically used as a springboard for embarking upon grammatical digressions, which in certain instances, and most notably in Vācaspati's subcommentary, could be interpreted as imputing the sphoṭa theory to Yoga.[41] The sūtra itself states that 'word' (*śabda*), 'meaning' (*artha*), and 'mental representation' (*pratyaya*), though commonly conflated, can be distinguished by means of meditation (*saṃyama*) upon the differences between them.[42] However, drawing such a distinction between these aspects of a communicative utterance hardly amounts to an affirmation of the sphoṭa theory; and thus the 'most important point in favour of [the] identification' of the two Patañjalis seems very weak indeed.

Feuerstein (1989a: 3) has registered his 'profound ignorance about the historical personality of the author of the *Yoga-Sūtra*', and, under the circumstances, this seems a fair description of the scholarly situation. Roughly the same could be said regarding the *Yogasūtra*'s date, although on this matter there is a general concensus upon the period 100–300 CE.[43]

If we look now to the *Yogasūtra*'s commentaries, we see that one in particular has acquired such an eminent status that, of the others, most take the form of subcommentaries upon it. This is the bhāṣya that is universally attributed to Vyāsa (or 'Vedavyāsa'). Such an attribution is really equivalent to saying that we have no idea who composed the work, since *vyāsa* literally means 'arranger' or 'compiler' (and, according to V. Bhāratī (2001: lii), 'analysis' as well). The term has accumulated a somewhat overburdening weight of legendary associations, for it is to Vyāsa that the authorship of some of India's most vaunted religious and mythological works has been ascribed, including no less than the Vedas, the *Mahābhārata*, the Purāṇas, and the *Brahmasūtra*. In comparison with such esteemed and (with the exception of the last mentioned) voluminous material, a commentary on the *Yogasūtra* appears very small fare; but the association has stuck. Although the commentary is often referred to simply as the *Vyāsabhāṣya*, alternative titles include the *Yoga-* or *Yogasūtra-bhāṣya* and the *Sāṃkhyapravacana-bhāṣya*, the *Yogasūtra* itself being widely regarded as a 'verbal presentation' (*pravacana*) of the Sāṃkhya teachings. No scholar seriously entertains the thought that the author of the *Yogabhāṣya* could be identical with that of the *Brahmasūtra*, or indeed with the myriad authors that must have been required to produce the other works traditionally ascribed to Vyāsa. However, the association of the name with the *Yogabhāṣya* is significant because it is suggestive of the authority that has been accorded to this particular commentary. Estimates of its date gravitate towards the fifth and sixth centuries CE.

Opinions on how useful the *Yogabhāṣya* is in assisting our comprehension of the *Yogasūtra* vary widely. At one extreme there is the view that Vyāsa is a 'great Yoga authority', whose commentary 'illuminates our understanding of Patañjali's thought' (Whicher 1998: 2, 28). It has even been speculatively suggested (V. Bhāratī 2001: lii) that the *Yogabhāṣya* might be an autocommentary (*svopajñaṭīkā*) by Patañjali himself. At the other extreme is the view that the commentary is in many instances, and perhaps in most, an unhelpful distraction from the genuine meaning of the sūtras, and that its author tries to impose upon the Yoga material an interpretation unduly biased towards Sāṃkhya.[44] Between these two extremes is a continuum of viewpoints, each of which regards the *Yogabhāṣya* as being more or less useful in its exposition of the classical text. My own view is that both of the extreme positions just outlined are, for separate reasons, unwarranted. The *Yogabhāṣya* certainly appears, on occasions, to be following its own agenda, and thus can be said to be imposing certain interpretations upon the original text; but to characterize this imposition as Sāṃkhya philosophy being foisted upon an independent Yoga system is highly misleading. Vyāsa's interpretation might lack subtlety and sophistication in places, but the Sāṃkhya viewpoint is already present in the *Yogasūtra* itself. Moreover, in many instances he furnishes us with extrapolations of the sūtras that are either highly plausible or at any rate worthy of exegetical consideration. In addition he helps to embed the sūtras within the broader context of the Sāṃkhya and Yoga traditions, especially by his insertion of quotations from earlier exponents of related philosophies (whose names we sometimes learn only from later subcommentaries, most notably that of Vācaspati). My own assessment of the *Yogabhāṣya* leads me to treat it, along with the other commentaries upon the *Yogasūtra*, critically and discerningly, neither ignoring it nor accepting its interpretations as indubitable.

The *Yogasūtra* has been the subject of a great number of commentaries, many of which (as noted above) take the form of subcommentaries upon Vyāsa's *Yogabhāṣya*. Descriptions and summaries of these texts can be found elsewhere (e.g. Arya 1986: 9–13; Feuerstein 1998: 312–15). I shall do little more than provide a list of titles and authors, along with approximate dates and a minimal amount of descriptive comment.

Tattvavaiśāradī: a subcommentary (*ṭīkā*) by Vācaspatimiśra upon the *Yogabhāṣya*. (Either mid-ninth or late tenth century CE.)[45]

Rājamārtaṇḍa or *Bhojavṛtti*: a commentary upon the *Yogasūtra* by Bhojarāja, also known as Bhojadeva (1019–1054 CE), which is largely independent of the *Yogabhāṣya*.

Kitāb pātanjal: a loose rendering into Persian by Al-Bīrūnī (eleventh century CE) of the *Yogasūtra* plus an unspecified commentary.[46] Al-Bīrūnī is also responsible for a translation into Persian of a Sāṃkhya text, which he ascribes to Kapila.

Yogasūtrabhāṣyavivaraṇa: a subcommentary composed by a certain Śaṅkarabhagavatpāda. The commentator's name has inevitably generated theories that he may have been the famous Vedāntin, Śaṅkarācārya, prior to a conversion from Yoga to Advaita (see e.g. Hacker 1968). Although such speculations have not entirely been laid to rest, the currently prevailing view is that the vivaraṇa belongs to the fourteenth century CE, which is several centuries later than Śaṅkarācārya.[47]

Sarvadarśanasaṃgraha: a major work by Mādhava, a fourteenth-century Vedāntin in the lineage of Śaṅkarācārya. It summarizes sixteen philosophical systems in an order that, predictably, implies the supremacy of Advaita Vedānta. Although not strictly a commentary, the chapter on Yoga provides a fair account of the classical system and, in doing so, serves to illustrate the high status that this system held during the medieval period. A separate chapter on classical Sāṃkhya is also included.

Yogasiddhāntacandrikā: a commentary (*bhāṣya*) upon the *Yogasūtra* by Nārāyaṇatīrtha (late fifteenth or sixteenth century CE). A follower of Vallabhācārya's 'pure non-dualist' (*śuddhādvaita*) interpretation of Vedānta, Nārāyaṇatīrtha adopts a strongly devotional (*bhakti*) approach to yoga both in this substantial commentary and in his shorter vṛtti entitled *Sūtrārthabodhinī*. In both works the author relates certain aspects of Tantric symbolism (e.g. *cakra*s and *kuṇḍalinīśakti*) to the classical Yoga system.

Yogavārttika: a subcommentary (*vārttika* or *ṭīkā*) on Vyāsa by Vijñānabhikṣu (sixteenth century CE), who is also responsible for the more concise *Yogasārasaṃgraha* ('Compendium of the essence of Yoga'). Vijñānabhikṣu has a particular philosophical position that he tries to promote through all his works, including his commentaries. It consists in an attempted synthesis of the major Indian systems of thought, with his own interpretation of Vedānta as the umbrella under which the other systems are subsumed.

Yogānuśāsanasūtravṛtti, also known as *Pradīpikā* or *Pradīpa*: a summary, in large part, of Vijñānabhikṣu's vārttika by one of his own disciples, Bhāvāgaṇeśadīkṣita (*c.* late sixteenth century CE).

Bṛhatī ('Great') and *Laghvī* ('Short'): two subcommentaries (*vṛtti*s) on Vyāsa by Nāgeśabhaṭṭa, also known as Nāgojībhaṭṭa (*c.* late sixteenth century CE), who is well known for his works on grammar and Vedānta. Like Vijñānabhikṣu and Bhāvāgaṇeśa, Nāgeśa makes it his aim to demonstrate that a unifying soteriological thread connects the classical Sāṃkhya and Yoga position with that of the principal sources of Vedānta, especially the Upaniṣads, the *Bhagavadgītā* and the *Brahmasūtra*. As in the previous cases, this project tends to involve a suppression of distinctively non-Vedāntic elements in the Sāṃkhya and Yoga material.

Maṇiprabhā: a short subcommentary on Vyāsa by Rāmānandayati (sixteenth century CE).

More recent commentaries include the following. From the eighteenth century: Sadāśivendra's *Yogasudhākāra*; from the eighteenth or nineteenth century: Anantadeva's *Padacandrikā*, Rāghavānanda's *Pātañjalarahasya* and Rāmabhadradīkṣita's *Patañjalicarita*; and from the twentieth century: Baladevamiśra's *Pradīpikā* and Hariharānanda Āraṇya's *Bhāsvatī*. With a growing popular interest in certain aspects of yoga in the West, commentaries upon the *Yogasūtra* have probably never been so prolifically manufactured nor so readily available as they are today. This is not, however, to say that the sharpness of philosophical analysis and depth of soteriological insight conducive to composing such commentaries are always as prevalent as might be desired.

Post-classical developments

During the centuries immediately following the period to which the *Sāṃkhyakārikā* and *Yogasūtra* have been ascribed, there appears to have been a significant growth, or possibly a resurgence, in the loosely affiliated panoply of sects and lineages that are commonly bundled together under the term 'Tantra' or 'Tantrism'. This is relevant to my present survey for various reasons, one of which is the Tantric emphasis upon bipolarity symbolism, and another of which is the promotion within Tantric lineages of yogic methods of contemplation, often in highly ritualized forms.

The bipolarity symbolism adopted by many Tantric groups takes the form of a divine opposition between masculine and feminine deities. In Hindu and Jain traditions, the masculine deity typically represents knowledge (*jñāna*) or consciousness (*cit*), and is in himself inactive. The feminine deity, meanwhile, stands for 'power' or 'energy' (*śakti*) and the capacity to act and manifest in any number of forms. For adherents of Śaiva and Śākta sects, the masculine deity would be some version of Śiva, often in one of his ferocious aspects such as Bhairava, and the feminine counterpart would be Pārvatī (or Durgā, Bhairavī, etc.), whereas for Vaiṣṇavas the deities would be versions of Viṣṇu (or Nārāyaṇa) and Lakṣmī (or Nārāyaṇī, etc.). In Vajrayāna Buddhism, and in Buddhist Tantra more widely, the poles are reversed, the feminine being static 'wisdom' or 'insight' (*prajñā*) and the masculine being dynamic 'compassion' (*karuṇā*) (cf. A. Bharati 1965: 200 ff.).

There is an obvious parallel between the kind of polarity symbolism just outlined, at least in its non-Buddhist varieties, and the encounter between *puruṣa* (a passive, masculine spectator) and *prakṛti* (a dynamic, feminine performer) that is depicted by Sāṃkhya. Many who have looked at the issue agree that the parallel is too close to be coincidental, although in view of the obscurity that pervades ancient and early medieval Indian history, determining a direction of influence between Tantra and Sāṃkhya is far from straightforward. Historical accounts of Sāṃkhya and Yoga often give only scant attention to Tantra, preferring to stick to the less ritualistic and less symbolically elaborated strands of Indian soteriology. Scholars with a particular interest in Tantra, meanwhile, have been less reticent to express opinions on the relationship. Agehananda Bharati, for example, asserts that the polarity symbolism of Tantra 'has its philosophical background in the Sāṃkhya system', which he, like many others, holds to be 'the oldest systematized metaphysical school in India' (1965: 204). A related suggestion is that several of the principal concepts associated with Sāṃkhya are so widely disseminated throughout Indian culture that they are taken up and assimilated by various religious and philosophical groups, including those characterized as Tantric, without there being any identifiable line of transmission.[48]

A renegade stance on the Sāṃkhya–Tantra relation has been taken by Chattopadhyaya, who claims that Tantrism is much older than it is commonly assumed to be, and that Sāṃkhya, rather than being a major source of Tantric concepts, is in fact 'an explicit philosophical re-statement of the fundamental theoretical position implicit in Tantrism' (1968: 362). Chattopadhyaya's broader theory is that Tantrism (and hence Sāṃkhya) has its origin in popular non-Vedic tribal traditions that antedate the Upaniṣads and are essentially materialist in orientation (see, for example, Chattopadhyaya 1968: xvi ff.). These speculations are highly eccentric and are heavily influenced by their author's idiosyncratic interpretation of Marxist historicism. We need not burden ourselves with such ideological encumberances, however, in order to acknowledge a close relation between Sāṃkhya and Tantra.

In many Tantric systems there is an explicit avowal of monism, or 'non-dualism' (*advaita*), which might appear to contradict the connection with Sāṃkhya. Such avowals tend, however, to occur at the theoretical level without being realized in Tantric symbolism, which remains flagrantly dualist. In certain systems, the metaphysics of classical Sāṃkhya, comprising twenty-three manifest categories and two unmanifest ones, is embellished in an attempt to form a conceptual bridge between the mutually irreducible principles of puruṣa and prakṛti on the one hand, and a monistic absolute on the other. For example, in the medieval non-dualist Śaiva school of Kashmir, which superseded the earlier dualistically-inclined Śaivasiddhānta and whose most notable exponent was Abhinavagupta (tenth century CE), eleven extra categories are added, making a total of thirty-six. The supreme principle is Śiva (also called Bhairava, Parameśvara, etc.), and all the lesser principles are manifestations of the feminine 'power' (*śakti*) that always accompanies him and which is expressed as active compassion or 'grace' (*anugraha*).[49] Thus we see that there is an attempt in Kashmiri Śaivism to affirm the self-sufficiency and pre-eminent authority of the absolute Śiva while simultaneously enthroning a feminine principle alongside him. This manoeuvre is achieved by the use of poetic metaphors that leave the ontological status of Śakti profoundly ambiguous. She is 'non-different' (*avibhāga*) and not to be conceived as 'separate' (*bheda*) from Śiva, and yet she is lauded as a goddess (*devī*) in her own right.[50] Thus the adorning of the Sāṃkhya theoretical framework with extra layers of metaphysico-symbolic complexity, which we see exemplified in Kashmiri Śaivism, results in a heightening of emotional evocativeness while at the same time serving to dilute and cloud important philosophical distinctions.

The overlaying of Sāṃkhya's metaphysical categories with additional symbolic motifs is echoed in the ways in which Yoga, as a practical discipline, is treated within Tantric traditions. The well-known eight-limbed (*aṣṭāṅga*) system laid out in the second and third chapters of the *Yogasūtra* is often discernible as an implicit foundation; but in the Tantric material far more emphasis tends to be placed upon the application of mantras and visualizations as methods of meditation. To some extent such methods are anticipated in the *Yogasūtra*'s third chapter (esp. 3.29–34), in which the effects of sustained meditation upon quasi-physiological energy plexuses (*cakra*s) and channels (*nāḍī*s) are briefly mentioned as part of a varied assortment of meditation techniques. But in the Tantric literature can be found suggested visualizations of diagrammatic emblems (*yantra*s) and pictorial scenes that involve such rich and intricate complexity and close attention to detail that the pithy half-sentences of the *Yogasūtra* appear arid by comparison.[51]

Much of the Tantric material highlights the role of 'vital energy' or 'breath' (*prāṇa*, *vāyu*) as the medium of psychophysical transformation; the proposed methodology being to accumulate the vital energy within the central conduit (*suṣumnā-nāḍī*) in order to thereby thermically stimulate and awaken the still more potent source represented as a coiled serpent in the 'root' energy plexus (*mūlādhāra-cakra*). The specific methods for arousing the serpent – who is referred to variously as *kuṇḍalī*, *kuṇḍalinī*, *bhujaṅgī*, etc. – include those of *haṭha-yoga* ('forceful yoga'); that is, the application of breathing techniques and bodily contractions in order to engender a prolonged – and, in theory, indefinite – suspension of respiration, known as *kevala-kumbhaka* ('absolute retention') or *prāṇāyāma* ('extension [of the retention] of prāṇa').[52]

Prāṇāyāma is a key component of the classical aṣṭāṅga system (*YS* 2.49–53), and thus there is no obvious incompatibility between Yoga in its classical and its Tantric versions at a practical level. The differences consist largely in the ways that the goal of the practice is conceived and represented: the classical formulation being to pacify mental activities in order that consciousness, or the 'seer' (*draṣṭṛ*), can 'abide in its own form' (*svarūpe 'vasthānam*) (*YS* 1.2–3), whereas in haṭha-yoga, as in Tantra more generally, the goal is represented as a transpersonal union of the feminine and masculine poles within the crucible of the human organism.

Among modern-day Yoga teachers, whether in India or elsewhere, who take a relatively traditional approach to the subject (as opposed to the widespread approach that treats Yoga as little more than a form of fitness training), a sharp distinction tends not to be made between classical and Tantric teachings. Both of these sorts of teachings are commonly combined together – along with elements from other sources, such as the Upaniṣads, *Bhagavadgītā* and Āyurveda – as part of an eclectic pedagogical repertoire. Although this eclecticism has probably increased as traditional texts have become more widely and easily available in printed editions, there are strong indications that a blurring of philosophical distinctions has been underway for several centuries. For example, in some of the later commentaries upon the *Yogasūtra* – notably those by Vijñānabhikṣu, Bhāvāgaṇeśa and Nāgeśabhaṭṭa – there is an attempt to reconstruct Sāṃkhya and Yoga in ways that make them compatible with a monistic interpretation of Vedānta, and this is a trend that continues among many Indian commentators today.

Now, to complete this summary of post-classical developments, I need to say something about a couple of sūtra texts, each of which represents a distinct expression of Sāṃkhya without either duplicating or commenting upon the *Sāṃkhyakārikā*. These are, respectively, the *Tattvasamāsasūtra* ('Assemblage of truth sūtra') and the *Sāṃkhyasūtra* (sometimes referred to as the *Sāṃkhyapravacanasūtra*). Despite the anonymity of available manuscripts, both works have attracted followers who have ascribed their authorship to Kapila, the legendary originator of the Sāṃkhya catechism. Such ascriptions have been dismissed by most scholars on two main grounds. The most significant of these is the absence of any reference to either of the works in accounts of Sāṃkhya philosophy up to and including Mādhava's treatment in the *Sarvadarśanasaṃgraha* (fourteenth century CE); and the other is the first appearance of commentaries upon the two works only in the late fourteenth century – in the case of the *Tattvasamāsasūtra* – and in the second half of the fifteenth century in that of the *Sāṃkhyasūtra*. Together, these factors suggest that the *Tattvasamāsasūtra* dates from the fourteenth century, while the *Sāṃkhyasūtra* is a product of either the late fourteenth or early fifteenth century.

The *Tattvasamāsasūtra* is a slender composition, comprising a mere twenty-five sūtras, the last of which is commonly thought to have been added by the unknown author of the commentary called the *Kramadīpikā* (*c.* late fourteenth century). The sūtras are highly condensed, most of them consisting of just two or three words. They amount to little more than subheadings, the implications of which are left for commentators to fill in. As expanded and interpreted by the *Kramadīpikā*, and also by later commentaries such as the *Tattvayāthārthyadīpana* of Bhāvāgaṇeśa (*c.* late sixteenth century), the *Tattvasamāsasūtra* offers nothing that significantly differentiates its version of Sāṃkhya from that of Īśvarakṛṣṇa.

The *Sāṃkhyasūtra* is a work of far greater length than the *Tattvasamāsasūtra*, and of the *Sāṃkhyakārikā* as well. It comprises a total of 527 sūtras, spread over six chapters; and much of its content is of significant philosophical interest. The earliest existing manuscript of the *Sāṃkhyasūtra* also contains a commentary (*vṛtti*) by Aniruddha, which Garbe (1888) has plausibly assigned to the late fifteenth century. The other well-known commentary on the *Sāṃkhyasūtra* is

Vijñānabhikṣu's *Sāṃkhyapravacanasūtrabhāṣya* (*c*. 1550–1600 CE). In common with its author's other works, this commentary seeks to promote a form of monistic Vedānta and to accommodate the Sāṃkhya material to this position.

In the *Sāṃkhyasūtra* itself there are signs that it may have been composed in part to demonstrate Sāṃkhya's conformity with key utterances from the Upaniṣads. Crucially, for example, the Upaniṣadic declarations of the singularity of the self – which would appear to contradict the classical Sāṃkhya doctrine of a multiplicity of selves – are interpreted to mean that the multiple selves share a common nature (*jāti*) and are, to that extent, 'non-dual' (*advaita*) (*SS* 1.154). Although such efforts to harmonize the respective pronouncements of Sāṃkhya and Vedānta are not an entirely novel development, they are carried out in the *Sāṃkhyasūtra* and its commentaries with more noticeable self-consciousness than in previous works. In pre-classical texts, the overlap between 'Sāṃkhyan' and 'Vedāntic' doctrines had probably been largely due to the high degree of conceptual and terminological fluidity that existed in those times. Then came the classical period, during which the distinctions between philosophical viewpoints were sharpened. And now, with the *Sāṃkhyasūtra* and some other post-classical works, there seems to be a move to bring Sāṃkhya and Yoga into more obvious concurrence with *śruti*, that is, the 'heard' (or 'revealed') ejaculations of the Upaniṣadic – or, more broadly, Brāhmaṇic – tradition.

It is perhaps in part because of the apologetic and diluted character of certain portions of the *Sāṃkhyasūtra* that this text has failed to supplant the *Sāṃkhyakārikā* as the foremost exposition of Sāṃkhya philosophy, although this may also be due to the greater concision of Īśvarakṛṣṇa's composition, and to the patent spuriousness of the claims made concerning the *Sāṃkhyasūtra*'s authorship. Whatever the reasons may be, modern-day presentations and discussions of Sāṃkhya typically treat the *Sāṃkhyakārikā* as primary, with the *Sāṃkhyasūtra* being drawn upon, if at all, only in a secondary capacity.

For the sake of completeness I should mention that, in addition to those of Aniruddha and Vijñānabhikṣu, commentaries upon the *Sāṃkhyasūtra* have also been written by Mahādevavedāntin (*Vṛttisāra*, *c*. 1650–1700 CE) and Nāgeśabhaṭṭa (*Sāṃkhyasūtravṛtti*, *c*. 1700–1750 CE), and that further commentaries upon all three main Sāṃkhya works (i.e. the *Sāṃkhyakārikā*, *Tattvasamāsasūtra* and *Sāṃkhyasūtra*), along with occasional original expositions of the Sāṃkhya teachings, have continued to be written and published up to the present day.[53]

2

THE RELATION BETWEEN THE TWO DARŚANAS

The model of the development of Sāṃkhya and Yoga that was adopted in Chapter 1 – and which I have called the gestation or ontogenic model – is one that is commonly accepted by scholars, although the acceptance, one suspects, may often be due more to the unavailability of a more satisfactory account than to any positive features that the model possesses. The model, it should be noted, radically contravenes the view of the systems' origins that is taken by the traditions themselves. On the most prevalent of traditional understandings, the Sāṃkhya teachings – of which Pātañjala Yoga (i.e. the Yoga of Patañjali) is merely a restatement with an especially practical emphasis – were conceived in the mind of a great seer named Kapila, who subsequently dictated them to his disciple, Āsuri, from whom a strict pedagogical lineage developed. The last few verses of the *Sāṃkhyakārikā* testify to this origination story, with Īśvarakṛṣṇa himself being portrayed, not as an innovator, but as a faithful transmitter of an already existing body of knowledge. The ontogenic model undermines this origination story by dispensing with the notion of a spiritual master's revelatory intuition and replacing it with a tale of the incremental formalization of disparate ideas. This formalization is supposed to have taken place over a period of several hundreds of years, during which period what began as vague and often mythologically encumbered pronouncements acquired increased definition and philosophical acuity. If Kapila has any place at all in this latter version of events, then it is as a man who – at some unspecified moment in history – made a significant contribution to the formalization process.

Notwithstanding the high level of acceptance it has received, there remains a serious problem with the ontogenic model of Sāṃkhya's and Yoga's development. This consists in the fact that what the model requires us to believe is that a complex and relatively cohesive body of thought and practice could emerge as the result of a series of more or less haphazard events in the minds of an indefinite number of protagonists over the course of many generations. That such a thing could occur is perhaps not impossible, but it is highly improbable and also starkly at odds with what ordinarily occurs in the formation of a philosophical system.

Martin Heidegger once noted, with reference to the thought of ancient Greece, that 'what is great can only begin great', and that something small and primitive in its origins can serve only to diminish philosophical thinking rather than to enhance it in any way (1961: 15). This need not be taken to mean that a great philosophy must be brought into the world already *fully fashioned*. Rather, what I take Heidegger's suggestion to be is that there must, from the start, be a greatness of insight. Schopenhauer, in a remark concerning the origins of philosophical systems more generally, draws a distinction between philosophies that comprise *a system of thought* and those which, like his own, consist in a *single thought* (1969, I: xii f.). The former, he holds, must always possess an architectonic structure, supported by firm foundations, whereas the latter tend to be more 'organic' in nature, in the sense that their parts are mutually supportive. Both kinds of philosophies can be great; for, although Schopenhauer conceives of his entire philosophical output as having given expression to a single thought (a conception which is, of course, open to question), he at the same time considers it to be in large measure a response to the great work of Kant, who was the architectonic system-builder *par excellence* (ibid.: xv). In any event, the point here is that, whether a philosophy is 'architectonic' or 'organic' – or (as I suspect is most often the case) a hybrid of these two ideals – it must have a discernible *unity* or *integrity*; and it is hard to see how this could be present in a set of disconnected fragments that have, enigmatically, coagulated in a lump.

My task in this chapter is not primarily to overturn the ontogenic model that I have just brought into question. To do so convincingly would require far closer attention to historical details than that which can be given here. My main task is, rather, to justify my decision to speak about Sāṃkhya *and* Yoga (and occasionally about 'Sāṃkhya–Yoga') instead of treating these two as separate and autonomous philosophies. The chapter divides into three sections. First I discuss some competing theories concerning the historical relationship between the two darśanas; second, I inquire whether the two systems' methodologies are discrepant with one another; and third, I argue that although Sāṃkhya and Yoga are by no means identical, in the case of their metaphysics it is plausible to treat them as adhering to the same basic framework of principles.

The historical relation

Not all researchers who have looked at the history of Sāṃkhya and Yoga have been attracted by the ontogenic model. Richard Garbe, for example, did not accept it, but neither did he accept the traditional account of a unitary and Brahmanically orthodox lineage of transmission. He held, rather, that, although the Sāṃkhya system must owe its origin to the genius of a single mind, it is essentially a non-Vedic, or non-Brahmanic, current within Indian thought. A weakness in Garbe's argument is his claim that Sāṃkhya stems from, and has been promoted by, the *kṣatriya-varṇa*, that is, the Indian social group responsible for governance and military defence.[1] This seems implausible due to the absence of any discernible kṣatriya influence in the particular contexts where the term *sāṃkhya* occurs. What we tend to find instead is Sāṃkhya – and in many cases Yoga as well – being associated with the renunciation of possessions and status in order to follow a path of quietist contemplation. Admittedly, such an approach to life does not sit easily with the Brahmanic emphasis upon ritual sacrifice, which is directed more towards the accumulation of personal merit than to the permanent liberation from experiential existence. Neither, however, does it accord with the typically 'this-worldly' activities and aspirations of warriors and politicians. Furthermore, if we are to regard the asceticism represented by Sāṃkhya and Yoga as non-Brahmanic, then there is a sense in which the whole Upaniṣadic tradition is equally non-Brahmanic, since the ideal of the sagely renunciant absorbed in contemplation and transcending worldly attachment is an image that pervades much of the Upaniṣadic landscape, not merely those passages that have a distinctively Sāṃkhyan flavour.

Without wishing to get deeply embroiled in ongoing debates over ancient Indian history, I think a few remarks need to be made here concerning the complicated nature of India's religio-cultural heritage. What is often simplistically construed as a linear path of development – from the invocatory mantras brought together in the Vedic 'collections' (*saṃhitā*s), to the systematized philosophies, and on to contemporary Hinduism – is, as Julius Lipner has suggested, better depicted as a convoluted banyan tree with 'new branches and roots forever springing up or down as others wither away' (1994: 5). Among these branches and roots – and perhaps forming the main trunk itself – is a number of traditions of ritual worship, whose practices are formalized in the Brāhmaṇa texts that were appended to the Saṃhitās. Interwoven with these traditions are various pedagogical lineages, often linked to founding preceptors, that are oriented less towards ritual performance and more towards ascetic discipline. These ascetic lineages find their voice in the Āraṇyakas and Upaniṣads, both of which categories of texts have been appended to the Brāhmaṇas and Saṃhitās, thereby establishing the fourfold division of *śruti*.[2]

It is, I believe, with the ascetic traditions of India that Sāṃkhya and Yoga can most plausibly be held to have their origins; not necessarily as pre-Vedic, nor as reactions to Brahmanic hegemony, but as lineages that, having begun with an individual or small group of philosopher-sages, then followed a line of descent running from guru to disciple. Over time, because a single teacher can have several disciples, a number of lineages would tend to develop; and in the absence of written documents, it is inevitable that interpretive variations would slip into the teachings transmitted along divergent streams. It seems likely that, as Garbe proposes (1917: 54 f.), the specimens of Sāṃkhya and Yoga doctrines in the Upaniṣads, *Mahābhārata*, Purāṇas, as well as some other places, are the result of those doctrines' having been borrowed or assimilated from already existing schools or minor traditions. The alternative view – which, though rarely articulated explicitly, implies that the systems of Sāṃkhya and Yoga somehow evolved out of fragments gleaned from the various available textual sources – is, to my mind, founded upon a misunderstanding of how philosophical systems in general are established and of the traditional process of doctrinal transmission in India in particular.

Before moving on to discuss a selection of views of the historical relation between Sāṃkhya and Yoga, it is worth mentioning an interesting variation on the 'evolutionary' story of their development. What I have in mind is the proposal, put forward by Paul Deussen at the end of the nineteenth century, that Sāṃkhya and Yoga did indeed emerge via a process of gradual metamorphosis of more ancient sources, but that, far from constituting a progressive integration of a number of disparate threads, this process amounted to a 'natural disintegration' of an originally superior philosophy (Deussen 1919: 245; cf. 235 ff.). According to this proposal, the earliest Upaniṣads – especially the *Bṛhadāraṇyaka* and *Chāndogya* – are inspired by an exalted monistic idealism, which in the subsequent metrical and later prose Upaniṣads can be seen to decline, via pantheism and cosmogonism,[3] to theism and eventually to atheism; this last position being, on Deussen's view, embodied in the Sāṃkhya system. The final destination in this abysmal descent is a form of deism, which Deussen attributes to Yoga. It differs from the 'atheistic' Sāṃkhya only in the respect that, 'from considerations of practical convenience', it appends to that system a personal, yet essentially inactive, deity (Deussen 1919: 238–39).[4]

Deussen's analysis is illuminating insofar as it draws attention to the diversity of metaphysical viewpoints that can be detected within the Upaniṣads. However, his arrangement of these viewpoints into a linear schema comprising several discrete stages is simplistic, and presupposes a level of certainty pertaining to Upaniṣadic chronology that neither he nor any subsequent researcher has been capable of validating. Worse than this, moreover, is Deussen's characterization of Sāṃkhya and Yoga as forms of 'atheism' and 'deism' respectively. Such terms, being derived from western theological discourse, can be highly misleading when applied to ancient Indian thought, unless they are heavily qualified. Deussen is perhaps unique among scholars in his attribution of deism to Yoga, although 'atheism' and 'theism' continue to be bandied around in relatively recent works on Sāṃkhya and Yoga, as though these terms presented no semantic difficulties in an Indian context. This issue requires further attention, and I shall return to it in the third section of this chapter. Now, however, as a route by which I might introduce my own thoughts upon the relation between Sāṃkhya and Yoga, I shall outline a broad classification of alternative conceptions of this relation. Such conceptions can, I think, be placed into one or other of four main categories, namely

1 the *single system* thesis,
2 the *divergence* thesis,
3 the *grafting-on* thesis and
4 the *separate systems* thesis.

I shall say more about each of these in turn.

(1) According to the 'single system' thesis, Sāṃkhya and Yoga have, from their beginnings, constituted not two distinct systems but, rather, two parts (or halves,

aspects, poles, etc.) of a unified enterprise. One part (Sāṃkhya) gives primary emphasis to theoretical matters, and the other (Yoga) is mainly practical in orientation, but both are harmonized within the compass of a theory–practice unity, directed towards a common spiritual goal. Chakravarti exemplifies this position when, speaking of Sāṃkhya and Yoga, he states that 'The former is specially busy with the theoretical investigation, whereas the latter deals with the practical side. Speaking briefly, the two systems are nothing but the concave and convex side of the same sphere' (1975: 65).[5] Proponents of this view are apt to use the conjunct expression 'Sāṃkhya–Yoga' not merely as a shorthand for 'Sāṃkhya *and* Yoga', but to designate a single system that combines these two aspects. It is a common feature of this view, or perhaps a sub-species of it, that Sāṃkhya is seen as the more comprehensive side of the partnership, and that Yoga is merely a compartment or 'school', to be referred to as 'Pātañjala-Sāṃkhya' (e.g. Dasgupta 1922: 229).[6] In support of this view it is sometimes noted that the most important commentators upon the *Yogasūtra* have been unanimous in regarding Yoga as an 'exposition' (*pravacana*) of Sāṃkhya, and that the very phrases 'Patañjali's exposition of Sāṃkhya' (*Pātañjala sāṃkhya-pravacana*) and 'Yoga doctrine' (*yoga-śāstra*) appear as synonyms in the colophons traditionally inserted at the end of each chapter of Vyāsa's *Yogabhāṣya* (cf. Chakravarti 1975: 73).

It should be noted that the 'single system' thesis that I have just outlined is often proposed in terms that are sufficiently vague to leave the precise nature of the relation between *classical* Sāṃkhya and Yoga unspecified. When Sāṃkhya and Yoga are described as 'twins', or aspects of the same 'sphere', it is rarely, if ever, implied that the Yoga of Patañjali perfectly reflects the Sāṃkhya of Īśvarakṛṣṇa. Rather, what appears to be meant is that Yoga (of which Patañjali's is the best-known version) shares enough in common with expositions of Sāṃkhya (of which Īśvarakṛṣṇa's is the most ostensibly coherent) for the classical forms of Sāṃkhya and Yoga to be regarded as complementary and not antagonistic. The imprecise way in which the suggestion is often made, however, results in a blurring of the distinction between the 'single system' thesis and that to which I shall now come, namely the 'divergence' thesis.

(2) The 'divergence' thesis conceives of classical Sāṃkhya and Yoga as being derived from a single system but as having diverged from one another at some point along a more or less complicated sequence of transmissions, which 'sequence' is perhaps better pictured as a bushy plant with multiple branches than as a chain of orderly links. On this view, then, the two classical systems are related to one another more as cousins than as twins. This is, in essence, the view that I take; and furthermore, it is probably – if one looks behind the rhetoric of the ontogenic model – the most prevalent way in which the Sāṃkhya–Yoga relation is understood. Dasgupta advocates it at one place, suggesting that 'we have lost the original Sāṅkhya texts, whereas the systems that pass now by the name[s] of Sāṅkhya and Yoga represent two schools of philosophy which evolved through the modifications of the original Sāṅkhya school' (1930: 2). We need not, I think, assume that there ever were any 'original Sāṃkhya texts', at least not in the form

of complete and standardized verbal compositions. The teachings may have been passed on orally in a fairly loose structure for decades or centuries before more definitive versions were fixed. Such loose transmission would have facilitated modification along different lineages; and thus it is hardly surprising that, when the teachings come to be written down by scribes within those different lineages, a number of variant forms is produced.

A point that is often taken for granted but which needs to be stated explicitly is that the *Sāṃkhyakārikā* and the *Yogasūtra* are clearly composed for different purposes. Both of them comprise a set of statements in a pithy form that is relatively amenable to memorization; and both, it is fair to assume, are intended for the instruction of initiated disciples by their more learned mentors. However, whereas the *Sāṃkhyakārikā* is an exposition of the theoretical principles underlying a particular form of soteric practice, the *Yogasūtra* is to a far greater extent a guide to the practice itself. This significant difference of purpose needs to be borne in mind whenever claims are made concerning apparent philosophical discrepancies between the two darśanas, and especially with regard to the issue of their respective methodologies, which I shall come to later. It is also relevant to the third position on the Sāṃkhya–Yoga relation, the 'grafting on' thesis.

(3) This 'grafting on' view can, once again, be found in the work of Dasgupta, although it has been around since at least Garbe's time. In common with the first two theses, it proposes that classical Sāṃkhya is an exposition of a much older body of teachings; but unlike those theses, it holds that classical Yoga is a more artificial construction, amounting to little more than a collection of technical instructions plus a few ad hoc doctrines that have been attached, or 'grafted on', to an already existing (presumably preclassical) version of Sāṃkhya. Garbe makes the point as follows:

> The metaphysical basis of the Yoga system is Sâṃkhya philosophy, whose doctrines Patañjali so completely incorporated into his system that that philosophy is with justice uniformly regarded in Indian literature as a branch of the Sâṃkhya. At bottom, all that Patañjali did was to embellish the Sâṃkhya system with the Yoga practice, the mysterious powers, and the personal god; his chief aim had, no doubt, been to render this system acceptable to his fellow-countrymen by the eradication of its atheism.
>
> (Garbe 1899: 14–15)

The latter assertion, concerning Patañjali's primary motivation, seems on the face of it highly implausible, although it has not been universally rejected by subsequent scholars.[7] The suggestion that the 'chief aim' of the *Yogasūtra*'s compiler was to achieve popular acceptability for the Sāṃkhya philosophy seems extremely unlikely, especially when one considers that the text is composed in a style so condensed as to be barely intelligible to a general reader. However, leaving aside this dubious assumption about Patañjali's motivation, the extract from

Garbe exhibits two metaphorical descriptions of the Sāṃkhya–Yoga relation that are worth highlighting. One is that the former system is 'incorporated into' the latter, and the other is that Yoga amounts merely to an 'embellish[ment]' of Sāṃkhya (though, as usual, it is left unspecified whether it is *classical* Sāṃkhya or some broader category that is being referred to). Both metaphors evoke a kind of parasitic relationship, in which the founder of Yoga makes use of Sāṃkhya in a way that suits his own purposes.

The 'grafting' metaphor derives once again from Dasgupta, who says of Patañjali that he 'not only collected the different forms of Yoga practices, and gleaned the diverse ideas which were or could be associated with the Yoga, but grafted them all on the Sāṃkhya metaphysics' (1922: 229). The major problem with this thesis is that it assumes that the contemplative discipline of Yoga and the metaphysical framework of Sāṃkhya can come into being independently of one another, when there is good reason to suppose that Sāṃkhya metaphysics is, at least in part, a theoretical formalization of truths held to have been *revealed* through Yogic contemplation. Admittedly, there are difficulties involved in establishing precisely how theory and practice are related in Sāṃkhya and Yoga; however, in view of the metaphysically saturated terminology in which these darśanas express their soteric aspirations, a convincing argument would be required to show that the techniques of Yoga could simply float free of what appear to be firm metaphysical moorings. And no such argument has been forthcoming.

(4) The final thesis within this fourfold classification is that according to which Sāṃkhya and Yoga began as separate systems and remain so in their classical forms. Owing to the significant overlap in the theoretical content of the two systems, it is doubtful whether any serious researcher could maintain that they have evolved along entirely separate paths. However, there is a view, prevalent among many scholars, that the respective methodological approaches of Sāṃkhya and Yoga differ radically from one another; and at least one vociferous modern commentator has asserted that this alleged methodological difference 'initiated important conceptual and doctrinal divergencies which further increased the chasm between [the two] schools of thought' (Feuerstein 1980: 116). While it seems right to me to acknowledge that there are differences of various kinds between Sāṃkhya and Yoga, the suggestion that these differences constitute a 'chasm' must surely be misleading. In the next section I shall address the issue of methodology in relation to the two systems. Before coming to that, however, I should say a little more about Feuerstein's thesis.

It is in *The Philosophy of Classical Yoga* that Feuerstein most vigorously pushes his 'chasm' thesis. What he is eager to show is that 'Classical Yoga is exactly what its protagonists claim: an autonomous *darśana* with its own characteristic set of concepts and technical expressions', and that the 'popular scholarly impression according to which Classical Yoga is some kind of parasite, capitalising on the philosophical efforts of Classical Sāṃkhya, is . . . in need of urgent revision' (1980: ix–x). An initial problem with this thesis is that it is not at all clear who Feuerstein has in mind when he refers to 'protagonists' of classical Yoga.

It cannot be the authors of the traditional commentaries on the *Yogasūtra*, for these invariably and liberally invoke Sāṃkhyan concepts in order to explain the sūtras, and generally stress not Yoga's autonomous status but its continuity with Sāṃkhya thought. Indeed, one of the tasks that Feuerstein sets himself is to 'combat the overpowering influence exercized by Vyāsa's scholium' (p. ix), for the very reason that he considers Vyāsa to have 'superimposed the views of his particular school on the philosophy of Patañjali', rather than having provided a neutral, more trustworthy, exegesis (p. 51). Since the other major commentaries generally take Vyāsa as their starting-point – and even where they do not, they nevertheless interpret Yoga in the light of Sāṃkhya – it is doubtful whether any protagonists of classical Yoga fit Feuerstein's description. Indeed, not even the *Yogasūtra* itself explicitly declares its own position to be 'autonomous'; on the contrary, it portrays itself as an exposition of a long-established tradition. Thus it would appear that Feuerstein, while claiming to be standing up for a position taken by classical Yoga itself, is really constructing a thesis out of his own interpretation of Yoga *vis-à-vis* other Indian philosophies and Sāṃkhya in particular. That I consider there to be errors in that interpretation will become evident in the following section, although I shall not restrict the discussion to Feuerstein's views alone.

Methodologies

It is frequently said of Sāṃkhya and Yoga that the principal difference between them consists in their discrepant methodological approaches. Feuerstein makes this point by claiming that, 'whereas Classical Sāṃkhya relies heavily on the power of ratiocination and discernment, Classical Yoga, like any other yogic tradition, is founded on a philosophy which encourages personal experimentation and direct "mystical" verification' (1980: 113). Whicher, similarly, contrasts Sāṃkhya's 'theoretical/intellectual analysis' with Yoga's stress on 'the necessity of personal experimentation and practical meditational techniques' (1998: 53). The description of Sāṃkhya as a rational, or rational*ist*, system goes back to the nineteenth century. Garbe, for example, subtitled his major work on Sāṃkhya 'A System of Indian Rationalism',[8] and in another monograph he states that, of all Indian philosophies, Sāṃkhya 'claims our first and chief attention, because it alone attempts to solve its problems solely by the means of reason' (1899: 29). Davies likewise remarks that 'The system of Kapila, called Sānkhya or Rationalistic, . . . contains nearly all that India has produced in the department of pure philosophy' (1894: v).

There is nothing inherently inaccurate about attributing rationalism to Sāṃkhya if 'rationalism' is understood in the weak sense of a propensity to employ rational arguments in support of propositions. For Sāṃkhya undoubtedly does have such a propensity, and there are many places in the *Sāṃkhyakārikā* where at least the rudiments of rational arguments are displayed. The attribution becomes problematic, however, when 'rationalism' is taken in a stronger sense to imply that Sāṃkhya's methodology relies exclusively upon reason and, in that respect, is to be contrasted with Yoga, which – as we have seen in the remarks of Feuerstein and Whicher above – is regarded as being more mystically inclined. There are, as far as I can see, three main problems here. One is that a conclusion is being jumped to from too little evidence; second, evidence favourable to an alternative conclusion is being overlooked; and third, two distinct kinds of methodology are being conflated. This third problem is crucial, and so I shall deal with it first.

The two kinds of methodology that need to be distinguished might be called 'metaphysical' and 'soteric' respectively. What I mean by 'metaphysical methodology' is the set of tools and processes by means of which a metaphysical conclusion is arrived at. 'Soteric methodology', on the other hand, comprises the techniques that a person or school advocates as an effective way of achieving a desired salvific end. The relationship between these two types of methodology is not straightforward. It may turn out for any particular school or system that in some ways the two types overlap and reflect each other and in other ways they diverge. What remains clear, however, is that a question, asked of a philosophical system, such as: How has this system arrived at its metaphysical conclusions? is not equivalent to the question: How does this system propose to achieve salvation? The major problem with the claim that Sāṃkhya is 'rationalist', as it is normally stated, is that these two questions are conflated, and the fact that rational arguments are employed in the *Sāṃkhyakārikā* to support certain metaphysical assertions is taken as evidence that Sāṃkhya regards its goal of spiritual liberation as being achievable by means of theoretical reason alone. We see this conflation at work when Keith, for example, observes that, for Sāṃkhya, 'The knowledge which results in liberation is the realization that the spirit is not one or all of the [prakṛtic] principles' and that 'The attainment of this knowledge through consideration of the facts of existence results in the cessation of the creative activity of nature' (1949: 97–98). Although 'consideration of the facts of existence' certainly has a large part to play in Sāṃkhya's working out of its metaphysical schema, it is highly doubtful that Keith's description here adequately represents the sort of radical psychological transformation that is required if Sāṃkhya's final salvific step is to be made.

There is an undeniable tension between the claim that Sāṃkhya's methodology (both metaphysical and soteric) is purely rational and the claim that its goal is a state in which rational processes are transcended. This tension is rarely confronted by interpreters. In Radhakrishnan's discussion of Sāṃkhya, for example, we see him at one place declaring Sāṃkhya to be 'a notable attempt in the realm of pure philosophy', whose very name indicates 'the fact that it arrives at its conclusions by means of theoretical investigation' (1927, II: 249),[9] and then, in a later passage, describing the goal of Sāṃkhya as a state of mental passivity, 'which no breath of emotion or stir of action disturbs' and which 'seems to be an extinction of individuality' (ibid.: 313, 314). While it may well be true to say that Sāṃkhya arrives at its metaphysical conclusions, at least in part, 'by means of theoretical investigation', it is difficult to believe that such investigation would be sufficient for establishing the state of pure passivity to which Radhakrishnan refers. And yet Radhakrishnan, like many other advocates of the 'rationalist' interpretation of Sāṃkhya, leaves us to assume that rational methods are, for Sāṃkhya, soteriologically as well as metaphysically adequate.

I mentioned above that proponents of the 'rationalist' interpretation of Sāṃkhya have tended to jump to a conclusion on insufficient evidence and to overlook important contra-indications. These points deserve expansion. First it needs to be said that, although the *Sāṃkhyakārikā* contains no explicit statement of its methodology, whether metaphysical or soteric, it does provide some significant suggestions. In order to treat these suggestions discerningly, however, it is necessary to remove the blinkers that the assumption of Sāṃkhya's 'rationalism' places upon us. Many interpreters have tended to see the arguments – or rudiments of arguments – that occur in the *Sāṃkhyakārikā*, and to then assume that, as far as Sāṃkhya is concerned, ratiocination is the means of not only generating metaphysical truths but of achieving spiritual liberation as well. This assumption leads such interpreters to overlook potentially anomalous features of the Sāṃkhya material, or to interpret those features in ways that bring them into conformity with the overall 'rationalist' assumption only at the expense of exegetical fidelity.

Among the suggestions made in the *Sāṃkhyakārikā* concerning its soteric methodology, two of the most significant occur in verses 2 and 64, each of which I shall now discuss in turn. *SK* 2 provides both a negative and a positive statement on the matter of the most effective way of truncating the 'distress' (*duḥkha*) alluded to in the text's opening verse. On the negative side, it declares that neither the 'perceptible' (*dṛṣṭi*) nor the 'heard' (*ānuśravika*) methods are successful; and on the positive side, it asserts that the 'best' or 'superior' (*śreyas*) approach involves the 'discrimination of [or between] the manifest, the unmanifest, and the knower'.[10] For our immediate purpose it is not necessary to go into any detail about these three factors. What I wish to focus on is the notion of discrimination itself. The term used in the verse I'm discussing is *vijñāna*, which has etymological associations with the English word 'knowledge'. The prefix *vi-* may here be taken to indicate that the sort of knowledge in question is of an especially refined or elevated quality, and hence terms such as 'discrimination' and 'discernment' are often given as translations of *vijñāna*. In itself, 'discrimination' leaves it ambiguous whether the cognitive act at issue is one that involves rational mediation or is, instead, one of purely intuitive awareness; and in many contexts (including, for example, the interpretation of Sanskrit Buddhist texts) *vijñāna* would be assumed to mean the latter – that is, 'awareness' or 'consciousness' – and would be translated accordingly. A term which is very close in meaning to *vijñāna* – and which for most purposes can be regarded as its synonym – is *viveka*. This occurs six times in the *Yogasūtra*, and, like *vijñāna* in the *Sāṃkhyakārikā*, is commonly rendered as 'discrimination' or 'discernment'.[11] However, whereas *vijñāna* is routinely assumed, by those who favour the 'rationalist' interpretation of Sāṃkhya, to consist in rational cognitive operations, *viveka* as it occurs in the *Yogasūtra* is taken to involve direct intuition. Feuerstein, for example, says of *vijñāna* that it 'is by no means synonymous with *prajñā* or gnostic insight as acquired in *samādhi*', but is, rather, 'an intellectual act of continuously reminding oneself that one is not this body, this particular sensation, feeling or thought'. And he adds that 'This is the famous *neti-neti* ["not this, not this"] procedure of the Upaniṣadic sages applied in the most rationalistic manner possible' (1980: 115; my square brackets). It is not at all clear to me why Feuerstein should regard the method he describes here as 'rationalistic', or even 'rational'. It appears to consist in the adoption of an attitude of non-attached witnessing that is a key component of numerous meditative systems, including that of Yoga. It can certainly be said to involve 'an intellectual act', but whether it is properly 'rational' seems debatable. Indeed, what we see here is an equivocation in Feuerstein's use of terms such as 'rational' and 'intellectual' that is, I think, fairly common among those who characterize Sāṃkhya as 'rationalist'. On the one hand, he seems to want to use these terms to denote the engagement of logical reasoning skills, while on the other hand he wants to use them in a much looser sense to cover virtually any act of cognition or mentation.

Whereas Feuerstein talks about Sāṃkhya's 'rationalism' specifically in relation to the term *vijñāna*, Whicher is, we might say, less discriminating in this regard, and uses the terms *vijñāna* and *viveka* interchangeably. In common with Feuerstein, however, Whicher considers Yoga to be striving for a more direct form of knowledge, or more elevated state of being, than that which Sāṃkhya is aiming at: 'Yoga, in its program of purification, goes beyond the position of classical Sāṃkhya... which seems to rest content with a discriminating knowledge (*viveka*) leading to a final isolation of *puruṣa* or absolute separation between *puruṣa* and *prakṛti*' (Whicher 1998: 288). As Whicher sees it, Sāṃkhya's 'conceptual means of discrimination (*vijñāna*) is not sufficient... for the aspiring yogin.... In Yoga, immortality is realized through consistent practice and self-discipline, and is not something to be demonstrated through inference, analysis, and reasoning' (ibid.: 53). I should mention at this point that Whicher's interpretation of the goal of Yoga is unusual, first because he considers it to be entirely different from that of Sāṃkhya, and second because he imagines it to be an embodied state of indefinite duration in which experience and action have been 'purified' but not (as in more standard interpretations) discontinued (cf. ibid.: 275 ff.). This interpretation enables him to portray the goal of Sāṃkhya in a way that, on most accounts, would exactly coincide with that of Yoga while maintaining that the latter darśana seeks a loftier destination.[12] Although Whicher seems to be interested in Sāṃkhya only to the extent that he can contrast it with Yoga, his view gives rise to the same problem that was noted earlier in relation to Radhakrishnan's work. This is the problem of how (in Whicher's phrase) an 'absolute separation between *puruṣa* and *prakṛti*' – that is, between the pure subject of consciousness and the source of experiential content – can be instigated by 'conceptual means of discrimination'. To express the tension more starkly: what Whicher and others are suggesting is that Sāṃkhya advocates purely rational methods for the achievement of a state in which all mentation has ceased – including, of course, rational thought itself. While it is not out of the question that rational methods could play a part in such an endeavour, it seems evident that at some point in the process a leap has got to be made beyond the rational. This conclusion is, I think, supported by a careful reading of *SK* 64, to which I shall now turn.

When it comes to understanding Sāṃkhya's soteric methodology there is no expression more important than *tattvābhyāsa*, a two-word compound comprising *tattva* and *abhyāsa* that occurs at *SK* 64. Although, as with *vijñāna*, it is impossible to settle the matter of *tattvābhyāsa*'s meaning from material internal to the *Sāṃkhyakārikā* alone, we do have the advantage in this case of an occurrence of almost precisely the same expression in the *Yogasūtra*, which can serve as a valuable point of comparison. *SK* 64 reads in full:

> Thus, from the assiduous practice of that-ness (*tattvābhyāsa*), the knowledge arises: 'I am not', '[this is] not mine', 'not I'; which [knowledge], being free of delusion, is complete, pure, and singular.

Here I have translated *abhyāsa* as 'assiduous practice', since it is generally understood to indicate a form of practice that is repeated and sustained; and I have used the most literal available translation of *tattva*, namely 'that-ness'. *Tattva* is often assumed by modern commentators to be a generic term for any one of the ontological categories of Sāṃkhya, in which case tattvābhyāsa is regarded as the practice of enumerating, or discriminating between, these categories. Interpreters who are already committed to a 'rationalist' view of Sāṃkhya's soteric methodology of course take such enumeration or discrimination to be carried out at the level of rational thought. There is, however, nothing in the *Sāṃkhyakārikā* to validate such a reading of *tattva*; and thus, although tattvābhyāsa undoubtedly has something to do with discriminating between the ontological categories, the expression itself is perhaps best understood in more general terms as 'the practice of discerning the true state of things'.

It is evident from the context within which *SK* 64 occurs that the knowledge that is said to arise from the performance of tattvābhyāsa consists in puruṣa's self-recognition. It is because puruṣa is conceived as a non-phenomenal subjective principle that this self-recognition must be expressed in purely negative terms, as a dissociation with the complex of factors that comprises empirical reality. If we were to be in any doubt that the statements 'I am not, [this is] not mine, not I' are to be attributed to puruṣa, these doubts should be removed by a consideration of *SK* 65, which informs us that 'Then puruṣa, abiding [in itself] like a spectator, sees prakṛti, who has returned to inactivity'. There are, admittedly, huge conceptual difficulties associated with any attribution of cognitive states to a principle of pure (contentless) consciousness, and these will be discussed later in this study (chiefly in Chapter 7). For now, I think it is fair to assume that the knowledge being alluded to at *SK* 64 is of a supra-rational kind.

The comparison to be made with the *Yogasūtra* concerns sūtra 1.32, where the expression *eka-tattvābhyāsa* occurs. This expression is translatable as 'practice of singular that-ness' and is best understood as denoting the discipline of concentrating single-pointedly upon an object or principle. In the context of Yoga, such concentration is typically taken by interpreters to involve rational processes only in its early stages.[13] Its primary purpose is the pacification of mental activities (*citta-vṛtti*) and the engendering of a mode of cognition unmediated by conceptual machinations. Since we have no reason to believe that *tattvābhyāsa* should mean one thing in the *Yogasūtra* and something entirely different in the *Sāṃkhyakārikā*, I propose that in both texts the term refers primarily, not to a strictly rational exercise, but to sustained and focused contemplation, which is held to result in a profound intuition of puruṣa's distinctness from prakṛti.

I should make it clear that I do not mean to underplay the importance of the rational component in Sāṃkhya's methodology. The *Sāṃkhyakārikā* does, as I have noted, employ rational arguments, and it is this feature of the text that, to a large extent, distinguishes it as properly philosophical rather than merely dogmatic or mythopoetic. Such arguments are less evident in the *Yogasūtra*, and this, as we have seen, has often been taken to indicate a distinctvely non-rational methodology on the part of Yoga. I have argued that this characterization – of Sāṃkhya as 'rationalistic' and Yoga as 'non-rational' or 'mystical' – is simplistic. The *Yogasūtra* is primarily a practical treatise; its chief task is to pithily expound Yoga's soteric methodology, comprising a range of techniques designed to engender radical physiological and psychological changes in the practitioner. The *Sāṃkhyakārikā*, meanwhile, has the main purpose of presenting the theoretical background of Yoga, and hence it is far more appropriate to find therein a number of arguments accompanying its propositions, many of which concern matters that can broadly be described as metaphysical. Despite the difficulties involved in establishing the precise relation between rational thought and supra-rational meditation in the soteric practice of Sāṃkhya and Yoga, I can see no good reason for maintaining that the two systems advocate divergent methodologies for achieving their salvific goal.

Metaphysical framework

Despite the common assumption that the respective methodologies of Sāṃkhya and Yoga are poles apart, the majority of researchers acknowledge that, for the most part, there is relatively little that divides the two darśanas when it comes to metaphysics. (Indeed, for this very reason it seems surprising that the assumption of a radical methodological discrepancy should be so prevalent; for, although there is nothing exceptional about the same or similar conclusions being reached via different routes, when it comes to the postulation of elaborate metaphysical systems, the chances of this occurring become vanishingly remote.) There is, however, one particular question of metaphysical importance upon which Sāṃkhya and Yoga are widely held to be at odds, namely that of whether there is a God. In the remainder of this chapter I shall first address this question and then discuss the extent to which the two darśanas are in agreement over metaphysics more generally.

The assumption that God, or 'the Lord', is the major bone of contention between Sāṃkhya and Yoga is ubiquitous within the secondary literature. As we saw exemplified by Deussen earlier in this chapter, the two darśanas are often contrasted with one another on the grounds that Yoga is 'theistic' (or, as Deussen idiosyncratically puts it, 'deistic') whereas Sāṃkhya is 'atheistic'. Sustenance for these characterizations is obtained, not only from a particular way of reading the classical texts, but also from more ancient sources, such as the *Mahābhārata*, in certain portions of which Sāṃkhya and Yoga are indeed portrayed as being, respectively, 'without the Lord' (*anīśvara, nirīśvara*) and 'with the Lord' (*seśvara*, sc. *sa-īśvara*) (cf. Brockington 2003: 15).

It should be noted at the outset that the notions of theism and atheism are highly problematic here. When it is claimed that Sāṃkhya is 'atheist' or 'non-theist', this is not generally taken to mean that Sāṃkhya denies the existence of all supernatural agencies that might, in western parlance, be called 'gods' or 'deities'. For example, in the *Yogakathana* portion of the *Mahābhārata*, despite being represented as *anīśvara*, Sāṃkhya is not accused of denying the existence of the Vedic gods (Brockington, ibid.); and it is evident from verses 53 and 54 of the *Sāṃkhyakārikā* that classical Sāṃkhya postulates a 'divine' (*daiva*) realm, described as eightfold and an abundance (*viśāla*) of 'lucidity' (*sattva*, lit. 'being-ness'). This realm is contrasted with organic nature, which is fivefold and abounds in 'darkness' (*tamas*), and with the middle or human realm, which abounds in 'activity' or 'energy' (*rajas*) and on this model is not subdivided. Correspondingly, when Yoga is described as 'theistic', what is at issue is not Yoga's recognition of Vedic or other tutelary deities. Rather, it is Yoga's specific postulation and adulation of a singular being known as *īśvara* that is of concern.

The concept of *īśvara* in the *Yogasūtra* comprises several elements. It is first introduced in a series of seven sūtras in the first chapter (*YS* 1.23–29), where the practice of *īśvara-praṇidhāna* is announced, apparently as one of the means by which a state of spiritual absorption may be achieved. *Praṇidhāna* can mean 'worship' or 'obeisance' or 'submission' in the religious sense; and it can also mean 'contemplation' or 'meditation upon'. Hence *īśvara-praṇidhāna* stands for a form of contemplative or devotional practice directed towards Īśvara. The practice is described as involving the repeated recitation (*japa*) of the 'pronouncement' or 'word of praise' (*praṇava*), which is universally accepted as being the monosyllabic mantra *oṃ*. This mantra is defined as Īśvara's 'vocalization' or 'sonic indicator' (*vācaka*), and its repetition is said to 'manifest' or 'bring into being' (*bhāvana*) its 'meaning' (*artha*) and result in the 'inward-directedness of consciousness and also the disappearance of obstacles' (*YS* 1.29). It would seem, therefore, that this is a highly abstract form of meditation rather than something that involves the worship of an obviously personal deity.

Īśvara-praṇidhāna is also mentioned at three places in the *Yogasūtra*'s second chapter (*YS* 2.1, 32 and 45), but at none of these is any additional information provided about either the form of practice or the concept of *īśvara*. The primary definition of *īśvara*, given at *YS* 1.24, reads:

> Untouched by detrimental dispositions, by actions and their fruitions, and by the reservoir thereof, Īśvara is a special self.[14]

The expression 'special self' (*puruṣa-viśeṣa*) is crucial, as it implies that Īśvara is not to be regarded as constituting a distinct ontological category. The Lord is special, and hence in a certain respect unique, but he is a member of the category of selves or conscious subjects (*puruṣa*s). His specialness would seem to consist in his freedom from actions and his immunity to the psychological drives or dispositions (*kleśa*s, lit. 'afflictions') that lead thereto. According to the teleological Sāṃkhya–Yoga eschatology, the underlying purpose of empirical existence is to engender the liberation of all conscious subjects from what is understood by these systems to be the affliction of worldly experience.[15] Lived experience is both an entrapment – which comes about only as the consequence of a primordial 'misperception' (*avidyā*) – and the opportunity for the recognition of one's essential distinctness from empirical reality. All of us who have yet to fulfil our spiritual destinies are selves conjoined with, or captivated by, the display of phenomena; we feel ourselves to be active participants in the display rather than the inactive 'seers' (*draṣṭṛ*s) that we truly are. Īśvara, meanwhile, is eternally pure and transcendent, undefiled by worldly engagement. At least, this is the impression we get from *YS* 1.24.

To the list of apophatic characteristics of Īśvara that *YS* 1.24 provides, the following sūtra adds that, 'Therein [i.e. in Īśvara] the seed of all knowledge is unsurpassed'.[16] Although this is usually taken to mean that Īśvara is omniscient, the phrase 'seed of all knowledge' suggests that the knowledge is potential rather than actual. For Sāṃkhya and Yoga, every conscious subject is a 'seer' (*draṣṭṛ*)[17] and a 'knower' (*jña*, *SK* 2) insofar as it is that principle in which, or *to* which, all experience, and hence all cognitive episodes, occur. It is, then, not out of place that Īśvara should be described as a source of knowledge. The knowledge is, presumably, in a potential and ungerminated state due to Īśvara's detachment from the world: he has the power to know all things, but it would appear that this power remains dormant.

The picture that has so far been sketched of the Lord as a transcendent being – somehow conscious but beyond the world of ordinary experience – appears to shift at *YS* 1.26, where we are informed that, 'due to his temporal unrestrictedness', the Lord is the *guru* – that is, the spiritual guide and preceptor – 'of the earlier ones'.[18] Commentators agree that these 'earlier ones' are the renowned teachers of the Sāṃkhya–Yoga lineage. Of them all, Īśvara is the primordial guru, for there has never been a time when he was not awakened to spiritual truth. If we are to take this characterization literally, then it suggests that he is capable of intervening in worldly affairs in order to dispense teachings for the benefit of pre-liberated beings. This, I think, is a difficult notion to accommodate within the overall Sāṃkhya–Yoga account of what it is to be a liberated self in general, and the eternally liberated Lord in particular. What makes it especially difficult is the tension between inactive aloofness on the one hand, and immanent participation on the other. There are, no doubt, ways of interpreting the concept of 'primordial guru' figuratively, which would facilitate at least a partial resolution of the tension.[19] But since I can see no way of satisfactorily determining the exegetical validity of such an interpretation, I am reluctant to enter into speculations of this sort.

What is of immediate concern is whether Yoga's inclusion of the Lord within its theoretical framework constitutes a significant difference between this framework and the one expounded by Sāṃkhya. In my view, it does not; and I say this for two main reasons. First, as I have already indicated, the Īśvara of Yoga is not a distinct ontological category but is instead a special instance of the generic category of selves. While it is indeed surprising that Sāṃkhya – if it accepts the concept of Īśvara at all – should fail to mention it in the exposition of its metaphysical schema, this failure does not entitle us to presume that the concept is positively rejected. In the Yoga system, we should recall, the Lord is introduced in the context of a repertoire of meditative techniques. He – or the mantra which is held to invoke him – is a focus for sustained contemplation; but this mode of contemplative discipline is only one among many. Since the *Sāṃkhyakārikā*'s concern is more with presenting a metaphysical schema than with divulging practical instructions, the Lord may simply not have fallen within its rubric.

My second reason for denying that Yoga's 'Lord' sharply demarcates this system from Sāṃkhya is that Sāṃkhya does in fact have a concept of a primordial guru or teacher very similar to the Īśvara described at *YS* 1.26. Towards the end of the *Sāṃkhyakārikā* it is stated that the foregoing 'esoteric knowledge of the self's end (or purpose, *artha*)' has been 'disclosed by the highest seer' (*SK* 69). This 'highest seer' (*paramarṣi*), although not named explicitly, is undoubtedly the legendary founder of Sāṃkhya known as Kapila. Despite the nominal difference, the role of Kapila within the Sāṃkhya system is strikingly similar to that of Īśvara within Yoga. In both cases we have a figure whose ontological status is ambiguous between that of an incarnate human being and an unworldly pure awareness; and in both cases, too, this figure is regarded as the original source of the philosophical teachings, which have been handed down along a line of spiritual masters. That Īśvara and Kapila are considered synonymous by some important players within the Yoga tradition is inferable from Vyāsa's apparent endorsement of this view. At *YBh* 1.25, within the context of discussing Īśvara's compassionate proclivities, Vyāsa quotes Pañcaśikha as saying: 'The primal knower (*ādividvat*), the highest seer (*paramarṣi*), informing a self-produced mind, gave the teachings, out of compassion (*karuṇā*), to Āsuri, a seeker after knowledge.' This passage closely resembles *SK* 70, which tells us that 'the quiet one (*muni*) first passed on this supreme method of purification, compassionately (*anukampayā*), to Āsuri; Āsuri, again, to Pañcaśikha, and by him the teaching was widely disseminated'. It is the fact that Vyāsa inserts the quotation from Pañcaśikha without qualification that implies that, as far as he is concerned, the 'highest seer' – who is without question the Kapila of Sāṃkhya – is the very same as the Īśvara of Yoga.

Now, the fact that an Īśvara–Kapila identity claim appears to be approved of by Vyāsa is by no means conclusive; but I think, when combined with the other points I have highlighted, it gives us grounds to be very cautious indeed before embracing the standard opinion of modern commentators that 'The main difference between the Sāṃkhya and Yoga . . . lies in the fact that the former is . . . atheistic while the latter is . . . theistic' (Chakravarti 1975: 65).

I wish now to show why I consider it legitimate to speak of *a* metaphysics of Sāṃkhya and Yoga rather than of two separate metaphysical positions that must be scrupulously distinguished on every occasion. As I hope has been made clear earlier in this chapter, my view is not that classical Sāṃkhya and Yoga should be conflated into a single unified system. I think they probably derived from a single source, but they represent moderately divergent streams flowing from that source. With regard to metaphysics, however, I think they share enough in common to be unproblematically regarded as equivalent in most respects; and when I use the term 'metaphysics' here I am, in the main, using it in the broad sense of a theory of what exists, of what the relations between existent entities are, and of what makes those entities possible. For the most part I shall use 'metaphysics' interchangeably with 'ontology', and will use expressions such as 'metaphysical schema' and 'metaphysical framework' to refer to the set of principles or categories that a philosophical system postulates as existing (although 'existing' should not necessarily be assumed to constitute a homogeneous ontological status – there may be 'degrees' of existence). In actual fact it is not really necessary for me to put forward an argument here, since the near-equivalence of Sāṃkhya and Yoga in the area of metaphysics is generally accepted. However, I shall point out some of the similarities and differences that I see between the two systems, on the understanding that a more elaborated account of the metaphysical framework as a whole will be developed over subsequent chapters.

The fundamental metaphysical distinction that Sāṃkhya and Yoga share is between, on the one hand, the self or conscious subject and, on the other hand, that which is experienced. Roughly speaking, we could call these two factors the subjective and objective principles, or simply the subject and object, although it must be remembered that they become subject and object only in relation to one another. Considered independently of that relation, they are merely *potentially* subject and object. In the *Sāṃkhyakārikā* the two principles are generally referred to as *puruṣa* and *prakṛti* (or *pradhāna*), whereas the *Yogasūtra* more often uses the terms *draṣṭṛ* ('seer') and *dṛśya* ('seen' or 'seeable'), but the basic distinction remains the same. Both darśanas regard the second of these principles as having three constituents or properties, or more literally 'strands' (*guṇa*s),[20] and as having a manifest and an unmanifest aspect. The precise nature of the relationship between these two aspects is not made very explicit in either text, although in many instances the analogy of flowing or surging is used to represent how the manifest aspect of prakṛti arises from the unmanifest one.[21] It is, for both systems, the 'conjunction' (*saṃyoga*) of the two co-fundamental principles – potential subject and potential object – that initiates the transformation of the latter principle into its manifest forms; and again for both systems, it is the dawning of the subject's knowledge of its non-identity with those manifest forms that initiates their dissolution back into their unmanifest ground.[22] The subject's awakening to its self-sufficiency and purity is the envisaged *eschatos* of both darśanas, and they both refer to this fully awakened state as *kaivalya*, literally 'aloneness' or 'solitude'. Furthermore, they concur that it is the very purpose (*artha*) of prakṛti's manifestation, and hence of the whole of life and experience, to bring about the conditions in which this awakening can occur.[23]

Thus we can see that the metaphysical commonalities between Sāṃkhya and Yoga are abundant. Now let me point out some differences. There are, for a start, differences of terminology, and in certain instances it is difficult to tell whether these harbour more significant conceptual discrepancies. In the cases so far mentioned – that is, Yoga's preference for *draṣṭṛ* and *dṛśya* where Sāṃkhya tends to use *puruṣa* and *prakṛti/pradhāna* – there is no indication of any conceptual disagreement. In other cases, however, it is less easy to tell. For example, the Yoga term *citta* (usually translated as 'mind') could be a precise synonym of the Sāṃkhya term *buddhi* ('awareness-of', 'discernment') or, alternatively, it might be intended in Yoga to stand for the three mental factors – namely *buddhi* plus *ahaṃkāra* and *manas* – that are brought together by Sāṃkhya under the term 'the inner instrument' (*antaḥkaraṇa*). A third possibility is that Yoga is simply less rigorous than is Sāṃkhya with respect to its specification of psychological capacities, and that *citta* is sometimes equivalent to *buddhi* and at other times more like *antaḥkaraṇa*.

The main reason why it is difficult to be certain in cases such as the one just outlined is that nowhere within the *Yogasūtra* are we given a comprehensive list of metaphysical categories, and hence there is nothing with which to directly compare the far more systematic exposition of categories that proceeds from *SK* 22. The nearest thing we get to a list such as this within the *Yogasūtra* is a fourfold categorization of the 'levels of the strands' (*guṇa-parvāṇi*) at *YS* 2.19, and this is by no means explicit in its wording. The four levels, or divisions, in question are:

1 the specific or particular (*viśeṣa*),
2 the non-specific or non-particular (*aviśeṣa*),
3 the mere mark or indicator (*liṅgamātra*) and
4 the unmarked or unmanifest (*aliṅga*).

The task of mapping Sāṃkhya's unmanifest prakṛti plus twenty-three manifest categories onto this fourfold schema is feasible although not straightforward. The last two of the four Yoga divisions are relatively easy to account for: the fourth, *aliṅga*, is undoubtedly unmanifest prakṛti, which – in addition to just plain *prakṛti* or *pradhāna* – Sāṃkhya calls *avyakta* (the unmanifest, *SK* 2, 10) and *mūlaprakṛti* (fundamental productivity or procreation, *SK* 3); and the third, *liṅgamātra*, must surely be the equivalent of Sāṃkhya's *mahat* ('the great'), which it also calls *buddhi*. The first and second divisions are a little more problematic, however. The terms *viśeṣa* and *aviśeṣa* do occur in the *Sāṃkhyakārikā*, as characterizations of the five elements (*bhūta*s) and five modes of sensory content (*tanmātra*s)[24] respectively (*SK* 38); and hence there is some chance that they are being used similarly in the *Yogasūtra*. However, even if we were able to situate these elements and modes of sense-content within Yoga's fourfold model, this would still leave a further twelve Sāṃkhya categories unaccounted for.

At this point in the mapping-on process most commentators, both traditional and modern, defer to Vyāsa's opinion on the matter; for in his commentary on *YS* 2.19 he manages to slot each of the remaining Sāṃkhya categories into one or other of the first two Yoga ones. To be more exact, he places Sāṃkhya's 'egoity' (*ahaṃkāra*)[25] in the 'non-specific' (*aviśeṣa*) division, and he places *manas* plus the five sense-capacities and five action-capacities in the 'specific' (*viśeṣa*) division. (The whole of Vyāsa's comparative model is represented in Table 2.1.) Although Vyāsa does not support his analysis with arguments, it may be pointed out in his defence that the sixteen principles he assigns to the 'specific' division are also grouped together – and indeed referred to as 'the sixteen' (*ṣoḍaśaka*) – at *SK* 3, where they are said to share the distinct status of being produced (*vikāra*) without themselves being productive.[26]

On the face of it, then, there seems to be no good reason for supposing the fourfold division of principles at *YS* 2.19 to be incompatible with Sāṃkhya's ontology. While it is admittedly a little frustrating that the *Yogasūtra* contains no more detailed exposition of its categories than this one, the consistency between Sāṃkhya and Yoga on other theoretical matters should, I think, give us confidence that they are closely aligned on this matter as well. I therefore take it to be reasonable, for the purposes of this study, to speak of 'the metaphysics of Sāṃkhya and Yoga' as a relatively integral whole while acknowledging that Yoga's presentation of the metaphysical principles is rudimentary in comparison with Sāṃkhya's. The question remains, of course: What advantage is served by treating Sāṃkhya and Yoga together in this way? In my view, the advantage is that, when we study Sāṃkhya and Yoga together as two complementary streams emanating from a single source as opposed to two separate and competing enterprises, we obtain a more fully rounded picture of their overall purpose. Reading the *Sāṃkhyakārikā* in isolation from the *Yogasūtra* is analogous to reading the list of

Table 2.1 Correspondence between the respective ontological categories of Sāṃkhya and Yoga (in accordance with Vyāsa's commentary on *YS* 2.19)

Terms used at Yogasūtra *2.19*	*Terms used in the* Sāṃkhyakārikā
aliṅga – unmarked, unmanifest	*avyakta* – unmanifest (*SK* 2, 10); also called *mūlaprakṛti* – fundamental productivity (*SK* 3)
liṅgamātra – mere mark, indicator	*mahat* – the great (e.g. *SK* 22); also called *buddhi* – awareness-of, discernment (e.g. *SK* 23)
aviśeṣa – non-specific, non-particular	*ahaṃkāra* – egoity (e.g. *SK* 24); plus five *tanmātra*s – modes of sensory content (*SK* 24, 25, 38)
viśeṣa – specific, particular	five *bhūta*s – elements (*SK* 38); plus five *buddhīndriya*s – sense capacities (*SK* 26); plus five *karmendriya*s – action capacities (*SK* 26); plus *manas* – mentation (*SK* 27)

ingredients in a recipe without having any instructions on what to do with those ingredients (and in several instances not even knowing what sort of entity the ingredient is). Admittedly, the two texts do not dovetail neatly with one another. Whether considered individually or in each other's light they leave the would-be interpreter with a large number of gaps to fill in or work around; and thus the hermeneutic situation is not as simple as the 'single system' thesis implies.

Sāṃkhya and Yoga are not merely the theoretical and practical sides of a single system, for they each contain elements of both of these aspects. They do, however, each have a primary focus or emphasis, and this is legitimately characterized as theoretical in the case of Sāṃkhya and practical in that of Yoga. A study that includes them both, and which looks to the one in order to help explain certain features of the other, is therefore in a stronger position to understand the metaphysics that Sāṃkhya and Yoga largely share than one which views the two systems as antagonistic or (as Feuerstein hyperbolically puts it) divided by a 'chasm'.

3

ANALYSING EXPERIENCE

Kantian and phenomenological philosophy

One of my principal aims in this study as a whole is to show that the metaphysical framework that is for the most part shared by Sāṃkhya and Yoga is best regarded as the result of a close analysis of experience rather than as a cosmogony or creation myth. Since there are several ways in which the phrase 'analysis of experience' can be understood, it will be incumbent upon me, over the course of the work, to clarify the sense in which this phrase can fruitfully be applied to Sāṃkhya–Yoga metaphysics. In order to get this clarification under way, I shall in this chapter introduce two quite distinct approaches to the analysis of experience, each of which has in its own way been highly influential within modern western philosophy, and both of which I think have important contributions to make – by way of providing valuable analogies – to our understanding of Sāṃkhya and Yoga.

The first of the western approaches to be discussed here is that developed by Immanuel Kant in his so-called 'critical' period, which was momentously announced by the publication in 1781 of the first edition of his *Critique of Pure Reason*, and which continued until Kant's death in 1804. The second approach is that which has become known by the term 'phenomenology' and has been closely associated with a number of continental European thinkers in the late nineteenth century and throughout much of the twentieth century. Most notable among these is Edmund Husserl, who did not invent the term 'phenomenology' but did much to promote its use in philosophy. Although I shall be partly concerned with Husserl's work, the task of broaching the phenomenological method is best carried out, in my view, by examining the work of his principal teacher, Franz Brentano. It is also in Brentanian phenomenology – which Brentano himself termed 'empirical psychology' – that we find the elements of this approach that are most informative for the interpretation of Sāṃkhya and Yoga that I wish to develop.

It will come as no surprise to the reader that what I am offering here is a highly selective treatment of the western philosophical viewpoints concerned. While endeavouring not to paint a distorted picture of these viewpoints, a good deal of their complexity – not to mention the complexity of exegetical arguments surrounding them – will of necessity have to be glossed over. The goal at the forefront of my mind will, of course, be to highlight those areas of the viewpoints that relate most directly to points I wish to make later regarding Sāṃkhya and

Yoga, and I shall include a section at the end of the present chapter where I spell out some of the ways in which the material discussed here is relevant to the study as a whole. Anyone who wishes to follow up remarks that I make concerning Kantian and phenomenological philosophy will, I hope, find useful the references to primary and secondary literature in the text and notes.

Kant and the problem of metaphysics

Even by the standards of great philosophers, Kant was an exceptionally broad-ranging thinker. Among those subjects in which he was interested and to which he made important contributions are astronomy, the philosophies of science and religion, ethics, aesthetics and of course metaphysics. In all of these areas, but perhaps most explicitly in the last mentioned, Kant was eager to distinguish between, on the one hand, those items that constitute the proper subject-matter of reasonable human inquiry and, on the other hand, those that transcend the compass of rational thought. It is, thinks Kant, when reason tries to overreach its own limitations that it veers into dogmatism, and its claims then become vulnerable to the attacks of sceptics, whose own zealousness threatens to undermine our commitment even to legitimately discovered truths. The best way of defeating scepticism, therefore, is to be clear and honest about what can, and what cannot, be known by us, while also acknowledging that not all our relations to objects of thought are epistemic ones. On Kant's view, the big three traditional questions of religious metaphysics – namely: whether the soul is immortal, whether we have free will, and whether there is a God – are incapable of being settled by means of theoretical reason. We can think of them as bare possibilities; but because our concepts of these things cannot be grounded in experience, the things themselves can never become objects of knowledge (cf. Kant 1992: 590). They remain objects of faith; which, for Kant, is not to diminish their status within the firmament of metaphysics – it is merely to clarify the nature of our relationship to them. He has, as he famously puts it, denied knowledge 'in order to make room for faith' (Bxxx).

There is, then, a sense in which Kant rules out the possibility of metaphysics; but only to the extent that it is traditionally conceived. What Kant seeks to replace the old speculative metaphysics with is a more empirically grounded approach; that is, one that takes as its starting-point the complex nature of experience and inquires how such experience is possible. Kant labels this approach 'transcendental philosophy' (or 'transcendental reflection') because it concerns the conditions of experience, which, by definition, cannot themselves be experienced (and hence can be said to *transcend* it) but which can nevertheless be known by virtue of the very fact of experience's possibility. The line of argument in transcendental reflection therefore goes as follows:

1 Experience is possible
2 It is a necessary condition of experience's possibility that *p*
3 Therefore *p*.

On this model, *p* stands for a proposition to the effect that some factor or factors must be in place, or must play a certain role in a broader process, if experience is to have the characteristics that it does. In practical terms, what the transcendental method involves is a systematic abstraction from experience of all those features that are particular to the experiential episode concerned in order to arrive at the most general features. Indeed, what is sought are the *universal* characteristics of experience, that is, those which show up in every particular experience; for it is these universal characteristics that Kant considers to be necessary conditions of any possible experience. Kant calls them transcendental conditions that are knowable *a priori*, that is, prior to any particular experience but only insofar as we are experiencing beings capable of reflecting upon our own experience in general. The purpose of transcendental reflection is to show that, if experience *x* occurs, then precisely *these* elements must be in place; and it is the excavation of these elements that constitutes the Kantian metaphysical enterprise. He calls his project a mere series of preliminary investigations, or *prolegomena*, which must be undertaken before metaphysics proper can get underway; but in actual fact Kant's own approach is doing the work of metaphysics, a fact which he acknowledges when he refers to it as 'the metaphysics of metaphysics' (Kant 1967: 95). The factors that he comes up with as transcendental conditions have an intriguing ontological status. Kant is often said to have offered an inventory of those features of experience that are brought to it *by us* (or by the experiencing subject, or by the mind), as though he were presenting us with a breakdown of the various faculties that together make up our 'cognitive apparatus'. In many respects this is not an unfair way of reading Kant, and my own interpretation will in part be based on it. However, if we were to ask 'Where is this set of apparatus located?', there is no easy answer to be given. In some sense it is 'in the mind', but it is not 'mental' in the sense that a thought or other 'inner experience' might be considered mental. And it is decidedly not (*pace* the physiological Kantianism of Schopenhauer for example) in the brain; for the brain is an empirical object, and as such is conditioned by our cognitive apparatus and cannot itself be the condition thereof. The transcendental conditions are thus the machinery that give rise to experience, but for this very reason they have no empirical properties of their own.

The major distinction that Kant makes in his analysis of experience is between the receptive component and the active or spontaneous one. The receptive component, or capacity, he calls *sensibility*; and the spontaneous one he calls *understanding*. It is through sensibility that we receive the material of representations from whatever it is that lies 'outside' us, although neither 'material' nor 'outside' are to be taken here in spatial terms. In receiving this material, sensibility attributes to it the forms of space and time; and the material plus these forms constitute what Kant calls 'intuitions' (*Anschaaungen*). Kantian intuitions are representations, and for most purposes can be thought of as sensations or perhaps sensings, but they are not yet experiences, that is, conscious episodes. In order for experiences to occur – whether they are perceptual (i.e. of 'external' objects) or mental (i.e. involving thought) – there must, in Kant's view, be a 'subsumption' of intuitions under a concept or set of concepts. As Kant sloganistically puts it: 'Thoughts without content are empty, intuitions without concepts are blind' (*CPR* A51/B75), and here I take Kant to be using the term 'thoughts' in a wide sense to cover experiences in general. As I interpret it, the claim is that in the absence of concepts we could have mere sensations but they would not be sensations *of* anything, and hence they could never amount to a genuine perceptual experience or cognitive event. Just as something other than the forms of space and time was considered by Kant to make up the 'material' of intuitions, now we have intuitions themselves being portrayed as the 'material' of experiences, with concepts providing the form. We should be careful not to think of these concepts as thoughts that we can be aware of; they do not arise *in* experience, but are conditions *of* experience. Kant calls them *a priori* categories of the understanding. Before I say more about them, however, I want to mention a point of controversy concerning Kant's argument for the ideality of space and time.

There is no dispute over the fact that Kant regards all our representations – that is, all our thoughts and perceptions – as having the form either of time alone (in the case of 'inner', purely mental, representations) or of both time and space (in the case of 'outer', sense-perceptual, representations). Furthermore, he certainly regards these forms as features of experience that are not given to sensibility by anything outside it, but are the forms of sensibility itself, through which representation is possible. The controversy begins when we ask why Kant believes, as he undoubtedly does, that spatiotemporal dimensions are exclusively the properties of sensibility, and could not belong to anything that had not already entered into sensation; why, that is, they could not belong to things-in-themselves. According to a recent, somewhat renegade suggestion by Paul Guyer, Kant argues 'that space and time can *only* be mere forms of representation *because* they cannot be properties of things in themselves' (Guyer 1989: 148), the more standard view being that, for Kant, 'space and time cannot be properties of things in themselves *because* they are subjective forms of representation' (ibid.; cf. Allison 1983: 7). Whichever of these interpretations we favour, we seem to be left with an assumption on Kant's part of considerable magnitude, namely that space and time cannot be *both* forms of sensibility *and* properties of things in themselves. This 'third' or 'neglected' alternative is sometimes known as 'Trendelenburg's alternative', after Adolf Trendelenburg, who observed (in 1862) that 'even if we concede the argument that space and time are demonstrated to be subjective conditions which, in us, precede perception and experience, there is still no word of proof to show that they cannot at the same time be objective forms' (quoted in Gardner 1999: 107). Kant responds to this sort of objection in his *Prolegomena* (4: 289–90),[1] where his argument seems to be that there is simply no comparison that can be made between something that occurs in sensation and a property of a thing-in-itself. Space and time must *either* belong to sensibility *or* to things-in-themselves; it makes no sense to think of them as belonging to both. The argument, as Gardner remarks, 'remains far from decisive' (1999: 110).

Whatever we make of Kant's arguments, what he takes himself to have established in the part of the *Critique* known as the 'Transcendental Aesthetic' is that the objects we encounter in experience are appearances only and not things-in-themselves. About things-in-themselves nothing positive can be known, since knowledge concerns only representations and the transcendental factors that make representations possible. Kant does not view this conclusion as epistemologically depressing. On the contrary, he heralds it as the key to overcoming scepticism about the external world. Having declared it to be 'a scandal of philosophy and universal human reason that the existence of things outside us . . . should have to be assumed merely *on faith*' (Bxxxix n.), he presents his own position as a way of giving dignity back to philosophy: it is no loss to us that we cannot know things-in-themselves, for these are simply the objects we *do* know, thought of in terms of what they are independently of our knowing them. Appearances are all we should ever hope and expect to know, and we know them, according to Kant, immediately.[2] Objections to this view have been raised from many quarters, and I shall mention some of them later in this chapter.

Now I want to return to Kant's formulation of the categories of the understanding. It will be recalled that, for Kant, in order for intuitions or sensings to become full-blooded experiences, they must be 'subsumed' under a concept. This means that a judgement must be made with respect to them. They must in each case be judged to be a representation *of something*, and this act of judging requires the employment of concepts, which employment – or the faculty responsible for such employment – Kant calls the understanding. As Kant puts it in the *Prolegomena* (4: 300), in order for experience to arise, 'The given intuition must be subsumed under a concept, which determines the form of judging in general with respect to the intuition, connects the empirical consciousness of the latter in a consciousness in general, and thereby furnishes empirical judgements with universal validity'. In some passages Kant brings in – in addition to sensibility and the understanding – a third faculty, namely the imagination. In some ways this third faculty spans the gap between the other two, although in other respects it seems to be merely the functioning of the understanding. The imagination's role is to assist in the performance of synthesis – of intuitions along with concepts – that is needed in order for coherent experiences and a cohesive empirical world to emerge. Before I say more about it, however, let me introduce the specific categories that Kant identifies.

The use of the term 'categories' in philosophy can be traced back to Aristotle, who specified ten principles by means of which being can be characterized. These ten are: substance, quantity, quality, relation, place, date, position, state, action and affection.[3] Kant describes Aristotle's schema as 'an effort worthy of an acute man', but complains that because Aristotle had no systematic method by means of which to arrive at his principles, the schema lacks integrity and concision (*CPR* A81/B107; cf. *Prol.* §39). In contrast, then, to Aristotle's somewhat baggy collection, Kant regards his own set of categories as comprising the core principles to which all *a priori* concepts can be traced. He divides the set into four classes, each of which includes three categories, thereby making twelve in total. These are represented in Table 3.1.

Table 3.1 Kant's categories of the understanding (as given at *CPR* A80/B106)

I. Quantity	*II. Quality*	*III. Relation*	*IV. Modality*
(1) unity	(4) reality	(7) inherence and subsistence	(10) possibility–impossibility
(2) plurality	(5) negation	(8) causality and dependence	(11) existence–non-existence
(3) totality	(6) limitation	(9) community (reciprocity)	(12) necessity–contingency

According to Kant, in order for experience to occur three main transcendental 'acts' must be performed. First, the sensory manifold must be apprehended as an intuition and not as a merely disparate array. For example, the momentary parts of a sound must be taken to form one continuous episode, otherwise no sound whatsoever could be heard. Kant calls this act, in one place, 'the *synopsis* of the manifold *a priori* through sense' (*CPR* A94), but elsewhere 'the synthesis of apprehension'. Second, for the intuition to become an empirical representation, it must be related to earlier versions of itself, as intuitions of a certain type. This involves retaining intuitions and being able to imaginatively reproduce them in ways that relate appropriately to one's current situation, and hence Kant calls it 'the synthesis of reproduction in the imagination' (A100 f.). Finally, to appreciate that an empirical representation is of a certain type, it is not enough merely to reproduce previous representations of that type in imagination; one must, additionally, *recognize* the equivalence between them, and hence 'the synthesis of recognition in the concept' is required (A103 f.). This recognition will include an acknowledgement of the general context within which two or more representations can be encountered as representations of the same thing, this general context being that of a single unified consciousness. It is this unified consciousness – which Kant calls 'the synthetic unity of apperception' – that makes possible the experience of an empirical world as opposed to a disharmonious set of experiential packages, and Kant regards it as 'the supreme principle of all use of the understanding' (B136). All individual experiences must, if they are to cohere into an experience-whole, share the status of belonging together under the common designation 'I think…' (or: 'I am conscious of…'). In other words, for Kant self-consciousness is essential for consciousness *per se*, although the 'self' of which one is conscious is nothing over and above the unity of experience that one spontaneously takes to be one's own.

Recapitulation and some criticisms of the Kantian view

In the Introduction to the *Critique*'s second edition Kant famously compares his own project to that of Copernicus (Bxvi ff.). I would interpret his remarks on this matter as follows. Just as Copernicus, in order to devise a correct theory of the relation between the sun and the planets, had needed to think of the real situation as being other than what appears to us to be the case, so, in order to discover how knowledge and experience are possible, we must reconsider the relation between the knowing subject and the world of objects it experiences. Although, from our standpoint here on earth, the sun appears to move across the sky, a proper scientific investigation exposes the fact that it is the earth that travels around the sun. Similarly, although we ordinarily – both pre-theoretically and in pre-critical philosophical reflection – assume that our experience of objects conforms, or at least corresponds to some degree, to the intrinsic properties of the objects themselves, if we are not to fall prey to scepticism about the possibility of knowledge, then we must reorient our view in such a way that empirical objects – insofar as they *are* empirical – are understood to be constructed through the very process of their coming into experience.

The reason why the pre-critical view (or 'pre-Copernican' one, in Kant's metaphor) leads to scepticism is, roughly speaking, that if our experiences are held to be *of* things-in-themselves and yet, *qua* experiences, not to *be* those things, then there always remains an epistemic gap between the experience and the thing, and hence we can never know the extent to which our experience does or does not conform to its object. Kant's view reframes this situation by postulating that our experiences are not *of* things-in-themselves at all; they are, instead, *of* appearances, but there is no epistemic gap between the appearances and our experience of them because, in effect, the appearances and experiential content are one and the same.

There are, inevitably, many objections that could be, and have been, raised to Kant's position, and I will be able to do little more than mention a few of them here. The three I have selected are all targeted at Kant's notion of the thing-in-itself. Two are from Schopenhauer and the other is from Hegel and Bradley.

Schopenhauer is broadly sympathetic to Kant's enterprise, and regards his own work as being in large part a development of Kant's, with elements of Platonism, Vedānta and Buddhism thrown into the mixture.[4] He is especially sympathetic to the Kantian distinction between appearances and things-in-themselves, and takes this as the starting-point of his own philosophy, albeit with some qualifications. The chief difficulty that he has with Kant's formulation of the distinction – and he was not the first to draw attention to this point[5] – is that it seems to be based on the assumption that the manifold of raw sensory material which constitutes the content of our intuitions cannot manifest spontaneously of its own accord, but must be derived from something outside us; in other words, every sensation must have an extra-mental *cause*. This assumption is problematic in view of Kant's conviction that 'causality–dependence' is one of the categories of understanding; that is, is one of the relations in terms of which objects are cognized, and cannot therefore legitimately be ascribed to that which is independent of all subjectivity (cf. Schopenhauer 1969, I: 436, 502). The same criticism might, of course, be made with regard to the categories themselves: if the categories *in toto* are held to play a part in causing experiences to occur, then causality cannot itself be one of them. It would seem that causality is a necessary condition not only of the possibility of experience, but of the possibility of anything's *generating* experience as well, and hence it cannot be coherently regarded as merely a category of the understanding. Schopenhauer's own way out of this problem is not very satisfactory, for he wants to do two incompatible things. On the one hand he wants to retain the Kantian ascription of causality to our perceptual apparatus,[6] while on the other hand he wants to transform the unknowable things-in-themselves into a monistic principle of self-objectifying will, thereby ascribing causal agency to that which logically precedes the causal relation (which is precisely what Kant was being accused of in the first place).

A secondary error that Schopenhauer finds in Kant's notion of things-in-themselves is that which has just been hinted at in the reference to Schopenhauer's monism, namely their supposed plurality. Whereas Kant, in speaking (as he often does) of *things* in themselves, implies that there are several, perhaps innumerable, such items, Schopenhauer points out that numerical attributions can apply only to temporal and spatiotemporal entities and that the thing-in-itself always remains unaffected by space and time. Strictly speaking, the thing-in-itself could not even be designated as singular, for this too is a numerical attribution. However, if we are to refer to it at all, we cannot avoid all quantifying terms, and the singular is more appropriate than any alternative – as long, that is, as we remember that it is 'not one as an object is one, for the unity of an object is known only in contrast to possible plurality' (ibid.: 113).

That the Kantian thing-in-itself can be properly spoken of neither as singular nor as non-singular might awaken a suspicion that it is a very peculiar type of thing indeed. Schopenhauer, as I have noted, wants to hang on to some version of it, but there have been many other philosophers who prefer to reject it on the grounds of its incoherence. One of these who has been especially influential is Hegel, who complains that the Kantian thing-in-itself cannot legitimately be regarded as transcendent of thought: it is merely the '*caput mortuum*' that remains when we abstract the bare identity of an object from all its properties. It makes no sense to speak of it as something unknowable to us, for it is precisely the thing that we do know, only stripped of all positive determinations (cf. Hegel 1975: 72 [Zusatz to §44]). The British absolute idealist F. H. Bradley nicely captures the paradoxical status of the Kantian thing-in-itself when he writes that:

> The Unknowable must, of course, be prepared either to deserve its name or not. But, if it actually were not knowable, we could not know that such a thing even existed. It would be much as if we said, 'Since all my faculties are totally confined to my garden, I cannot tell if the roses next door are in flower.'
>
> (Bradley 1969: 111)

The problem that has been raised here is one that all philosophers with idealist inclinations must face. If one is committed to the view that the knowable can exist only in relation to a conscious knowing subject, then one has denied oneself the possibility of saying anything intelligible about the way reality is independently of the domain of subjective consciousness. If one is not to be inconsistent, therefore, one must delimit the whole of reality to a single consciousness, which position is, of course, open to the charge of solipsism. This issue is one that Husserl struggled with in his own idealist phase; and since it is also one that Sāṃkhya was alert to, I shall be giving it some further attention in Chapter 7. Now, however, let us examine some more general features of phenomenological theory and methodology that are pertinent to Sāṃkhya and Yoga.

Phenomenology and descriptive psychology

The term 'phenomenology' has been around in philosophical discourse since the eighteenth century, and was used on occasions by Kant and some of his German contemporaries.[7] It gained increased prominence when it was taken up by Hegel in *The Phenomenology of Spirit* (1807). According to most interpreters, Hegel's phenomenology consists in the investigation and description of the grand historical process in which 'consciousness' (construed transpersonally) progresses towards a state of absolute knowledge, this being the identity of knower and known (the 'for-itself' and the 'in-itself'). Hegel regarded phenomenology as a rigorous science, and this sense of the term was carried through into the late nineteenth and early twentieth centuries in the work of Franz Brentano, Carl Stumpf and Edmund Husserl. However, for the likes of Brentano and Stumpf, and the early Husserl, phenomenology was no longer the explication of a world-historical narrative; rather, it became the careful and sustained attempt to describe and analyse experience of a more everyday kind. Whether it has ever become genuinely scientific remains a moot question.

I specified just now that it was for the *early* Husserl that phenomenology was no longer the explication of a world-historical narrative. This qualification is necessary because in his later work, and especially in the book that he came close to completing in his final years,[8] Husserl shows a growing interest in history, albeit primarily the history of western philosophical ideas. He never succeeded in marrying his views on the evolution of western thought with his commitment to an all-encompassing 'transcendental subjectivity', but at times the attempt to combine these themes brings him close to Hegelian absolute idealism. I shall say more about Husserl's ideas shortly, although, as noted earlier, my initial concern will be with Brentano.

Brentano (1838–1917) is commonly characterized as a 'forerunner', rather than an advocate, of phenomenology.[9] It is true that he referred to his own approach as 'descriptive psychology' or 'psychognosy' in preference to 'phenomenology'. However, it is also true that what he meant by these terms could with perfect legitimacy be called phenomenology, and that in Brentano's work we find the seeds of much of what was to become known as phenomenology in the twentieth century, including the idealist, and potentially solipsistic, tendencies of Husserl.[10] Brentano places himself within the empiricist tradition of western philosophy and psychology, and declares of himself that 'My psychological standpoint is empirical; experience alone is my teacher. Yet I share with other thinkers the conviction that this is entirely compatible with a certain ideal point of view' (1973: xv). I take it that, by referring to 'a certain ideal point of view', Brentano is simply acknowledging that in order to do psychology it is not enough to merely *have* experience – one must also *theorize* about it, and such theorizing inevitably involves the 'ideal' realm of thought.

Brentano's primary methodological tool is what he calls 'inner perception', and he is quick to distinguish this from 'inner observation', otherwise known as 'introspection' (ibid.: 29). According to Brentano, one can never truly observe one's own mental states because the process of observation changes the state itself. For example:

> If someone is in a state in which he wants to observe his own anger raging within him, the anger must already be somewhat diminished, and so his original object of observation would have disappeared. The same impossibility is also present in all other cases. It is a universally valid psychological law that we can never focus our *attention* upon the object of inner perception.
>
> (Ibid.: 30)

As I understand it, Brentano's 'inner perception' involves one's making precisely the sort of attitudinal shift that Husserl had in mind when he 'discovered' the so-called 'phenomenological reduction' about thirty years after the publication of Brentano's best-known work.[11] Whereas, ordinarily in day-to-day life and also in natural scientific research, we take the phenomena that we perceive via our senses to be objects and events 'out there in the world', when we engage in Brentanian 'inner perception' we continue to perceive the same phenomena but we treat them as being 'in the mind' or 'in consciousness' as opposed to outside it. This attitudinal shift is, in effect, an act of imagination, for it consists in considering the same phenomena that constitute our everyday experience from an alternative standpoint.[12] Brentano holds that when objects are viewed in this way – that is, purely as phenomena and not as mind-independent entities – we have apodictic knowledge of them. This is because we have abolished the distinction between appearance and reality: all we are concerned with is the appearance. However, while sensations and perceptual phenomena can be treated in this way when one is in a cool and reflective mood, if one wishes to also study states of mind such as the anger that Brentano referred to above, then a supplementary method must be employed. Brentano thus advocates the use of memory; for, although we cannot introspect our mental states directly, if we can remember them we are thereby able to observe certain of their characteristics. While admitting that, unlike inner perception, memory is fallible, Brentano adds that without some trust in the power of memory not only would psychology be impossible, but so would all other sciences (p. 36).

As far as Brentano is concerned, the subject matter of descriptive psychology is the various types of phenomena that occur as presentations (*Vorstellungen*) in consciousness. He divides these into two main categories, namely mental phenomena and physical phenomena. His conception of physical phenomena has frequently been considered by critics to be inappropriately named, since he includes under this heading not only what we would ordinarily call physical objects as they are presented in consciousness, but also the content of feelings and sensations, mental images and even concepts. Essentially, he classes as a physical phenomenon anything that can be construed as the object or content of a conscious mental state, and he classes the conscious mental states themselves as mental phenomena or mental acts. As examples of mental phenomena he mentions: 'hearing a sound, seeing a colored object, feeling warmth or cold', plus judging, recollecting, expecting, inferring, holding a conviction or opinion, doubting and having an emotion (p. 79).

Among the chief characteristics of mental phenomena, Brentano includes their exclusive availability to inner perception (and hence their privacy to a single conscious individual), and their invariable appearance as part of a unity. The success of these as characteristics that distinguish mental from physical phenomena is open to question, since on Brentano's use of the term, 'physical phenomena' must be regarded as privately available and as part of a unified consciousness as well. After all, if physical phenomena are the *contents* of mental ones, then the privacy and unified nature of the latter must apply also to the former. A more successful criterion of distinction, and indeed the one to which Brentano himself gives most emphasis, is therefore that of intentionality: mental phenomena are intentional in the sense of being *of* or *about* something, whereas physical phenomena are the very things that are intended. The following passage is probably the most widely quoted of any that Brentano ever wrote:

> Every mental phenomenon is characterized by what the Scholastics of the Middle Ages called the intentional (or mental) inexistence of an object, and what we might call, though not wholly unambiguously, reference to a content, direction toward an object (which is not to be understood here as meaning a thing), or immanent objectivity. Every mental phenomenon includes something as object within itself, although they do not all do so in the same way. In presentation something is presented, in judgement something is affirmed or denied, in love loved, in hate hated, in desire desired and so on.
>
> (Ibid.: 88)

To this statement Brentano adds that 'This intentional in-existence is characteristic exclusively of mental phenomena. No physical phenomenon exhibits anything like it. We can, therefore, define mental phenomena by saying that they are those phenomena which contain an object intentionally within themselves' (p. 89).[13] Like 'intentionality' itself, the term 'inexistence' has acquired in modern English a sense at variance to that which Brentano is operating with. It is clear from his own account, however, that he means by it not 'non-existence' but 'existence *in*' or, more precisely, 'containing something existentially'. Since he regards physical phenomena as contained within mental ones, Brentano attributes to them a lower grade of existence. Both mental and physical phenomena can be intended: physical ones are intended by mental ones, and mental ones can be intended by higher order mental acts such as remembering. Hence both types of phenomena have intentional existence; but, according to Brentano, mental phenomena 'are those... which alone possess real existence as well as intentional existence. Knowledge, joy and desire really exist. Color, sound and warmth have only a phenomenal and intentional existence' (p. 92).

The distinction between mental and physical phenomena that Brentano developed laid a foundation for much of the phenomenological work that was to come subsequently, as did his stipulated (if not always strictly practised) delimitation of the appropriate sphere of descriptive psychology to that of consciousness itself. Husserl's early work, up to and including the second volume of his *Logical Investigations* (1901), broadly accepts the Brentanian framework, albeit with some reservations and terminological alterations. Perhaps Husserl's most substantial disagreement was over the intentionality of mental phenomena. Whereas, as we have seen, Brentano regards this as a mental phenomenon's defining characteristic, Husserl thinks that not all mental phenomena are intentional. In certain cases – such as sensations of pleasure and pain, and some desires and volitions – there may be an experience (i.e. a mental phenomenon in Brentano's terminology) which is not directed towards any discernible object.[14] A pleasurable feeling, for example, though provoked by some event outside itself, may then persist long after the event has ceased to be present to consciousness. Although I do not have space to enter into this dispute in detail, in Brentano's defence I would point out that, when he claims that a sensation – whether of pleasure, pain, or anything else – is intentional, he does not, on the whole, mean that it is always directed at, or provoked by, a determinable object. As I understand him, he means, rather, that any sensation may be analysed into the sensing-act and the feeling-content, and this act–content distinction is perfectly consistent with Brentano's overall approach. Husserl did not see consistency of this kind as a virtue because, with regard to sensations, he considered the act–content distinction to be inappropriate; on Husserl's view, the sensation and its content are identical.[15]

From Husserl's own point of view, the disagreements that he had with Brentano in the *Logical Investigations* were relatively minor when looked at in the light of subsequent developments in his thinking. A clear indication of this point is that, whereas in the Introduction to the first edition of *Logical Investigations* vol. 2 Husserl defined 'phenomenology' as 'descriptive psychology' – thereby approximating his general strategy to that of Brentano – in the second edition (1913) he replaced the passage in which this definition occurred with one that goes out of its way to define phenomenology in *contrast* to descriptive psychology. The distinction, Husserl thinks, lies in the fact that, while descriptive psychology deals with psychological states (such as perceptions, judgements, feelings, volitions, etc.) as 'the real states of animal organisms in a real natural order', phenomenology 'does not discuss states of animal organisms... but perceptions, judgements, feelings *as such*, and what pertains to them *a priori* with unlimited generality' (1970a, I:[16] 261–62). The contrast to which Husserl seeks to draw attention here seems contrived, for the sort of descriptive psychology that Brentano and the early Husserl himself engaged in was never concerned solely with the description of the *particular* mental states of conscious living beings; such description was always a means to the end of devising a *general* classification of mental states. Thus Husserl appears to be trying to impose a distinction where there is no significant difference, and this is a tendency of his that we see also in his accounts of what he considers to be his greatest methodological innovation, namely the *phenomenological reduction*.

From phenomenological reduction to metaphysical idealism

In an article on phenomenology written for the *Encyclopaedia Britannica*, Husserl says of the '*method of "phenomenological reduction"*' that it is 'the foundational method of pure psychology and the presupposition of all its specifically theoretical methods' (Husserl 1981: 24). He thereby implies that the reduction is not itself a 'theoretical method'. It is, rather, the adoption of a particular attitude or standpoint from which one imagines – that is, voluntarily assumes it to be the case – that everything within one's field of consciousness bears no relation to anything beyond consciousness itself. It is called a 'reduction' (or *epoché*, to give it the Greek name often used by Husserl) because it involves 'reducing' all phenomena to the status of *mere* phenomena, viewing them as appearances alone and not as entities whose existence is independent of the consciousness in which they are now revealed. The technique might just as well be termed the 'expansion of subjectivity', since it enlarges the boundary of one's own consciousness to the extent that everything – literally everything one can possibly experience in perception or thought – is encompassed by it.

As I noted earlier, Husserl's reductive approach was anticipated by Brentano in his method of 'inner perception', which similarly consists in putting aside the presupposition that the objects of consciousness transcend consciousness itself; and hence it can hardly be regarded as a profound development on Husserl's part. Indeed, Husserl himself sees pre-echoes of the reduction in the work of earlier philosophers, and especially in the method of systematic doubt formulated in Descartes's *Meditations*. Just as Descartes set out to establish an apodictic basis for knowledge by rejecting all claims upon which the slightest shadow of doubt could be cast, so Husserl, under the flag of phenomenological reduction, 'suspends' (or 'puts out of play' or 'brackets') all speculations concerning the trans-subjective ontological status of phenomenal items. Or, at least, this is what Husserl professes to be doing. When we turn to those works of his that were published in or subsequent to 1913, however, we find a blurring of phenomenological and ontological vocabularies that makes it virtually impossible to interpret Husserl's position as anything other than an absolute idealism, according to which the only thing that ultimately and truly *is*, is consciousness itself, which Husserl calls variously 'Absolute Being' and 'transcendental subjectivity'. This is especially true of passages such as the following:

> It is clear that... Consciousness, considered in its "*purity*", must be reckoned as *a self-contained system of Being*, as a system of *Absolute Being*, into which nothing can penetrate, and from which nothing can escape.
>
> (Husserl 1931: 153)

> Every imaginable sense, every imaginable being, whether the latter is called immanent or transcendent, falls within the domain of transcendental subjectivity.
>
> (1977: 84)

Thus we see that Husserl's radicalism resides not in the method of phenomenological reduction, which is really nothing new, but rather in his overstepping of the very prohibition that he had laid down as the criterion of proper phenomenological investigation, the prohibition, namely, against maintaining ontological commitments that are unsusceptible to experiential verification. Against Brentano, and against Kant – each of whom, in his own way, admitted that there must be *something* extraneous to consciousness which causes our sensations[17] – Husserl delimits all existence to consciousness itself. Since he acknowledges the undesirability of a solipsistic position, and yet cannot see any possibility of a reality outside of a unified consciousness, he finds himself awkwardly committed to a universe of windowless monads *à la* Leibniz. Although this is surely among the most outlandishly speculative of all metaphysical conceptions, Husserl maintains in his *Cartesian Meditations* that it has emerged as a result of following purely phenomenological methods.[18]

The relevance of Kantian and phenomenological thought

The points at which phenomenology and Kantian critical philosophy intersect with, and become relevant to, my explication of Sāṃkhya–Yoga metaphysics will, I hope, reveal themselves as this study progresses. My purpose in this chapter has been to highlight some salient features of the philosophical approaches concerned in readiness for the re-emergence of certain of these features in the discussion of the Indian material that is to follow. In order to make the relevance more explicit, however, it will be helpful if I partly anticipate that discussion by here outlining some specific similarities.

We have seen in this chapter that, although all the philosophers mentioned were deeply committed to the task of analysing experience, between (and, indeed, within) each of their individual approaches, there is considerable room for variation. My contention is that Sāṃkhya and Yoga are also involved in an analysis of experience, and that their approach, while being identical neither to Kant's nor to that of Brentano or Husserl, nevertheless contains elements in common with each. The orientation of Sāṃkhya and Yoga is, as I interpret it, phenomenologically reductive in the sense that it takes as its primary site of inquiry the field of consciousness, as opposed to a realm of objects that is believed to exist independently of anyone's experience. The metaphysical or ontological schema presented in the *Sāṃkhyakārikā* contains within it a distinction between intentional acts and their intended objects or contents that is analogous to Brentano's distinction between mental and physical phenomena. Like Brentano, though unlike Husserl, the Sāṃkhya schema regards sensations as intentional. It refers to the five sense modalities as 'awareness-capacities' (*buddhīndriya*s) and to each of the five modes of sense-content as 'merely that' or 'that alone' (*tanmātra*), which term is perhaps suggestive of the ineffability of qualitative sense-experience.

Analogous to Kant's distinction between the matter and form of intuitions is the Sāṃkhyan distinction between the five modes of sense-content (*tanmātra*) and the five 'elements' (*bhūta*s). The comparison is, admittedly, rather tenuous; for, although the Sāṃkhya elements include 'space' (*ākāśa*), they do not appear to include time, and the other four elements do not have any place in Kant's conception of the sensible forms. However, the mere presence in the Sāṃkhya philosophy of a form–matter distinction with regard to perceptual objects indicates a subtlety of analysis that, while less elaborated than Kant's, is nevertheless comparable to it.

Of particular interest is the Sāṃkhya category of 'egoity' (*ahaṃkāra*), which we find as 'I-am-ness' (*asmitā*) in Yoga. Defined as 'the thought of oneself' (*abhimāna*) at *SK* 24, this can refer both to the moral defect of pride or conceit and to the mere thought of one's *being* a self. When considered in the light of this latter definition, Sāṃkhyan egoity is very much like the Kantian 'I think' (or 'unity of apperception'), for in both cases there is a conception of a certain ability – namely the ability to formulate oneself as a subject of experience – as being a necessary condition of experience's possibility. A further resemblance to Kantian thought can be found in the Sāṃkhyan *manas* ('mind' or 'mentation'), which seems to play a role similar to that of the Kantian imagination, at least insofar as the latter can be considered responsible for the synthesis of sensory experiences under the common condition of experiential unity.

With regard to the defining metaphysical dualism of Sāṃkhya–Yoga, namely that between the 'self' (*puruṣa*) and the 'primordial producer' (*prakṛti*), despite there being nothing to match this dualism in any of the western philosophies considered here, Kantian vocabulary can be helpfully invoked in order to clarify what is going on in the Sāṃkhya–Yoga system. Essentially, the dualism seems to consist in an encounter between a transcendental subject (conceived as simple and structureless) and a transcendental source of the forms and material constituents of experience. This latter source is inferred, by means of a rudimentary transcendental deduction known as the *sat-kārya-vāda*, to have an unmanifest or noumenal aspect. It is also inferred to have a threefold structure, comprising three 'strands' (*guṇa*s) that are, in my view, best construed as necessary conditions of all possible appearance.[19]

I hope enough has been said to vindicate my claim that certain components of Kantian and phenomenological philosophy can serve to illuminate parts of Sāṃkhya and Yoga metaphysics. With these conceptual tools in the bag, I shall in the next chapter begin tackling some persistent assumptions about Sāṃkhya and Yoga that I consider to be inadequately grounded. Central among these is the assumption that Sāṃkhya and Yoga uphold what one scholar has recently described as 'a thoroughgoing realism' (King 1999: 65).

4

THE IMPUTATION OF REALISM

In philosophical discourse 'realism' usually concerns the relation between a subject of experience – that is, a conscious mind – and a class of objects, which may be more or less broad in scope. If one is a realist about a certain object or thing, then one believes that the thing in question exists independently of one's experiencing it, whether in perception or as an object of thought. Because the range of things about which one could have such a belief is extremely wide, the term 'realist' does not, in itself, have a definite meaning.[1] Strictly speaking, when one asserts of anyone that he or she is a realist, one ought always to specify what it is that the person is a realist about. Correspondingly, when one ascribes *anti-realism* to someone, one ought to spell out exactly which class of objects the person is denying subject-independent reality to. In practice, however, the terms 'realism' and 'anti-realism' often get bandied around in philosophical discussions without their frame of reference being stipulated. In many, perhaps most, cases this is of little importance, since the relevant objects will be determinable from the discursive context. But in certain instances the meaning of the terms remains thoroughly opaque due to a lack of clarity and precision on the part of the discussants.

Anyone who reads even a small amount of the available interpretive literature on classical Sāṃkhya and Yoga will, before long, encounter some particular claims about these Indian systems. Two of these claims have been discussed already in Chapter 2 above, namely that: (1) Sāṃkhya is 'rationalist' whereas Yoga is 'mystical', and (2) Sāṃkhya is atheistic whereas Yoga is theistic. Both of these claims, when expressed as simply as this, are in my view highly misleading. Among the other claims routinely made about Sāṃkhya and Yoga are: that they are metaphysically dualist, that they believe prakṛti to be a material principle, and that they are philosophically realist. These three claims are closely related, since prakṛti is one of the two poles that are regarded as making up the metaphysical dualism, and it is prakṛti and its emergents that Sāṃkhya and Yoga are held to be realist about. What complicates the interpretive situation, however, is that the imputation of realism is often made, first, without a coherent explanation of what prakṛti and its series of emergents *are*, and hence, second, without any account of how this form of realism relates to the sorts of viewpoints with which the term realism has been more typically associated in western philosophy. The temptation for interpreters – once prakṛti has been defined as a material principle – is to regard 'prakṛti', 'material principle', and '*the world*' as equivalent terms, and then to either state explicitly, or else leave it to be assumed, that what Sāṃkhya and Yoga are realist about is *the world of material objects*. There is, however, a major problem with this interpretation, which starts to reveal itself as soon as one examines the descriptions of the two co-ultimate metaphysical principles – namely puruṣa and prakṛti, or the 'seer' (*draṣṭṛ*) and the 'seeable' (*dṛśya*) – that are presented in the classical texts.

In this chapter I wish to place in question the imputation of realism to Sāṃkhya and Yoga, and to argue that such an imputation can be sustained only when unwarranted simplifications and conflations are made in relation to the complex positions of these philosophies. I do not wish to dispute the claim that Sāṃkhya and Yoga are metaphysically dualist; dualism is indeed one of their defining characteristics. I shall argue, however, that the nature of the dualism – and hence the nature of its two polar principles – needs to be properly understood before we can assume that it makes any sense, in the context of Sāṃkhya and Yoga thought, to speak of the relation between an experiencing subject and a world of mind-transcendent objects. The argument cannot be completed in a single chapter, for it requires a detailed examination of the concept of prakṛti, and this examination will take place mainly in Chapter 5. Here, however, I shall get the argument under way, first by critically scrutinizing some of the core assumptions that are made in the exegetical literature on Sāṃkhya and Yoga, and second by focusing more sharply upon a particular passage in the *Yogasūtra* that has been seized upon by many commentators (both traditional and modern) as evidence of Yoga's realism and its opposition to idealism.

The standard interpretation of Sāṃkhya and Yoga (and some of its shortcomings)

Probably the best way of grasping why Sāṃkhya and Yoga have so frequently been assumed to be realist is to begin by outlining the main features of what has become the standard interpretation of these systems. Although variations occur between the versions presented by different interpreters, there exists a widely accepted set of core principles, which can be summarized as follows:

1 Sāṃkhya and Yoga are metaphysically dualist. They hold that reality comprises two mutually irreducible entities (or 'substances' or 'principles'), which are most commonly referred to as puruṣa and prakṛti.
2 Puruṣa is the principle of subjectivity or consciousness. Only in its presence can experience take place. There is a multiplicity – indeed, an infinity – of puruṣas, which in themselves are numerically distinct despite being qualitatively indistinguishable from one another.
3 Prakṛti is the principle of objectivity and materiality. It comprises three co-essential constituents or, more literally, 'strands' (*guṇa*s). When these are

undisturbed and in equal tension with one another, prakṛti remains unmanifest (*avyakta*). When they are disturbed and out of equilibrium, prakṛti becomes manifest (*vyakta*). It is normally assumed that prakṛti is singular.

4 The disturbance of the guṇas occurs due to the 'presence' or 'proximity' (*sannidhāna* [*TK* 20]) of puruṣa, and therefore this presence may be regarded as a 'catalyst' that stimulates or 'excites' the guṇas into action, even though puruṣa itself remains passive.[2] There was never a time, however, when puruṣa and prakṛti were not compresent, and thus the guṇas must, in actuality, have always been active. Despite the 'beginninglessness' of their conjunction (*YBh* 2.22), it is possible for puruṣa and prakṛti to separate, and thus for equilibrium to be established between the guṇas.

5 The process of prakṛti's manifestation consists in a series of 'real transformations' (Feuerstein 1980: 32; Organ 1975: 211), which together form an evolutionary chain. The whole of empirical reality – the cosmos or world – is produced through this process. 'Real transformation' may be taken to imply that the prakṛti-generated world is not constitutionally dependent upon puruṣa, despite the fact that it could not have manifested without puruṣa's presence, and that it manifests solely 'for the purpose of puruṣa' (*puruṣārtha*).

6 The 'purpose of puruṣa' is twofold. It comprises, on the one hand, having experience or 'enjoyment' (*bhoga*) of the world and, on the other hand, transcending experience and abiding in a state of self-contained 'aloneness' (*kaivalya*). Since experience is inherently dissatisfying and distressing (*duḥkha*), the former purpose must be regarded as subordinate and auxiliary to the latter.

7 The goal of kaivalya is achieved through the attainment of a self-revealing knowledge. For Sāṃkhya this knowledge is arrived at as a result of rational thinking, whereas for Yoga it is acquired by means of supra-rational meditation.

8 Although kaivalya involves only an epistemic and not an ontological change in puruṣa, it does involve the 'dissolution' (*laya*, *pratiprasava*) of manifest prakṛti into its unmanifest source (cf. *SK* 65; *YS* 4.34), which (because the manifestation is 'real') can be regarded only as an ontological change.

With respect to the issue of realism, the two most important points in the above summary come under numbers 1 and 5. I shall therefore focus upon these, although, as we will discover, these cannot be considered in isolation from other matters. Point 1 is important because the proposal that prakṛti is not ontologically reducible to puruṣa may be construed as an assertion of prakṛti's subject-independent reality. In short, there is *something* that exists independently of consciousness. Point 5 pushes this assertion further and claims that not only is the metaphysical ground of the empirical world real, in the sense of being subject-independent, but so is the empirical world itself. I shall say a little more about each of these points in turn.

A point that needs to be made straightaway is that the modern interpretation of the puruṣa–prakṛti dualism has tended to be heavily influenced by the mind–body dualism common to western metaphysical debate, the most paradigmatic version of this dualism being that of Descartes. For Descartes, since a substance is that which requires nothing else in order to exist, strictly speaking the only genuine substance is God.[3] However, less strictly we can regard as substances those things that depend for their existence upon nothing other than God; and this definition allows in, on Descartes's view, *res cogitans* ('thinking things', minds, souls) and *res extensae* ('extended things', bodies, material objects) (Descartes 1985, I: 210).

Interpreters of Sāṃkhya and Yoga are generally reluctant to speak of puruṣa as a substance. This is probably because, in spite of the long history of expressions such as 'spiritual substance' and 'immaterial substance' in western philosophy, there remains a sneaking suspicion that 'substance', if not a precise synonym of 'matter', at least *implies* it.[4] No such qualms need interfere with the characterization of prakṛti, however. To this principle the term 'substance' is freely applied, as, for example, when Radhakrishnan declares that 'Prakṛti is the fundamental substance out of which the world evolves' (1927, II: 266),[5] or Davies defines it as 'a blind unconscious force, or rather a primal substance' (1894: 105 n.2). Indeed, some modern commentators have not merely defined prakṛti in terms of substance, but have translated it as such (on occasions endowing 'Substance' with a capital initial).[6] More common, however, are phrases that involve 'matter' or 'nature'. The majority of translators of Sāṃkhya and Yoga texts render *prakṛti* and its synonyms by expressions such as 'primordial matter' (Jhâ 1896), 'primordial nature' (Larson 1979), and 'primal nature' (Suryanarayana Sastri 1948). And in commentarial or critical literature written in European languages, we frequently find talk of such things as 'the Unmanifested or primal matter' (Davies 1894: 17), 'primal virgin matter' (Zimmer 1953: 225), 'primitive matter' (Garbe 1899: 10; Macdonell 1900: 391), and 'sheer materiality' (Larson 1980: 307). All of these terms are presumably intended to accord prakṛti the status of being an ultimate and self-existent substance in something approximating the Cartesian sense. Thus, although no interpreter would be reckless enough to equate puruṣa and prakṛti with Cartesian minds and bodies, the basic picture of a metaphysical substance-dualism is ascribed in common to both philosophies.

As an aside, it is appropriate to note here that, in order for a philosophical position to be externally realist – that is, realist with regard to empirical objects – it need not necessarily be dualist. Far from it. Physicalism (or materialism), for example, is monist in the sense that it proposes that everything, including supposedly 'mental' states and events, can be 'reduced to' (i.e. explained exclusively in terms of) physical states and events. Yet physicalists are certainly realists about empirical objects. That is, they hold that the objects we commonsensically take to be external to our minds are indeed external to our minds (insofar as they are external to our brains) and would continue to exist even if all conscious beings were annihilated (albeit, perhaps, not with precisely the same properties that we assume them to have in perceptual awareness).[7] Conversely, it is not necessary for a philosophy to be monist in order for it to be *anti-realist* about empirical objects (and hence 'idealist' in the most usual sense of this term). Although Kant, for example, would not wish to commit himself to either a monist or a dualist metaphysics – as to do so would, from his point of view, be to overstep the boundary of reason – it is nevertheless conceivable that a metaphysics could combine an affirmation of the unknowability of the thing-in-itself with a denial that the conscious subject can be reduced to that thing. In Chapter 6, I shall propose that this is in fact very close to the stance taken by Sāṃkhya and Yoga. But a good deal of background interpretive work will need to be done first.

The view of Sāṃkhya and Yoga that puruṣa and prakṛti are co-ultimate ontological principles is, on its own, a very minimal kind of realism. While it shows that the two Indian systems are realist about at least these two principles, in itself this is not of much philosophical interest. After all, everyone has to be a realist about *something*. As Descartes pointed out in the second of his *Meditations*, the very act of doubting the existence of things requires the existence of a doubter (and even if one refuses to grant this – as Nietzsche did for example[8] – the existence of *the doubt itself* cannot be denied); therefore a *complete* scepticism ends in self-contradiction. The minimal kind of realism that has just been attributed to Sāṃkhya and Yoga is not entirely trivial, however, since it is a necessary precondition for the more interesting kind that is asserted in point 5.

In point 5 we have the assertion of an ostensibly more familiar sort of realism, namely that which consists in the claim that 'the world' – that is, the extensive realm of things and events that we have experiences of and thoughts about – does not depend upon puruṣa for its existence, but is produced out of unmanifest prakṛti via a process of material changes or evolutions. It is this notion that Richard King, whom I quoted at the end of the last chapter, has in mind when he declares of Sāṃkhya: 'The school upholds a thoroughgoing realism. The world around us is real and independent of our perception of it being a series of material evolutes (*pariṇāma*) deriving from *prakṛti*' (1999: 65). And King is far from being alone in holding this view. Arthur Macdonell voiced it a hundred years earlier; by Sāṃkhya, he said, 'The world is maintained to be real, and that from all eternity; for the existent can only be produced from the existent' (1900: 391). Before him John Davies, in a discussion of the Sāṃkhya view of perception, wrote that Kapila (to whom Davies attributes the classical Sāṃkhya teachings) 'accepted our sense-perceptions as representating a real external world, which exists in itself, and not merely as a projection of our sensations or thoughts', and he adds that 'The Vedāntist doctrine, that the material world is only *māyā*, or illusion, was not held by him' (1894: 103). The contrast with Vedānta – by which term is typically meant the *Advaita* ('non-dualist') Vedānta of Śaṅkara – is a relatively common feature of claims concerning the realism of Sāṃkhya and Yoga. Arthur Keith draws it when he writes that 'nature [prakṛti] is essentially other than spirit [puruṣa]: it is not, as in Vedānta, a production of ignorance, but is as real as spirit itself' (1949: 89); and so does Eliade when he remarks that 'For Sāṃkhya and Yoga, the world is *real* (not illusory – as it is, for example, for

Vedānta)' (1969: 9, original emphasis). Later in this chapter I shall call attention to some statements made by Śaṅkara which show that he did not consistently hold the empirical world to be illusory; but let us now inquire whether there is any plausibility in the obviously widespread view that Sāṃkhya and Yoga regard it as real.

In the opening sentence of the above paragraph I noted that, according to point 5, the world does not depend upon puruṣa for its existence. In a western philosophical context it would be normal to describe external realism as the view that the world does not depend for its existence upon *the mind* or, in other words, upon our 'cognitive apparatus' or 'perceptual equipment', etc. With regard to Sāṃkhya and Yoga, however, it cannot be described in this way, since what is meant by 'the world' is not at all what is normally understood by this expression in western philosophical parlance, and neither of course is *puruṣa* equivalent to 'mind', 'cognitive apparatus', or similar constructions. This point is crucial, for it not only highlights the inappropriateness of designating prakṛti as 'the world', but also – as I hope to show in this and the subsequent two chapters – ultimately undermines the whole realist interpretation as it is generally formulated.

Taken in its broadest sense, 'the world' can mean simply 'everything that exists' or 'the whole of reality'. In that case, when applied to the philosophy of Sāṃkhya and Yoga, it would encompass both prakṛti and puruṣa. In discussions of realism and anti-realism, however, 'the world' invariably stands in opposition to the cognizing subject or mind. When we ask in such discussions whether the world is mind-independent, we are clearly not including 'mind' within 'the world', for it would be unintelligible to ask whether the mind is independent of itself. Nor can we be including mental states, contents, faculties and suchlike; for these, too, could not be thought of as mind-independent (cf. Alston 2002: 1). When, however, Larson (or any other interpreter of Sāṃkhya or Yoga) says that 'The *puruṣa*, which is consciousness, witnesses every level of the manifest world, and the manifest world does what it does because of or for the sake of *puruṣa*' (1979: 176), the phrase 'the manifest world' must not be regarded as excluding the mind and its contents. On the contrary, it must be regarded as referring *primarily* to the mind and its contents, and only secondarily to anything that exists outside it. For no interpreter of the systems concerned – even one who insists that everything to do with prakṛti is in some sense 'material' – would seriously deny that at least the majority of prakṛti's manifest forms is presented as being mental.

Puruṣa, meanwhile, can indeed be designated as consciousness, just as Larson designates it in the quotation above. This assessment is supported by puruṣa's being identified with *cetana* (*SK* 55), which is itself best translated as 'consciousness', and (at *SK* 19) with such states as 'seer-ness' (*draṣṭṛtva*) and 'witnessing' (*sākṣitva*), which latter term the quotation from Larson also alludes to. Yet puruṣa is patently not the kind of experiencing subject or self with which 'the world' is normally contrasted in western philosophy. Although many varied conceptions of such a subject exist in the western tradition, the most prevalent of these include its being complex and active, possessing a range of faculties (capacities, powers) by means of which it is able to engage with the world – to perceive it, think about it, and make more-or-less voluntary decisions to act in it, often in ways that have ethical implications.[9] Indeed, in western parlance, 'subject' and 'self' (and in earlier times 'spirit' and 'soul') have often been used interchangeably with 'mind' and 'person', thereby bolstering an assumption that the subject of experience must possess the kinds of properties that are typically attributed to minds, such as those of being able to undergo certain 'states' and intentionally hold certain perceptual and conceptual contents. It has come to be widely accepted, especially since Kant, that the mind, and hence the subject, must be *active*, as experiences and knowledge could not possibly arrive in our minds already fully formed. Whether one holds that one's perceptual experiences and conceptual knowledge fairly accurately represent the way the world is (*à la* realism) or bear no resemblance to that world whatsoever because a spatiotemporal realm of objects cannot exist independently of an experiencing subject (*à la* idealism), it cannot plausibly be maintained that we (*qua* cognizers or experients) play *no part* in the construction of the world as we experience it.

In Sāṃkhya and Yoga philosophy, however, puruṣa is neither complex nor active, although it is very definitely the 'experiencer' or 'enjoyer' (*bhoktṛ* [*SK* 17]). Most of the capacities that, in western thought, have tended to be ascribed to the subject – such as concept-formation, making judgements, recollecting things and events, initiating bodily movements – are, in Sāṃkhya and Yoga, placed very firmly within the purview of prakṛti. Even the very notion of being a self – an ego or 'I' (*aham*) – is a function of the essentially nonconscious prakṛti (*SK* 24). All that is left for puruṣa seems to be an impassable, undiscriminating, bare consciousness. Indeed, it cannot even be held to properly *perceive* anything, or to be aware *of* anything at all, since this intentional kind of consciousness belongs to – or, rather, is – buddhi.[10] In both Sāṃkhya and Yoga, perception (*dṛṣṭa*, *pratyakṣa*) is one of the three modes of valid cognition (*pramāṇa*), which is in turn a 'mental modification' (*cittavṛtti*) and, as such, cannot be attributed to puruṣa (cf. *YS* 1.2–7). Indeed, for this reason it is difficult to determine exactly in what sense puruṣa is to be regarded as an 'experiencer' at all. The term *draṣṭṛ*, meaning 'seer' (the one who sees), is used synonymously with *puruṣa* in the *Yogasūtra*, thereby suggesting an ability to see or perceive in some way. And in that text, as well as in the *Sāṃkhyakārikā*, the whole process of prakṛti's manifesting is said to be for the dual purpose of puruṣa's 'enjoyment' (*bhoga*) or 'seeing' (*darśana*) of prakṛti on the one hand, and its 'liberation' (*apavarga*, *kaivalya*) on the other (*YS* 2.18; *SK* 21). As mentioned above, however, we also find in both texts statements that identify puruṣa with the more abstract quality of 'seer-ness' (*SK* 19) or 'mere seeing' (*dṛśimātra* [*YS* 2.20]), which terms imply an attempt to dissociate puruṣa from any *particular* experiences and to characterize it as a kind of potential awareness – something 'within which' or 'to which' particular phenomenal events can occur.

The concept of puruṣa seems to require, then, that we distinguish between, on the one hand, experiential contents and the acts that intend them (to use Brentanian terminology), both of which fall under the category of prakṛti, and on the other hand, the fundamentally non-empirical pure subject – the 'subject that is never the object' as J. Ghosh puts it (1977: 2, 21). This latter subject can be said, analogically, to provide the conscious location in which phenomena reveal themselves, but cannot be said to cognize them itself.

It now becomes evident why the dualism at the heart of Sāṃkhya and Yoga philosophy is badly misrepresented when its counterposing principles are said to be 'consciousness' (or the 'conscious subject') and 'the world' respectively. Puruṣa is indeed, in some sense, a conscious subject, but it is held (albeit somewhat ambiguously) to be, in itself, non-intentional. The intentional relation – that is, the relation between an intentional act and its content – is something that, for Sāṃkhya and Yoga, is internal to prakṛti. Prakṛti, in its manifest state, comprises the repertoire of mental events and processes that make experience of a world possible, while puruṣa is, at least for the most part, aloof from such events and processes. Thus, what we are faced with in Sāṃkhya–Yoga metaphysics is not a mind–world dualism as typically understood in the tradition stemming from Descartes, but something which, though hard to pin down exactly, can provisionally be termed a subject–experience dualism (where 'experience' is construed as including both acts – or powers to act – and the contents thereof). 'The world' – *qua* subject-independent realm of entities – is not in the picture.

Owing to the peculiar and (to many western thinkers at least) unfamiliar nature of the basic Sāṃkhya–Yoga metaphysical position, one might expect to find frequent and lengthy explanations of precisely why the term 'realism' may appropriately be applied thereto in the writings of those interpreters who regard it as so applicable. Such explanations are not, however, forthcoming; indeed, where we do not find merely an absence of explanation, the most that tends to be offered is a half-explanation that leaves a high degree of ambiguity concerning the nature of the imputed realism. Francis Catalina, for example, says of Yoga that it 'is a realistic, mystical and scientific school of thought' (a curious combination!), and adds that 'It is realistic in its insistence upon the reality of the phenomenal world and that a normal evaluation of the perceptions of the sense be made' (1968: 138). By 'a normal evaluation of the perceptions of sense', I can only presume that Catalina means an evaluation that judges these perceptions as representing objects that exist independently of the perceptions themselves; which claim, combined with that of the 'reality of the phenomenal world', strongly implies that the realism being referred to involves the relation between perceiving subjects and an external world of objects, and this is precisely what I have argued amounts to a misrepresentation of the Sāṃkhya–Yoga position. Of course, many interpreters believe that Yoga *does* affirm the existence of physical objects in a subject-independent spatiotemporal world, and for some of them this belief is based upon a string of statements in the *Yogasūtra*'s fourth chapter which is taken to be an attempted refutation of the Yogācāra Buddhist 'consciousness-only' doctrine. I will come to this supposed refutation in the next section. The point of immediate interest, however, is that the statement quoted from Catalina above – which is not untypical of those who attribute realism to Sāṃkhya and Yoga – implicitly equates prakṛti with the world of subject-transcendent objects.

As a further illustration of this implicit equation let me give an example from the work of Anima Sen Gupta. Having declared that 'The philosophy of Sāṁkhya is not merely a dualistic system; it is also a realistic and rationalistic system', she then goes on to give some account of what she means by 'realistic system':

> A realistic system, as we know, is a system which believes that the object of cognition is different from and independent of cognition. In the opinion of a realistic philosopher, the object of valid cognition (pramājñ[ā]na) is never non-existent or unreal (asat). It is only the object of an erroneous cognition which can be regarded as asat in some sense or other.
>
> (Sen Gupta 1982: 2)

Sen Gupta, like Catalina above, is here talking about the relation between objects and our cognitions of them, and not about the relation between prakṛti and puruṣa as they ought, in my view, to be understood. Since she offers this definition of realism in order to explain the sense in which Sāṃkhya's position should be construed as such, she clearly believes that Sāṃkhyan realism is realism about the external world.

Elsewhere Sen Gupta acknowledges the fact that, for Sāṃkhya, the cognition and the cognized object both fall upon the prakṛtic side of the puruṣa–prakṛti dualism; that is, they are both constituted by prakṛti's three co-fundamental 'strands' (*guṇa*s). But she then goes on to confuse the issue by attempting to contrast the Sāṃkhya position with idealism. The passage is worth quoting at some length since it exemplifies the way in which the distinction between the puruṣa–prakṛti relation and the cognition–object relation is often blurred in accounts of Sāṃkhya's (and Yoga's) putative 'realism':

> [The] guṇas . . . form the realistic setting of the Sāṁkhya school. Knowledge and its objects belong to the realm of *guṇas* which are totally independent of the *puruṣa*. An idealistic system holds that in the acquisition of knowledge, consciousness contributes every item and that the object of knowledge is convertible into consciousness. The classical Sāṁkhya, however, holds that the stuff of which the object of knowledge is composed is radically distinct from consciousness and is also independent of it. The whole world, therefore, rests on a principle which is as eternal and independent as the spiritual principle. Thus, according to Sāṁkhya, both matter and spirit are equally real, although matter, being an obstacle in the path of liberation, is of inferior value.
>
> (Sen Gupta 1982: 66, my underlining)

This is a very confusing passage, and I will not endeavour to unravel all its tangled knots. The main thing I want to point out is the highly ambiguous – indeed, multivalent – use of the term 'consciousness'. For a start, in the assertion that, for the idealist, 'consciousness contributes every item [in the acquisition of knowledge]', 'consciousness' appears to have the sense of 'cognizing subject' or 'mind'. When, however, it is added that on such a view 'the object of knowledge is convertible into consciousness', 'consciousness' is now being used to mean the content of the cognition itself considered as merely mental. (By 'is convertible into', I take Sen Gupta to mean 'is ontologically reducible to' or 'is (numerically) identical to'.) This slide from one sense of 'consciousness' to another sets a precedent for the further slide that occurs between the term's third appearance and that of the expression 'spiritual principle'. The third occurrence of 'consciousness' could be read in either of the two earlier senses; and yet when Sen Gupta goes on to assert that 'The whole world, therefore, rests on a principle which is as eternal and independent as the spiritual principle', she has assumed a quite different meaning for the term 'consciousness' in the preceding sentence, namely the *pure* consciousness that we associate with (i.e. that *is*) puruṣa. This, of course, is not at all straightforwardly equivalent to the sense of a 'cognizing subject' and is in no measure equivalent to that of cognitive content. By means of this semantic promiscuousness Sen Gupta is able to convince herself that the dualism between 'matter and spirit' (i.e. prakṛti and puruṣa) is equivalent to, or at least implied by, a realist position concerning the existence of physical objects, when in fact, as I have been arguing, the two positions are *by no means* equivalent. In defence of the sort of equivalence that Sen Gupta implicitly proposes, one might point out that, insofar as puruṣa does not, according to Sāṃkhya and Yoga, actively contribute anything to the objects of cognition and experience, it is true to say that these systems regard the objects as being real independently of the conscious subject. This, however, would again be to impose a Cartesian paradigm upon the puruṣa–prakṛti dualism. The categories that make up prakṛti's manifest aspect are not Cartesian extended material objects; they include such things as intentional awareness (*buddhi*), egoity (*ahaṃkāra*), sense-capacities and their sensory contents. And hence when Sāṃkhya talks about prakṛti, and Yoga talks about the 'seeable' (*dṛśya*), what is at issue is not a world that stands, in itself, outside of experience, but the set of factors that together make the experience of a world possible.

It is my view, then, that the characterization of Sāṃkhya and Yoga as realist is thoroughly inappropriate and misleading. If the term 'realist' is to be applied to these systems at all, then we must be clear about which items they are claiming to be real, and what sense is being given to 'reality'. Prakṛti is real insofar as its existence is not dependent upon anything else. It cannot, however, be regarded as ontologically mind-independent, because it *is* the mind, or at least includes the mind. This last point – albeit expressed somewhat imprecisely here for the sake of brevity – is not controversial among interpreters of Sāṃkhya and Yoga. The problem is that many of these interpreters, as we have seen, fail to remain mindful of the largely (or perhaps exclusively) psychological nature of prakṛti, and fall prey to the temptation to use simple-sounding, but vague, expressions such as 'the world'.

The nature of prakṛti as I interpret it will receive further attention in Chapters 5 and 6. The remainder of this chapter will examine a passage in the *Yogasūtra* that is frequently cited by proponents of the realist interpretation of Sāṃkhya and Yoga as evidence for this view.

Yoga's alleged refutation of Buddhist idealism

It is a series of sūtras in the Kaivalyapāda, the fourth (and final) chapter of the *Yogasūtra*, that is widely held to contain a polemic against a theory attributed to the Yogācāra school of Mahāyāna Buddhism. This Buddhist school is estimated to have flourished in India from the fourth to the twelfth centuries CE, and is championed by such figures as Maitreya, Asaṅga, Vasubandhu and Sthiramati (cf. T. E. Wood 1991: ix). It is well known for holding a particular doctrine (*vāda*) that has typically been interpreted as idealism of an absolute, or monistic, kind.[11] The central principle of its doctrine is referred to as, among other things, *vijñāna* and *vijñapti* – each of which terms can, depending upon the context, be translated as 'consciousness', 'cognition', 'discernment', etc. – or sometimes as *citta*, which again can be rendered as 'consciousness' or 'mind'. The doctrine itself is called by such names as *vijñānavāda* ('consciousness[-only] doctrine') and *vijñapti-mātratā* ('aloneness of consciousness'); and these are taken to be indicative of the view that reality is exclusively mental. Since the early 1980s this idealist interpretation has been criticized by some scholars, who contend that Yogācāra's approach does not amount to the postulation of a supreme mental principle, and is better construed as, for example, 'realistic pluralism'[12] or phenomenology.[13] The interpretive situation has therefore become very complicated, and I do not intend to enter into this dispute here. For my present purpose, what needs to be noted is that those scholars who regard the *Yogasūtra* as containing an anti-Yogācāra critique bring to the issue two important presuppositions. One of these is that Yogācāra's vijñānavāda is a form of absolute idealism, and the other is that an attack on such idealism is equivalent to a defence of realism (about the physical world). I shall argue that the passage in question is neither realist nor anti-idealist, and exhibits no signs of being directed against Yogācāra or any other form of Buddhism.

The passage in question begins at *YS* 4.14 and continues through to 4.22, or 4.23 according to James Woods (1914: xli). Although there is no explicit reference to the vijñānavāda in any of these sūtras, several traditional commentators from Vyāsa onwards have taken them to be polemical in nature, and have, in their respective commentaries, vented their own opposition to the vijñānavāda. Modern scholars have, on the whole, accepted the traditional interpretation of the passage, and have cited it as evidence both of Yoga's (and, indirectly, Sāṃkhya's) alleged realism and of the *Yogasūtra*'s date being not earlier than the third century CE.[14] Regarding the latter claim, Woods proposes that, although we cannot be certain that the version of the vijñānavāda 'attacked by the [Yoga-]Sūtra must be the idealism of Vasubandhu', there remains a 'great' probability that it is (pp. xvii–xviii). This supposition is based almost entirely upon the inclusion in Vācaspati's commentary of a reference to a *vijñānavādin* (i.e. an advocate of the vijñānavāda), whom Woods thinks is unlikely to be anyone other than Vasubandhu (p. xviii). Woods shows no sign of having considered the fact that, whether or not Vācaspati was referring to Vasubandhu, such a reference would not in itself be sufficient to indicate that the original sūtra also had this particular Buddhist in mind, or any Buddhist for that matter. Notwithstanding the tenuousness of the evidence in its favour, however, the view that the sūtras are indeed criticizing Vasubandhu has become commonplace.

As I noted in Chapter 1, Surendranath Dasgupta challenges Woods' assessment of the *Yogasūtra*'s likely date, although not on the grounds that Woods has attached undue significance to Vācaspati's commentary. Rather, Dasgupta alleges that the whole of the Kaivalyapāda is an interpolation, and that it therefore cannot be used to place a limit on the antiquity of the other three chapters (Dasgupta 1922: 229–30). If Dasgupta is right about the Kaivalyapāda's being a later addition to the *Yogasūtra*, then even if it did contain passages expressing pro-realist and anti-idealist sentiments this in itself would not be sufficient for us to conclude that the Yoga system as a whole advocates external realism. Since, however, it is unlikely that the issue of the *Yogasūtra*'s integrity will be conclusively resolved one way or the other, it is worth asking the question whether the series of sūtras that purportedly argues in favour of realism does in fact expound such a position. Probably the most important of the sūtras to consider are 4.14 and 15, as it is these two that attract the most vociferously anti-idealist rhetoric from some traditional commentators, and which have been cited by several modern scholars as most explicitly exhibiting Yoga's realism. Let us, then, examine each of these two sūtras in turn.

YS 4.14 comprises the following brief statement: *pariṇāma-ekatvād vastu-tattvam*. A fairly literal translation would be: 'Due to the oneness of the modification, the "that-ness" of an object.' Owing to the fact that the preceding sūtra (4.13) designates the 'strands' (*guṇa*s) as the 'essence' (*ātman*) of objects that are either 'manifest' (*vyakta*) or 'subtle' (*sūkṣma*, i.e. imperceptible), the expression *pariṇāma-ekatva* may be taken to stand for the unity of the modifications of these strands. *Vastu-tattva*, meanwhile, can be understood as the existence of an object, literally the fact *that it is*. Neither 'that-ness' nor 'existence' is, however, an unequivocal term; for, as Kant pointed out, one can believe that, ultimately, the existence or being of an object (*qua* thing-in-itself) is independent of the object's being perceived, while at the same time believing that the object's *formal* (apparent) existence is thoroughly subject-dependent. In other words, we might speak of objects as 'empirically real' without thereby committing ourselves to the view that those objects have formal, spatiotemporal, existence independently of their being perceived by anyone. In the case of the expression *vastu-tattva*, it is not at all clear whether *tattva* is to be taken in the sense of empirical existence or, alternatively, transcendent existence (i.e. existence unconditioned by perceptual acts or capacities). Any interpreter who has decided in advance that Yoga's position is realist about perceptual objects is likely, of course, to give it the latter sense. In my view, however, such a reading becomes unsustainable as soon as we recall that the process of 'modification' (*pariṇāma*) – by means of which objects come to be experienced – is not at all independent of perceptual capacities. On the contrary, it could be described as the emergence of the factors that make perceptual experience possible. Chief among these factors are our perceptual capacities, by which phrase I mean to denote the Sāṃkhya categories of buddhi, ahaṃkāra, manas, and the buddhīndriyas and karmendriyas. Thus, if pariṇāma is the process by which, not only objects, but also our capacities to have those objects as part of our experience, emerge, then the unity or integrity of that process can hardly be considered responsible for the subject-independent reality of the objects. The fact is, as far as I can see, that pariṇāma – the modification of co-fundamental ontological strands – is the making possible of empirical reality, and hence it is empirical objects, not transcendent ones, whose existence is dependent upon pariṇāma's 'oneness'. What I take 'oneness' ('unity', 'integrity') to mean here is the coherence of a particular configuration of ontological strands. It is this configuration (*pariṇāma-ekatva*) that gives rise to, or is equivalent to, the formal existence of particular empirical objects (*vastu-tattva*).

Whether the interpretation I have just offered is, or is not, found to be acceptable, now that I have introduced the wording of the sūtra itself we can turn to what the commentators Vyāsa and Vācaspati have to say about it. Vyāsa evidently holds that, contrary to my own reading, the sūtra asserts the object's independence of the subject's awareness or cogniscence (*vijñāna*) of it. He refers to an opposing opinion, according to which physical objects are unreal in a way that is analogous to the unreality of dream images. The view that Vyāsa attributes to his opponent is as follows: 'there is no object (*artha*) that is unaccompanied by cognition (*vijñāna*); there is, however, knowledge (*jñāna*) that is unaccompanied by an object, as in a dream' (*YBh* 4.14). The terms *vijñāna* and *jñāna* are here being used as synonyms or near-synonyms. I have translated them, on etymological grounds, as 'cognition' and 'knowledge' respectively, although their sense in this extract seems to be closer to 'phenomenal presentation', that is, a mental image which may or may not represent some independently real entity. Briefly stated, the view mentioned by Vyāsa is that with which Yogācāra Buddhism is typically associated, namely that the objects encountered in waking consciousness are merely apparent and, like dream-images, have no substantial basis independent of consciousness itself. As I have noted above, it remains a matter of contention whether Yogācārins genuinely reject the possibility of a reality outside of consciousness – thereby committing themselves to absolute idealism – or whether, alternatively, they merely regard any assertion concerning such a reality as epistemologically illegitimate (which position would be closer to Brentanian phenomenology). If Vyāsa's remark is indeed an attack on Yogācāra's position, then it would appear that he takes that position to be idealist; he certainly regards it as untenable, a mere attempt to 'conceal (*apahnava*) the true nature of the object (*vastu-svarūpa*) [by asserting that] the object is a mere fabrication of knowledge[15] (*jñāna-parikalpanā-mātra*)' (*YBh* 4.14). He does not, however, provide any arguments to support his objection; he merely declares that 'the object stands presented as "this" (*idam*) by its own power'.[16] Sen Gupta quotes this statement and explicates it as follows: 'The object of cognition is always revealed in cognition as something given, as *idam*, and such a revelation is due to *viṣaya*'s [i.e. the object's] own power of intelligibility' (1982: 3). This appears to be realism in its most naive form. Rather than addressing the vijñānavādin's point, that the appearance of an object in consciousness cannot in itself be taken as evidence that the object exists independently of consciousness, Vyāsa merely dogmatically reasserts the contrary, that is, that the appearance of independence in a perceived object is itself sufficient to demonstrate that the object exists in its own right. This response, of course, merely begs the question against the sceptical Yogācārin. However, in view of my present purpose, what is still more important to highlight is the fact that there is nothing in the original sūtra (4.14) to warrant Vyāsa's remark. Indeed, the remark seems to diverge from the sūtra's insistence that the existence ('that-ness') of the object is due, not to its own inherent power, but to the integrity of the modifying activities of the guṇas; and, on what I consider to be the most plausible interpretation of the guṇas (which will be elaborated in Chapter 5), these are determining factors of the object *as experienced* and not as a transcendent entity.

Vācaspati's gloss on Vyāsa's commentary to *YS* 4.14, despite its considerable length, boils down to little more than the flat denial of the vijñānavāda that we find already in Vyāsa. According to Vācaspati, from the premise that all objects are accompanied by an awareness (*vedyatva*) of them, it does not necessarily follow that the object has no existence other than its appearance in consciousness. The vijñānavādin's proposal (on the idealist reading of Yogācāra) that a perceived object is nothing other than the perceptual datum itself is therefore, on Vācaspati's view, a mere conception (*vikalpa*), which has no power to override our intuitive conviction that the perceived object transcends our perception of it. Neither Vyāsa nor Vācaspati (nor, indeed, Sen Gupta, who approvingly refers to both commentaries) denies the central claim of the vijñānavādin, which is equivalent to Berkeley's observation that the existence of things is revealed to us only in consciousness; they merely deny the famous Berkeleyan conclusion that the being of a thing therefore consists in its being perceived (*esse* is *percipi*).[17] There is no subtlety in their argument; it consists in the bald assertion of naive realism, according to which, because the world *appears* to comprise a range of spatially extended and temporally enduring physical entities, it must in reality be so comprised. It is not, in my view, an argument worthy of classical Sāṃkhya and Yoga, which systems are primarily concerned with the disclosure and categorization of psychosensory acts and contents that underlie, as conditioning factors, all our experiences, including our experiences of supposedly external, physical objects. So if the realist assertions of the likes of Vyāsa and Vācaspati are not to be regarded as genuine expositions of the original text – or if such genuineness is at least highly questionable – then whence did they derive?

It is well known that Vācaspati was something of a philosophical mercenary in the sense that he composed commentaries on several systems and was able to give the pretence of advocating each of them even where their standpoints were at variance to one another. He is generally held to have written eight major works (or seven if one regards his *Nyāyasucīnibandha* as an appendix to his *Nyāyavārttikatātparyaṭīkā*), all but two of which are commentaries or subcommentaries on other works. In addition to Sāṃkhya and Yoga, he commented upon Nyāya, Pūrva-mīmāṃsā, and Vedānta; and it is his subcommentary to Śaṅkara's *Brahmasūtrabhāṣya* (*BSBh*) that constitutes his most extensive work, known as *Bhāmatī* ('Illumination'). It is therefore evident that Vācaspati had a thorough familiarity with Śaṅkara's *Bhāṣya* even if we cannot state categorically that he was a committed advaitin himself. With this in view, it is interesting to note the similarity between Vācaspati's criticism of the Yogācāra vijñānavāda in his subcommentary to Vyāsa's *Yogabhāṣya* and Śaṅkara's own assault on this viewpoint at *BSBh* II.2.27–28.

A rudimentary form of realism is already staunchly asserted at *BSBh* I.1.2, where Śaṇkara declares that: 'the valid knowledge of the true nature of a thing is not dependent on human notions. On what does it depend then? It is dependent on the thing itself'.[18] Then, at *BSBh* II.2.27–28, he engages in a protracted attack on the vijñānavāda. To discuss this in detail would be a distraction from my main purpose, but I shall summarize the most salient points. First it should be noted that Śaṅkara, though hardly sympathetic to any rival school, can be said without exaggeration to have possessed a particular loathing for Buddhism in its several varieties, and to have seized any opportunity that availed itself to unleash his vitriol. Notwithstanding this antagonistic attitude, Śaṅkara provides a fair account of the vijñānavādin's position. He notes, interestingly, that according to the vijñānavāda, although an external object may exist independently of consciousness, knowledge of the object cannot arise unless the object is presented in consciousness. We therefore, on this view, have no cognitive access to the object's inherent nature, but only to the object *as cognized*, that is, as an appearance. It is on this basis that the vijñānavādin treats the object (insofar as it is epistemically available to us) and the content of one's cognition of it as identical. What is of particular interest in this portrayal of the vijñānavāda is that, by virtue of its admission that things may exist in a non-cognized (or perhaps even non-cognizable) state, it avoids the categorical denial of transcendent entities that is typical of absolute idealism and replaces it with a phenomenological neutrality concerning the ultimate ontological status of cognized objects.

The important point for us here is not whether Śaṅkara's summary at *BSBh* II.2.27 does justice to the vijñānavāda; that is a matter for scholars of Yogācāra Buddhism to decide. It is, rather, that in the subsequent discussion (at *BSBh* II.2.28) Śaṅkara ignores the distinction I have just highlighted – that is, between an ontological denial of a thing and a phenomenological agnosticism about that thing's subject-independent existence – and simply imputes to his hypothetical Buddhist opponent the ontological denial before proceeding to counter this view with a dogmatic realism. This is of interest to us because it exemplifies a tendency that is exhibited by other critics of the vijñānavāda, including the Yoga commentators Vyāsa and Vācaspati.

Brahmasūtra II.2.28 states, with characteristic brevity: *na-abhāva upalabdheḥ* – 'not non-existent, because of perception'. Śaṅkara takes this to mean, as we might express it in modern parlance, that because the act of perception is necessarily intentional, it must be directed towards an object that is external to itself, and that, therefore, to hold that the object exists merely as perceived (having no existence 'in itself') is a contradiction: 'it cannot be', asserts Śaṅkara, 'that the very thing perceived is non-existent'.[19] This claim seems surprising, since it appears to overlook the many occasions when we readily admit to having perceived something – or having *taken ourselves* to have perceived something – as external that later turns out to have been, in whole or in part, mental; typical examples being dream images and hallucinated objects. The only way in which a statement such as Śaṅkara's might be justified is if 'perceived' were to be understood as necessarily connoting 'perceived veridically'. In this case it would indeed be true to say that one can perceive a thing only if that thing genuinely exists; however, it would also be trivial, since it would be true merely by definition, and would fail to address the problem of how to tell whether one's perceptions are veridical. It is precisely this problem that is brought to a focus by the vijñānavādin's dream analogy, since dreams offer a clear illustration of objects appearing to us that, when considered from a viewpoint outside of the dream, seem to possess no 'external' (supra-mental) ontological ground. Śaṅkara himself discusses dreams (at *BSBh* II.2.29), and proposes that their difference from waking experiences consists in their being subject to sublation. But this merely begs the question how we can know that our waking experiences are not to be sublated by some superior, perhaps yet unrecognized, mode of consciousness (which is close to what is advocated in the *Māṇḍūkyakārikā* (e.g. 1.7, 14) of the advaitin Gauḍapāda and in other works of Advaita Vedānta).

In his constructed interlocution with the Yogācāra advocate, Śaṅkara berates him for using the expression 'as though external' (*bahirvat*) in relation to perceived objects, for he thinks that the very use of this expression proves that the Yogācārin, like the rest of us, really does believe that the objects are external (see *BSBh* II.2.28). It would seem that, as far as Śaṅkara is concerned, there is no place for an appearance–reality distinction in this context: it is enough that the objects we perceive as external should *appear* to be external in order for us to determine that they really are external. Śaṅkara thus exhibits in his *Bhāṣya* the same uncritical espousal of realism that we encounter in Vācaspati's subcommentary on *Yogabhāṣya* 4.14. Now, since the same basic viewpoint is taken in the *Yogabhāṣya* itself, which text is generally held to have preceded Śaṅkara by over two centuries, it would be unwarranted to suggest that Vācaspati's position on vijñānavāda is derived solely from his immersion in Śaṅkara's works. However, the similarity between the viewpoints of Śaṅkara, Vyāsa and Vācaspati on this matter is, I think, sufficiently close to indicate that the latter two commentators need not have obtained their opinions from an exclusively Sāṃkhya–Yoga context. On the contrary, the realist response to the vijñānavāda would appear to have been common currency among various schools, and thus its occurrence in the Yoga commentaries need not be taken as strong evidence of its presence in the *Yogasūtra* itself.

Having inquired into *YS* 4.14 and two of the commentaries upon it, let us now turn to *YS* 4.15, which reads: *vastu-sāmye citta-bhedāt tayor vibhaktaḥ panthāḥ*. This can be rendered as: 'Due to the sameness (i.e. continuity) of the object and the dividedness of the mind (*citta-bheda*), these two are distinct levels.' In some translations the expression *citta-bheda* is taken to mean a multiplicity of minds, and on such a reading the sūtra presents a version of the 'experience of a shared world' argument for the independent reality of physical objects. That is to say, if the same object is experienced by several minds, the object itself must be independent of any particular mind (and therefore, by implication, independent of all minds). Sen Gupta ostensibly accepts this interpretation, stating that 'one and the same object can be presented to many buddhis or cognitions. So, the object cannot be of the form of any one of these cognitions' (1982: 3).[20] The terminology here is ambiguous, however. By 'cannot be of the form of any one of these cognitions', I would at first assume Sen Gupta to mean 'cannot exclusively belong to…'. What she then goes on to say, however, is that: 'one and the same object can arouse different kinds of cognitions in different minds. That which arouses different cognitions can never be of the form of any one of these cognitions' (ibid.). Thus Sen Gupta has managed (albeit by following Vyāsa's lead) to interpret the sūtra as saying the exact reverse of what we might have expected. That is, rather than its being the *sameness* of an (experienced) object in relation to several cognizing minds that indicates the mind-independence of the object, this independent status is revealed, according to Sen Gupta, by the *difference* between the various experienced versions of the object (as occurring in or to different minds). The argument is invalid since the conclusion does not follow from the premise. Why should the fact that several minds, or persons, have different experiences of an object constitute evidence in favour of the mind-independence of that object? Surely what constitutes such evidence is the fact that, *despite* any (relatively minor) discrepancies between their respective experiences, the several individuals can all agree that they are experiencing the *same* object. Thus it is what their experiences have in *common* that is crucial, not how they differ. It should be added, however, that even this commonality of experience – which is the basis of the 'shared world' argument – is not decisive in favour of realism; for as Kant has shown, it is possible to formulate a version of idealism in which the sharedness of the world is accounted for by the uniformity (or at least profound compatibility) of the subjects' respective modes of experiencing or, as it is often expressed, their cognitive apparatus. Therefore neither version of the argument imputed to *YS* 4.15 is effective in establishing realism with regard to external objects.

The fact that the argument *imputed* to the sūtra is a failure does not, on its own, prove that the imputation is wrong. It could be that the sūtra itself is at fault. If a close examination of the sūtra can reveal a more tenable meaning, however, then this would provide firmer grounds for discarding, or at least seriously reconsidering, the existing interpretation. So what, then, is *YS* 4.15 saying? It is undoubtedly saying something about the relation between mind (*citta*) and its object (*vastu*); principally that these items belong to separate *panthans*. *Panthan* is a synonym of *pathan*, both terms being cognate with the English 'path' and having, as in the case of this English term, the metaphorical sense of a more-or-less systematized approach adopted in pursuit of a desired result as well as the literal meaning of a pre-defined route or road along which one travels. In the present context, most scholars are agreed that *panthan* means a 'way of being' or 'level (of existence)',[21] and thus a semantic connection is evoked with *YS* 2.19, in which the levels or divisions (*parvans*) of the 'seeable' (*dṛśya*) constituted by the guṇas are listed. It therefore comes as no surprise that the mind and its object should be designated as different 'levels', for it is precisely an awareness of the various levels of manifest reality that followers of Sāṃkhya and Yoga aim to cultivate. Unmanifest prakṛti and its twenty-three manifestations can be divided into groups or levels in various ways, and the way that is used in *YS* 2.19 consists in a fourfold division (cf. pp. 53–54 above). Although it is not necessary to discuss the four divisions in detail here, I shall provide an outline of how I consider *vastu* and *citta* to be related to them.

Whether one interprets *vastu* to mean a mind-independent entity or an object as perceived by a conscious subject, it can nevertheless be agreed that it must be dependent upon prakṛti and the manifest modes thereof; which is to say, upon all four levels of the 'seeable' (*dṛśya*) listed at *YS* 2.19. According to the standard realist interpretation, the five 'elements' (*bhūtas*), which are included in the first level (*viśeṣa*: 'specific'),[22] are the immediate material causes of the vastu, while these elements are in turn 'caused' by the constituents of level two, and so on back to level four, namely the unmanifest (*aliṅga*) itself. My interpretation differs insofar as I regard the relation between the modes of prakṛti as one of transcendental conditionality rather than material causality. The elements, for example, are dependent upon the preceding modes in the sense that those modes are the conditions of the elements' possibility, but not in the sense that those modes are somehow transformed into the elements. Nor, in my view, are the elements properly material entities; rather, they stand for the forms that must accompany sensory contents (*tanmātras*) if the subject is to have experience of an external environment. This interpretation will be presented more fully in Chapter 6. Here all that needs to be said is that, on both the realist and my non-realist account, the vastu is dependent upon the four levels of the 'seeable'.

Now, with regard to *citta*, in the present discussion I have so far translated this term merely as 'mind'. In certain instances the term can be considered synonymous with the 'inner instrument' (*antaḥkaraṇa*) of Sāṃkhya, while in others it is closer to *buddhi* alone. Indeed, the traditional commentators tend to use *citta* and *buddhi* fairly interchangeably. In the context of the four levels that I have been dealing with, buddhi is the sole occupant of level three (*liṅgamātra*) whereas antaḥkaraṇa – comprising buddhi plus egoity (*ahaṃkāra*) and the synthesizing aspect of mind (*manas*) – must be spread over three levels (*viśeṣa*, *aviśeṣa* and *liṅgamātra*). In whichever of these two ways we understand the term *citta*, however, it is evident that it must be regarded as belonging to a different level (or set of levels) than its object, vastu.

So if we ask again, what *YS* 4.15 is saying, I think some clarity has been added in the above discussion to what is likely to be meant by the statement that mind and object constitute 'distinct levels (of reality)'. But this leaves unspecified the reason that is given for their being regarded in this way. The expression *citta-bheda* is inherently ambiguous, and I do not think it is determinable whether the author of the sūtra intended to denote the split between the minds of separate individuals or, alternatively, between the different states of a single mind. *Vastu-sāmya* is less ambiguous (if we leave aside the question whether vastu is or is not mind-independent), seeming to indicate the spatiotemporal continuity of an object. I take it, then, that what is being said at *YS* 4.15 is as follows: Due to the fact that (a) there is a general conformity between an external object as experienced by different minds at the same time (and/or by the same mind at different times), and (b) the minds themselves (and/or the various mental states of a single mind) are evidently distinct from one another, the object and the mind that perceives it must be separate levels (modes, categories) of reality. There is no reason why this interpretation should be controversial. It becomes controversial only when we ask in what sense the vastu is dependent upon the (other) manifest modes of prakṛti. For the answer to this question, however, we must search *elsewhere* than *YS* 4.15, and therefore this sūtra cannot possibly be treated as an argument for, or even a statement of, external realism.

There is considerably more that could be said about the allegedly anti-idealist section of the Kaivalyapāda, but I hope the above discussion is sufficient to show that the interpretation of the relevant sūtras is by no means cut-and-dried. Contrary to the assertions of some scholars, the sūtras themselves are not unambiguously realist, although a form of realism can be read into them if one assumes in advance that this is their author's position. As we have seen, traditional commentators such as Vyāsa and Vācaspati do make such an assumption, but the eagerness of these commentators to besmirch the vijñānavāda and their general hostility to Buddhism (most explicit in the case of Vācaspati) ought to make us wary. It is likely that philosophical vendettas are being waged at the expense of accurate exegesis. In opposition to the traditional interpretations, I have proposed alternative readings of the two key sūtras, which readings undermine the assumption that the sūtras are inherently realist. In the remaining chapters, unencumbered by the imputation of realism, I shall endeavour to flesh out the non-realist interpretation that has so far been only hinted at.

5

THE NATURE OF PRAKṚTI

Sāṃkhya is renowned for its metaphysical schema of twenty-five categories and for the careful – some would say obsessive[1] – attention it gives to the enumeration of the individual components of that schema. Yoga is widely held to have added a twenty-sixth principle, namely *īśvara*, but to have otherwise adopted the Sāṃkhya model, at the heart of which is the claim that the whole of reality can be reduced ultimately to two co-fundamental principles, typically referred to as *puruṣa* and *prakṛti*. The other twenty-three principles derive in some way from the 'combination' or 'conjunction' (*saṃyoga*) of these two co-fundamentals. The twenty-three derivates are generally described as 'products' or 'evolutes' of prakṛti, which 'emerge' or 'arise' when the equilibrium of the three guṇas (the threefold constitution of prakṛti) is disturbed by the presence (*saṃnidhi*) of puruṣa.

According to the standard interpretation, which I outlined towards the beginning of Chapter 4, the metaphysical schema amounts to a cosmogony, which is to say that it presents an account of the order in which the various entities that make up the cosmos came into being. Having been in some mysterious way 'stimulated', 'catalysed', 'intelligized' or 'vitalized' by puruṣa's presence,[2] the guṇas proceed to reconfigure themselves to produce a succession of entities, beginning with the most 'fine' or 'subtle' and ending with the most 'coarse' or 'gross'. Since, on the standard view, prakṛti is a material principle, all twenty-three of her evolutes must also be regarded as material. The fact that most of them are patently mental in nature is held by many interpreters to be unproblematic as long as the multipurposed and conveniently undefined expression 'subtle matter' is applied to them. The production of three-dimensional physical objects out of elements whose origin can be traced to the psychic factor of 'egoity' (*ahaṃkāra*), and further to 'discernment' (*buddhi*), is also accounted for on the grounds that all these things are material *in some sense*. They are material, and of course 'real', even though they all dissolve back into unmanifest prakṛti when puruṣa realizes that he is not of their nature. It is, I think, unsurprising that this story – which becomes increasingly incoherent the more closely it is scrutinized – finds little favour among modern philosophers, whether in India or elsewhere, and is on the whole treated as a mere historical curiosity as opposed to a world-view deserving of serious attention. In Chapter 4, I challenged the realist assumption upon which the standard interpretation of Sāṃkhya and Yoga is based. In this chapter I shall prepare the ground for a radical reinterpretation of the metaphysical schema by examining some of the principal doctrines that underpin it. Chief among these doctrines are: (a) the theory of causation known as the *satkāryavāda*, (b) the supposed materiality of prakṛti, and (c) the analysis of prakṛti into three constituent 'strands' (*guṇa*s). Each of these will be looked at in turn.

Creation, manifestation and causality

SK 3 distinguishes four ontological genera on the basis of whether each is creative or created, or both, or neither. The four genera are as follows:

1 *Mūlaprakṛti*, 'fundamental productivity'. This is by definition creative, and is itself uncreated (*avikṛti*).
2 The seven principles referred to simply as 'the great (*mahat*) and others'. From verses that occur later in the *Sāṃkhyakārikā* it can be inferred that, in addition to mahat (which is also called *buddhi*), the seven principles comprise ahaṃkāra plus the five modes of sensory content (*tanmātra*s). These are all both creative and created (*prakṛti-vikṛti*).
3 A group of sixteen principles, comprising manas, the five sense-capacities (*buddhīndriya*s), the five action-capacities (*karmendriya*s), and the five elements (*bhūta*s). These are all merely created (*vikāra*), and are not themselves creative.
4 The conscious subject (*puruṣa*). This is 'neither creative not created' (*na prakṛti na vikṛti*).

It has been remarked upon by several scholars that this fourfold division of reality bears a startling resemblance to a similar categorization employed by the ninth-century Irish theologian Joannes Scotus Eriugena.[3] The most relevant passage, from Eriugena's *Periphyseon* ('On the Division of Nature'), reads:

> The division of nature (*divisio naturae*) seems to me to admit of four species through four differentiae. The first is the division into what creates and is not created; the second into what is created and creates; the third, into that which is created and does not create; the fourth, into what neither creates nor is created.
>
> (Eriugena 1976: 2 [I.441b–442a])[4]

It is not beyond the realms of possibility that this aspect of the Sāṃkhya philosophy could have found its way from India to the royal court in France where Eriugena worked, for communications did exist in medieval times between India and Europe, via Persia. But whatever the source of Eriugena's quaternary schema may be, the reason for my mentioning it here is principally to draw attention to a further point in the Irishman's philosophy that might have a bearing upon how we interpret Sāṃkhya. The point of interest is Eriugena's definition of creation as 'self-manifestation... self-externalisation, revelation' (Moran 1989: 250), none of which terms suggests the kind of separation between a divine creator and his creation that is normally associated with Christian cosmogony. It is, I want to argue, by viewing the relation between the unmanifest and manifest aspects of prakṛti as one of self-manifestation that we can make better sense of Sāṃkhya–Yoga metaphysics than by assuming, as many interpreters have done, that it is one of material causation.

The verses most pertinent to this issue are *SK* 8 and 9, which deal, respectively, with the imperceptibility of unmanifest prakṛti and the ontological status of its manifestations. Referring to unmanifest prakṛti, *SK* 8 states that it

> is imperceptible (or ungraspable, *anupalabdhi*) due to its subtlety, not its non-existence (*abhāva*). It is graspable (*upalabdhi*) via its effects (*kāryata*). *Mahat* and the others are its effects and are with-the-nature (*sarūpa*) and without-the-nature (*virūpa*) of prakṛti.

While this verse makes it clear that unmanifest prakṛti, though not directly accessible to us, can be 'grasped' – that is, inferred to exist – due to its 'effects', it does little more than hint at how these 'effects' are related to it. The traditional commentaries are far from helpful on this point, tending as they do to present merely a string of analogies in place of an explanation. The sorts of analogies that typically occur include the respective relations between cloth and its threads, sesame oil and the seeds from which it is pressed, and rice grains and the stalks from which they are obtained by threshing (cf. e.g. *TK* 9). A further analogy of this kind concerns the relation between a jar and the clay from which it is made, and this is exemplified well in the following passage:

> A lump of clay is shaped by the potter as a jar. Here nothing that did not exist before comes into existence, but there is only change of position in space of the particles of the stuff. Any one who could see the clay in minute portions will see that those portions are only rearranged in a particular manner in the jar. But those who see the whole and are familiar with the use of a jar, will call it a jar and in common parlance may say that a thing that was not in existence before has come into existence. In reality, however, there is only a spread of the mass of clay in a particular manner.[5]

The main problem with this and similar analogies is that they describe a relation between two manifest spatiotemporal objects, one of which derives from the other due to the intervention of a conscious agent. The lump of clay, for example, is not an unmanifest jar – it is simply a lump of clay. It can be formed *into* a jar only by the action of a potter. In the case of prakṛti and its effects, however, we are concerned with the relation between something that is *un*manifest on the one hand, and its manifestation or *appearance* on the other.

The crucial point with regard to prakṛti is that it is not, in itself, a manifest object existing in time and space. It is defined as being the *opposite* of that which is, among other things, 'conditioned (or caused, *hetumat*), non-eternal (*anitya*), non-pervasive (*avyāpin*), [and] active (*sakriyā*)' (*SK* 10). Put in positive terms, this means that it is:

(a) unconditioned;
(b) eternal (in the sense of being *atemporal*, as distinct from being continuously enduring);[6]
(c) non-spatial (i.e. without spatial limitations, and hence without location or form);[7]
(d) inactive.

Therefore no comparison or analogy between it and something manifest can do justice to the nature of prakṛti. It becomes manifest only in the 'presence' of, or in 'conjunction' with, puruṣa; and thus if anything is to be regarded as the cause of prakṛti's manifestation it is this presence, albeit not an active or efficient cause in the way that a potter who turns clay into a jar is active. It would seem to be more plausible to say that prakṛti is not really 'turned into' anything; it is merely the case that in the presence of consciousness prakṛti has an appearance, a form, and can thus be said to *manifest*, whereas in the absence of consciousness – that is, 'in itself' – prakṛti has no appearance, and remains unmanifest.

The so-called 'effects', or manifestations, are, then, thoroughly contingent upon the compresence of puruṣa and prakṛti, and it is with this precarious conditionality that I think the ostensibly paradoxical last line of *SK* 8 is grappling: the manifest principles are similar to unmanifest prakṛti insofar as they share its 'nature' (*rūpa*),[8] but are dissimilar insofar as, by definition, they are manifest and it is not. This issue of the relation between manifest and unmanifest prakṛti parallels to some extent that of the relation between appearances and things-in-themselves in Kant's philosophy. It cannot, in truth, be a relation of causation – with unmanifest prakṛti being the 'cause' of its own manifest forms – for causation implies temporal succession; and that which is unmanifest – in the radical sense of this term that is attached both to unmanifest prakṛti and to Kant's thing-in-itself – stands 'outside' time. Yet there is certainly a sense in which the manifest forms are profoundly and inescapably *dependent upon* their unmanifest ground, and it is perhaps for this reason – that is, to indicate this relation of dependence or conditionality – that the author of the *Sāṃkhyakārikā* uses the terms 'cause' (*kāraṇa*) and 'effect' (*kārya*) apparently synonymously with 'unmanifest' (*avyakta*) and 'manifest' (*vyakta*) respectively.

Turning now to *SK* 9, this is commonly regarded as 'the locus classicus for the *satkāryavāda*' (Halbfass 1992: 56), the latter being the so-called 'theory of the pre-existent effect'. The standard view is that the kārikā presents a theory of causation, according to which an effect constitutes not a novel creation but merely a realization or objectification of something that already existed *potentially* in its cause.[9] Such a theory would be plausible only if the notion of cause were restricted to *material* cause.[10] One could propose, for example, that a jar exists 'potentially' in a lump of clay as one of the clay's possibilities; that is, the clay has the potential to take the form of a jar under specific circumstances. It would be far less plausible – and perhaps unintelligible – to suggest that the jar exists potentially *in the potter* (or, more precisely, *in the action of the potter*). The potter's action is the occasion for the clay's becoming – that is, actualizing its potential to be – a jar; but it makes no sense to call the action itself a potential jar. And for reasons such as this the satkāryavāda is indeed normally taken to be a theory of *material* causation.

There is some textual justification for this reading, notably the occurrence of the expression *upādāna-grahaṇāt* among the reasons given for holding the *satkārya* view at *SK* 9. 'Material cause' is one of the meanings of *upādāna*, although curiously the word's etymological derivation is *upā-√dā*, 'to appropriate to oneself' (cf. MW: 213). *Grahaṇa* means 'to grasp', both literally and figuratively; and hence the expression as a whole can be translated as: 'because a material cause is "taken"'. Larson's translation reads: 'because of the need for an (appropriate) material cause' (1979: 258), which is very loose. Suryanarayana Sastri is a little closer to the mark with: 'since there is recourse to the (appropriate) material cause' (1948: 23); but when one reads his explanation of the verse it is clear that his translation has been influenced in a particular direction by Gauḍapāda's commentary. Gauḍapāda takes *upādāna-grahaṇa* to refer to the sort of selecting process someone engages in when choosing milk rather than, say, water in order to make yoghurt. This accounts for Suryanarayana Sastri's parenthetical insertion of the word 'appropriate', which is not warranted by the original Sanskrit. Larson presumably shares this interpretation since he makes the same insertion. If it was really this kind of selection that the author of the kārikā had in mind, however, then it would be a peculiar argument to put forward in the present context. It should be remembered that the verse immediately follows *SK* 8, which I have been examining above and which asserts the knowability of prakṛti via its manifest 'effects'. In this light, *SK* 9 would make more sense if it were understood to be elaborating why or how it should be the case that prakṛti can be known (i.e. known to exist) in this way, rather than as proposing reasons for holding that effects 'pre-exist' in their (respective) material causes. A more context-sensitive interpretation of *upādāna-grahaṇa* might view it as an observation of human psychology instead of a claim about the objective necessity of causes. It is not so much that there is a 'need' for a cause (as Larson puts it), but rather that we, *qua* rational subjects, are predisposed to assume the existence of one: we 'grasp' (*grahaṇa*) the cause in the sense of taking there to be one. With this psychological reading in view, let me now present what I consider to be the most tenable interpretation of the expression *satkārya* itself.

As I have noted already, *satkārya* is these days generally translated as 'existent effect' or 'pre-existent effect'. There is, however, an alternative rendering of the expression, which was suggested by John Davies in the late nineteenth century, before the now standard reading acquired its current inertia. 'The phrase [*satkārya*]', Davies writes,

> does not mean 'an existent effect,' but that what *is* formally existent is necessarily an effect. Causality is implied as an absolute condition of all formal being. *Asadakaraṇāt* (literally from non-existence, non-cause) implies that there is an identity in the terms non-existence and non-cause, and that we cannot conceive of formal existence as uncaused: only the unformed *Prakṛiti* (Nature) is without a cause, having existed eternally.
> (1894: 30, my underlining)

On this interpretation, then, *satkārya* can be rendered as 'that which is [formally] existent (*sat*) is an effect (*kārya*)', which assertion implies that whatever is encountered as manifest (and only that which is manifest *can* be encountered, that is, experienced perceptually or conceptually) must have a cause. Although Davies doesn't quite spell out its Kantian implications, the remark that 'we cannot conceive of formal existence as uncaused' places causality very firmly within the structure of our own thought and experience, as a conditioning *a priori* factor – a transcendental category of the understanding, as Kant would call it – as opposed to an intrinsic feature of the relations between things-in-themselves.

Again, however, we should pause to remind ourselves that it is not a cause in any straightforward sense of the word that is being talked about here. Rather, it is the unmanifest ground of the manifest categories; and these categories are not themselves empirical objects, but are the factors that must be in place, as components of experience, if objectual perception is to be possible. The soteriological project of Sāṃkhya and Yoga is to reveal, first, the dependence of these factors upon prakṛti and puruṣa, and second the total unconditionality of puruṣa itself. The part that the satkāryavāda seems to be playing in that project is to propose that anything manifest *must* have an unmanifest ground. The terseness of the exposition in *SK* 9, as elsewhere in the classical texts, leaves it unclear whether this 'must' is to be taken as wielding the force of a metaphysical necessity or merely a conceptual one. If it were merely conceptual, then the claim would be that we cannot conceive of anything's having formal existence without at the same time conceiving of that thing's being, in itself, beyond form; but from this alone no conclusion could be drawn as to whether there is a pre-formal level of existence. If, on the other hand, the necessity is to be taken as metaphysical, then the claim would be that our inability to conceive of form without an underlying formless reality indicates that there really is such an underlying reality. The fact that unmanifest prakṛti is, for the most part, spoken of in classical Sāṃkhya and Yoga as though it were a genuine metaphysical reality leads me to suspect that, even if these systems did draw a distinction between conceptual and metaphysical necessity, they laid little weight upon it.

As Davies and I read it, *SK* 9 can, in short, be understood as containing a transcendental argument for the existence of unmanifest prakṛti. Beginning from the fact of manifest existence, in the form of the various generic constituents of our everyday experience, we can observe that there is, for us, an irresistible urge to assume that all of this experience must have an unmanifest ground, and hence we are obliged to postulate the existence of that unmanifest ground. Owing to the brevity with which the argument is put forward, I do not feel it would be appropriate to enter into a critical discussion of its merits or defects. However, I hope enough has been said on this matter to show that a more philosophically astute, and contextually coherent, reading of the satkārya doctrine is available to us than that which takes it to consist in the implausible and only barely intelligible claim that effects pre-exist in their causes.

Prakṛti and materiality

I have been talking above about prakṛti as that which is both the 'unmanifest ground' of the constituents of all possible experience and, in its manifest aspect, the constituents themselves; and I have tried to steer away from the insinuation that prakṛti is material in nature. I am among a small number of scholars who consider 'matter' to be an inappropriate translation of *prakṛti* in the context of Sāṃkhya and Yoga,[11] but at the same time I am aware of the severe difficulties involved in avoiding this kind of terminology. Since puruṣa can be defined as empty or 'pure' consciousness, it must be prakṛti that provides the content – and hence in a very broad sense the 'matter' – of experience. Although matter in the sense of 'content' need not imply *physicality* (think, for example, of the content of a thought, dream, or story), the danger of speaking of prakṛti as representing matter in this broad sense is that it is liable to get tangled up with the scientific usage of the term to denote the physical stuff – divisible into microscopic particles – of which the whole material universe is composed, and to which (at least from a reductive materialist standpoint) every existent thing can be reduced. Some scholars have added considerable confusion to the interpretation of prakṛti by suggesting that its three co-essential components can be compared with certain particles conceptualized in modern physics, such as atoms or the subatomic constituents thereof.[12] Responsibility for such speculations must in part be apportioned to Vijñānabhikṣu, who sought to distinguish the guṇas as conceived by Sāṃkhya from those of the Vaiśeṣika darśana by referring to the former as 'substances' (*dravya*s);[13] but, all the same, this doesn't excuse the flagrant misappropriation of scientific concepts by modern scholars.

It is not uncommon for modern exegetes to express qualms about using terms such as 'matter' and 'material' with reference to prakṛti, but to go ahead and use them in any case. Radhakrishnan is a slight exception to this tendency insofar as he prefers the term 'substance', or 'fundamental substance' (1927, II: 266), and declares that prakṛti 'is not a material substance' since it 'gives rise not only to the five elements of the material universe, but also to the psychical' (p. 274). In the absence of any account of what a non-material substance might be, however, Radhakrishnan's use of 'substance' in place of 'matter' amounts more to a merely terminological difference than to a clear conceptual one. Larson, meanwhile, is quite open about the difficulty he has had in finding an adequate translation of *prakṛti* in its unmanifest aspect. 'It cannot be characterized as "stuff",' he reflects,

> for such a notion, whether understood as subtle or gross 'stuff,' can only arise when *puruṣa* is present... The usual translations such as 'nature' or 'matter' are useful as general designations, *so long as they are not confused with our Western notions of nature and matter*, which frequently imply more than the Sāṃkhya notion would allow.
>
> (1979: 167, emphasis added)[14]

Larson finally plumps for an expression that even he finds 'awkward', namely ' "an undifferentiated plenitude of being"... – i.e. the simple fact or presence of being apart from consciousness' (ibid.). Such misgivings do not prevent him, however, from making liberal use of such phrases as 'primordial nature' and 'primordial materiality' in his major published works on Sāṃkhya (esp. 1979, 1987), nor from asserting elsewhere that 'The notion of *prakṛti* in Sāṅkhya philosophy implies a closed causal system of reductive materialism – "reductive materialism" in the sense that all thinking, fantasizing, imagining, feeling, and willing can finally be reduced to a modality or function of sheer materiality' (1980: 307).

The stipulation that 'matter' and 'nature' can be regarded as appropriate translations of *prakṛti* only 'so long as they are not confused with our Western notions' of such terms is an odd one, for it would seem to suggest that absolutely nothing has been added to our understanding of prakṛti by the use of such translations. If, in order to stand in place of a foreign term, a familiar English one has to be radically redefined or so heavily qualified that the new meaning is entirely out of step with that which it usually has, it might legitimately be asked whether we would not have done better to stick with the original foreign term. It may turn out that certain terms cannot be translated by any single word or expression without generating serious confusion; and in such circumstances the sensible option would seem to be to retain the original term while doing one's best to define its semantic range as clearly and comprehensively as possible.[15] Inadequate translations place the interpreter who uses them in a position of perpetual backtracking, where a requirement is felt to frequently distinguish between a term's normal usage and the use one is making of it. This tendency is illustrated well in the following passage from a study of the concept of prakṛti by Knut Jacobsen:

> *Prakṛti* is not ordinary matter like earth or air. It does not occupy space since space is a product of materiality. *Prakṛti* is a substance but matter in the sense of 'atoms'... is not the ultimate material cause of the world... The material principle is not mental but also not material in the ordinary sense of the word... *Prakṛti* is material in the sense that it is non-conscious.
>
> (Jacobsen 1999: 225)

By trying to dissociate his own use of terms such as 'matter' and 'material' from their ordinary senses, Jacobsen ends up offering a purely negative definition of 'material' as that which is 'non-conscious'. Although he does not explicitly mention Aristotle, the concept that Jacobsen, along with Larson and others, seems to be somewhat inelegantly searching for resembles that of Aristotle's *prōtē hýlē*, which became the *materia prima* of medieval scholastic philosophy. As Ernan McMullin has helpfully noted:

> the existence of unqualified changes, and of a multiplicity of totally different sorts of substances, was for Aristotle a primary fact of our experience. If one is to explain *this* fact, the sort of 'underlying nature' required will not be a substantial stuff with recognizable properties, but rather an indefinite substratum, the featureless correlate of substantial form.
>
> (1963: 7)[16]

Aristotle's form–matter distinction is, then, useful for understanding what certain interpreters are trying to get at in their notion of prakṛti as 'primal matter'; but this is not to say that it is genuinely useful in understanding the concept of prakṛti itself. While Aristotle's definition of matter as 'the primary substratum of each thing, from which it comes to be without qualification, and which persists in the result'[17] is undoubtedly broad enough to be compatible with the Sāṃkhya–Yoga notion of prakṛti, it fails to even hint at prakṛti's most crucial feature, namely its status as the source of the manifest factors that, in combination with one another, generate experience.[18] These factors are 'manifest' in the sense that, through their interplay a world of myriad phenomena is established; but in isolation from one another they lack empirical representability. Among the categories of manifest prakṛti there are several purely formal factors, such as the capacities for intentional consciousness (*buddhi*) and relating experiences to oneself as experient (*ahaṃkāra*). There are also specific kinds of mental act, such as the five sense-capacities (*buddhīndriya*s) and five modes of awareness of bodily action (*karmendriya*s). None of these factors is in any obvious sense 'material'. The nearest thing we get to 'matter' among the Sāṃkhya categories are the tanmātras; for these are the five varieties of sensory content, and as such provide the matter which, when intended by the sense-capacities, constitutes the five basic types of sensation. It is the five 'elements' (*bhūta*s) that are commonly regarded as the most patently physical of the manifest categories. As I shall explain in Chapter 6, however, these are best understood as physical only in the sense that they are the perceptual forms in which we encounter physical objects; and such forms are not themselves physical.

Thus we see that, in applying terms such as 'matter' and 'form' to prakṛti and its manifestations, we have to be careful to specify the sense in which these terms are being used. In explicating the schema of twenty-three manifest categories it can, as we have begun to see above, be useful to employ the form–matter distinction as well as the act–content distinction; and although these two distinctions are not interchangeable, they do overlap in certain respects. With regard to prakṛti in its entirety, that is, in both its manifest and unmanifest aspects, the term 'matter' can be applied only if we are willing to speak of everything that is not the pure subject – including acts and formal structures of experience as well as experiential content – as material. And if we do use 'material' in this broad sense, then we ought to take special care not to conflate it with its narrower sense of mere experiential content.

Before moving on to discuss the threefold constitution of prakṛti, there is one more thing in the above-quoted passage from Jacobsen that deserves comment since it is particularly troubling from a philosophical point of view. This is the statement that prakṛti 'does not occupy space since space is a product of materiality.' Although Jacobsen is not explicit on this point, what I take him to mean is that since one of the five bhūtas, namely *ākāśa*, is normally identified in whole or in part with 'space', and since the bhūtas are among the manifestations of prakṛti, prakṛti as it is in itself cannot be regarded as existing in space.[19] This is a perfectly valid point to make. But Jacobsen expresses it badly due to his use of 'materiality' to stand for prakṛti. The statement that 'space is a product of materiality', if it is not to be regarded as absurd, requires some considerable justification; and yet such justification is not forthcoming from Jacobsen. In most, and perhaps in all, contexts where the concept of matter occurs, the existence of space and time is presupposed. An entity's being material generally implies that the entity is extended in space and that it endures over time; and hence spatial extension has typically counted as a defining characteristic of material entities. Descartes, for instance, in one place defines 'body' (i.e. any material thing) as 'whatever is capable of being bounded by some shape, and comprehended by some place, and of occupying space in such a way that all other bodies are excluded' (1970: 68). Aristotle's *prōtē hýlē* is a broader concept than Descartes's space-occupying thing, but still it is at least questionable whether such a 'primal matter' does not also require a 'primal space' in which to exist. For Kant, matter is the content of appearances, to be distinguished from the form, which is provided by the subject's faculty of sensibility. Although Kant's statements on this point are not free of ambiguity, it would seem that he construes *sensations* (i.e. sensory content) as the data, and hence as the matter, of appearances, and time and space as their forms. Thus, on Kant's view, time and space are determinations of matter and have logical precedence over it, but neither matter nor form are ascribable to things-in-themselves (cf. *CPR* A267–8/B323–4).[20]

On my interpretation of Sāṃkhya and Yoga, prakṛti is the source of both form and matter in the Kantian senses of these terms; that is, it is the source of the raw sensory material and the formal categories that give perceptual shape to that material, including the form of space. Thus, if we talk of prakṛti itself as 'materiality' (or a 'material principle', etc.), we must acknowledge that, in this instance, we are using the term to mean something far broader (and vaguer) than sensory material. In order to sharpen up our concept of prakṛti, let us now turn to the issue of its threefold 'constitution'.

The three 'strands' of prakṛti

According to the standard interpretation, in which prakṛti is held to be a 'material principle', its three constituent 'strands' (*guṇa*s) are likewise construed as material in nature. It was noted in the preceding section that they have been assumed by some scholars to be similar, analogous, or even identical to certain particles – atomic or subatomic – derived from the theoretical repertoire of modern physics. The following extract from Feuerstein exemplifies this view:

> The *guṇas* can be described as being the ultimate building-blocks of the material and mental phenomena in their entirety. They are not merely qualities or properties, but actual entities or 'reals' (S. Dasgupta . . .) and as such non-distinct from the world-ground itself. They are the indivisible atoms of everything there is, with the exception of the Self (*puruṣa*), which is by definition *nir-guṇa*.
>
> (1980: 34, my underlining)[21]

There is, however, little textual justification for this 'building blocks' interpretation. Indeed, when one examines the key passages in the classical texts where the three guṇas are discussed, it is hard to imagine how they could be supposed to be atomic particles at all. *YS* 2.18 states that the 'seeable' (*dṛśya*, i.e. *prakṛti*) is 'of the nature (*śīla*) of shining-forth (*prakāśa*), activity (*kriyā*), and steadiness (*sthiti*),' and notes that its twofold purpose is 'experience (*bhoga*) and liberation (*apavarga*)'. This characterization is echoed at *SK* 13, where it is said that the first of the guṇas, *sattva*, is 'light' (*laghu*, i.e. not heavy or dense) and, as in the sūtra just quoted, 'shining forth' or 'luminous' (*prakāśaka*); the second guṇa, *rajas*, is 'exciting' (*upaṣṭambhaka*) and 'mobile' (*cala*); and the third, *tamas*, is 'heavy' (*guru*) and 'enveloping' (*varaṇaka*). Here it is mentioned that the guṇas co-operate to fulfil their collective purpose 'like a lamp' (*pradīpavat*, cf. *SK* 36).[22] We are told, at *SK* 12, that the guṇas' 'essences' or 'essential characteristics' (*ātmaka*s) are, respectively, 'gladness (*prīti*), perturbation (*aprīti*), and stupefaction (*viṣāda*),' and that their 'ends' or 'purposes' (*artha*s) are, again, 'shining-forth (*prakāśa*), engagement (*pravṛtti*), and restraint (*niyama*)'. Their relation to one another is there said to involve 'subjugation (*abhibhava*), support (*āśraya*), generation (*janana*), and intercourse (*mithuna*)'.

So what overall impression is to be gleaned from these various accounts? In most instances, contrary to Feuerstein's protestation, the descriptive terms seem to denote qualities or properties of objects, and nowhere could they be taken to denote substances (or 'reals'), still less material particles. In some of the descriptions they have a more subjective and emotional flavour, notably the reference to 'gladness' etc. at *SK* 12, whereas in the case of such characteristics as 'engagement' and 'restraint' they could be understood either subjectively *or* objectively. The several references to *prakāśa* in relation to sattva indicate that this guṇa concerns a thing's power to be seen or known. This interpretation accords with Radhakrishnan's assessment that sattva is the 'tendenc[y] to manifestation'

(1927, II: 266). The most literal translation of *sattva* is 'being-ness'; and if we recall the discussion of *satkārya* earlier in this chapter we might note that *sat* can, with some legitimacy, be understood as '*formal* being/existence', that is, the existence of a thing insofar as it appears or is a constituent of an appearance. In this light, *sattva* could be defined as the quality of manifestability – the capacity of a thing to become apparent or to contribute toward the becoming apparent of a thing. It makes some sense that the categories of manifest prakṛti are imbued with this quality, for they, though not themselves particular appearances, are the conditioning factors that make appearances, and hence experience, possible. Having defined *sattva* in this way, we can perhaps begin to comprehend why prakṛti's unmanifest aspect is held to consist in the dormancy of the guṇas. For if something is going to become manifest, then it must possess the power or capacity to do so; and yet the very fact of its *becoming* manifest implies that its prior state was one of unmanifestness. According to Sāṃkhya and Yoga, prakṛti is unmanifest independently of puruṣa, but manifest in puruṣa's presence. Since puruṣa is present to prakṛti beginninglessly, prakṛti's independent unmanifestness cannot be understood as temporally prior; instead it must be ontologically or metaphysically prior, in the sense that, in the absence of puruṣa, unmanifestness is prakṛti's natural state.

If we now consider the other two guṇas, namely rajas and tamas, we see that the latter is represented as embodying such qualities as stability, inertia, limitation and boundedness, while the former encapsulates the countervailing qualities of instability (mutability), mobility, expansiveness and unboundedness. It does not require a great leap of imagination to notice that each of the tendencies typified by these two sets of qualities is present to varying degrees in manifest phenomena, and that there may be something about the interplay between them that invariably accompanies manifestation. Davies has said of rajas that it 'is rather the cause of an impetus than the impetus itself, the moving force rather than the motion' (1894: 38). I think this is right: it is the *capacity to move*, or (to use classical Greek terms) the *energeia* that makes the *ergon* (action) possible. Anything that was completely static (immobile, inert) could not manifest, for manifestation itself requires some kind of impulse or drive. If, however, there were no check on such an impulse – nothing to constrain and delimit it – then the motion would be at risk of increasing towards infinite velocity in no specific direction (or, in other words, in all directions at once), which would inevitably preclude the integration that is necessary for anything to become manifest. And this is where tamas enters the picture, it being precisely the delimiting tendency that prevents disintegration and furnishes any manifest entity with the congruity and cohesion that must be in place if it is to manifest at all.

Although any proposal concerning the reasoning behind the doctrine of the three guṇas must, due to the very nature of the case, be highly speculative, it seems to me that the most plausible explanation is that the doctrine is the result of something approximating transcendental reflection upon experience. I agree with Feuerstein that the guṇas 'are experientially derived concepts' (Feuerstein 1980: 38);

but whereas he means by 'experientially derived' that the guṇas can be objects of immediate perception (albeit in yogically-induced 'non-ordinary states of consciousness' (ibid.: 39)), my understanding of the guṇas is that they are held by Sāṃkhya and Yoga to be the absolutely basic criteria for anything's appearing or becoming manifest. As such, they cannot be available to perceptual awareness in themselves; their existence – as necessary conditions of manifest being – can be known only by means of reasoning *a priori*. It is for this reason, I think, that at *SK* 8 prakṛti is said to be imperceptible, though knowable via its 'effects'. What is added to this statement in the doctrine of the guṇas is that, not only can prakṛti's existence be inferred, but something can be known about its constitution as well, scilicet: that it must comprise the three powers of manifest existence (*sattva*), mutability (*rajas*) and limitation (*tamas*).

A pertinent remark on this issue of whether the guṇas are perceptible is made in a quotation that Vyāsa includes (apparently with approval) in his commentary on *YS* 4.13. The quotation, which Vācaspati attributes to the *Ṣaṣṭitantra*, reads: 'The ultimate nature of the guṇas is not understood by way of perception (*dṛṣṭipatha*). That which is available to perception is like *māyā*.' The expression 'like māyā' (*māyā-iva*) is interesting here. *Māyā* is often translated as 'illusion', and assumed to stand for a generative power which, through its own creativity, establishes a veil that obscures the underlying reality. Vācaspati takes the expression in Vyāsa's commentary to mean that although what is available to perception is *like* māyā, that is like an illusion, it is not *in fact*, or not *entirely*, illusory (*TV* 4.13). This equivocal description resembles Kant's account of the world of appearances, or 'the world as representation' as Schopenhauer famously termed it: it is real insofar as it constitutes actual experience – which is to say, it is empirically real – but it cannot be held to be real in itself. The appearance masks the ultimate reality; yet, paradoxically, it also reveals it, for it is only through its *appearing* that reality can be known as anything at all.[23] That, at least, is the Kantian–Schopenhauerian claim. The position of Sāṃkhya and Yoga is different in two main respects. First, it treats prakṛti not as merely the 'in itself' of so-called external phenomena, but as the source also of the mental acts that intend those phenomena; and second, far from regarding speculations concerning the constitution of unmanifest prakṛti as being off-limits, it postulates the 'three strands' (*triguṇa*) as that constitution.

I now wish to draw attention to two interpretive difficulties that threaten to scupper any attempt to make sense of the guṇa doctrine. The first is the root problem of the guṇas' ontological status: what sorts of things, exactly, *are* they? The second is that of their relation to space and time. In view of what the classical texts say about the guṇas, it certainly seems amiss to regard them as substances, or material entities, or anything to do with the sorts of concepts that Feuerstein and others invoke from particle physics. However, we can see why the substance interpretation is tempting; for any alternative – such as capacity, quality, property, power, tendency, etc. – seems to require the existence of a substance in order to be instantiated. If, for example, sattva is taken to be the capacity to manifest, rajas the capacity to move or change, and tamas the capacity to inhibit movement, then it is unclear how such capacities could exist in themselves independently of some substantial entity that possesses them. It makes sense to speak of a thing, say an apple, as being manifest (and *ipso facto* as having the capacity to manifest), and as undergoing change (and thus having mutability) while also being relatively stable (and thus having the power to desist from change). But if we remove the apple itself and try to consider, each on its own, the three capacities or qualities that were attributed to it, they become curiously abstract and ephemeral. The apple – and any other manifest entity – must possess the capacities in question; yet to postulate the capacities as constituents of the entity would seem to be to make a category mistake.

Insofar as the possession of the qualities for which the three guṇas stand is a necessary condition for anything's being a manifest thing, the guṇas themselves may legitimately be deemed to be necessary conditions of this kind. Indeed, in the Sāṃkhya–Yoga doctrine of prakṛti I think we can now observe the result of a two-tier transcendental reflection upon experience: at one level the manifest categories are inferred to be the necessary constitutive elements of the complex repertoire of our experiential possibilities, while at a deeper level, the guṇas are inferred to be the irreducible conditions for manifestation, and hence for experience in general. They are 'constituents' of prakṛti merely in the sense that *prakṛti* is the collective term for them.

Now, on the problem of the guṇas' relation to space and time, it was noted earlier in this chapter that prakṛti has been held – even by those, such as Jacobsen, who adopt a materialistic interpretation – to be the *source* of space (and of time as well), and that according to such a view neither prakṛti as a whole nor any of its three guṇas can be considered to exist *in* space or time. Various statements in the traditional literature support this view. With regard to time, Gauḍapāda comments that, whereas some have said that 'time matures beings, time consumes (or "takes", *saṃharati*) the world; time watches while others sleep, time cannot be overcome, [Sāṃkhya's reply would be that there are only] three types of things (*padārthas*) – the manifest (*vyakta*), the unmanifest (*avyakta*) and puruṣa – and time fits into one of these categories, [i.e.] it is manifest' (*GBh* 61).[24] The author of the *Sāṃkhyasūtra* appears to be a little more specific about the origin of space and time, stating that 'space (*diś*) and time (*kāla*) [arise] from ākāśa and the others' (*SS* 2.12). But the statement is ambiguous owing to the fact that both *diś* and *kāla* can, in the same way as their English equivalents, refer to either a particular space (in the case of *diś*) or time (in the case of *kāla*) or, alternatively, to space and time in general, that is, as abstracted from any specific spatial areas or temporal periods. The commentator Vijñānabhikṣu takes it to be the *particular* (*khaṇḍa*, literally 'broken', 'fragmentary') kinds of spaces and times that are being referred to here. He concurs with another commentator, Aniruddha, that ākāśa, when limited by certain 'conditioning factors' (*upādhis*), 'is called "space" and "time"' (*SSV* 2.12, cf. *SPBh* 2.12), but adds that space and time in themselves (i.e. in the abstract sense of these terms) are held not to arise from ākāśa but to be its source. They are in fact, says Vijñānabhikṣu, 'eternal... specific properties of prakṛti' (*SPBh* 2.12).[25] Thus what starts off looking like an affirmation of the derivative nature of space and time becomes in the hands of the traditional commentators, and especially in those of Vijñānabhikṣu, a statement of the irreducibility of these principles. Space and time are accorded the status of eternal existents, and are thereby placed on a par with the three guṇas as inherent qualities of prakṛti. Such interpretive manoeuvres seem highly dubious, and ought not to be considered as the final word on the Sāṃkhya position. For one thing, it is generally agreed that the *Sāṃkhyasūtra* post-dates the *Sāṃkhyakārikā* by approximately a millennium, and that its author was influenced by philosophical viewpoints extraneous to classical Sāṃkhya; and for another thing, being a sūtra text, the *Sāṃkhyasūtra* tends to leave itself open to competing interpretations, of which those of Aniruddha and Vijñānabhikṣu are noteworthy but not definitive.

Notwithstanding Vijñānabhikṣu's assertion that space and time are 'specific properties' (*guṇa-viśeṣa*) of prakṛti, the predominant view among scholars is that, according to classical Sāṃkhya and Yoga, the terms 'space' and 'time' do not denote real (mind-independent) properties or entities, but refer merely to qualities that are attributed to empirical objects by the cognizing mind. An important – perhaps the *most* important – source of this view is Vyāsa's commentary on *YS* 3.52 (which appears as 3.51 in some editions), in which the commentator says of time that, though 'devoid of object' (*vastu-śūnya*), it is 'a mental construction (*buddhi-nirmāṇa*) and follows [i.e. accompanies] the cognition of a word (*śabda-jñāna*)'. The terminology here echoes *YS* 1.9, where *vikalpa* is defined as 'following word-cognition, devoid of object'.[26] Thus, at least on Vyāsa's account, time is a *vikalpa*, that is, a form of intuition that invariably accompanies cognitions but which has no mind-independent existence. This appears to be an undiluted proclamation of what, in Kantian terms, we might call the ideality of time. If we look at the commentary on *YS* 3.52 as a whole, however, it becomes apparent that Vyāsa is not quite making such a proclamation. Instead he is proposing an atomic theory of time, according to which time is, in reality, nothing other than a succession of indivisible momentary units (*kṣaṇa*) and it is merely our ordinary view, wherein time is conceived in terms of artificial durations, such as hours and days and nights, that is a mental construction. The moments are genuinely existent, and follow one another in a procession; and it is to such a procession of moments, says Vyāsa, that the yogin refers by means of the term 'time' (*YBh* 3.52).

Thus, although the respective views of Vijñānabhikṣu and Vyāsa on time seem significantly different from one another, they have in common the fact that two types of time are distinguished, one of which is merely empirical and the other of which has a subject-independent reality. (And the same distinction is made by Vijñānabhikṣu with respect to space.) Again, however, we cannot be sure that such a distinction was endorsed by the classical darśanas. I noted earlier in this chapter that the description of prakṛti at *SK* 10 can be interpreted as proposing that the characteristics of prakṛti include its being 'unconditioned, eternal (atemporal), and non-spatial'. It is only *manifest* prakṛti that is 'non-eternal' (*anitya*, i.e. temporal) and 'non-pervasive' (*avyāpin*, i.e. subject to spatial constraints). Therefore it would seem fair to surmise that, even though it is not stated explicitly in the *Sāṃkhyakārikā*, the implicit view therein is that time and space obtain only within empirical reality – the realm of thought and perception – and cannot be ascribed to the unmanifest ground of that reality, comprised of the three guṇas in their dormant state.

Having come this far we can now formulate the problem that exists concerning the guṇas' relation to time and space. One aspect of the problem is as follows. If the guṇas are qualities (or properties, powers, etc.), then they must be qualities of some entity; and the sort of entity that possesses qualities must exist temporally (in the case of both physical and mental entities) or both temporally and spatially (in the case of physical ones). If it were to be accepted, *à la* Vijñānabhikṣu's claim, that the guṇas are substances as opposed to qualities, the problem would not thereby be avoided; for the difficulty involved in conceiving how three substances could be distinguished from one another in the absence of spatiotemporal dimensions is comparably as serious as that of conceiving how qualities could exist independently of any entity that possessed them. As Schopenhauer was keen to point out, 'time and space are the *principium individuationis*' (1974a: 148, cf. 1969, I: 112 f.). Which is not to say that they are necessary conditions for existence *per se*; for if that were so then time and space themselves would be precluded from existing (even as merely ideal forms). It is to say, rather, that they are the principles that enable anything to be discerned as identical to itself and distinct from other things, that is, to stand out from the world in general. Thus it is far from clear that three things, namely the guṇas, can intelligibly be posited as existing 'prior to' time and space and as being, collectively, the source thereof. (It is presumably for this sort of reason that Vijñānabhikṣu asserts the 'eternal' existence of space and time, as elements of prakṛti alongside sattva, rajas and tamas.)

A second aspect of the problem, which is really implicit in what has already been said in relation to time, concerns the notion of the guṇas as 'process'. The ways in which the guṇas are said to relate to one another – namely, 'subjugation, support, generation and intercourse' (*SK* 12) – are suggestive of processes, which must of course take place over a period of time.[27] This processive nature of the guṇas is recognized by several interpreters, and is reflected in, for example, Larson's preferred translation of *triguṇa* as 'tripartite constituent process' (see esp. Larson 1987: 65 ff.). Again, then, the guṇas cannot intelligibly be conceived to interact independently of time. And even on the assumption that they remain dormant until animated by the presence of puruṣa the problem cannot be avoided, since any transition from dormancy to activity, or from potentiality to actuality, can happen only *in time*. Indeed, the notion of dormancy itself implies temporal duration; for it can be meaningful only in opposition to activity, which must be a genuine possibility for whatever entity the notion is applied to. (In a similar way, temporal duration is implicit in the concept of immutability, as it is only *over a period of time* that something can remain unchanged.)

These problems are daunting, but it is not necessary that they be resolved here in order for the interpretation of the guṇas that I have proposed to be taken seriously. The riddles of space and time are ones that have intrigued and frustrated metaphysicians throughout history, and it would be asking too much to expect a fully satisfactory account of them to spring forth from texts as laconic as the *Sāṃkhyakārikā* and *Yogasūtra*. If we take Kant as an example, we see that part of his project for setting metaphysics upon a firmer footing was to reinterpret space and time as 'forms of sensible intuition' and, as such, as being contributions brought to experience by the experiencing subject, rather than subject-independent realities (cf. *CPR* A22/B36 ff.). But those who hold spatiotemporal dimensions to be real and independent of our forms of intuition can easily point the finger at Kant and ask: If sensibility is a capacity for receiving sensory material (which claim seems to be among those made in the opening passage of the 'Transcendental Aesthetic'), then from where if not from *outside itself* is such material received? If it be affirmed that it is indeed received from outside, then some kind of spatial relation prior to the engagement of the relevant form of intuition (i.e. space) has already been admitted. And with regard to time, does the application of temporal form to incoming sense-material not itself imply a process, thereby implying further that time is already in place?[28] These problems are similar to those touched upon in the preceding few paragraphs of this chapter; and in some form or other they afflict any philosophical attempt to explain space and time in non-realist terms.

Despite the outstanding conceptual conundrums that have been alluded to, it still strikes me that 'necessary conditions of manifestation in general' comes closest to expressing the meaning of the guṇas in Sāṃkhya and Yoga. In Chapter 6 attention will be focused upon the categories that, while being dependent upon the guṇas, are themselves the conditions of experience.

6

THE EMERGENCE OF THE MANIFEST PRINCIPLES

The classical exposition of prakṛti's twenty-three manifest principles, or categories, occurs in the portion of the *Sāṃkhyakārikā* beginning at verse 22 and ending at verse 38. The names of these principles are well known, and their respective and collective functions have received a great deal of attention in the secondary literature. However, what remains only very dimly understood, and constitutes a source of perennial agitation and bewilderment to scholars, is the nature of the relations between the principles and, connected with this, the reason for the order in which they are said to emerge being as it is. Radhakrishnan gives voice to this agitation when he remarks that 'It is difficult to understand the precise significance of the Sāṃkhya account of evolution, and we have not seen any satisfactory explanation as to why the different steps of evolution are what they are' (1927, II: 274). He can see no logic in the nature or order of the principles, and concludes that these things must be the result of 'historical accidents' rather than any process of deductive reasoning on the part of Sāṃkhyan philosophers (ibid.).

In this chapter I shall argue that the kind of bemusement exhibited by Radhakrishnan in the passage from which I have just quoted inevitably arises if one assumes at the outset that the schema of principles represents a cosmogonic narrative. Through the lens of such an assumption, the schema cannot but appear to be the arbitrary figment of a mythic imagination. The Sāṃkhya account offers no explanation of why 'the great' (*mahat*), also known as buddhi ('awareness', 'discernment'), should figure as the first product of unmanifest prakṛti, nor of how or why it comes to give rise to 'egoity' (*ahaṃkāra*), nor indeed of how egoity in turn gives rise directly or indirectly to the other twenty-one principles. Moreover, when the principles are conceived of as each being single, material, and cosmological, it becomes impossible to formulate how they might be related to conscious human individuals; and thus Sāṃkhya metaphysics is made to appear incongruous and irrelevant to the soteric enterprise of self-revelation.

In this chapter, after discussing the standard way in which the purportedly 'evolutionary' schema has been interpreted, I shall propose an alternative reading, according to which the principles are understood as categories resulting from an analysis (which might well be called a *transcendental* analysis) of the constitutive features of experience, and the order they are enumerated in represents, not the temporal sequence of their emergence, but the relations of conditionality, or dependence, between them. A further claim on my part will be that this alternative, non-realist and non-cosmogonic, interpretation enjoys relative success where others have suffered dismal failure in enabling us to make sense of the relation between metaphysics and soteriology in Sāṃkhya and Yoga.

Cosmos and psyche

In response to the problem alluded to above concerning how, if the manifest principles are cosmological, they can be held to bear upon the internal lives of conscious and intelligent persons, it has been postulated by some interpreters that the principles must be both cosmological and psychological at the same time. Radhakrishnan exemplifies this position well:

> Buddhi, as the product of prakṛti and the generator of ahaṁkāra, is different from buddhi which controls the processes of the senses, mind and ahaṁkāra. If the former is identified with the latter, the whole evolution of prakṛti must be regarded as subjective, since the ego and the non-ego are both the products of buddhi. This ambiguity is found in the other products of prakṛti also.
>
> (1927, II: 268)

Radhakrishnan has clearly discounted in advance the possibility that 'the whole evolution of prakṛti must be regarded as subjective,' for he does not give it a second thought. It would, after all, conflict with a common presupposition to which Radhakrishnan evidently subscibes, namely that, according to Sāṃkhya, a mind-independent reality of physical objects somehow derives from the more obviously psychological principles. Rather than question this presupposition, Radhakrishnan prefers to double the number of principles, positing two buddhis and two ahaṃkāras, and we may presume (since he considers the same 'ambiguity' to exist in them all) two of each of the other principles as well.

Ian Whicher appears to share this dichotomous conception of the manifest principles, but adds that the cosmic aspect must have ontological priority over the psychological one, because the former 'turns... into the psychological' when we (i.e. puruṣa – the true self within us) falsely identify with it. 'It would', says Whicher, 'be a grave mistake to assert, as does S. Dasgupta, that the cosmic and individual *buddhi* for example, have the same ontological status' (1998: 71). However, having claimed that the principles in their psychological aspect 'have no ontological reality,' Whicher does not explain what sort of thing a 'cosmic' intellect might be. Statements that '*Mahat* or cosmic knowing is the first created essence of *prakṛti*, as real as *prakṛti* herself' (ibid.) may possess a rhetorical grandiloquence, but in the absence of any account of how 'knowing' can be 'cosmic' they fail to inform us of what Sāṃkhya is held to have been getting at.

The notion of a cosmic–psychological bifurcation is conspicuous by its absence in the original texts. Neither the *Sāṃkhyakārikā* nor the *Yogasūtra* anywhere speaks of a cosmic and a psychological buddhi; it is merely a single (kind of) buddhi, or in the case of Yoga a single (kind of) citta, that is spoken of. And the same applies to the other manifest principles. As an exegetical strategy, therefore, the bifurcation thesis is exceedingly unparsimonious. It is my view that, not just the majority, but all of the manifest principles can best be understood as psychological, and that in order to interpret them and their interrelations in a coherent manner we need to leave aside the 'cosmic' dimension. This is not to say that Sāṃkhya's own presentation of the schema does not invite a cosmogonic reading; in some ways such a reading is indeed the most natural and literal. I think it has to be acknowledged, however, that in trying to decipher a largely esoteric work such as the *Sāṃkhyakārikā*[1] a literal reading will not always be the most hermeneutically plausible. In certain instances a more sophisticated interpretive approach is called for if we are to discern the meaning being alluded to in equivocal or figurative passages. In this study my principal criterion has been – where two or more alternative interpretive options present themselves – to favour that which, other things being equal, appears to be the most philosophically coherent.

'Vertical' and 'Horizontal' ontologies

Wilhelm Halbfass, in contrasting Sāṃkhya ontology with that of Vaiśeṣika, proposed that we distinguish between 'vertical' and 'horizontal' ontologies. 'Both of these systems present elaborate lists of world constituents', he says:

> However, the Sāṃkhya does so in a 'vertical' manner; that is, in an enumeration of successive stages (i.e., the primeval 'nature,' *prakṛti*, and its twenty-three evolutes).
>
> The Vaiśeṣika, on the other hand, is the most representative case of a 'horizontal' enumeration and classification of world constituents. It lists its cosmic factors and 'categories' of reality *not as successive stages in a scheme of evolution, but in a horizontal, synchronic arrangement, which includes, however, certain structures of dependence and subordination.*
>
> (Halbfass 1992: 48–49, my italics in the last sentence)

Although this statement by Halbfass accurately represents the standard interpretations of Sāṃkhya and Vaiśeṣika respectively, it misses the underlying meaning of the Sāṃkhya schema. The part of the statement that I have emphasized is intended to refer to Vaiśeṣika ontology. I do not wish to dispute that it fairly describes that system's approach. I do, however, wish to contend that, if we apply it also to the Sāṃkhya schema, then that schema makes far more sense than it does when viewed as 'an enumeration of successive stages'. It would, of course, be foolish to claim that the *Sāṃkhyakārikā* 'lists its cosmic factors . . . in a horizontal, synchronic arrangement'. Clearly it does not (and, as noted above,

I would question whether its factors are best construed as 'cosmic' in any case). What I think *can* legitimately be claimed, however, is that the ostensibly diachronic ontological exposition in the *Sāṃkhyakārikā* symbolically, or analogically, represents a set of synchronically related principles.

Before I explain why I take this view, it is worth noting that Halbfass was not the first to describe Sāṃkhya ontology in terms of a 'vertical' – 'horizontal' distinction. The distinction was also used by van Buitenen, only with the difference that he held Sāṃkhya's schema – or 'description of world evolution' as he called it – to be partially vertical and partially horizontal (1957a: 16).[2] Van Buitenen's point is that the descent from prakṛti to buddhi and then to ahaṃkāra is a case of 'vertical evolution', whereas 'From the *ahaṃkāra* on this pattern is abandoned: its evolution becomes a ramification' (ibid.). The eleven indriyas ('powers', 'capacities') – comprising the five sensory capacities, the five action capacities, and manas – are all derived from ahaṃkāra, as are the five tanmātras, from which come (in 'vertical' fashion this time) the five elemental forms (*bhūtas*). '[T]he function of the *ahaṃkāra* in the evolution process is much more complicated than those of *pradhāna* and *mahān*', notes van Buitenen. 'By itself it creates the whole phenomenal world, not in successive evolutions, but immediately; it is the father of the world but its ways are mysterious' (ibid.). Despite van Buitenen's account having preceded that of Halbfass, it nevertheless strikes me as being the more accurate of the two. Still, however, I would say that its accuracy lies only in its ability to describe how the manifest principles are presented in the *Sāṃkhyakārikā*. It does not take us very far towards a comprehension of the underlying meanings of the relevant passages.

My interpretation of Sāṃkhya ontology concurs with the interpretations of Halbfass and van Buitenen insofar as all three of us construe that ontology as an account of the factors that together bring 'the world' into being. Where my interpretation diverges from those others is in what might be called its *subjectivization* of the concept of 'the world'. When van Buitenen speaks of ahaṃkāra creating 'the whole phenomenal world . . . immediately', I think he paints the situation with too broad a brush. Ahaṃkāra does indeed make possible the experience of a world, but this occurs not through an instantaneous *fiat*. What follows from ahaṃkāra is not the world 'out there', but a set of intentional acts and contents, which are conditions for perceptual experience. At no point in its ontological exposition does Sāṃkhya invoke the realist notion of a subject-independent world: the entire set of principles arises only in the presence of the transcendental subject (*puruṣa*) and concerns factors internal to the instigation of experience. To make this point clearer, let us now examine in detail the passage in the *Sāṃkhyakārikā* that begins at verse 22.

The order of emergence

SK 22 offers the following précis of the ontological categories:

> From prakṛti, mahat; from that, ahaṃkāra; and from that, the group of sixteen; from five of those sixteen, the five bhūtas.

Most translators of this verse tend to insert additional words to provide some information about the nature of the relations between the various principles mentioned. This tendency is illustrated in the following extracts from three translations (key words have been underlined by myself):

> From Prakriti issues Mahat . . . ; from this . . . issues Self-consciousness (Ahankâra), from which proceeds the set of sixteen; from five of these sixteen, proceed the five gross elements.
>
> (Jhâ 1896: 61)
>
> From Primal Nature proceeds the Great One . . . thence individuation, [etc.].
>
> (Suryanarayana Sastri 1948: 46)
>
> From *prakṛti* (emerges) the great one (*mahat*); from that (comes) self-awareness (*ahaṃkāra*); [etc.].
>
> (Larson 1979: 262–63)

Thus, although the original verse tells us very little about the relations concerned, it has commonly been assumed that they involve an issuing, procession, or emergence of some kind. While such terminology is perfectly consistent with certain expressions used in other verses, most notably *pariṇāmata* and *sarga*, we should be wary of taking them too literally. The term *pariṇāma*, literally 'bending around', is usually rendered as 'transformation' or 'modification'. It is prevalent within the *Yogasūtra*, wherein it occurs eleven times, and was touched upon in Chapter 4 above in connection with its appearance in *YS* 4.14. In the *Sāṃkhyakārikā*, it occurs only twice: at *SK* 27 in the expression 'specific modifications of the *guṇas*' (*guṇa-pariṇāma-viśeṣa*), and at *SK* 16, as *pariṇāmata* ('modifiable' or 'transformable'). The context of this latter occurrence is that the unmanifest (*avyakta*) is being described as, in part, 'the source (or "cause", *kāraṇa*) [of all manifest things], operating due to the combination of the three guṇas, transformable (*pariṇāmata*) like flowing water (*salilavat*) due to the specific [nature] of each of these guṇas that underlie it.' The simile of flowing water is also pertinent to the other term that is of particular interest here, namely *sarga*, which is etymologically cognate with the English word 'surge', via the Latin *surgere* ('to rise up'), from which we also get 'source' (cf. Partridge 1966: 683). At *SK* 21 we encounter the phrase *api saṃyogas tat kṛtaḥ sargaḥ*, which can be translated as 'from this union proceeds creation' (Jhâ 1896: 60).[3] However, since *saṃyogas* (= *saṃyogaḥ*) is in the nominative and not the ablative case, an alternative and slightly more accurate rendering would be: 'that conjunction indeed *is* creation, surgence' (emphasis added), the conjunction in question being that of puruṣa and prakṛti. In any event, taking into account *SK* 16, the meaning of the present passage would seem to be that, when in conjunction with puruṣa (passing over, for the time being, precisely what 'in conjunction' amounts to), prakṛti is modified or transformed in such a way that it 'swells' or 'surges forth' as a formal creation, which comprises – as we learn in the subsequent verse – the twenty-three manifest principles.

Now, what I have just given is a fairly literal interpretation of the relation between prakṛti and its manifestations as suggested at *SK* 21. In competition with the terminology of 'transforming' and 'surging', however, is that of manifestation itself. The term 'manifestation' is, in many contexts, highly ambiguous, and hence can be philosophically troubling. To say that *X* is a manifestation of *Y* could, conceivably, mean any of several things, including for example:

(a) *Y* has transformed into *X* ('What was once a caterpillar now manifests as a butterfly');
(b) *X* exists or occurs because of *Y* ('The symphony is a manifestation of the composer's laborious effort');
(c) *X* is the appearance of *Y* to a subject.

In the cases of (a) and (b) above, the fact that *X* is a manifestation of *Y* implies the temporal priority of *Y*; (c), however, is equivocal on this point. On the one hand, *X*'s being an appearance to a subject of *Y* could mean that *X* and *Y* are numerically and qualitatively identical to one another – that is, they are the *same thing* – but that, with regard to *X* the subject is in a position to perceive (or understand, or in some other way cognitively appreciate) it, whereas he or she was not in such a position with regard to *Y* ('The book I'd been looking for did not become manifest until I looked behind the bookcase – and there it was!'). In this instance, the temporal priority of the unmanifest over the manifest is implied, even though the crucial factor is the relation of a subject to the object and not the state of the object itself. On the other hand, *X*'s being a manifestation of *Y* could mean that *X* and *Y* are the same thing considered in terms of two distinct *aspects*, namely a manifest and an unmanifest one. This is the Kantian thought: that the very same thing can, at one and the same time, be conceived as *appearance* and *thing-in-itself*. Insofar as it is experienced by a subject, it is the one thing, and insofar as it is not so experienced it is the other.

I do not want to propose that the Sāṃkhyan concept of unmanifest prakṛti is equivalent to the Kantian thing-in-itself. It definitely is not. Whereas Kant employs the expression 'things-in-themselves' to denote only objects considered in their non-empirical aspect, prakṛti (in itself) is the unmanifest aspect of both the objectual content of experience and subjective intentional acts. In Kantian terms, therefore, prakṛti is the noumenal correlate of both, on the one hand, the pre-experiential sensory manifold, and on the other, the sensible forms and conceptual categories by virtue of which the sensory manifold comes to be recognized as the external world. Notwithstanding the non-equivalence of the Kantian and Sāṃkhyan conceptual frameworks, the analogy between them on this point is, I think, philosophically instructive.

The precise nature of the relation between the manifest and unmanifest aspects of prakṛti is not fully worked out in the classical texts of Sāṃkhya and Yoga. In place of clear explanations, we generally find unelaborated similes; and thus it is probably impossible to resolve the issue of whether the relation is to be conceived along the lines of a (roughly) noumenal–phenomenal dual-aspect theory, or something more like a process in which what was previously noumenal changes into – or generates out of itself – that which is phenomenal. The language of 'surging' or 'emerging' suggests the latter, whereas other passages suggest the former. At *SK* 2, for example, it is stated that the best method of eradicating the threefold dissatisfaction (*duḥkha*) referred to in the opening verse of the text is to acquire 'discerning awareness' (*vijñāna*) of 'the manifest, the unmanifest, and the knower.' I take this to imply that the manifest and unmanifest aspects of prakṛti co-exist and can, as a result of the right sort of sustained contemplation, be distinguished from one another. Of course, someone who holds that unmanifest prakṛti is an infinite reservoir of matter – or an 'undifferentiated plenitude of being' as Larson puts it (1979: 12, 167) – might contend that such a reservoir is capable of giving rise to any number of real finite entities without diminishing its own existence, and that the co-existence of unmanifest and manifest prakṛti can thus be accounted for without recourse to a dual-aspect interpretation.[4] Such a reading is supported by, for example, *YS* 4.2, which asserts that 'The transformation (*pariṇāma*) into another type (*jāti*, i.e. ontological class or category) is due to the outpouring (*āpūra*) of prakṛti.' Whichever way we understand the classical metaphors, it is evident that, according to Sāṃkhya and Yoga, in becoming manifest prakṛti does not cease to be, in itself, unmanifest.

Having remarked upon the relation between unmanifest prakṛti and the manifest schema as a whole, let us now consider each of the manifest principles in turn, in the order in which they are presented in the *Sāṃkhyakārikā*. The first principle has two quite different names, the reason for which is nowhere fully explained. One of these names, *mahat*, means simply 'that which is great, mighty, supreme'; and the other, *buddhi*, has the broad sense of 'awareness' as well as a range of more specific senses that come into play in particular contexts. As a general rule, the term *mahat* is used when the manifest principles as a collective group are being referred to, notably in the expression 'mahat and the others', some version of which occurs four times in the *Sāṃkhyakārikā* (*SK* 3, 8, 40, 56). *Buddhi*, meanwhile, is used when something is being noted that is of relevance either to this specific principle (*SK* 23, 49) or to the three 'inner' mental instruments (*antaḥkaraṇa*s [*SK* 35]), of which buddhi is one, as distinct from the ten 'outer' instruments (cf. *SK* 33). As I mentioned in Chapter 4, buddhi is defined as *adhyavasāya* (*SK* 23), which term also features in the definition of perception at *SK* 5, and may be translated as 'ascertainment' or 'discernment'. Buddhi is said to have two poles, one *sāttvika* (light, luminous, positive) and the other *tāmasa* (dark, negative). The first of these comprises 'virtue (*dharma*), knowledge (*jñāna*), emotional non-attachment (*virāga*), and masterfulness (*aiśvarya*)', and the second comprises the opposite qualities (*SK* 23). These various mental qualities or dispositions are referred to later in the text as *bhāva*s (*SK* 40, 43, 52), a term which can denote any kind of 'being' or 'state of being'. In the context of Sāṃkhya philosophy the bhāvas seem to play a role similar to that of the *saṃskāra*s and *vāsanā*s of Yoga, both of which latter terms indicate mental traits or habitual patterns of response (or, better perhaps, pre-conscious psychic traces that *impel* such responses). Whether we call them bhāvas, saṃskāras, or vāsanās, there are certain types of these mental factors that are deemed worthy of cultivation, and others that are to be eradicated. Eventually all of them must be left behind if the soteric goal of puruṣa's aloneness (*kaivalya*) is to be realized (*SK* 67–68). Thus we find, for example, that in Yoga one of the principal expressions applied to the mental state in which all saṃskāras have been pacified or dissolved is 'seedless' (*nirbīja-*) samādhi (*YS* 1.51, 3.8), which expression reflects the view that saṃskāras are seeds of puruṣa's misidentification.

What emerges from the above points is that buddhi is best regarded as encompassing a range of mental states, dispositions and capacities, although it is most particularly associated with discerning awareness, which might otherwise be termed intentional (object-directed) consciousness, as distinct from the 'pure' (contentless) consciousness with which puruṣa – considered in itself – is identified.[5] Taking all of its various associations into account, the common translation of *buddhi* as 'intellect' is not inappropriate, although in most contexts I regard 'awareness' or 'intentional consciousness' as closer to the mark. In this light, it may seem surprising that the majority of interpreters of Sāṃkhya and Yoga nevertheless regard buddhi (along with the entire schema of manifest principles) as 'material'.[6] If one is to treat something that is patently mental as also being material, then it would be not merely helpful, but an urgent necessity, to explain the sense in which these terms are being used; for in western philosophy 'mental' and 'material' (or 'mind' and 'matter') have frequently been defined in opposition to one another. Although some modern-day reductive physicalists and functionalists declare simply that 'the mind is the brain' (e.g. Dennett 1991: 33), on the whole philosophers are more careful to stipulate that, while mental states such as those of intentional consciousness 'are *realized in* the neurophysiology of the brain' (Searle 1983: 15, original emphasis), there remains a place for the concept of ontologically subjective events, which are not equivalent to physical ones. As we saw in Chapter 5, however, those who adopt a materialist interpretation of prakṛti tend to fall far short of explaining what they mean by 'matter' or 'material', and consequently end up using apparently paradoxical expressions to refer to certain of prakṛti's modes, such as 'mental material principles' (Jacobsen 1999: 225), without giving us any good reason to regard these expressions as anything other than nonsense.[7]

Turning now to the second manifest principle, ahaṃkāra, we find that it is tersely defined as *abhimāna* (*SK* 24), which term can denote self-conceit and pride or the mere having of a thought of oneself.[8] As was noted in Chapter 1, van Buitenen has proposed an interesting theory that ahaṃkāra, as a concept, has its origin 'in the ancient upaniṣadic speculations on a self-formulating, self-creating primordial personality' (1957a: 21), whose verbal ejaculation '*aham*!' ('I!') constitutes his self-formulation, which in turn constitutes the cosmos (ibid.: 19). If interpreted with a realist bias this equivalence between self-formulation and universal creation sounds implausible, and might at best be treated as an extravagant creation myth. Van Buitenen himself notes (ibid.) that the distinction 'between macrocosmos and microcosmos' seems to be absent in the ancient texts to which he is referring (principally early portions of the *Bṛhadāraṇyaka-* and the sixth chapter of the *Chāndogya-upaniṣad*). However, he does not take what would seem to be the obvious next step, which is to regard the 'macrocosmic' (i.e. cosmogonic) story as a mythopoetic exposition of an essentially idealist notion, namely that the individuation of the subject does not merely coincide with the manifestation of the world, but is its *precondition*.[9] In my view, sense can be made of Sāṃkhya's position only if the idealist notion just mentioned is taken to be the basis of the claim that from ahaṃkāra (i.e. due to the concept of selfhood, which can be known *a priori*) 'the rolling forth (*pravartate*) of the twofold emergence (*sarga*) [occurs],' comprising on the one hand the ten 'capacities' (*indriya*s) plus the synthesizing faculty of mind (*manas*), and on the other hand the five modes of sensory content (*tanmātra*s) (*SK* 24).

Let us, then, look a little closer at these factors that are contingent upon 'the thought of oneself', beginning with the 'powers' or 'capacities' (*indriya*s). There are either ten or eleven of these, according to whether we include manas among them or place it in a separate category. The ten are divided into two sets of five, named respectively *buddhīndriya*s and *karmendriya*s. The former – literally 'awareness capacities' (*buddhi-indriya*s) – comprise 'seeing (*cakṣus*), hearing (*śrotra*), smelling (*ghrāṇa*), tasting (*rasana*), and touching (*tvac*)' (*SK* 26). Several translators take the verse just quoted to refer to sense organs: 'eye, ear, nose, tongue and skin'.[10] But, as I read it, the original text is concerned much less with organs – or with the faculties of sense (i.e. sight, audition and so on) – than with the modes of sensory act, by which I mean the types of phenomenological episode known as *seeing, hearing, smelling*, etc.

The second fivefold set – namely 'action capacities' (*karma-indriya*s) – comprises 'speaking (*vāc*), clasping (*pāṇi*), foot (*pāda*), anus (*pāyu*), and genitalia (*upastha*, lit. "under-part")' (*SK* 26). Here the terminology is less evidently 'active' than in the case of the buddhīndriyas. Although *vāc* and *pāṇi* could be interpreted as vocal and manipulative powers respectively, *pāṇi* could just as well be translated as 'hand'; and the terms for the remaining three karmendriyas do not really lend themselves to being translated as anything other than the names of particular organs. However, two verses later, at *SK* 28, the karmendriyas are characterized in terms of their functions or modes of operation (*vṛtti*), which are, respectively, 'speaking (*vacana*), grasping (*ādāna*), wandering (*viharaṇa*), excreting (*utsarga*), and intense pleasure (*ānanda*).'[11] Here we appear to have a list of physiological activities, with the exception of the last, ānanda, which is a feeling-tone of extreme pleasure or delight. It is possible that, just as a particular feeling is here being linked with the genitals, so the other four karmendriyas are intended to represent feelings associated with certain parts of the body rather than the actions or body parts themselves. 'Grasping' and 'wandering' could very easily relate to modes of proprioceptive or kinaesthetic awareness; that is, awareness of the position and movement of limbs and other body parts.[12] And speaking and excreting, too, could be thought of in terms of the sensations that accompany these acts. Understanding the karmendriyas in this way would explain why they are placed alongside the buddhīndriyas: all ten indriyas are sense-capacities, only the buddhīndriyas are exteroceptive, i.e. concerned with awareness of the world external to one's own body, whereas the karmendriyas are introceptive, i.e. concerned with awareness of one's own body.

Manas is defined as being 'of the essence' (*ātmaka*) of both sets of indriyas, and thus as being at least analogous to an indriya itself; and also as *saṃkalpaka*, which can be translated as 'resolve' or 'decision' (*SK* 27). For etymological reasons, *manas* is normally translated simply as 'mind'; but this is somewhat misleading, given that in Sāṃkhya philosophy it evidently stands for a specific component of what in English we very loosely designate as 'the mind'. Davies acknowledges this point when he notes that 'The Latin *mens* and our *mind* correspond to it [*manas*] in origin but not in meaning' (1894: 63). But then, unduly influenced by some unhelpful assumptions, he offers the following contrast between manas and the western concept of mind:

> In our Western philosophy, mind is usually considered as an expression for the rational faculties of the soul, and as opposed to matter; but in the view of Kapila [i.e. classical Sāṃkhya], it is not a part of the soul, but is itself a form of matter from a material source (*Prakṛiti*).
>
> (Ibid., my square brackets)

The point I take Davies to be trying to make here is clouded, in part, by his equivocal use of the term 'soul'. Having first used it to denote a multi-facultative entity, he then subsequently uses it to stand for the puruṣa of Sāṃkhya. Since puruṣa is a pure subject, devoid of faculties, the fact that manas 'is not a part of [it]' ought not in itself to be taken to indicate that the concept of manas is out of step with that of a set of rational faculties. Davies' principal assumption, however, is that manas, along with all of prakṛti's other manifestations, is 'a form of matter' and that it is *this* that distinguishes it from western conceptions of mind. For reasons given in Chapter 5, I remain doubtful about the wisdom of describing prakṛti and its manifestations, without qualification, as 'material'.

It is generally agreed that manas is an organizing faculty, by which sensations are gathered and arranged into perceptual episodes (Davies calls it 'the *sensorium commune*' (1894: 63)). This interpretation, rightly in my view, emphasizes Sāṃkhya's insistence on the active and constructive role of the mind in the generation of experience. Indeed, I am inclined to regard manas as the synthesizer of sensory information, much in the way that Kant saw the imagination. Although it is rarely picked up by commentators, there may also be a connection between manas and conative operations, which are experienced as acts of volition.[13] This connection is suggested by the occurrence, in manas's definition, of *saṃkalpaka*,[14] and might be strengthened if we were to regard the karmendriyas as physiological acts, the co-ordination of which manas is responsible for, rather than as modes of introceptive awareness (which is in fact my preferred interpretation). Some interpreters have associated not manas but buddhi with volition, and Jhâ even uses 'will' as a direct translation of *buddhi* (1896: 62). Contrariwise, others have identified manas with intellect (e.g. Zimmer 1953: 317, 321 n. 45). Unfortunately the textual resources available to us are insufficiently explicit to conclusively resolve these matters.

It is worth reiterating at this point that Sāṃkhya has a collective term for the three components of the mind that have so far been discussed, those being buddhi, ahaṃkāra, and manas. The term is 'inner instrument' (*antaḥkaraṇa*), and is used in two slightly differing ways. At *SK* 35 it is used in a way that implies that each of the three mental components just mentioned is itself an 'inner instrument', while at *SK* 33 it clearly stands for a unitary but threefold instrument or faculty. In either case, the inner instrument is to be distinguished from the outer (*bāhya*) one, which comprises the five buddhīndriyas and five karmendriyas; and the inner and outer instruments together form a single yet complex structure known simply as 'the instrument' (*karaṇa*). The outer instrument is related to 'present time' (*sāmpratakāla*) whereas the inner instrument is related to the 'three times' (*trikāla*), which I take to mean that, while sensory representations are restricted to the present moment, thought can range over the past (in memory) and the future (in anticipation) as well as the present (*SK* 33).[15] The terms 'inner' and 'outer' are presumably intended to indicate, not spatial determinations, but the fact that the operations of the former type – namely intentional consciousness (*buddhi*), egoity (*ahaṃkāra*), and the synthesis of sensory events (*manas*) – are internal to the mind, whereas sensations ostensibly derive their content from extra-mental sources, that is from the external environment in the case of the buddhīndriyas and from the organic body in the case of the karmendriyas. At *SK* 35 the relation between the inner and outer instruments is described analogically as follows:

> Since buddhi, together with the other [two] inner instruments, is immersed in (*avagāhate*) all objects, this threefold instrument is the chamber (*dvārin*) and the remaining ones [i.e. the ten indriyas] are the doors (*dvāras*).

In this translation of the verse I have followed Suryanarayana Sastri's suggestion (1948: 66–67) that *dvārin* refers to 'that to which channels lead' and not, as other translators have supposed, a 'warder', 'gate-keeper', or 'door-keeper' (cf. e.g. Davies 1894: 71; Jhâ 1896: 76; Larson 1979: 266; and also MW: 504). According to the analogy (as Sastri and myself read it), the sensory and action capacities are the 'doorways' through which information concerning external objects is conveyed to the cognizing mind, although it should be noted that the verse makes no claim concerning the ontological status of the putatively external objects themselves.

Next to be considered among the manifest principles are the tanmātras, which, like manas and the ten indriyas, are held to 'roll forth' from ahaṃkāra. The doctrine that the tanmātras derive from, or are in some way contingent upon, egoity is highly significant. It is not always given the attention it deserves, however, in large part because of the serious difficulties it generates for the external realist interpretation of Sāṃkhya. These difficulties have led some scholars to express bafflement at the whole concept of the tanmātras, a case in point being Frauwallner, who concludes 'that no valid ground is found in the [Sāṃkhya] system to make its introduction . . . appear intelligible' (1973, I: 272). Such interpreters tend to assume that the tanmātras are something like 'material essences', which in some unspecified way 'generate the five gross elements' (Larson 1987: 50), and that these 'gross elements' (*bhūtas*) in turn constitute, or are themselves, perceptible physical entities.[16] The major problem here is this: on the one hand, the tanmātras are supposed to give rise to physical objects, which are real in the sense of being mind-independent; and yet on the other hand the tanmātras are themselves derived from a mental principle, namely ahaṃkāra, thus making them and anything that follows from them thoroughly mind-dependent. As long as the realist assumption is retained, this would seem to be an irresolvable paradox. Rather than reject the assumption of realism, however, what many interpreters have done is to invoke a concept that has now become a bulwark of Sāṃkhya and Yoga exegesis, namely 'subtle matter'.

With the exception of the bhūtas, which are described as 'gross' or 'coarse' matter, the term 'subtle matter' – or one of its synonyms such as 'subtle substance' or 'subtle material' – is routinely applied in the secondary literature to all the manifest principles, and occasionally to unmanifest prakṛti and the guṇas as well. A smattering of quotations will suffice to illustrate the point:

> [Buddhi] is material, but of the subtlest form of matter.
>
> (Davies 1894: 17–18)

> [Buddhi] is regarded as the subtle substance of all mental processes. It is the faculty by which we distinguish objects and perceive what they are. The functions of buddhi are ascertainment and decision.
>
> (Radhakrishnan 1927, II: 267)

> With the co-operation of rajas [ahaṃkāra dominated by tamas] is transformed into subtle matter, vibratory, radiant and instinct with energy, and the tanmātras of sound, touch, colour, taste and smell arise.
>
> (Ibid.: 271)

> The world develops according to certain laws out of primitive matter, which first produces those subtile substances of which the internal organs of all creatures are formed, and after that brings forth the gross matter.
>
> (Garbe 1899: 10)

> [A tanmātra is] undifferentiated and causal stuff and is just subtle or psychic matter.
>
> (K. C. Bhattacharyya 1956, I: 175)

> [T]he guṇas are non-intelligent subtle substances...
>
> (Dasgupta 1922: 259)

From this selection of extracts an impression can be gleaned of the kinds of ambiguities and confusions that the concept of subtle matter attracts. In the first of the two quotations from Radhakrishnan, for example, it is far from clear what is meant by the phrase 'the subtle substance of all mental processes.' It could mean that the principle being described, namely buddhi, is a non-physical substance that constitutes mental phenomena, if it were not for the fact that, in the next two sentences, we learn that buddhi is a 'faculty' with specific 'functions'. Although a faculty might belong to a thing that is constituted by a particular substance, I do not see how a faculty can itself be a substance, however 'subtle' it is assumed to be. Then, from Garbe, we get the claim that, according to Sāṃkhya, prakṛti 'produces' certain 'subtile substances' and then goes on to '[bring] forth the gross matter'; but he neglects in this passage to point out that, on the realist view to which he subscribes, the so-called gross matter is supposed to *derive from* or *evolve out of* the subtle substances. It is understandable why one might be tempted to play down this fact, especially if one is inclined, like K. C. Bhattacharyya for example, to treat 'subtle' as equivalent to 'psychic'; for how, after all, could a psychic (i.e. mental) entity be the material source of a 'gross' (physical) one? But ignoring the interpretive problem doesn't make it go away.

Some other scholars have been considerably less reticent about admitting that, on their reading, real physical entities must be held by Sāṃkhya to be the end-products of the same chain of evolution to which buddhi and the other patently mental principles belong. Again, however, such scholars have tended to blur the issue by referring to these latter principles as 'subtle' instead of 'mental'. Indeed, this term 'subtle' has been used – sometimes with tedious repetitiveness – to imply that the evolutionary chain is a graded continuum from unmanifest prakṛti at the top end to the bhūtas (interpreted as physical particles) at the bottom, with no sudden and inexplicable leap from mental to material stuff. Sen Gupta is one such interpreter, and the following passage illustrates not only her 'gradual evolution' theory but also the zeal with which the term 'subtle' can on occasions be employed:

> According to Sāṁkhya, the evolutionary change means gradual change from more subtle to less subtle. *Prakṛti* is the subtlest of all the constitutive principles of the world. So, the first evolute should be such which is less subtle than *Prakṛti* but more subtle than the succeeding categories. This is possible only if *sattva guṇa* becomes the predominating

> *guṇa* in the first category. (Subtlety can be generated in a category merely by increasing the *sattva guṇa*.)
>
> (Sen Gupta 1982: 98)[17]

The word 'subtle' derives from the Latin *subtīlis*, 'finely woven', and has a range of meanings, including 'delicate, elusive... imperceptible, intangible... [and] refined' (*Webster's*: 2281). The expression 'subtle matter' is not unheard of in western philosophy. Descartes, for example, uses it to denote 'particles of indefinite smallness' that are produced by the collision of 'violently agitated' matter with 'other bodies' (1985, I: 258).[18] But none of this helps us very much in trying to make sense of passages such as the one just quoted from Sen Gupta.

I do not mean to imply that 'subtle' should be banished from the interpretive literature on Sāṃkhya. It is in fact the most appropriate translation of the Sanskrit term *sūkṣma*, with which it may share some remote etymological ancestry,[19] and *sūkṣma* (along with *saukṣmya*, 'subtlety') is undoubtedly made use of in the *Sāṃkhyakārikā* (at *SK* 7, 8, 37 and 39) and in the *Yogasūtra* as well.[20] Indeed, when discussing *SK* 8 in the last chapter we saw prakṛti's 'subtlety' (*saukṣmya*) being cited as the reason for its imperceptibility; and it would be fair to presume from this that – since prakṛti is known via its manifest modes – these modes are held to be, as Sen Gupta says, 'less subtle' than unmanifest prakṛti. Furthermore, Sen Gupta is right to draw a connection between a thing's 'subtlety' and the extent to which the quality of sattva prevails in that thing, although I don't think the relation is quite as straightforward as she implies. The parenthetical remark that she makes at the end of the passage quoted above suggests that sattva is somewhat analogous to a chemical constituent that can be added to or subtracted from an entity in order to increase or decrease its level of 'subtlety'. If this were true, then that which is most 'subtle' of all, namely unmanifest prakṛti, would contain the highest proportion of sattva. But this is not the case; rather, prakṛti in itself is held to comprise the three guṇas in a state of perfect equilibrium.

As I see it, the link between subtlety and sattva resides in the notion of 'purification', which, though invoked more explicitly in Yoga than in Sāṃkhya, is nevertheless present in both systems. In the *Yogasūtra* the term *sattva* appears to be used as a synonym of *buddhi*. It is to be purified to a level at which it becomes indistinguishable from the puruṣa (*YS* 3.35, 55). In a sense, an expression such as 'purity of sattva' is pleonastic, for *sattva* can itself stand for clarity and purity.[21] But when *sattva* is used in place of *buddhi*, then what is meant by its 'purification' is, I presume, the cultivation of the moral discipline, perceptual acuity, and alertness that the Yoga system as a whole is intended to promote. 'Subtlety' enters the picture when we consider the kinds of things that can become objects of knowledge for the 'purified' or 'cultivated' buddhi. The advanced stages of Yoga practice are said to allow 'subtle objects' (*sūkṣma-viṣaya*s) to become the foci of sustained meditation (*YS* 1.44); and since 'the unmanifest (*aliṅga*) is the ultimate object of subtlety' (*YS* 1.45), it may be inferred that the expression 'subtle objects' here encompasses all, or most, of the manifest principles.[22] There are, of course, many questions that might be raised in this connection, such as how buddhi could become a meditative 'object' if buddhi is itself the medium through which meditation occurs; but to try to resolve such questions here would take us too far off our main track. The immediate point to be made is that Sen Gupta's claim, that increasing sattva increases subtlety, would be expressed more precisely if one were to say that, by means of the cultivation of the quality of purity, for which *sattva* in most contexts stands, increasingly difficult-to-comprehend (and hence 'subtle') aspects of the psychosensory apparatus are revealed to consciousness. This way of expressing the claim gives due weight to the epistemological implications of 'subtle', and rightly diminishes the ontological significance that is normally read into the term. In short, 'subtle' should be taken primarily to indicate an object's degree of accessibility to a knower, and not its material constitution.

The issue that prompted the above discussion of the term 'subtle' was that of how something physical – namely the bhūtas as they are typically construed – can derive, directly or indirectly, from something mental. The standard account – according to which all of the manifest principles are 'material', including ahaṃkāra and the tanmātras (which constitute the bridge between ahaṃkāra and the bhūtas) – is in my view incoherent. It is vitiated by its failure to explain, firstly, how mental principles can also be material ones, and, secondly, how mind-independent entities can 'evolve' from mental ones. My alternative to this account involves a recasting of the tanmātras and bhūtas as, no longer 'subtle' and 'gross' material items, but *modes of sensory content* and *forms of ostensibly external objects* respectively. A useful way of approaching an explanation of what I mean by these two expressions will be to consider how the five tanmātras are understood by traditional commentators.

Although the five tanmātras are not individually named in the *Sāṃkhyakārikā*, there is a consensus among the Sanskrit commentators that this group comprises sound (*śabda*), tactile feeling (*sparśa*), visual appearance (*rūpa*), flavour (*rasa*), and odour (*gandha*) (see e.g. *TK, GBh* and *YD* on *SK* 38). There should, therefore, be nothing controversial about my referring to the tanmātras as the five modes of sense-content, for this is the most literal interpretation of the traditional view. Where my interpretation differs from the standard modern one, however, is in its refraining from conceiving the tanmātras as anything *besides* sense-contents. I see no reason, for example, to regard them as the sorts of 'material essences' that Larson and others have assumed them to be, largely because I am not convinced that such expressions have any clear sense.[23] Terms such as 'subtle element' and 'primary element', which are widely favoured as translations of 'tanmātra',[24] can be justified by references to (a small number of) commentarial sources. Vyāsa commenting upon *YS* 1.41, for example, distinguishes three grades of objects to be apprehended in meditation, the first of which is *bhūta-sūkṣma* ('subtle element' or 'subtle entity'), and the other two of which are 'gross support' (*sthūla-ālambana*) and 'worldly divisions' (*viśva-bheda*, i.e. macroscopic objects). The translation 'subtle element' does not conflict with my interpretation of the tanmātras, as long as (*qua* sense-content) it is understood to mean a constitutive element of *sensations* and not of mind-independent physical entities. This understanding differs significantly from the common view that the tanmātras physically constitute – or 'give rise to' via 'a process of condensation' (Eliade 1969: 21) – the bhūtas, which in turn physically constitute the entire external world, including our own bodies.[25] By way of an examination of the bhūtas I shall elaborate how my interpretation of their relation to the tanmātras differs from the one just mentioned.

As in the case of the tanmātras, the bhūtas, though not individually named in the *Sāṃkhyakārikā*, are universally agreed to be the five elements, these being the four that are common to many ancient cultures – namely: earth (*pṛthivī* or *kṣiti*), water (*ap*), fire (*tejas*) and air (*vāyu* or *marut*) – plus *ākāśa* (or *vyoman*), which is normally translated these days as 'space' (the older translation as 'ether' having fallen out of favour).[26] An atomic or corpuscularian interpretation – according to which the elements are physical atoms – has been adopted by the majority of modern commentators. Dasgupta typifies it when he states: 'All gross things are formed by the collocation of the five atoms of kṣiti, ap, tejas, marut, and vyoman. The difference between one thing and another is simply this, that its collocation of atoms or the arrangement or grouping of atoms is different from that in another' (1922: 255). Usually it is implied that these atoms are, on their own, too small to be perceived, and hence that they are 'gross' only in the sense that they are constitutive elements of perceptible entities. There are, however, certain scholars who have taken the bhūtas themselves to be perceptible. K. C. Bhattacharyya, for one, asserts with regard to Yoga that it 'holds that bhūta emerges out of tanmātra in the form of *perceivable* sthūla ["gross", physical] atoms in the first instance, out of which again sthūla complex objects emerge as immanent pariṇāmas [transformations]' (1956, I: 243, emphasis and square brackets added).

Whether the bhūtas are conceived of as perceptible or imperceptible, the view according to which they are physical atoms is, I think, badly mistaken. For one thing, it requires us to ignore the fact that there are said to be only *five* bhūtas, and instead postulates an indefinite number, albeit divided into five *types*. But then, even if we allow the number five to refer to types rather than individual tokens, it remains far from clear why atomic particles should be referred to as 'earth', 'water', 'fire', 'air' and – most puzzling of all – 'space'. Notwithstanding extravagant, and apparently ad hoc, theories that have interpreted ākāśa, for example, as a 'proto-atom' (whatever such a thing might be),[27] it has to be admitted that, if the bhūta doctrine does concern atoms, then the names given to these atoms must be either tenuously symbolic or entirely arbitrary. But let us consider the names of the bhūtas a little more closely. What, for instance, could be meant by designating something as 'earth'?

Surely earth, or soil, in the literal sense is something complex, with various constitutive parts. If we consider, however, that the term *pṛthivī* can mean 'earth' in the sense of the ground upon which we stand and roam around, as can its virtual synonym *kṣiti*, then it seems plausible to ask whether this first bhūta might not be best conceived as the quality of hardness or solidity. And, following this initial speculation, *ap* might be understood as the general quality of liquidity rather than the specific liquid represented by the chemical formula H_2O; *tejas* as luminosity or heat; and *vāyu* as gaseousness. Having relinquished the assumption of atomism, when we come to *ākāśa* there is no need to think of it as anything other than space.[28]

I am proposing, then, that the first four of the bhūtas are most intelligibly understood, not as atoms, but as forms or states of being displayed by physical objects, and that the fifth, ākāśa, is best regarded as space. Space may also of course (following Kant) be termed a form of physical objects, and as such is the form that is a necessary condition for all the others. By 'states of being' – or, as I put it earlier, 'forms of ostensibly external objects' – I mean, essentially, the forms taken by physical objects *in our experience*, and do not mean to imply any commitment to the existence of those objects independently of experience.

There is nothing especially novel about this kind of phenomenological interpretation of the bhūtas. It is fairly widely accepted in Abhidharma Buddhism, for example, where four bhūtas (or *mahābhūta*s, 'great elements') are typically referred to, these being the same as in Sāṃkhya and Yoga but with ākāśa left out. Herbert Guenther, speaking of the Buddhist mahābhūtas, notes that 'There are four such "great elementary qualities": earth-, water-, fire- and air-basis',[29] and adds the following interesting remarks:

> Their names have been derived from the 'objects' which common-sense assumes, although the Buddhists never had the association of objects in our sense of the word. 'Earth' is the symbolic expression for all that is solid and able to carry a load, 'water' for all that is fluid and cohesive, 'fire' for all that is light and moving.
>
> (Guenther 1974: 146)[30]

Nor am I the first to spot that this line of interpretation is equally applicable to Sāṃkhya. J. Ghosh does so in his introductory essay to Āraṇya (1977). Of the bhūtas, argues Ghosh, 'it must be said that they are not extramental, since it is inconceivable, for instance, how a thing may be hard or soft without being felt as such' (1977: 7). Although this way of making the point risks begging the question against the external realist, as an interpretation of the Sāṃkhya position I think Ghosh's statement is correct. Ghosh did not, however, provide much more than a skeletal account of how each of the manifest principles relates to the others and fits into Sāṃkhya's overall metaphysical schema; and hence there remains considerable work to be done before the task of propounding a coherent non-realist interpretation of Sāṃkhya and Yoga metaphysics is complete. In the remainder of this chapter I shall endeavour to carry this task a little further.

The analysis of experience

One way of formulating the underlying question to which the metaphysical schema of Sāṃkhya and Yoga is a response, is to put it in terms similar to those which Kant used to frame his own inquiry: What are the necessary conditions for the arising of experience; or: what makes experience possible? Any attempt to address this question is likely to involve a close examination of experience and a cataloguing of its principal features, along with an ordering of those features with regard to their interrelations of conditionality; and this, I maintain, is very much what we find in Sāṃkhya, and to a lesser extent in Yoga as well. Thus, although the question itself is not stated explicitly in the classical texts of these darśanas, there is nothing arbitrary or inapposite about the suggestion that it represents a key entry-point into their metaphysical schema. Indeed, the fact that the soteriological orientation of Sāṃkhya and Yoga is avowedly founded upon the need to overcome suffering and dissatisfaction (*duḥkha* [*SK* 1; *YS* 2.16]), combined with the diagnosis that experience is *inherently* dissatisfactory (*YS* 2.15) and rooted in misperception (*avidyā* [*YS* 2.24]), indicates that a disclosure of the necessary conditions of experience is precisely what, from the viewpoint of Sāṃkhya and Yoga, needs to take place.

The fundamental dualism for which Sāṃkhya and Yoga are well known is often characterized as one between subject and object, but such a characterization is too loose to capture what is going on in the analysis that these systems perform; and if it is not treated with due caution then it runs the risk of perpetuating unhelpful realist presuppositions. We see this in interpretive passages such as the following extract from Jadunath Sinha: 'According to the Sāṁkhya–Yoga, perception depends upon two metaphysical conditions. In the first place, it implies the existence of an extra-mental object. In the second place, it implies the existence of the self (*puruṣa*)' (1958, I: 124). The mistake Sinha makes here is the one with which we are familiar from Chapter 4, namely that of conflating the puruṣa–prakṛti duad with the mind–world relation. Prakṛti, whether considered in its manifest or its unmanifest aspect, is not 'an extra-mental object'. There is nothing in the Sāṃkhya–Yoga concept of prakṛti that implies externality in relation to the mind. Within the schema, distinctions are made between 'inner' (*antaḥ*) and 'outer' (*bāhya*) types of principle (*SK* 33), and also between those principles that form the 'instrument' (*karaṇa*) and those that constitute the 'object' (*kārya*) of experience (*SK* 32); but both of these are best construed as intrapsychic distinctions. The 'inner–outer' split appears to be between mental factors that are conditions of intentional consciousness *per se* (i.e. including perception and thought) and other such factors that, being exclusively directed towards sensory elements, are conditions solely of perceptual experience. The 'inner' comprises awareness (*buddhi*), egoity (*ahaṃkāra*), and mental synthesis (*manas*), and the 'outer' comprises the ten 'capacities' (*indriyas*). These thirteen principles together constitute the 'instrument', which 'grasps, holds, and illuminates' its tenfold object (*SK* 32), this object being composed of the five modes of sense-content (*tanmātras*) plus the five states of being (*bhūtas*).[31] While this object may be taken to represent a world external to the mind, the objectual representation itself appears within consciousness, and is to that extent mental rather than mind-independent. Nowhere within the Sāṃkhya–Yoga schema do we find any explicit references to a world of objects whose reality transcends their being objects *for a subject*.

I noted above that I take the order in which the manifest principles are presented in the *Sāṃkhyakārikā* to be a consequence of the relations of conditionality that are held to operate between them. I now need to say a little more on this point. As we have seen (Chapter 4), the use of the ablative case at *SK* 22 is standardly assumed to indicate a relation of something approximating causality via material transformation between each of the ontological principles and its respective successor. Such an assumption inevitably implies that we are dealing with a diachronic narrative; and hence, if my synchronic reading of the Sāṃkhya schema is to sound plausible, this ostensible diachronism needs to be accounted for. I think the way of accounting for it is to treat the ablative inflections in the aforementioned verse as indicative of relations of conditionality and dependence other than material causality. That is to say that when, at *SK* 22, we read that 'From prakṛti [comes] the great; from that, egoity,' and so forth, the term 'from' might alternatively be read as 'due to' or 'because of', which terms, though equally valid translations of the Sanskrit ablative, are less committal when it comes to temporal implication. In order to see how a reading of the 'emergence' of the manifest principles could possibly play out when 'emergence' (*sarga*) is treated figuratively, let us briefly run through the manifest categories again, this time with a view to considering the sense in which each of them might be said to be 'conditioned by' that which is ontologically but not temporally prior to it.

Buddhi is the first of the manifest principles, and as such is conditioned only by unmanifest prakṛti. Its other name, 'the great' (*mahat*), probably has something to do with the fact that it, as awareness or intentional consciousness *per se*, makes all the other manifest principles possible.[32] If an analogy were to be sought within western philosophy, I think F. H. Bradley's 'centre of immediate experience (or immediate feeling)' would come fairly close.[33] On Bradley's view, there is a primary level of feeling – 'a felt totality' (1914: 200) – that is prior to, and hence contains, the division between self and not-self. Although Bradley conceives this primary level as being non-intentional and not yet fully conscious, his distinction between 'feeling' and 'consciousness' is not, in my view, sustainable. As I see it, there may subjectively be a level of feeling in which no appreciation of a subject–object dichotomy obtains; yet upon subsequent reflection, if the state is to count as 'feeling' at all, it must be admitted that it had a content, and hence that a distinction along the lines of the one Brentano makes between act and content is applicable. With this proviso, then, 'centre of immediate experience' strikes me as being among the best ways of formulating the notion of buddhi. It is the awareness of a field of phenomenal content, out of which may be said to emerge specific experiential qualities and episodes, but which in itself is undifferentiated.

Ahaṃkāra is the arising of self-consciousness within the phenomenal field already demarcated by buddhi. It is the distinguishing of the experiential content as 'mine' and hence of myself as an experiencer. It is thus dependent upon buddhi for its very possibility. Of course, neither ahaṃkāra nor buddhi is the true or authentic metaphysical self, which status belongs exclusively to puruṣa in each conscious individual. Puruṣa is the ultimate subject – the one who has the experience – while buddhi is the having of any experience whatsoever, and ahaṃkāra is the having of that experience *as one's own*. 'Rolling forth' (*pravartate*) from ahaṃkāra is what translates literally as the 'twofold surgence' (*dvividhaḥ...sargaḥ*) of the ten indriyas plus manas on the one hand, and the five tanmātras on the other (*SK* 24). I take this to mean that the self-ascription of experiential episodes is a necessary condition for one's having sensations, and hence perceptual experiences of any kind. To borrow an expression from Kant, the concept or judgement 'I think' or 'I cognize' (*cogito*) is the 'vehicle' of all experiences.[34]

With regard to the relation between the indriyas and the tanmātras, we find at *SK* 34 the following statement:

> Of these [i.e. the ten indriyas], the five buddhīndriyas have specific and nonspecific objects [i.e. the bhūtas and tanmātras]. Speaking manifests (*bhavati*) sound-phenomena (*śabda-viṣaya*) [alone], whereas the remaining [karmendriyas] [manifest] all five [types of] phenomena.

There is no problem here in assuming that the terms 'specific' (*viśeṣa*) and 'nonspecific' (*aviśeṣa*) refer to the bhūtas and tanmātras respectively, because four verses later, at *SK* 38, it is in exactly these terms that the bhūtas and tanmātras are defined. At *SK* 34, then, it is being claimed that, whereas the five sense-capacities (*buddhīndriya*s) are oriented towards both objectual forms (*bhūta*s) and modes of sense-content (*tanmātra*s), the action-capacities (*karmendriya*s) are associated with the five modes of sense-content alone. The first part of this statement seems unproblematic. Clearly the sense-capacities will be concerned both with the forms displayed by empirical objects – such as hardness, liquidity, etc. – and with the sensory feelings that we automatically regard as the results of external stimulation. It is, after all, these forms and sense-contents that provide the materials out of which our perceptual world is constructed. The second part of the statement is more difficult to comprehend; for, although it is evident why speaking might be described as manifesting sound, it is less clear why the four remaining action-capacities – which I have identified as powers of proprioception, kinaesthesia and excretory and erotogenic sensation – should be said to manifest (or bring into being, *bhavati*) all five modes of sense-content. There is certainly, however, more sense in regarding all five of these modes as being involved with the action-capacities when the latter are understood to be varieties of awareness of bodily action as opposed to the bodily actions themselves (or, for that matter, the organs that perform them).

The term *viṣaya* has a fairly broad semantic range: roughly speaking, it denotes a sphere or terrain with which something is concerned. Thus, in translating *viśeṣa-aviśeṣa-viṣayāṇi* as 'specific and nonspecific *objects*', it would be misleading to conceive of these objects as determinate physical entities such as stones, trees, cats, and tables. Rather, in this instance the 'objects' are really component *elements* of objects in the more familiar sense, the elements in question being the bhūtas and tanmātras. In my translation of *SK* 34, I render *viṣayā* and *viṣayāṇi* as 'phenomena' rather than 'objects' because the phrase 'speaking manifests sound-phenomena' is both less cumbersome, and in my view closer to the sense of *vāg bhavati śabda-viṣayā*, than would be an alternative construction such as 'speaking has sound-objects as its manifestation'. But nothing of significance hangs upon this decision. Certain other translations of the statement, such as Larson's 'Speech only has sound as its object' (1979: 266),[35] make little sense when 'speech' is taken literally to mean the act of talking. While we might, in English, consider speech to have the making of sound as its object, where, by 'its object', we mean its *end* or *purpose*, this alternative sense of 'object' is not available in the Sanskrit *viṣaya*. If, however, we take 'speech' to stand for the *awareness* of one's own speech, then to say that the object (or content) of this act is sound would be more intelligible. Larson's translation is therefore perfectly compatible with my interpretation of the karmendriyas as modes of physiological awareness.

The task of synthesizing the manifold sensations into coherent perceptual experiences falls, according to Sāṃkhya, to manas. Manas is itself dependent upon ahaṃkāra, since without the binding power of a unified self-concept there would be no one to whom the sensations could be attributed, and hence no means by which they could be brought into a contiguous whole. We do not find in Sāṃkhya anything comparable to the Kantian twelvefold structure of conceptual categories of the understanding. But the postulation of an *a priori* concept that is a necessary condition of experience is nevertheless present in the concept of ahaṃkāra.

This just leaves the relation between the tanmātras and bhūtas to be accounted for. The *Sāṃkhyakārikā* says very little about this relation beyond the fact that the bhūtas derive from, or are in some way dependent upon, the tanmātras (*SK* 38). Several traditional commentaries propose that the relation is one-to-one in the sense that each of the five bhūtas derives from one out of the five tanmātras. Thus, as the author of the *Yuktidīpikā* puts it, 'space is due to the sense-content sound, air is due to . . . tactility, fire is due to . . . visual appearance, water is due to . . . flavour, [and] earth is due to . . . odour' (*YD* 38c).[36] Although it is certainly possible that this sort of one-to-one relation is what the author of the *Sāṃkhyakārikā* had in mind, the original verse could just as well be read to mean that the bhūtas, as one generic category, are dependent upon the tanmātras, as another generic category. In terms of the interpretation that I have developed here – of the tanmātras and bhūtas as modes of sense-content and formal states of perceptual objects respectively – the one-to-one thesis is hard to make sense of. In some cases there is an obvious connection between particular members of each category. If, for example, we regard *tejas* as representing light, then it is easy to see why this should be linked with visual content (although, admittedly, not so clear why light should be *dependent* upon it). And, similarly, the connection between liquidity (*āpas*) and the flavoured content of a gustatory sensation is not too oblique; although neither is it very precise, since it is not only liquids that can be tasted. In other cases, however, the connections are very oblique indeed, such as that between 'earth' (which I am taking to represent hardness and solidity) and the odorous content of an olfactory sensation, or between 'air' (gaseousness) and the tactual content of a touch sensation. These incongruities can be dissolved by replacing the one-to-one thesis with the generic category thesis; that is, by treating the claim that the bhūtas are dependent upon the tanmātras as simply the claim that our encountering objects with discernible formal properties depends upon our being able to receive contentual sensations.

Thus we can see that the sequential exposition of the manifest principles in the *Sāṃkhyakārikā* becomes susceptible to coherent explication when we take it to represent the relations of conditionality between synchronic (i.e. simultaneously existing) features of any possible experiential episode. When, on the other hand, the sequence is treated as a temporal narrative concerning the successive emergence of 'real' trans-empirical entities, whether psychological or cosmological, not only does the exposition appear arbitrary and the metaphysical schema as a whole lack determinate structure, but the relevance that this schema has for the soteriological enterprise of Sāṃkhya and Yoga remains thoroughly obscure. It is to this issue of soteriological relevance that I shall now turn.

The soteriological relevance of the metaphysical schema

The question of how metaphysics and soteriology are related in Sāṃkhya and Yoga is one that has for the most part bemused those interpreters who have given it anything approaching the degree of attention it deserves. We saw early on in this chapter that Radhakrishnan found it 'difficult to understand the precise significance of the Sāṃkhya account of evolution' (1927, II: 274). Larson expresses a similar point, but with a little more specificity:

> On the one hand, we are told that *buddhi, ahaṃkāra, manas*, the senses, etc. evolve or emerge one after another. At the same time we are told that the *liṅga* transmigrates from life to life... [T]he theory of evolution has very little to do with the problem of salvation, since in any given life, evolution is already accomplished before that particular life begins... Clearly the exposition of the *Sāṃkhyakārikā* on this point leaves much to be desired.
>
> (1979: 196)

In this passage Larson is assuming that, according to Sāṃkhya, prakṛti evolves into a kind of proto-person called a *liṅga*, comprising the psychological characteristics which, in combination with a physical body, constitute a complete biological human being. Such an interpretation gains justification from certain statements in the *Sāṃkhyakārikā*, most notably the assertion at *SK* 40 that the liṅga comprises 'mahat and the others, down to the subtle [i.e., presumably, the "subtle elements" or tanmātras]', and that 'without enjoyment, [and being] endowed with dispositions (*bhāvas*), [it] wanders (*saṃsarati*) [from one lifetime to another]'. On my view, however, the liṅga need not be conceived as a quasi-organism that *has* or *undergoes* experiences. Indeed, it ought not to be conceived in such a way, since, strictly speaking, neither prakṛti as a whole nor any of its particular manifestations is a subject of consciousness, puruṣa alone being endowed with this latter status. Instead, the liṅga – *qua* 'sign', 'cipher' or 'mark' – is better conceived as the fluctuating experiential content of any individual conscious subject, 'content' here being construed broadly to encompass the various acts and forms as well as the more obviously contentual factors into which the Sāṃkhya system analyses experience. When the liṅga is understood in this way – as experiential sphere rather than psychological subject – then the problem of why the 'evolution' of the metaphysical principles should be 'already accomplished before [any] particular life begins' evaporates. The so-called 'evolution' is not a process that happens once, or even several times repeatedly; it is a symbolic model representing the interplay between diverse elements within the complex structure that makes up subjective experience. Each of its elements is itself a category standing for a type of phenomenon that arises within experience *per se*; and the arising and falling away of these phenomena is the ongoing process of *experiencing*.

Now, if we are to determine how Sāṃkhya's analysis of the structure of experience bears upon the soteric practice of sustained meditation, which is dealt with at some length in the *Yogasūtra* (albeit perhaps not in as much detail as we might prefer), then it will be useful to dwell for a moment upon this form of contemplative discipline. In describing this, I shall leave aside the ethical vows and the multiple postural and breathing techniques that have traditionally constituted important aspects of Yoga training (cf. *YS* 2.30–53), and focus on the meditation itself. This involves taking an object – which may, in principle, be any phenomenal or abstract entity but is typically either visual (such as an icon or a sacred diagram) or auditory (such as a mantra) – and concentrating incessantly upon this object to the exclusion of other sensory and conceptual items. Although not stated explicitly in the *Yogasūtra*, it is taken for granted by practitioners of Yoga that the object of meditation will be 'internal', i.e. mental and imagistic rather than sensorially imbibed. The noviciate will typically begin by using an external object, such as a visual depiction of a symbol or deity, but will be instructed by the guru to use this depiction only until it has successfully been reconstructed 'in the mind's eye'. Having performed such a reconstruction, and fixed one's attention upon it (*dhāraṇā* [*YS* 3.1]), one endeavours to sustain this level of single-pointed concentration to the point where it becomes genuine meditation (*dhyāna* [*YS* 3.2]). Eventually, according to the *Yogasūtra*, a depth of meditation will be achieved wherein the mind is completely absorbed in its object, and hence the 'object alone' (*artha-mātra*) is said to 'shine forth' (*nirbhāsa*) (*YS* 3.3, cf. 1.43).

This initial state of absorption or integration (*samādhi*, also termed *samāpatti*) is not the *terminus ad quem* of Yoga; rather, it is the *terminus a quo* for a series of degrees of meditative insight. The *Yogasūtra* refers to several distinguishable stages of samādhi, some of which involve cognition of the categories of prakṛti not cognitively available to us under ordinary conditions of reflection.[37] One of the two main poles of Yoga discipline consists in holding the cognized 'object' (or cognitive content) steady, this stabilizing of one's cognition being known as *abhyāsa* (*YS* 1.13). The other main pole is *vairāgya* – the non-attachment to, or dissociation from, the object of cognition; or, in other words, the cultivation of the inner knowingness that, in the case of each ontological category that comes to consciousness in profound meditation, one's true self is *not that* (cf. *YS* 1.15–16). Such knowingness is prefigured in the famous Upaniṣadic utterance *neti neti* (*na-iti na-iti*), 'not this, not this',[38] and is given expression at *SK* 64 as puruṣa's declaration that 'I am not (*na-asmi*), not mine (*na me*), not "I" (*na-aham*).' Larson interprets this latter statement as buddhi's assertion that 'I am not (conscious); (consciousness) does not belong to me; the "I" is not (conscious)' (1979: 274); but this is to turn the meaning of the verse on its head. There are, admittedly, significant difficulties attached to any ascription of knowledge – even a merely negative, dissociative kind of knowledge – to a principle of pure subjectivity such as puruṣa; for it seems paradoxical to propose that the pure subject can 'know' itself to be distinct from the very categories of manifest being that, under normal circumstances, make experience and knowledge possible. However, this is the sort of problem that frequently arises in connection with attempts to describe mystical (i.e. supra-ratiocinative) states of consciousness, and is far from being uniquely associated with Sāṃkhya and Yoga. Larson's alternative suggestion, it should be noted, is no less paradoxical; for it involves an essentially non-conscious principle, namely buddhi, having knowledge – which can only mean *becoming conscious of the fact* – that it is *not* conscious!

Since the goal of Sāṃkhya and Yoga is the self-abiding or 'aloneness' (*kaivalya*) of puruṣa, the achievement of which requires a cessation of puruṣa's false self-identification with that which is not-self (*anātman*, cf. *YS* 2.5 and 2.25), the knowledge of the ultimate metaphysical disjunction between puruṣa and prakṛti must *belong* to puruṣa, even if in some sense that knowledge can arise only by means of puruṣa's association with buddhi.[39] The aforementioned declaration at *SK* 64 is, in my view, an attempt to represent the dawning of puruṣa's disidentification with experience *in toto*. It is, so to speak, the 'last gasp' of experience – and hence of subject-object duality – before the 'seer' (*draṣṭṛ*), that which is in itself 'mere seeing' (*dṛśimātra* [*YS* 2.20]), 'abides in its own nature' (*YS* 1.3).

In the light of the above summarial account of Yoga discipline, I can see two main interpretive options concerning the soteriological relevance of Sāṃkhya's metaphysical schema. One is that it constitutes a report of meditative experience, an exposition of the insights gained into the nature of the mind and its processes during states of samādhi. A second possibility is that the schema was devised in advance of meditative experience via a process of rational reflection, perhaps analogous to that employed by Kant in his *Critique of Pure Reason* or by Brentano in his *Psychology from an Empirical Standpoint*. Both of these latter works, in their own particular ways, set out to expose the *a priori* conditions of experience in general without recourse to any kind of supra-normal intuition or introspective technique. Although, in the case of Sāṃkhya and Yoga it would appear that, ultimately, supra-normal intuition *is* being aimed at, the schema could, in principle, have been rationally constructed prior to its utilization as an intrapsychic 'map' for the meditating yogin.

The idea of the practical application of metaphysical schemata is not a new one. Feuerstein, for example, talks of 'ontogenetic models' as 'originally and primarily maps for meditative introspection, intended to guide the *yogin* in his exploration of the *terra incognita* of the mind' (1980: 117). As we saw in Chapter 2, however, Feuerstein is adamant that Sāṃkhya is wholly 'rationalistic' whereas Yoga relies exclusively 'on first-hand evidence (*pratyakṣa*)' (ibid.); and hence he fails to consider the possibility that a model, though rationally devised, may nevertheless perform an instructive role in meditation. When, therefore, Feuerstein asserts that 'These "maps" are records of internal experiences rather than purely theoretical constructions' and 'are descriptive rather than explanatory' (ibid.), we might be excused for wondering how a system such as Sāṃkhya, with its 'pronouncedly formalistic and rationalistic basis' (p. 113), was capable of coming up with a metaphysical schema which so closely parallels that of Yoga.

There is, as it turns out, no need to drive a wedge between the two interpretive options I have outlined. It is perfectly tenable, and indeed highly likely, that reason and meditative experience have been mutually reinforcing devices in the history of Sāṃkhya and Yoga, and that the respective schemata of these systems are both descriptive *and* explanatory. They describe, in what is evidently a highly abstracted and abbreviated manner, observations made during sustained inwardly oriented contemplation; and, at the same time, they are supported at certain points by arguments that appeal to the rational proclivities of the student, who has perhaps yet to enjoy the 'first-hand evidence' that will later (if the 'map' is followed correctly) verify the teachings.

Summary

In this chapter I have looked in some detail at the metaphysics of Sāṃkhya and Yoga, and have put forward what I consider to be a more credible interpretation than that which is commonly accepted. When construed as a representation of the sequential emergence of principles whose ontological status is in some ambiguous sense both cosmological and psychological, the schema of twenty-three 'manifest' categories appears baroque at best, and incoherent at worst. In place of this construal I have argued that the schema is more coherently interpreted as an analysis of experience, in which the ostensibly sequential relations may be taken to stand for relations of dependence between the various principles which together make experience possible. I have claimed that, not only does this interpretation of the schema as a metaphysics of experience reveal the internal logic of the system itself, but it also facilitates a fuller (though admittedly incomplete) understanding of how metaphysical theory and soteric practice combine to form an integrated whole.

7

FREEDOM FROM EXPERIENCE

Sāṃkhya and Yoga are not concerned with philosophy for its own sake. Like virtually all classical systems of thought in India, they were devised with a soteriological purpose in mind. This purpose is the attainment of release or liberation (*mokṣa*, *mukti*) from mundane existence, such existence being held, again in common with most Indian systems, to be inherently and irredeemably dissatisfactory.

The soteriological *telos* of Sāṃkhya and Yoga has, I hope, been an underlying presence throughout this study, for it certainly warrants being taken into account at every stage of the interpretive process. In this chapter I want to focus more sharply upon that telos, or *artha* ('end', 'purpose'), referred to in both the *Sāṃkhyakārikā* and the *Yogasūtra* as *kaivalya*, which term translates literally as 'aloneness' or 'solitariness'. In particular I wish to inquire into how the vision of this goal and the aspiration to achieve it cohere with the aspects of the Sāṃkhya and Yoga philosophies that have been discussed so far. I shall be arguing that the realist–cosmogonic interpretation of these darśanas has no way of accounting for kaivalya, and that any attempt to explain it that begins from the realist assumption regarding the manifestations of prakṛti can result only in confusion.

There is a sense, of course, in which kaivalya is radically inexplicable by any theory, for it does not fall within the domain of conceptualizable phenomena or states. Perhaps the greatest paradox, or irony, of Sāṃkhya and Yoga, and of other essentially mystical soteriologies, is their insistence that the liberation of the person involves, in effect, forsaking everything that marks one out as a person in the first place, including body, mind, memory and intentional consciousness itself. Notwithstanding this ultimately supra-rational orientation, however, it is not the case that anything goes when it comes to discussing kaivalya. It remains, I think, possible to distinguish between more and less plausible accounts, the main criterion for doing so being the extent to which any particular account succeeds in positioning kaivalya in coherent relation to the philosophies as integral wholes. This is not to say that the interpretation should be fudged in order to *make* it compatible with other elements in the systems. Close attention must be given to the texts at all times, and any inconsistencies pointed out. But a reasonable interpretive starting-point – indeed, probably the only genuinely workable starting-point – is to assume a high level of integrity on the parts of the systems concerned, and, from that basis, to piece them together in a way that utilizes the light from various elements to illuminate one another.

The central interpretive problem of kaivalya

The main problem hampering the interpretation of kaivalya in Sāṃkhya and Yoga for anyone who attributes a realist viewpoint to these systems is as follows. Kaivalya, according to both darśanas, involves the cessation of mental activity. This is made explicit in the *Yogasūtra*, where the very definition of *yoga* is given as 'the cessation (*nirodha*) of mental *vṛtti*s ("activities," "functions," "operations")' (*YS* 1.2), and it is implied in the *Sāṃkhyakārikā* by the fact that kaivalya is there stated to be attained upon puruṣa's 'split with the body' (*śarīra-bheda*) and the 'retreat from activity (*vinivṛtta*) of pradhāna', whose purpose (*artha*) has been accomplished (*SK* 68). Not only, then, does the mind cease to operate, but the entire world of ostensibly physical objects dissolves, leaving only an unmanifest and dormant prakṛti, plus of course the now solitary puruṣa, who abides purely 'in its own nature (*svarūpa*)' (*YS* 1.3). Since the attainment of kaivalya by one individual does not entail or engender the dissolution of the mental activities of other individuals, nor of the world those others experience, there would seem to be something about the dissolution that is particular to the kaivalyin alone (cf. *YS* 2.22).

The realist interpreter must address the following question: If the manifestations of prakṛti are real in the sense of being subject-independent, then how can it be the case that they cease or dissolve for the kaivalyin? The question generates a dilemma: Either (a) the manifestations do not *really* dissolve at all, but merely disappear from the 'view' or 'awareness' of the liberated puruṣa; the true self has, as it were, withdrawn its gaze from them and become enclosed or absorbed within its own being ('it contemplates itself' (Eliade 1969: 93)). Or (b) the manifestations were not independent after all, but were critically dependent upon an absence of self-knowledge on the part of puruṣa, and hence when that self-knowledge arises the manifestations no longer exist in relation to that puruṣa, even though they continue to do so for others. Each of these interpretive options is accompanied by serious difficulties, and this is perhaps why most interpretations tend not to be very explicit when it comes to the issue of kaivalya. Option (a) entails that kaivalya consists in a divestment of knowledge – a self-imposed exile or hibernation from reality – in which puruṣa remains cut off from a psychophysical world that continues to operate in its absence. This would, in principle, be compatible with the negative aspect of Sāṃkhya–Yoga eschatology, that is, the escape from the distress (*duḥkha*) that saturates worldly existence. But it would hardly concur with the positive aspect, which is expressed in the many proclamations to the effect that the path that leads from enthralment to emancipation is one of increasing discriminative knowledge and heightened awareness, not a shielding of oneself from that which is real and true. It would also contradict assertions that it is the manifestations of prakṛti that withdraw or retreat from view, and not puruṣa who blocks them out. The withdrawal is referred to as *pratiprasava* (*YS* 4.34), a 'return to the original state' (MW: 668) or 'flowing back to the source'; or as *prakṛtilaya* (*SK* 45), the 'dissolution of [or into] prakṛti'; neither of these terms suggests that the manifestations in fact continue more or less as they are, only without being 'seen' by puruṣa. In the poetic imagery of Īśvarakṛṣṇa's text, it is the tender and bashful (*sukumāra*) prakṛti who, having performed her dance for puruṣa, 'never again enters into puruṣa's sight' (*SK* 59–61).

As a consequence of these difficulties, what we tend to find in the interpretive literature are vague and unelaborated statements about kaivalya's being, for example, a 'pure isolation or abstraction... from matter' (Davies 1894: 48), which leave us unsure whether, once such a state has been attained, material objects continue to exist or not. Their continued existence might be implied in Larson's description of kaivalya as 'a kind of pure, translucent emptiness which transcends everything in the manifest and unmanifest world' (1979: 208), but here again it is not made explicit whether puruṣa's 'transcendence' is taken to leave the manifest world unscathed.

A further hedging manoeuvre that presents itself in this interpretive area is that of speaking of kaivalya's involving the cessation of the *relation* between puruṣa and prakṛti without specifying whether this cessation necessitates the discontinuance of manifest objects. Keith, for example, makes this move when he notes that 'the connection of spirit with matter terminates with the withdrawal of spirit into a condition of absolute freedom, which must, however, at the same time be absolute nonentity' (Keith 1949: 99). There is no question that the two spheres of reality – what Keith terms 'spirit' and 'matter' – are rent asunder in kaivalya, but there *is* a question whether, or in what sense, this rending coincides with the obliteration of prakṛti's manifest aspect; and this question remains unaddressed by statements about the termination of the relation (or 'connection') between the two co-fundamental principles. (Incidentally, Keith's decription of the liberated puruṣa's condition as one of 'absolute nonentity' sounds equivalent to declaring it to be completely annihilated. This cannot be what Sāṃkhya or Yoga have in mind, although it is admittedly very hard to provide any positive description of puruṣa's liberated condition.)

There is general agreement – except in rare cases such as Ian Whicher, whose ideas will be discussed below – that, in kaivalya, *experience* has been obliterated: 'It is the enstasis of total emptiness', as Eliade puts it, 'without sensory content or intellectual structure, an unconditioned state that is no longer "experience" (for there is no further relation between consciousness and the world) but "revelation"' (1969: 93). But, to reiterate the crucial question with regard to realism, what we wish to know is: In the absence of the 'relation between consciousness and the world', does there remain any objective (real, independent) world at all? Feuerstein, for one, proposes in certain places that there does, his boldest assertion to this effect coming in his commentary on *YS* 2.22. He translates the sūtra itself as follows:

> Although [the seen] has ceased [to exist] for [the *yogin* whose] purpose has been accomplished, it has nevertheless not ceased [to exist altogether], since it is common-experience [with respect to all] other [beings].
>
> (1989a: 74, Feuerstein's brackets)

And then he supplies the following assessment of it:

> This aphorism is as plain a refutation of mentalism as one can expect. The world is not a mere thought product which dissolves upon liberation. Objects are external to the mind and have their independent existence which is not affected by the event of Self-realisation. Emancipation is an individual achievement which abolishes man's false organismic identity and re-locates him into the Self. With the destruction of the consciousness complex the possibility of perceiving the external world, or perceiving the world externally, is likewise eliminated. But this absence of empirical perception does not conjure away the universe. It remains as real as before and continues to be experienced by those who erroneously identify not with the transcendental Self but with the phenomenal consciousness of a particular organism in space and time. Without this ontological assumption of the reality of the objective universe the emancipation of the very first liberated being would, logically, have entailed the annihilation of the cosmos and, by further implication, it would also have meant the emancipation of all other beings.
>
> (Ibid.)

The sūtra provides a 'refutation of mentalism', by which expression I take Feuerstein to mean a denial of idealism, only if one has already assumed that the Yoga position is realist. If this assumption has not been made, then the sūtra could very well be read as an *affirmation* of idealism, since it emphasizes the dependence of the 'seen' (manifest prakṛti, *dṛśya*) upon the 'seer' (*draṣṭṛ*, *puruṣa*). What I wish to draw attention to, however, is Feuerstein's assertion that, 'With the destruction of the consciousness complex the possibility of perceiving the external world...is likewise eliminated' even though the world 'remains as real as before'. Feuerstein uses 'consciousness' to translate *citta* (preferring 'Self' for *puruṣa*, as can be seen in the above passage); and thus by 'consciousness complex' he probably means the cognizing components of prakṛti, specifically the thirteenfold instrument (*karaṇa*) as it is called in Sāṃkhya (cf. *SK* 32). The dissociation of this complex from puruṣa – or, as Feuerstein puts it, its 'destruction' – would of course render external perception, along with any other mode of experience or cognition, impossible; and therefore this 'destruction' establishes an unbridgeable gap between puruṣa and the 'external world' (which world Feuerstein elsewhere refers to as the 'surface structure' of prakṛti as distinct from the 'deep structure', which is the psychosensory constitution of the empirical self (1980: 29)). Puruṣa has, in effect, been separated from the 'real world'; and hence, on this account, its liberation involves something approximating a state of voluntary ignorance, which, as I have indicated already, stands in stark contradiction to the overall gnostic orientation of Yoga and Sāṃkhya.

Let us now turn our attention to the second interpretive option, (b), that I outlined above, namely the view that the manifestations of prakṛti are *not* independent of puruṣa and hence do in fact dissolve in relation to the liberated puruṣa, though not for others. It might be presumed that this view entails the abandonment of the realist assumption and would therefore be unacceptable to any interpreter who holds that assumption. This would indeed be the case if such interpreters were consistent in their understanding of the relation between 'manifest prakṛti' on the one hand and the 'manifest world' on the other. Inconsistency on this point, however, enables the claim that manifest prakṛti *does* dissolve (disintegrate, demanifest) to be combined either with an insinuation that this dissolution does not include the 'manifest world' or with a non-committal silence about the fate of this world. Feuerstein can again be cited to illustrate the point, since his distinction between the 'deep' and 'surface' structures of prakṛti allows him to speak of 'the destruction of the consciousness complex' (manifest prakṛti as 'deep structure') while affirming the unbroken endurance of the 'external world' (manifest prakṛti as 'surface structure').

Thus we see that what I have referred to as two interpretive options can in fact be merged into one, but only by employing the disingenuous strategy of distinguishing two structural levels of manifest prakṛti. The strategy is disingenuous because it flagrantly ignores the fact that, according to any interpretation of Yoga and Sāṃkhya metaphysics (including the realist–cosmogonic one), the objects that populate the 'external world' *derive from* those which constitute the cognizing personality (or 'consciousness complex' as Feuerstein calls it). The sense in which they so 'derive' may be a matter of contention, but the fact that the 'surface structure' of objects could not exist without the 'deep structure' of the psychosensory apparatus is undisputed. This fact ought to preclude any assertion that, for Sāṃkhya–Yoga, the objects we ordinarily perceive can continue to exist once kaivalya has been attained, and ought, furthermore, to make it patently clear that the perceived objects are, according to these darśanas, merely appearances *for us*, without (as a Buddhist might say) any 'inherent existence' (*svabhāva*).

It is, in short, impossible to square any claim that in kaivalya the yogin's mind along with his body is dissolved into its unmanifest source, with the view that material objects exist independently of their being cognized. Thus, when Feuerstein says, at the beginning of his commentary on *YS* 4.34, that, 'Upon Self-realisation, the primary-constituents of Nature [i.e. the three guṇas]...cease to vibrate in the pattern characteristic of the *yogin*'s body and mind complex and become resolved into the unmanifest core (*prakṛti-pradhāna* = *aliṅga*)' (1989a: 145, Feuerstein's rounded parentheses, my square brackets), we are entitled to wonder what has happened to the mind-independent objects that he referred to earlier. We might wonder the same thing when, for example, Sen Gupta states that, 'As soon as *citta* gets merged in the *guṇas*, the vital function too stops automatically and the yogi is separated forever from the body' (1982: 139), or when Eliade remarks that 'Intellect (*buddhi*), having accomplished its mission, withdraws, detaching itself from the *puruṣa* and returning into *prakṛti*' (1969: 93).

It seems fair to conclude, then, that interpretations of Sāṃkhya and Yoga that take these systems to be realist about the empirical world stand no chance of presenting a coherent account of kaivalya, and this is indeed the conclusion I will draw. Before we can be sure of this, however, there is one further realist interpretation that needs to be considered, which is based upon a somewhat renegade re-reading of some key tenets of the Yoga system.

Ian Whicher's view of kaivalya as 'embodied liberation'

I noted at the beginning of the last section that the central problem for the realist interpretation of kaivalya is how to account for the fact that, according to Sāṃkhya and Yoga, the cessation of mental activities coincides with, or immediately precipitates, the dissolution of manifest entities, when those entities are supposed by the realist to exist independently of any experience of them. We have so far considered approaches that either skirt the issue or, in contradiction to the logical implications of the classical texts, baldly declare that despite the dissolution of the psychosensory components of manifest prakṛti the 'external world' persists. In recent years, however, a third approach has been articulated, in embryonic form by Christopher Chapple (see esp. 1996) and more fully by Ian Whicher (e.g. 1995, 1998, 2003). Essentially the approach involves a tentative (in Chapple's case) or forthright (in Whicher's) denial that kaivalya, as understood in classical Yoga, forecloses the possibility of mental activity and experience of an objective physical reality.

It should be noted at the outset that both Chapple and Whicher draw a distinction between the respective goals of Sāṃkhya and Yoga. Chapple holds that there is merely 'a slightly different interpretation of liberation' between the two systems (1996: 124), and that it amounts to little more than a matter of emphasis, with Yoga tending to place greater stress than Sāṃkhya upon 'the need for ongoing purification both on the path and at the penultimate phase of the quest for liberation' (p. 132). Whicher, meanwhile, regards the difference as more significant. He concurs with the common view that, for Sāṃkhya, kaivalya involves a total separation of puruṣa and prakṛti (e.g. 1998: 58), but makes the curious assertion that Yoga, far from wanting to disjoin them, in fact 'seeks to "unite" these two principles by correcting a misalignment between them, thereby properly aligning them, bringing them "together" through a purification and illumination of consciousness leading to the permanent realization of intrinsic being, that is, authentic identity' (1998: 4). 'Moreover', Whicher continues,

> Patañjali's Yoga *darśana* can be seen to embrace a maturation and full flowering of human nature and identity, a state of <u>embodied liberation</u> – one that incorporates a clarity of awareness with the integrity of being and action.
>
> (1998: 4, my underlining)

This could hardly be further from the idea that Yoga seeks a *transcendence* of worldly existence rather than merely a more harmonious accommodation to it. In view of this fact, it is fair to ask what textual justication Whicher brings forth in support of his highly contentious interpretation, and also what exactly he might mean by phrases such as 'embodied liberation' and 'integrity of being and action'.

Whicher's interpretation of classical Yoga appears to be largely constructed upon a translation of *YS* 1.2 that is unique to himself. The sūtra, which has been referred to already in this chapter, reads: *yogaś citta-vṛtti-nirodhaḥ*; and Whicher translates this as: 'Yoga is the cessation of [the misidentification with] the modifications of the mind' (1998: 1, cf. 1995: 47). The expression inserted in brackets by Whicher is crucial to his interpretation, and yet he does not attempt to justify its inclusion. Rather, he merely asserts it and then proceeds to examine the entire Yoga system in the light of this assertion, as though his translation of the aforementioned sūtra were uncontroversial. It is, however, extremely controversial, for it allows Whicher to claim that the goal of Yoga is not to induce the cessation of mental activities or 'modifications of the mind' (*citta-vṛtti*) themselves, but consists in merely the cessation of misidentification with those activities or modifications. The implication of Whicher's translation of this important sūtra is therefore that mental activities (states, modes) can continue *after* the attainment of Yoga's goal, and, moreover, that they can do so in a way that has been 'purified' of any misidentification with those activities or with the mind itself.[1]

The practice of inserting bracketed expressions into translations of the *Yogasūtra* (and other Indian texts) is extremely common among scholars, the justification being that without such insertions the meanings of the sūtras concerned would remain opaque or ambiguous at best, and entirely unintelligible at worst. The practice should, however, be treated with immense caution, both by the translator and by the reader; for the risk of imposing a meaning upon the text that was absent in its original formulation is significant. When a sūtra is perfectly intelligible without amendments then the insertion of additional wording is superfluous, and liable to be misleading. Now, in the case of *YS* 1.2, the sūtra provides a definition of *yoga* as *citta-vṛtti-nirodha*. Whicher, reasonably, translates the latter phrase as 'the cessation of the modifications of the mind', but then radically changes its meaning by inserting '[the misidentification with]' after 'the cessation of'.

In accordance with his overall emphasis on misidentification, Whicher's vision of the goal of Yoga is one in which the yogin is liberated from a false sense of identity but not from the world as such. On Whicher's view,

> *kaivalya* in no way presupposes the destruction or negation of the personality of the yogin, but is an unconditional state in which all the obstacles or distractions preventing an immanent and purified relationship or engagement of person with nature and spirit (*puruṣa*) have been removed.
>
> (1998: 277)

The issue of identity is deeply confused here, for it would appear that the yogin is supposed to 'engage' with puruṣa, which is not at all the same as *being* puruṣa.

Indeed, to engage with something precludes one's being that thing. Since, on most accounts, kaivalya consists in puruṣa's realizing *itself*, it seems far from clear that, on Whicher's description, the yogin's misidentification has been eradicated. Whicher adds to the confusion by asserting that 'cessation' (*nirodha*) need not 'imply being rooted in a conception of oneself that abstracts from one's identity as a social, historical, and embodied being' (p. 291). In other words, kaivalya (i.e. the completion of nirodha) involves the cessation of 'misidentification' with the personal mind but not an abstraction from one's socio-historical and biological existence. This is surely contradictory.

Contrary to Whicher's interpretation, I think there are strong indications that Yoga proposes a methodological strategy of renunciation that involves the relinquishment of identification with precisely the sorts of personal characteristics that we might call social, historical and bodily (or biological). Although there is a precedent for the concept of embodied liberation in Sāṃkhya and Yoga – namely the state referred to at *SK* 67, where 'direct knowledge' (*samyag-jñāna*) has been attained and yet bodily existence rolls on owing to the momentum of mental 'seeds' or 'impulses' (*saṃskāra*s) – this has no bearing upon Whicher's view, for two reasons. First, because it occurs in the *Sāṃkhyakārikā*, not the *Yogasūtra*, and Whicher does not accept that the two systems are consistent with one another on the point of kaivalya. And secondly, because even by Sāṃkhya the state of embodied liberation is held to be merely a temporary prelude to the complete severance between puruṣa and prakṛti that is announced at *SK* 68.

That both Sāṃkhya and Yoga conceive kaivalya to be a disembodied state is evident in the classical texts. A biological body, being part of our empirical world and perceived as an item within a wider physical environment, is thoroughly dependent upon prakṛti's manifestation. And, as the *Yogasūtra* and *Sāṃkhyakārikā* insist, puruṣa's aloneness coincides with the return of prakṛti and its three constituent strands to their original unmanifest homeostasis, their purpose having been fulfilled (*YS* 4.34, *SK* 68). Whicher gives his own peculiar twist to this notion of the guṇas' modifications coming to an end: 'This ending, it must be emphasized, does not mark a definitive disappearance of the *guṇa*s from *puruṣa*'s view', he says. Rather, the guṇas continue to operate, producing experience in the form of vṛttis; and the sole difference between the yogin's new state and that which preceded kaivalya is that he now no longer *identifies* with those vṛttis: 'Now the yogin's identity (as *puruṣa*), disassociated from ignorance, is untouched, unaffected by qualities of mind, uninfluenced by the *vṛtti*s constituted of the three *guṇa*s' (Whicher 1998: 277). In support of his view, Whicher cites Swāmī Hariharānanda Āraṇya's remark that, when cessation (*nirodha*) occurs, the guṇas 'do not die out but their unbalanced activity due to non-equilibrium that was taking place ... only ceases on account of the cessation of the cause (*avidyā* or nescience) which brought about their contact' (quoted in Whicher 1998: 380 n. 97, Whicher's ellipsis).[2] Āraṇya's statement, however, merely reiterates the familiar view that, by 'cessation of the guṇas', is meant not their complete annihilation but, rather, their abiding in a state of perfect repose. This tranquil state is the unmanifest (*avyakta*) condition of prakṛti, and thus, contrary to Whicher's demurral, its instantiation precisely *does* 'mark a definite disappearance of the guṇas from puruṣa's view', and hence a definitive end to experience.[3]

Whicher asks rhetorically how, if kaivalya is a disembodied and non-experiential state, there could 'be anyone around to articulate that it even exists'.[4] The question, though pertinent, has been dealt with by the Sāṃkhya and Yoga traditions. In the *Sāṃkhyasūtra* and its commentaries, for example, one who has attained the state wherein perfect discrimination (*viveka*) is enjoyed and yet the 'wheel' (*cakra*) still spins is referred to as a *jīvanmukta*, one who is 'liberated in life'. It is in this state, prior to forsaking the cogitating mind and organic body for good, that the sage is able to furnish disciples with illuminating teachings (*SS* 3.78–83). Such proposals, of course, raise several questions for every one that they answer: How, for example, if the liberated sage is merely waiting for the wheel impelled by past actions to stop spinning can she initiate the new actions that instructing students would involve? But we cannot expect to address such questions here. The immediate issue is the exegetical one of how the Sāṃkhya and Yoga traditions account for the existence of teachings that are attributed to enlightened sages, and I think this has been covered.

We can, then, leave aside the claim that kaivalya amounts merely to a 'purification', as opposed to a total cessation, of empirical existence, and begin to investigate whether there might, in the absence of the realist assumption, be a more satisfactory way of interpreting the soteric destination of Sāṃkhya–Yoga.

Aloneness and misperception

I noted above that kaivalya clearly seems to be conceived in both Sāṃkhya and Yoga as a disembodied state. It is worth saying more about this. Not only does kaivalya appear to be a state of disembodiment, but it is one of mindlessness as well, in the sense that all mental activities have ceased and puruṣa – the subject beyond the empirical mind – abides alone, in its 'own nature' (*svarūpa*), this nature being characterized by such terms as 'consciousness' (*cetana* [*SK* 55]), the 'power of consciousness' (*citiśakti* [*YS* 4.34]), and 'mere seeing' (*dṛśimātra* [*YS* 2.20]). Some important discrepancies and tensions do exist concerning the notion of kaivalya, and these will come to light in the course of the following discussion. They are, however, common to both Sāṃkhya and Yoga, and hence cannot be held up as important incongruities between the two systems.

It is right to note, as Chapple for example has done (1996: 124), that there is a difference of emphasis in the *Yogasūtra* as compared with the *Sāṃkhyakārikā*. The latter text makes it appear that, once the appropriate level of self-knowledge has been attained, it is just a matter of allowing the remaining impulses and habit-patterns (*saṃskāra*s) to run their natural course, and kaivalya will spontaneously supervene upon their exhaustion (cf. *SK* 67–68). The *Yogasūtra*, meanwhile, emphasizes the need for sustained meditative discipline, and for the active replacement of mental seeds of compulsive misidentification by seeds of deep insight, as a prelude to the state of 'seedless' (*nirbīja*) samādhi (*YS* 1.50–51). This difference of emphasis flows naturally, however, from the overall difference of orientation between the two texts, the *Yogasūtra* being primarily concerned with practical instruction and the *Sāṃkhyakārikā* with metaphysical categorization. Again, therefore, it need not be taken to represent a divergence in either doctrine or practice.

My main purpose now is to highlight some key problems stemming from the concept of puruṣa's liberation (*kaivalya*, *vimokṣa*), especially as it relates to the important notion of misperception (*avidyā*, *viparyaya*). And, as a way of approaching these problems, it will be useful to provide a brief survey of the occurrences of *kaivalya* within the two classical texts. The term appears four times in the *Sāṃkhyakārikā* and five in the *Yogasūtra*. On two of its four appearances in the former text the term constitutes the first part of the determinative compound expression *kaivalyārtha*, which is commonly translated as 'for the sake (or "purpose" or "end," *artha*) of [puruṣa's] liberation (*kaivalya*)' (*SK* 17, 21). This compound may reasonably be regarded as synonymous with *puruṣasyārtha* and *puruṣārtha* ('for the sake of puruṣa'), which occur at *SK* 36 and 63 respectively, and with *vimokṣārtha* ('for the sake of final release') at *SK* 56 and 58. Activity, or process, in general (*pravṛtti*) is said to be for the sake of kaivalya (*SK* 17), as is the very 'conjunction' (*saṃyoga*) of puruṣa and prakṛti which initiates that activity (*SK* 21). The conjunction just referred to is also for the purpose of puruṣa's 'seeing' prakṛti (*darśanārtha* [*SK* 21]); but it is fair to assume that this purpose is subordinate to that of puruṣa's final liberation, since prakṛti can be 'seen' only insofar as she is active, and activity, as has just been noted, is for the sake of kaivalya. A similar dual purpose is mentioned in the *Yogasūtra* (2.18), where the 'seen', in the form of the three guṇas, serves the 'purpose of experience (*bhoga*) and liberation (*apavarga*)'. Here again, experience ought to be understood as auxiliary and not co-ultimate, for everything that is experienceable must eventually be recognized as dissatisfactory (*duḥkha* [*YS* 2.15, cf. *SK* 55]).

At *YS* 2.25 it is stated that the 'aloneness of seeing' (*dṛśeḥ kaivalyam*) results from the 'non-existence' (or 'disappearance', *abhāva*) of conjunction (*saṃyoga*), which 'non-existence' results in turn from the non-existence or cessation of avidyā, about which I shall say more shortly. At *YS* 3.49–50, meanwhile, we are informed that kaivalya is due to non-attachment to even the 'vision of the otherness of sattva and puruṣa'. Thus kaivalya is not regarded as a state of discriminative knowledge; even the knowledge of puruṣa's non-identity with sattva, which latter term can here be taken to stand for purified buddhi or citta, must be relinquished. *YS* 3.55 adds that kaivalya consists in the 'sameness of purity of sattva and puruṣa'; which is a little incongruous, since one might have supposed (a) that nothing could attain an equivalence of purity with a principle so utterly non-phenomenal as puruṣa, and (b) that, in the absence of conjunction, buddhi (or citta) would have completely demanifested along with all the other modes of manifest prakṛti, and that it would therefore be unnecessary and inappropriate to speak of its 'purity'. As a tentative exegetical suggestion, I would say that, by 'purity', it could be precisely the unmanifest condition of buddhi that is meant; and that, insofar as both buddhi and puruṣa can be described as unmanifest – all mental content having been discontinued – the two principles have a level of purity that is equivalent, or at least analogous.

Turning again to the *Sāṃkhyakārikā*, it is noteworthy that kaivalya features among the principal characteristics of puruṣa, the others being: 'witnessing (*sākṣitva*), . . . equanimity (*mādhyasthya*), seer-ness (or awareness, *draṣṭṛtva*), and inactivity (*akartṛbhāva*)' (*SK* 19). The inclusion of kaivalya in this context suggests that 'aloneness' is puruṣa's natural state, and hence that the fulfilment of the soteric enterprise is best conceived as a re-establishment, or disclosure, of that natural state, rather than as a transition to some new condition. Related to this is the notion that it is prakṛti alone that undergoes activity and transformation, and that puruṣa, being essentially independent, never enters into genuine involvement with her. At *SK* 60, for example, it is said that, while prakṛti, 'endowed with qualities (*guṇavatī*), proceeds to serve his purpose in various ways without benefit to herself, *puṃsaḥ* (i.e. puruṣa), being without qualities, performs no active role.' And at *SK* 62 we find the following ostensibly unequivocal pronouncement:

> Surely, then, no one is bound, no one released, nor indeed is anyone transmigrating (*saṃsarati*, literally 'wandering'). Prakṛti in its several abodes (*āśrayā*, i.e. manifest forms) is transmigrating, bound, and released.

The situation appears to be clear: puruṣa undergoes no change whatsoever, whereas prakṛti transmigrates from one lifetime to another in a state of bondage until she is finally released. This, however, brings us to one of the crucial difficulties that I wish to draw attention to here. For if it is prakṛti that is released, then in what sense does she act 'for the sake of puruṣa'? In order for prakṛti's activity to be both purposeful and 'for another's sake' (*SK* 17, 60), puruṣa must have a need to be fulfilled; and this in turn necessitates that puruṣa must undergo a transition from a state of unfulfilment to one of fulfilment – howsoever we conceive of that fulfilment. The *raison d'être* of the whole set of principles that Sāṃkhya metaphysics depicts is puruṣa's liberation; and thus if it were really the case that prakṛti's activity serves to bring about only her own release, the system would collapse. And yet, at the same time, we can see how tempting it is to deny that a supremely transcendent principle such as puruṣa is in need of anything whatsoever.

The situation has therefore become far from clear; and since it would appear that the author of the *Sāṃkhyakārikā* was himself wavering between two incompatible accounts of puruṣa's status, it is doubtful that any amount of interpretive effort will succeed in resolving the problem. Eliade displays an awareness of this problem when he writes that:

> There is something of a paradox in the way in which Sāṃkhya and Yoga conceive the situation of Spirit (*puruṣa*); though pure, eternal, and

> intangible, Spirit nevertheless consents to be associated, if only in an illusory manner, with matter; and, in order to acquire knowledge of its own mode of being and 'liberate' itself, it is even obliged to make use of an instrument created by *prakṛti* (in this case, intelligence). Doubtless, if we view things in this way, human existence appears to be dramatic [a mere performance? – MB] and even meaningless. If Spirit is free, why are men condemned to suffer in ignorance or to struggle for a freedom they already possess? If *puruṣa* is perfectly pure and static, why does it permit impurity, becoming, experience, pain, and history?
>
> (1969: 31–32)

The sort of paradox described here is not unique to Sāṃkhya and Yoga. Indeed, something very close to it crops up in a large number of systems of metaphysics and soteriology, both in Indian traditions and elsewhere. The central problem is as follows. If one postulates an absolutely perfect, and unalterable, principle as the true identity of the sentient inhabitants of the manifest universe, then – whether that principle be called puruṣa, brahman, God, the One or anything else – the task of explaining how we, as patently imperfect and alterable individuals, came to misidentify ourselves with our sullied minds and corruptible bodies becomes, if not logically impossible, at least metaphysically recondite. For, as soon as the notion of a perfect principle's 'forgetting' or 'mistaking' itself is admitted, then the perfection of that principle would appear to have been severely compromised. If, as a defensive ploy, it is then suggested that no *ontological* imperfection has been attributed to the principle, merely an *epistemic* one, this cannot salvage the original position; for no concept of ontological perfection worthy of the name can contain within it the possibility of ignorance or self-delusion.

It is, no doubt, for reasons such as those just given that Siddhārtha Gautama, the reputed founder of Buddhism, opted to maintain a majestic silence on abstruse metaphysical questions, and urged his followers to pursue practical methods of alleviating their suffering in preference to getting hung up on abstract theory.[5] Indian monistic, or 'non-dualist', philosophies, meanwhile, have tended to double their difficulties by proposing that the perfect principle is not only the true identity of sentient beings, but is the source of all manifest phenomena as well. Proponents of non-dualism are obliged to hold that the supreme principle, despite its inherent immutability, was somehow able to project out of itself a phenomenal veil, which it then mistook for its own true self. Owing to the precarious and strained tenability of this view, it is usually not stated so explicitly, but is clouded and hedged by delegating responsibility for the manifestation of the world and the self-misunderstandings of sentient creation to a second principle, typically referred to in Advaita Vedānta for example as *māyā* ('creative illusion') or *avidyā* ('false knowledge', 'misperception').[6] This second principle – at least when referred to as māyā – ends up playing a role very similar to that of the prakṛti of Sāṃkhya and Yoga, and thus threatens to undermine the original claim of non-dualism.[7]

In classical Sāṃkhya–Yoga the term *māyā*, though employed by certain commentators,[8] does not appear in the primary texts. However, the notion of a primordial error underlying the way we, as empirical subjects, experience ourselves and the world is prominent in both systems. And it is to this notion of erroneous perception that I now wish to direct the discussion.

In the *Yogasūtra* it is said that the 'field' (*kṣetra*) from which all other mental afflictions (*kleśas*) grow is avidyā (*YS* 2.4), and the five main afflictions together constitute the 'root' (*mūla*) of all action (*YS* 2.12). *Avidyā* is defined as 'seeing the eternal, pure, delightful, and essential in [that which is] temporal, impure, distressing, and inessential' (*YS* 2.5).[9] It is thus claimed to be the source of the conjunction between the seer and the seen (*YS* 2.24), which conjunction becomes 'unmanifest' or 'non-existent' (*abhāva*) only upon the cessation of avidyā; and this cessation is equated with the 'aloneness of seeing' (*dṛśeḥ kaivalyam* [*YS* 2.25]). In the *Sāṃkhyakārikā* the term *avidyā* does not occur, although its synonym *ajñāna* is implicitly cited as one of the four 'dark' (*tāmasa*) modes of buddhi at *SK* 23.[10] At *SK* 47, meanwhile, the 'five misapprehensions' (*pañca-viparyaya*) are referred to as being among the fifty components of the 'phenomenal effusion' (*pratyaya-sarga* [*SK* 46]); and although these five misapprehensions are not named in the verse itself, they are plausibly interpreted by several commentators as being equivalent to the five kleśas of Yoga, including avidyā as the most primitive of the five (see esp. *TK* 47 and *YV* 1.8).[11]

Both the *Yogasūtra* and *Sāṃkhyakārikā* agree that the coming together or conflation of puruṣa and prakṛti is in some sense an act of misapprehension – a mistaking of the one thing for the other. 'Due to that conjunction (*saṃyoga*)', says *SK* 20, 'the liṅga, though nonconscious (*acetana*), appears as though it were conscious; and although agency is of the guṇas, the detached one (*udāsāna*, i.e. puruṣa) appears as though active'. And since it is this very conjunction that instigates the 'surgence' of manifest prakṛti, it is evident that the coming into being of experience itself is predicated upon a primordial error, and hence that the way things appear to us is held to be rooted in and impregnated with misunderstanding. It is for this reason that Whicher's contention that experience can continue in the absence of saṃyoga and avidyā must be a misinterpretation. Saṃyoga is the necessary precondition for experience, and avidyā is, in turn, the necessary precondition for saṃyoga. Thus, when avidyā is eradicated, the momentum that once gave rise to 'birth, life, and experience' (*YS* 2.13) can no longer be generated, and so, when the remaining psychic impulses (*saṃskāras*) have been exhausted, that's it – end of story.

If read in terms of a temporal narrative, the fundamental role of avidyā would be absolutely nonsensical; for its being the cause of saṃyoga would necessitate that a misapprehension could *precede* the existence (or at least the *manifest* existence) of that which is misapprehended, namely the combined modes of manifest prakṛti. We are therefore obliged to take a synchronic interpretive standpoint, and to see avidyā not as a temporally located causal antecedent, but as a transcendental (non-spatiotemporal) structuring condition of experience. It cannot rightly be translated as 'ignorance', for that would imply something wholly negative.[12] Avidyā has a positive aspect insofar as it makes possible the emergence of the constituents of experience and thus of the empirical world itself; but since, due to this very fact, experience is always a kind of delusion ('like *māyā*' [*YBh* 4.13]), avidyā is to be overcome and replaced by its opposite (*vidyā*, *jñāna*, genuine knowledge), which corresponds to 'the establishment of the power of awareness (*citiśakti*) in its own nature' (*YS* 4.34, cf. 1.3).

A synchronic approach does not, however, resolve the problem of what or whom avidyā is to be attributed to. If there are only two co-ultimate principles that have ontological priority over manifest existence, namely puruṣa and prakṛti, then avidyā must belong to one of these two. It cannot belong to prakṛti, since prakṛti, being non-conscious, is incapable of being in a state of knowledge or non-knowledge. And thus we are forced again to countenance puruṣa's being afflicted by delusion. Some interpreters have tried to blur the issue by referring to the owner of avidyā as 'the yogin' or 'the mind', or by using ambiguous phrases that leave the identity of the subject thoroughly obscure. When Whicher, for example, informs us that 'In the ordinary consensus reality of empirical existence the sense of self misidentified with any aspect of *prakṛti* thinks that it is the seer' (1998: 279, my underlining), who, precisely, is doing the misidentifying? And how can a 'sense of self' think anything at all, let alone 'that it is the seer'? Similarly, when Feuerstein describes avidyā (which he translates as 'nescience') as 'a fundamental category error which regards the Self as other than what it really is' (1989a: 63), the grammatical structure of the sentence implies that 'the Self' (*puruṣa*) is regarded 'as other than what it really is' *by* 'a fundamental category error'. This, since a category error cannot be an epistemic agent, would itself be a fundamental category error; and hence it cannot be what Feuerstein meant. But in any case the original statement cleverly avoids the issue of *who* regards puruṣa in this way. Later in the same passage Feuerstein asserts that 'we are all born in ignorance of our true nature and with the natural tendency of establishing our identity *outside* ourselves' (ibid., original emphasis). And so the answer to my query would seem to be obvious: it is *we* who regard puruṣa 'as other than what it really is'! But who are *we*? Surely, if our true self is puruṣa, then each of us *is* puruṣa. Indeed, it is utterly tautologous to say so. Thus it must be *puruṣa* who mistakenly regards *itself* 'as other than what it really is'. This is the only logical conclusion.

The question of who is afflicted by avidyā is equivalent to that of who is liberated, for liberation is release from dissatisfaction (*duḥkha*), and hence *from avidyā* – and hence also from experience as such. If it is puruṣa who is liberated, then it must also be puruṣa that was under the influence of avidyā, or who succumbed to the kind of misidentification for which avidyā stands. This is obviously problematic; for if puruṣa is the pure subject, then it is hardly a candidate for moving from a condition of affliction to one of liberation. For reasons such as this, the one who attains kaivalya is, as in the case of the possessor of avidyā, commonly referred to in ambiguous terms, as 'the yogin', 'the wise one', etc. When puruṣa is, at the same time, maintained to be eternally perfect, a paradox arises; for it is contradictory to claim that the yogin (who misidentifies himself with the empirical personality) is identical to puruṣa but that puruṣa never misidentifies itself. The ambiguous terminology, however, mischievously disguises this paradox, enabling the interpreter to regard the yogin and puruṣa as identical and as non-identical according to the particular explanatory exigencies of the moment.[13] But the incongruities do not end there. Further interpretive difficulties come to light when we consider the notorious characterization of puruṣa as multiple, which we shall now do.

Puruṣa and multiplicity

The doctrine of puruṣa's multiplicity has been one of the major targets of critics of the Sāṃkhya system in both traditional debates and modern scholarship. The classical statement of the doctrine comes at *SK* 18, which reads as follows:

> Due to various patterns of birth, death, and capacities, and to the disjunction of activities, puruṣa's multiplicity (*puruṣa-bahutva*) is established; and also due to contrariety of the three guṇas.

Essentially what we have here is the claim that, because sentient beings are born and die at different times, and because they exhibit different qualities and capacities and perform different activities while they are alive, they must each be regarded as a distinct self or consciousness. Although there is no such explicit statement of the doctrine in the *Yogasūtra*, it is certainly implied at *YS* 2.22, where the activities of prakṛti are said to have ceased in relation to one whose 'end is fulfilled' (*kṛtārtha*) but not to have ceased entirely, due to their 'commonality' (*sādhāraṇatva*), that is, their continuing in relation to others. Vyāsa's commentary on this sūtra distinguishes between the 'proficient' (*kuśala*) puruṣa, whose end has been fulfilled, and the 'non-proficient' puruṣas, for whom the 'seen' (*dṛśya*) continues to act; and some such distinction seems to follow unavoidably from the sūtra itself.[14]

Traditional criticisms of the doctrine have focused largely upon its apparent contradiction of *śruti*, that is, principally the Upaniṣadic utterances to the effect that all selves are ultimately one (see e.g. Śaṅkara's *BSBh* II.1.2). An attempt to counter such criticisms was made in the *Sāṃkhyasūtra* on the grounds that scriptural references to the non-duality (*advaita*) of the puruṣa, or *ātman*, ought to be understood as indicating *qualitative* and not *numerical* identity (*SS* 1.154). However unconvincing it may seem, this is the only defence open to Sāṃkhya if it is to try to align its doctrine of many selves with the received and lauded teachings of the Upaniṣads. The latter scriptures nowhere give any suggestion of a distinction between qualitative and numerical identity, but this is perhaps to their own detriment; for unless the plurality of empirical subjects is to be denied (which denial could lead only to solipsism) the claim that the supreme being (*brahman*, *paramātman*) is identical to the 'living' or 'embodied' self (*ātman*, *jīvātman*) must involve such a distinction.

Among modern scholars who have attacked the 'many puruṣas' doctrine, one of the least forgiving is Keith, who writes at one place that 'These spirits if examined are clearly nothing but abstractions of the concept of subject, and are philosophical absurdities, since in the abstract there can be but one subject and one object, neither, of course, being anything without the other' (1949: 60).[15] The point is a valid one: there is undoubtedly something absurd about the notion of a multiplicity of abstract subjects, existing independently of time and space, and unoccupied by any content whatsoever. Indeed, it is for reasons such as this that, in the western philosophical tradition, Leibniz's conception of an infinity of dimensionless 'monads' is generally regarded as little more than a historical curiosity. On the other hand, however, I suspect that Keith has been too quick to underestimate the profoundly problematic nature of the subject-matter being dealt with here. On the face of it he is right to highlight the fact that the 'number and individuality' of conscious individuals 'are conditioned by the possession of a different objective content in consciousness;' and that 'if this were removed there would remain nothing at all, or at most the abstract conception of subject, which could not be a multitude of individual spirits' (ibid.: 88). But if we consider that the very notion of a multiplicity of sets of objective content itself presupposes a multiplicity of conscious domains in which those sets can manifest, then, I think, we begin to glimpse the kind of conceptual terrain into which the Sāṃkhya philosophers were venturing.

Larson tries to excuse, or explain away, the 'many puruṣas' doctrine by asserting that 'it is hardly likely that the Sāṃkhya teachers were thinking of the plurality of consciousnesses as a set of knowable entities to be counted. They were thinking, rather, of a plurality of intellects through which the disclosure of contentless consciousness occurs' (1987: 80). Larson is probably at least partially correct here, for it is certainly the case that the individuatedness of self or consciousness cannot be appreciated in isolation from the intentional or experiential mode of consciousness for which *buddhi* ('intellect' in Larson's translation) stands. What I think he underplays, however, is the phenomenologically rooted nature of the doctrine, which I shall now say a little more about.

Phenomenologically speaking, we, as conscious subjects, are constantly being pulled in two directions. The relationship between our inmost subjectivity and the empirical world is a kind of Wittgensteinian duck–rabbit:[16] I can see myself as the 'duck' of individuated being, inhabiting a world comprised of myriad entities, some of which appear to be conscious in ways that resemble myself; or as the 'rabbit' of transcendental consciousness – what Wittgenstein himself, in his earlier work, refers to as 'the philosophical self' or 'metaphysical subject'. This latter self is 'not the human being, not the human body, or the human soul, with which psychology deals, but rather… the limit of the world – not a part of it' (1974: 70 [5.641]). But I cannot see – understand, know – myself to be the duck and the rabbit at the same time.

For a further perspective upon the same self-experiential conundrum, let us take note of the following passage from Edmund Husserl's *Cartesian Meditations*:

> I, the reduced 'human Ego' ('psychophysical' Ego), am constituted... as a member of the 'world' with a multiplicity of 'objects outside me'. But I myself constitute all this in my 'psyche' and bear it intentionally within me. If perchance it could be shown that everything constituted as part of my peculiar ownness, including then the reduced 'world', belonged to the concrete essence of the constituting subject as an inseparable internal determination, then, in the Ego's self-explication, his peculiarly own world would be found as 'inside' and, on the other hand, when running through that world straightforwardly, the Ego would find himself as a member among its 'externalities' and would distinguish between himself and 'the external world'.
>
> (1977: 99)

The two contradictory descriptions of puruṣa that are presented in the *Sāṃkhyakārikā* correspond in certain important respects to the two aspects of egoity identified by Husserl. The individuated puruṣa of *SK* 18 is analogous to Husserl's ' "psychophysical" Ego' – 'constituted... as a member of the "world"...' – while the pure self or consciousness of *SK* 19 ('witnessing..., aloneness, equanimous, seer-ness, and inactive') is more like what Husserl in many other passages calls the 'transcendental ego' (e.g. 1977: 23). Of course, puruṣa cannot in any respect be said to 'constitute' the world of objects, but it can be regarded (albeit loosely and analogically) as the arena within which objects are constituted. It stands for the sheer possibility of anything's appearing as an object, whereas prakṛti is that which shows itself as the conditioning factors of experience. Consequently, puruṣa might be said to 'bear [the "world"] intentionally within [itself]', as Husserl says of his constituting ego.

What should not be lost sight of, however, is the fact that Sāṃkhya and Yoga seem to attach a far more literal sense, than does Husserl, to the notion of 'purity' in relation to self and consciousness. For Husserl, 'pure consciousness' ('transcendental consciousness', 'transcendental subjectivity', etc.) is merely ordinary consciousness as viewed in terms of phenomena alone. It is still marked by the same objective content; the only difference between it and ordinary consciousness being that the 'natural attitude' has been suspended, this natural attitude consisting in the assumption that objects of experience are exemplaries of a real world that lies outside consciousness (cf. Smith 2003: 25). It is 'pure' merely in the sense that its contents are no longer tainted by any 'prejudice' concerning their ontological status (cf. ibid.: 19). Similarly, the pure, or 'transcendental', ego is not an *experienceless* ego, but is merely the ego as considered in terms of its *containing* its intentional objects rather than being itself just another entity within the (trans-egoic) world. For Sāṃkhya and Yoga, meanwhile, pure consiousness is not arrived at merely by means of an attitudinal shift.

More than being just the context in which experience can occur, it is also that which remains when all phenomenal content is removed. It is, or can be, a state of being in which the transcendental self or consciousness is neither drawn out of itself into a world of mental and physical events, nor even constitutes the boundary around those events, but abides instead solely in its own nature, as consciousness (awareness, 'seeing') alone. In this sense of 'pure consciousness', it is not only ontological prejudices that have been stripped away, but experience itself. I shall discuss this point further in the next section.

To sum up the present section it can be noted that, contrary to certain interpreters, I do not hold that the multiple puruṣa doctrine can be explained away, or that it can easily be brought into harmony with the doctrine of a pure, dimensionless and non-engaged self. Rather, I maintain that these two conceptions of self perpetually and awkwardly rub up against one another in Sāṃkhya and Yoga; and that this awkwardness, far from exposing some disastrous weakness in the two darśanas, in fact points up a genuine and inordinately intractable antagonism at the heart of what it is to be a conscious subject. Of course, we cannot be sure that the proponents of the classical systems were fully alert to this antagonism, for insofar as they make no direct reference to it, the impression is given that the descriptions of puruṣa at, for example, *SK* 18 and 19 are to be regarded as perfectly compatible. Whether these proponents were or were not aware of the full extent of the difficulty, however, I consider that anyone's ridiculing and disparaging the conception of puruṣa advanced in Sāṃkhya and Yoga without thoroughly thinking through the issues involved amounts to doing these systems a great disservice.

Consciousness without content

The concept of pure consciousness is highly controversial within western philosophy. The so-called 'Continental' stream of modern European philosophy has been strongly influenced by the phenomenological philosophy of Husserl and his predecessors such as Brentano, who defined consciousness in term of intentionality. Furthermore, representatives of the phenomenological movement have commonly read the doctrine of the essential intentionality of consciousness back into the history of philosophy. As James Edie, for example, puts it: 'most historical philosophers have acknowledged the intentionality of consciousness in the sense that all consciousness is *consciousness of something*, that consciousness is a self-transcending process oriented toward objects *other than* and *outside* itself' (1987: 7, original emphasis). Defining consciousness as necessarily intentional or object-oriented inevitably precludes the possibility of pure consciousness of the sort that is postulated, under terms such as *dṛśimātra* (*YS* 2.20) and *dṛśeḥ kaivalyam* (*YS* 2.25), in Sāṃkhya and Yoga as well as other comparable soteriological traditions.

In the Anglo-American analytic stream of philosophy, meanwhile, the philosophy of mind has been largely dominated by physicalist and functionalist approaches. Physicalism identifies mental states with brain states, or ascribes to mental states, at most, the status of being supervenient upon neurophysiological states (see e.g. Kim 1984), while functionalism holds mental states to be 'constituted by their causal relations to one another and to sensory inputs and behavioural outputs' (Block 1995: 189). Neither approach, therefore, has much of interest to say about the phenomenological dimension of mental episodes; nor are they well-suited to talking about the possibility of a state of consciousness that, though devoid of phenomenal content, is yet not equivalent to unconsciousness. While on physicalist and functionalist assumptions the existence of consciousness independent of the complex neurophysiological processes of the organic body is unthinkable, this is not a view shared by the Indian systems with which we are concerned. Sāṃkhya and Yoga declare, not only that the state of pure consciousness that they strive for is one in which the factors that give form to physical objects (including the human body) have receded into an unmanifest condition, but that the final goal of human life – and of manifest existence in general – involves a decisive split with the body (*śarīra*) and the detachment of consciousness, or the conscious subject, from the spatiotemporal world.

Within the area of research that deals with mysticism and mystical experiences the issue of pure consciousness has been an awkward bone of contention for many years, especially since the late 1970s. On one side of the debate are the proponents of what has become characterized broadly as 'constructivism' or 'contextualism', according to which both the *post hoc* reports of mystical experiences and, crucially, the *experiences themselves* are 'constructed' ('defined', 'conditioned', 'mediated', etc.) by the culturally derived concepts, beliefs, and expectations of the experiencing subject.[17] On the other side of the debate are those who propose an 'anti-constructivist' or 'decontextualist' view. This has been labelled more positively by Robert Forman as 'perennial psychology', but is not, according to him, to be identified with the 'perennial philosophy' promoted by an earlier generation of mystically inclined thinkers (Forman 1998: 3 ff.).

Forman and others argue that, although the constructive factors cited by constructivists do indeed play an important role in ordinary (non-mystical) experience, there is a particular category of human experience that transcends the influence of such factors because it supervenes upon the 'forgetting' or 'letting go' of cognitive operations. '[T]he key process in mysticism is not like a construction process', writes Forman, 'but more like one of unconstructing. Meditative procedures encourage one to gradually lay aside and temporarily cease employing language and concepts' (1998: 7). Such procedures, Forman claims, can lead eventually to a conscious state that is so contrary to ordinary modes of experience that the very term 'experience' barely seems applicable. This latter issue led Forman to coin the expression 'pure consciousness event', which he defines as 'a wakeful though contentless (nonintentional) consciousness' (1990: 8).

Both sides in the debate over mystical experience have had things to say specifically about Sāṃkhya and Yoga. Forman uses the notion of kaivalya in these systems as an illustrative example of what he means by 'pure consciousness event'. What is encountered as a result of the process of 'relinquishing mental activities' that these systems advocate is, says Forman, 'not something acquired from outside, learned, or even thought, for these would all be elements... within *prakṛti*. Rather, what is encountered in *kaivalya* is *puruṣa*, which is inherent *within the self itself*' (1998: 11). The use of terms such as 'encounter' as substitutes for 'experience' do not, of course, eradicate the problem of an implied intentionality. An 'encounter' requires duality just as much as an 'experience' does; and hence Forman's description of kaivalya as an encounter with puruṣa is highly problematic, since who would it be who does the encountering, if not puruṣa itself?

Later in the same essay, Forman struggles to find an appropriate vocabulary with which to indicate the kind of knowledge that is arrived at in the state of pure consciousness. Having briefly outlined 'knowledge by acquaintance' (i.e. the sort of knowledge that I claim to have when I declare, for example, that 'I *know* Mrs Smith') and 'knowledge about' (as in 'I know *that* Delhi is in India', etc.), Forman notes that neither of these epistemic modes can meet the task at hand.[18] He then suggests, instead, 'knowledge by identity' as a more suitable expression to delineate the state of knowing oneself to *be* consciousness, although he nevertheless repeatedly slips into talking of it as though it were the knowledge *that* I am aware.[19] There is a major difference between knowing '*that* I am and have been aware' and knowing oneself *as awareness* (or *as consciousness*). The former kind of knowledge is perfectly compatible with our everyday pre-mystical understanding of ourselves as individual psychophysical entities whereas the latter implies a radical shift of self-identification and, arguably, the abandonment of any phenomenal content associated with one's identity.

In contrast with Forman, Steven Katz refuses to admit the possibility of consciousness without content, and thus asserts that 'it is in appearance only that such activities as yoga produce the desired state of "pure" consciousness' (1978: 57). 'Properly understood', he continues, yoga

> is *not* an *un*conditioning or *de*conditioning of consciousness, but rather it is a *re*conditioning of consciousness, i.e. a substituting of one form of conditioned and/or contextual consciousness for another, albeit a new, unusual, and perhaps altogether more interesting form of conditioned–contextual consciousness.
>
> (Ibid.)

In support of this assertion Katz notes that each of the various traditions of yoga has a particular conception of its soteric goal, and that since the conceptions differ from one another the experiences determined by them (for on Katz's view conception *must* determine experience[20]) must also be different. Katz's assumption here seems to be twofold. First, in line with his overall epistemology, he is assuming that the results of yoga practice are in all cases determined by the conceptual formulation of the goal. Second, he is assuming that he, or any other suitably qualified researcher, can adequately comprehend the goal of a yoga school or tradition from textual descriptions alone. This twofold assumption furnishes Katz with the confidence to state, for example, that 'in Upanishadic Hinduism yoga is practised in order to purify the individual "soul" and then to unite it with Brahman or, as later represented in the Bhagavad Gita, with Krishna' (p. 57) as though it were obvious what such terms as 'soul' (which Katz is using here as a translation of *ātman*), *brahman* and *kṛṣṇa* mean. For if the meanings of such terms is not perspicuous then what justification can there be for talking as though (a) these terms refer to intentional objects and (b) the intentional objects themselves are at variance to those referred to by different terms (or even by the same terms) in other traditions?

The fact is, however, that the meanings of the metaphysical terms concerned are matters of dispute, both within and between the Indian traditions and among researchers from outside those traditions; and there is therefore no basis upon which to assert the nature and idiosyncrasy of a conceptualized goal by referring merely to a set of key terms that appear in textual descriptions, which descriptions are themselves often highly poeticized and aphoristic. I agree with Katz that, in order to understand – or get anywhere near to understanding – the mystical proclamations of religio-philosophical schools, we have to take account of the background theories of each school concerned. I disagree, however, that it is legitimate to assume from the outset that the background philosophy of any particular school wholly determines the nature and content – rather than merely the pre- and post-experiential interpretations – of its soteric outcomes. It might well turn out to be the case that in many, and perhaps all, instances the soteric outcome *is* 'mediated', 'shaped', etc. by theoretical factors; but we ought not to merely assume this *a priori*, as does Katz.[21]

For the purposes of the present study, the question as to whether the combined theoretical and practical technologies of Sāṃkhya and Yoga *really* result in a state of pure consciousness is in fact secondary. Indeed, it is a question that can be properly addressed only by means of first-hand experimentation with the proposed techniques, and by diligent psychological, and in certain instances psychophysiological, evaluation of such experiments.[22] The primary issue here is the hermeneutic one of whether the soteric goal of Sāṃkhya and Yoga *as formulated in the classical texts* can be best (most accurately) defined as a state of pure consciousness – or as something else. Katz's position on this issue is not to deny that pure consciousness is the state *aspired to* by those who follow the procedures Yoga recommends, but, rather, to rule out on epistemological grounds the possibility of such aspirations being fulfilled (see Katz 1978: 57, quoted above). His position is therefore highly inconsistent. On the one hand he advises researchers to treat the theoretical components of mystical traditions as evidence of the uniqueness and culture-specific nature of the experiences they engender, while on the other hand, when coming across theoretical accounts that speak of a contentless state of consciousness which is nevertheless not *un*consciousness, he declares that such accounts are inadmissible as evidence of the results actually achieved; since they conflict with his own 'contextual thesis', they must, he assumes, be epistemologically flawed.[23]

Katz's regarding proponents of Yoga as having profoundly misunderstood their own experiences need not, then, imply the hermeneutic invalidity of describing the goal of Sāṃkhya and Yoga, as conceived from within the systems themselves, as a state of pure consciousness. The argument between constructivists such as Katz and perennial psychologists such as Forman concerns the possibility of *attaining* pure consciousness; and this, though an extremely interesting and important issue in itself, is not my primary concern here.

There is, however, no getting away from the fact that the notion of pure consciousness is highly abstruse and problematic. Indeed, consciousness of any kind has eluded any fully satisfactory definition, and many philosophers have balked at the attempt. As John Dewey once noted:

> Consciousness can neither be defined nor described. We can define or describe anything only by the employment of consciousness. It is presupposed, accordingly, in all definitions and all attempts to define it must move in a circle.
>
> (Dewey 1886: 2)

Since consciousness is not a *thing* – or at least, if it is a thing, then it is a thing most unlike any other – it is impossible to have a clear conception of it independent of its phenomenal content. When one tries to think of consciousness in itself, it recedes inexorably away from one's cognitive grasp. Like a dog trying to catch its own tail, we cannot quite get hold of it no matter how quickly our thoughts run. Or, to use another simile, commonly found in Buddhist writings: just as the blade of a sword cannot cut itself, so it is impossible for consciousness to observe itself (cf. Wallace 1998: 67). Devoid of content, it would seem to possess no feature which could distinguish it from nothing at all; and yet, since consciousness itself – or, if one refuses to call it such, then whatever it is that makes phenomenal consciousness possible – is presupposed in all experience, all knowledge, all conception, it is evidently not absolutely nothing. Jean-Paul Sartre, though hardly a mystic himself, refers to consciousness, when 'purified of the *I*' (and hence of all contents whatsoever), as 'quite simply a first condition and an absolute source of existence' (1957: 106). And since it is this that we are talking about – the first condition of conscious (or manifest, or phenomenal) existence – then, if we are to call it something, 'pure consciousness' serves the purpose at least as well as any other expression.

Schopenhauer, who certainly *did* have a mystical streak in him, talks of the 'abolition of the will' as an event in which 'the world melt[s] away', leaving 'before us only empty nothingness' (1969, I: 411–12). But he is careful to note that it is 'for all who are still full of the will' that it is nothing, and that 'conversely, to those in whom the will has turned and denied itself, this very real world of ours with all its suns and galaxies, is – nothing' (p. 412). This point is very apt, for Schopenhauer's notion of the abolition or denial of the will is, as far as it is possible to tell in these matters, highly reminiscent of the relinquishing of activities, desires and habits that precipitates the transition from egoic or personal consciousness to supra-personal 'pure' or 'absolute' consciousness in Sāṃkhya and Yoga. And just as in Schopenhauer's account, the transition consists in a shift so decisive that it marks, not a mere alteration of perspective within phenomenal existence, but a complete perspectival reversal; or, one could say, a transcendence of perspectivity altogether.

Owing to the absolute otherness of the reality that is arrived at, many exponents of mystical soteriologies have opted to hold back from committing themselves to any metaphysical position concerning its ultimate nature. The Buddha's original emphasis on bringing an end to distress and dissatisfaction (Pali: *dukkha*), as distinct from offering positive descriptions of the transcendent state, is the prime example in this respect.[24] In the case of Sāṃkhya and Yoga, however, it is hard to deny that they conceive the final state to be one of pure consciousness.[25] Puruṣa, or draṣṭṛ, is almost invariably referred to in terms that implicitly or explicitly identify it as consciousness, and its 'aloneness' is thus the ground of consciousness – or consciousness 'in itself' – vacated of all content.[26] This, in my view, is the most plausible reading of, for example, *YS* 1.2–3, where the 'cessation of mental activities' is said to enable 'the seer (*draṣṭṛ*) [to] abide in its own nature'; and of *YS* 4.34, where *kaivalya* is defined as the 'returning-to-the-source of the qualities (*guṇa*s), devoid of [any further] purpose for puruṣa; or the establishment of the own-nature of consciousness-power (*citiśakti*)'. The same point is echoed at *SK* 68, according to which the 'inactivity of pradhāna, due to the fulfilment of its purpose, [facilitates] the attainment of aloneness, which is both singular and conclusive'. The end towards which all experience is directed has been achieved, and its conditioning factors have dissolved into their unmanifest ground. All that remains is puruṣa, that which stood behind experience as its witness and was shrouded thereby, and which now stands naked and totally alone.

8

CONCLUSION

As we saw in the last chapter, a positive description of the soteric goal of Sāṃkhya and Yoga is very hard to provide. It is clear, however, that these systems – in common with many others both in India and elsewhere – regard the purpose of life as being, in the end, its own transcendence. Lived experience is imperfect and dissatisfactory, and is generated by a primordial misapprehension, whereby the true self or seer falsely identifies itself with aspects of an empirical reality that are susceptible to change, decay and death. Consequently, the path to release involves a systematic disidentification with those impermanent and inherently mutable aspects. It is also clear that the final release is held to involve an epistemic transformation in which the self is in some sense revealed to itself, even if we cannot conceive of what such a revelation might consist in or say anything meaningful about it. The methods for inducing this self-revelation consist largely in the cultivation of self-discipline. This includes adherence to strict ethical codes, the performance of bodily cleansing procedures, the practice of arduous postural and breathing techniques, and, perhaps most importantly, the training of mental attention by means of sustained meditation. Without this practical dimension, the claims that are made in the texts of Sāṃkhya and Yoga would still be of some philosophical significance, but the motivation behind them would be thoroughly obscure.

Notwithstanding some residual uncertainties concerning the precise nature of the relation between rational cogitation and direct awareness in Sāṃkhya and Yoga, I think it has been firmly established in this study that the most plausible way of understanding these systems' metaphysical schema is as the outcome of a rigorous analysis of immediate experience and of the conditions of any possible experience. It therefore seems likely that the yogin, having acquired a state of relative mental quiescence through single-pointed meditation, then engages in a refined process of phenomenological analysis, which shades into metaphysical speculation upon the underlying conditions of the phenomenal constituents. When viewed as the product of this kind of inquiry, the metaphysical categories cease to look like a loose collection of disparate fragments, and instead take on the appearance of a cohesive whole. According to the investigation that I have undertaken in the forgoing chapters, the components of the metaphysical schema can be best presented as follows.

Unmanifest categories

- the pure subject of consciousness (*puruṣa*);
- the source of phenomena (*prakṛti*) – constituted by the three strands (*guṇa*s).

Manifest categories

- intentional consciousness (*buddhi*);
- egoity (*ahaṃkāra*);
- mental synthesis (*manas*);
- five capacities for outer sensation (*buddhīndriya*s);
- five capacities for bodily-action sensation (*karmendriya*s);
- five modes of sensory content (*tanmātra*s);
- five formal elements of sensible objects (*bhūta*s).

None of the manifest categories contains items that are external to the field of experience; and hence, contrary to the received view of Sāṃkhya exegesis, the schema harbours no implications of external realism.

Despite the assumptions of numerous commentators, beginning with Vyāsa, that the *Yogasūtra* includes an attempt to refute metaphysical idealism, my own examination of the relevant sūtras (in Chapter 4), and of classical Sāṃkhya and Yoga as a whole, has not convinced me that this is so. Indeed, I have found nothing to indicate that these systems are incompatible with idealism; and, if my view that the modes of manifest prakṛti can best be understood as constituents of experience is correct, then there is no reason to suppose that any mind-independent correlates of experienced phenomena are postulated by Sāṃkhya–Yoga. The doctrine that puruṣa's presence is necessary for the manifestation of prakṛti is, on the face of it, an affirmation of idealism, which fact has been recognized by some scholars.[1] But if we do construe it as idealism, it must be acknowledged to be idealism of a very peculiar sort. The manifestation of prakṛti amounts neither to a projection of the empirical world out of a self-positing subject (*à la*, for example, J. G. Fichte), nor to the imposition of a formal empirical structure upon a non-empirical thing-in-itself (*à la* Kant). Prakṛti's manifestation provides the conscious subject not with a world, but with the categories through which, or in terms of which, a world is experienced. These manifest categories are not fully-formed objects; they are the conditions that make objects possible for us.

A question concerning the relation between experienced objects and 'real entities' cannot get a foothold within the Sāṃkhya–Yoga framework. Does the desk in front of me exist independently of my perceiving it? It is not clear that such a question can meaningfully be asked from the Sāṃkhya–Yoga standpoint. The experiential episode that includes my perception of the desk is constituted by all the manifest principles – or, more precisely, by specific exemplifications of these generic principles – working in combination with one another. No mention is made by Sāṃkhya or Yoga of any 'real' object (such as a desk) that transcends its instantiation in an individual's experience. When I finally fulfil my purpose as an embodied conscious entity, and awaken to my non-identity with the body-mind complex, then the desk, along with the empirical world as a whole, ceases to exist for me; but it continues to exist insofar as it is experienced by others who are not yet awakened in this way (cf. *YS* 2.22). The implication here is clear: the desk's existence is equivalent to its appearing to one or more conscious subjects: *esse* is *percipi*.[2]

The distinction that is of primary importance to Sāṃkhya and Yoga is not that between an 'external' world of mind-independent entities, on the one hand, and an 'internal' world of mental experience, on the other. The metaphysical dualism at the heart of Sāṃkhya–Yoga philosophy is, on my interpretation, concerned with the so-called 'internal' world of experience alone. However, the two fundamental principles that constitute this dualism are not themselves items within experience; rather, they are the mutually ineliminable grounds of experience. This is why, although the details of the process by means of which the co-fundamental principles were arrived at are not laid bare in the classical texts, it is fair to presume that the process in question involved some sort of transcendental reflection: an inferential move from formal, perceptible, existence to the imperceptible conditions thereof. In the case of one of the two principles, prakṛti (in its unmanifest aspect), its imperceptibility is due, we are told at *SK* 8, not to its non-existence, but to its 'subtlety' (*saukṣmya*). Its existence can be inferred from its 'effects' (*kārya*), namely the manifest categories that are instantiated in experience. The other principle, puruṣa, remains imperceptible because it is itself the ultimate perceiver, the conscious subject, what in Yoga is termed the 'seer' (*draṣṭṛ*). This dualism is often viewed as the greatest weakness of Sāṃkhya and Yoga. Indeed, it has been held up as an illustration of their failure to achieve a fully 'philosophical' understanding of reality.[3] I, on the other hand, see dualism as an indication of their genuinely philosophical predilections. The authors of the *Sāṃkhyakārikā* and *Yogasūtra* appear unconcerned as to whether their teachings conform to those of the so-called 'heard' or 'received' wisdom (*śruti*), contained in the Vedic canon and more particularly in the principal Upaniṣads. By contrast, the Vedānta darśana, with its many branches and sub-branches, has expended countless words and hours of human effort in the attempt to read into the Upaniṣads a consistent set of doctrines. However, the Upaniṣads, being works largely of mystical inspiration rather than systematic philosophy, strenuously resist such attempts. (As van Buitenen once poignantly remarked, 'It is always difficult to prove one's case by calling on the upaniṣads as witnesses: they are at once too willing and too evasive' (1957a: 21).)

Monistic systems come up against severe difficulties when trying to account for experience. Modern versions of physicalism, for example, have a great deal to say about the neurophysiological *correlates* of phenomenal consciousness, but nothing of any interest to say about the experiences themselves, because experiences are simply not 'physical' in the relevant sense. Meanwhile, non-specific or 'neutral' monism – according to which physical and mental facts are reducible to facts about some more primordial, yet unknown (or unknowable), substance – offers an unhappy and unstable compromise: it attempts to retain the façade of philosophical respectability that monism is supposed by many to confer while simultaneously admitting the metaphysical dualist's point that mental things and physical things constitute two radically incommensurable kinds of reality. Such monisms therefore suspend philosophizing in favour of wishful thinking.[4] And finally, mental monism, or absolute idealism, by reducing even the ground of phenomena to the supreme ego (or mind, or spirit, etc.), forecloses the possibility of an encounter between those two things, which encounter ought to be considered the very precondition for experience to take place. Such a monism, if it is not to deny experience any existence at all (which denial would hardly be credible), is obliged to posit the spontaneous emergence of phenomena either out of nothing, as 'mere appearances' with no ontological foundation, or out of something that is, in its essence, a pure subject.

Classical Sāṃkhya and Yoga appear to have seen the pitfalls associated with monism and to have resisted its seductive lure. Given that experience exists, there must be both something that *appears* and something *to which* the appearing occurs. According to Sāṃkhya and Yoga, that which appears must have, as a bare minimum, the characteristics of formal existence (*sattva*), activity (*rajas*), and limitation (*tamas*). The range of specific experiential episodes can be analysed in such a way that it discloses twenty-three general features, which are the manifest principles of the Sāṃkhya–Yoga ontology. Whether we take these twenty-three principles to constitute the optimum set of universal constituents of experience is a question with which this study has not been concerned. The main point I have sought to establish is that the metaphysics of classical Sāṃkhya and Yoga does indeed result from an analysis of experience. Or, to put the point slightly differently: the metaphysics of these systems *makes sense* when it is interpreted as the result of an analysis of experience, whereas when it is taken to be a realist cosmogony – that is, a story about how the universe came into existence at some datable moment in prehistory – then it becomes incoherent.

Ironically, some interpreters have imputed to Yoga a superior status over Sāṃkhya on the grounds that, whereas the latter system is 'merely' rational in its approach, Yoga is founded upon immediate intuitive awareness of an underlying metaphysical reality. As I hope I made clear in Chapter 2, there is no warrant for such claims. The philosophies of Sāṃkhya and Yoga are motivated by a salvific impulsion, and are, due to this fact, perpetually teetering on the brink of a domain beyond theoretical reason. But up until the moment of final revelation, it would seem that rational philosophy is not abandoned, and nor is it compromised in order to align its insights more neatly with the putatively unerring proclamations of Upaniṣadic sages. The doctrine of metaphysical dualism is justified not on the basis of *ipse dixit* – 'thus it was said [in this or that Upaniṣad]' – but, rather, on the basis that, if experience is to occur at all, there must be at least *two* principles in play. A single undifferentiated principle is inadequate to explain the possibility of experience; which is why, in my view, so-called 'non-dualist' systems invariably sidestep any attempt to philosophically validate their central metaphysical claim, and rely instead on dogmatic appeals to the authority of scripture.[5]

This is not to say that either Sāṃkhya or Yoga restrains itself from ever exceeding the limits of theoretical reason. Take the concept of puruṣa as a case in point. The interpretation of puruṣa that I have put forward in this study is not especially controversial, at least not at the level of textual exegesis. Most interpreters are agreed that the puruṣa of classical Sāṃkhya and Yoga is, on the one hand, an ontologically self-sufficient principle of pure consciousness and, on the other hand, a world-experiencer of which there are innumerable individuated exemplars. It is also generally acknowledged that these two conceptions of puruṣa are in tension with one another. I have not tried to resolve this tension, since I strongly suspect that it emerges from the nature of the problem itself – that is, the question of ultimate selfhood – and not due to any theoretical inadequacy particular to Sāṃkhya–Yoga. Neither have I attempted to vindicate the Sāṃkhya–Yoga claim that, given the right forms of soteric discipline, puruṣa (as pure consciousness) can discontinue its engagement with empirical existence and arrive at a state of supreme liberation from dissatisfaction. To propose a philosophical argument for a thesis such as this would amount to an overstepping of the limits of rational discourse. I have therefore argued that – again from a purely exegetical point of view – a state of contentless consciousness is indeed the sort of concept that comes closest to capturing what Sāṃkhya and Yoga consider their ultimate goal to be, but that this claim cannot be rationally elucidated.

A central question, broached in Chapter 7 but about which more could be said here, is that of what exactly the proponents of Sāṃkhya and Yoga mean when they say, as they frequently do, that prakṛti acts 'for the sake of puruṣa' or 'for the sake of [puruṣa's] liberation'. The meaning of such statements is rarely, if ever, queried in the interpretive literature, and hence its obviousness would seem to have been taken for granted. But if taken at their word the statements concerned contain a significant and in no way obviously justified assumption, namely that experience *as such* is goal-oriented; that is, it all happens for a reason, with a specific end in view. I have discussed in Chapter 7 the main conceptual problem associated with the goal itself, which is that either (a) puruṣa is eternally (timelessly) disengaged from empirical reality, and thus has no need of 'liberation' or (b) puruṣa *becomes* engaged through misidentifying itself with the constituents of that reality and thus must be the sort of being who can make perceptual errors (and hence is not quite the 'pure consciousness' that we thought it was). But from neither of these interpretive options does it immediately follow that the totality of experience – and the sub-empirical processes that give rise to that totality – should be for the exclusive purpose of puruṣa's liberation; and in the case of option (a) in particular, since puruṣa is already 'liberated', such a claim would be incoherent. It is undoubtedly the case that, in view of the overall theoretical framework of Sāṃkhya and Yoga, it makes no sense to think that liberation could be achieved without experience; for it is only by disidentifying with experience (or the constituents thereof) that puruṣa can escape from the world of suffering. There is thus a sense in which experience-generating activity is indispensable to the pre-liberated puruṣa, and to that extent at least can be said to be for puruṣa's sake. This interpretation has the advantage of not implying – as some interpretations might – that prakṛti has it all planned out, so to speak; that is, that every experiential episode is merely a part of an unfolding process that leads inexorably to a predetermined outcome. As ever, the notion of a 'pre-liberated' puruṣa is in tension with that of puruṣa's being eternal in the atemporal sense, i.e. completely independent of time, and thus incapable of having either a *pre-* or a *post-*liberated state. But this is just one more instance of a tension that has already been noted.

A further interpretive possibility is that expressions such as 'for the sake of puruṣa' might be intended merely, or primarily, to emphasize the phenomenological point that – since nothing can manifest independently of consciousness – events, thoughts, images, perceptual objects, etc., are thus on every occasion *for us*, or *for the subject*. In this sense prakṛti is always the servant of puruṣa, and owes 'her' entire manifest existence to 'him'. (The symbolic framework of Sāṃkhya–Yoga scrapes uncomfortably against modern sexual–political sensibilities – but it is far from being unique among spiritual traditions in this respect.) Indeed, one of the alternative terms for prakṛti is *sva*, meaning 'one's own' or 'oneself'(cf. Latin *sui*), just as one of the synonyms of *puruṣa* is *svāmin*, the 'self-possessor' or 'owner' (*YS* 2.23). The empirical world and its conditioning factors belong to puruṣa. Whether puruṣa *needs* them is a vexed question to which there seems to be no available consistent response.

Saṃyoga, 'conjunction', is the state in which we ordinarily find ourselves, in which there is no epistemic distance between what is experienced and the experiencing subject. This state is described as 'beginningless' (*anādi* [e.g. *YBh* 2.22]) because, I presume, for each of us there is no identifiable moment at which one began to confuse oneself with the content of one's experience. This is simply our natural situation. One feels sensations and treats them as 'mine', as though it were really oneself that were affected by them. Yet the soteriological claim of Sāṃkhya and Yoga is not merely that, in treating sensations in this way, one is making an erroneous conflation, but that, furthermore, there is a method of disentangling the conflated factors, self and not-self. This method is the system of practice known as *yoga-abhyāsa*, or simply *yoga*, which, like *saṃyoga*, means 'conjunction' or 'union', only in this case what is being unified is the subject of consciousness. The misidentification with the not-self is systematically discontinued. In quiet, contemplative moments the dimensionless point of awareness 'withdraws' from felt sensations and discerns them as akin to ripples on a pool of water, arising and then dissipating. The 'I' undergoes no change, and neither does it 'remain unchanged' – it is beyond the categories of mutability and immutability. Likewise, when performing an action, one commonly imagines that 'I' am doing it, to serve some purpose, to satisfy some desire that I take to be mine. Yet if

I slow down, pause, consider more carefully what it is I am doing, I may start to see the action as part of an extended web of interconnected impulses, events, and reactions to events, none of which is genuinely initiated by the contemplative self that is now considering them. Rather, the desires and impulses seem to emerge from some deep, dark reservoir, and the action begins to take place even before I have consciously acknowledged the need to perform it. If both the desire, or will, and the action itself *precede* my awareness of them, how can they really be *mine*?

Once the sensations, desires, impulses to act, and – more inwardly still – the thoughts, and structuring concepts thereof, have been disidentified with, such mental contents do not disappear immediately; they continue to whirl around as though perpetually generating their own momentum, and 'I' – as pure consciousness – repeatedly get drawn back into that cascading torrent, the 'effusion of phenomenal episodes' (*pratyaya-sarga*). However, by means of continual practice – through sitting still, regulating and intermittently suspending the respiratory rhythm, attending to a specific mental object in order to reduce the phenomenal manifold to the barest minimum; and, having let go of the mental object, observing detachedly the inner space that remains, a little less cluttered than before – the degree of centredness, of stability, incrementally increases, and the whirling torrent becomes a steady stream. And I can well imagine that, eventually, it may become a mere trickle, and then a drip; and then – nothing (that can be imagined) at all.

This is the practice of yoga, and it is given theoretical expression in the philosophies of Yoga and Sāṃkhya. The relation between metaphysics and spiritual discipline is, for these systems, symbiotic: the metaphysics formally maps out and categorizes the gamut of generic constituents of experience whose specific instantiations are discerned and noted during periods of sustained contemplation; and in turn, it would seem, the contemplative process is informed by the metaphysical map. Insofar as phenomenal consciousness is the context within which the empirical world is encountered, the inquiry into the nature and conditions of experience brings the acolyte of Sāṃkhya–Yoga into a deeper acquaintance with the nature and conditions of the empirical world. This world is never taken to be a thing in itself, arising independently of conscious participation, although neither is it the product of a voluntary creative act. It is constructed through the interplay of all of the twenty-three manifest ontological categories, which are in turn conditioned by the three co-ultimate 'strands' (*guṇa*s) that constitute the source of productivity (*prakṛti*).

Although the interpretation of classical Sāṃkhya and Yoga developed in the present work leaves considerable scope for further refinement, as well as for divergent readings of particular details within the respective systems, I hope enough has been done to demonstrate the extreme unlikelihood that Sāṃkhya and Yoga are responsible for the sorts of crude cosmological speculations that have been avidly attributed to them by several generations of putative exegetes. What they are instead responsible for, I have proposed, is among other things an elaborate and insightful system of interrelated principles that is best construed as an Indian metaphysics of experience.

APPENDIX A

The text of the *Sāṃkhyakārikā*

Preliminary remarks

Below is the complete Sanskrit text, totalling seventy-two distiches, of the *Sāṃkhyakārikā* in both Devanāgarī and Roman script, plus a new translation into English by myself.[1] There is at present no critical edition of the *Sāṃkhyakārikā*, but differences between the available editions are very minor. In some instances I have mentioned discrepancies between different editions in notes, although it should not be assumed that every such discrepancy has been indicated. In preparing this appendix I have consulted all the editions and translations of the *Sāṃkhyakārikā* that are listed under 'Primary Sources' in the Bibliography, and of these I have given most attention to the respective editions and translations by Jhâ (1896), Suryanarayana Sastri (1948), and Larson (1979). I have also benefited greatly from the assistance of Monier-Williams' monumental *Sanskrit–English Dictionary* and also the *Glossary of the Sāṅkhyakārikā* by Digambarji *et al.* (1989).

I considered also including in this appendix a full translation of the *Yogasūtra*, but decided against it on the following two grounds. First, although the *Yogasūtra* is certainly a work of enormous importance for this study, it is not as systematic and coherent a text as is the *Sāṃkhyakārikā*. For this reason an understanding of the passages from the *Yogasūtra* that are quoted in the foregoing chapters of this study will not, in my view, be significantly enhanced by the inclusion of a translation of the text as a whole. In the case of the *Sāṃkhyakārikā*, however, the more systematic and progressive nature of its structure increases the usefulness of being able to read its verses within their broader context. Second, the textual form known as the *sūtra* is terse to the point of near-obscurity, and many passages require an accompanying commentary in order for any sense to be made of them. In view of this fact, by merely providing my own translation of the *Yogasūtra* I would not necessarily be clarifying for the reader anything concerning the meaning of the text, but would be adding just another more-or-less opaque version of it to the numberless editions that exist already. The *kārikā* style in which the

Sāṃkhyakārikā is composed is also apothegmatic, but far less stringently so than that of the sūtra; and the text is therefore more capable of standing on its own without the support of a verse-by-verse commentary. I could, of course, have translated the *Yogasūtra* with a commentary alongside it, but such a project would have been unduly extravagant for a mere appendix.

I freely admit that any translation will contain certain biases in favour of the translator's own particular interpretation of the original text. By being aware of this fact throughout the process of translation, however, I hope that I have avoided any serious distortions which might, had I been less alert, have slipped in. The inclusion of the original text will, in any event, make it easier for scholars of Sanskrit to detect any deficiencies in my translation. I have endeavoured to keep bracketed interpolations in the translation to a minimum, and the relatively brief elaborations of the text that I provide in endnotes are not intended to constitute anything approaching a full explanation. Inevitably this will leave the meaning of some *kārikā*s less than obvious. But my purpose here is principally to supplement the interpretive investigation that makes up the main body of this study, and not to either duplicate or try to surpass that investigation with an extensive exegesis.

The *Sāṃkhyakārikā* in Devanāgarī and Roman script, and in English translation

1 दुःखत्रयाभिघाताज्जिज्ञासा तदपघातके हेतौ ।
दृष्टे सा ऽपार्था चेन्नैकान्तात्यन्ततो ऽभावात् ॥ १ ॥

duḥkhatrayābhighātāj jijñāsā tad apaghātake hetau /
dṛṣṭe sā 'pārthā cen naikāntātyantato 'bhāvāt // 1 //

Due to the affliction of threefold distress, the inquiry into its removal [arises]; [if said to be] pointless because obvious [methods exist], this is not so, for such methods are neither singularly directed nor conclusive.

2 दृष्टवदानुश्रविकः स ह्यविशुद्धिक्षयातिशययुक्तः ।
तद्विपरीतः श्रेयान् व्यक्ताव्यक्तज्ञविज्ञानात् ॥ २ ॥

dṛṣṭavad ānuśravikaḥ sa hy aviśuddhikṣayātiśayayuktaḥ /
tad viparītaḥ śreyān vyaktāvyaktajñavijñānāt // 2 //

The heard [method] is like the obvious, as it is conjoined with impurity, corruption, and excess. The superior and opposite of that [comes] from the discrimination of the manifest, the unmanifest, and the knower.

3 मूलप्रकृतिरविकृतिर्महदाद्याः प्रकृतिविकृतयः सप्त ।
षोडशकस्तु विकारो न प्रकृतिर्न विकृतिः पुरुषः ॥ ३ ॥

mūlaprakṛtir avikṛtir mahad ādyāḥ prakṛtivikṛtayaḥ sapta /
ṣoḍaśakas tu vikāro na prakṛtir na vikṛtiḥ puruṣaḥ // 3 //

Mūlaprakṛti is uncreated; the seven – 'the great' (*mahat*) and the others – are creative and created; the sixteen, meanwhile, are [merely] created; *puruṣa* is neither creative nor created.

4 दृष्टमनुमानमाप्तवचनं च सर्वप्रमाणसिद्धत्वात् ।
त्रिविधम्प्रमाणमिष्टं प्रमेयसिद्धिः प्रमाणाद्धि ॥ ४ ॥

dṛṣṭam anumānam āptavacanaṃ ca sarvapramāṇasiddhatvāt /
trividham pramāṇam iṣṭaṃ prameyasiddhiḥ pramāṇād dhi // 4 //

The attainment of knowledge is based on [certain] ways of knowing; the accepted ways are three – perceiving, inferring and reception of verbal testimony – as these cover all ways of knowing.

5 प्रतिविषयाध्यवसायो दृष्टं त्रिविधमनुमानमाख्यातम् ।
तल्लिङ्गलिङ्गिपूर्वकम् आप्तश्रुतिराप्तवचनं तु ॥ ५ ॥

prativiṣayādhyavasāyo dṛṣṭaṃ trividham anumānam ākhyātam /
tal liṅgaliṅgipūrvakam āptaśrutir āptavacanaṃ tu // 5 //

Perceiving is the discernment of particular objects; inference, which is said to be threefold, is the tracing of the mark-bearer from its indicating mark; reception of verbal testimony, meanwhile, is reception of *śruti*.

6 सामान्यतस्तु दृष्टात् अतीन्द्रियाणाम्प्रतीतिरनुमानात् ।
तस्मादपि चासिद्धं परोक्षमाप्तागमात् सिद्धम् ॥ ६ ॥

sāmānyatas tu dṛṣṭāt atīndriyāṇām pratītir[2] *anumānāt /*
tasmād api cāsiddhaṃ parokṣam āptāgamāt siddham // 6 //

Inference by analogy ascertains what is beyond the sense-capacities; and what is unaccomplishable even by that is established by verbal testimony.

7 अतिदूरात् सामीप्यात् इन्द्रियघातान्मनो ऽनवस्थानात् ।
सौक्ष्म्याद् व्यवधानात् अभिभवात् समानाभिहाराच्च ॥ ७ ॥

atidūrāt sāmīpyāt indriyaghātān mano 'navasthānāt /
saukṣmyād vyavadhānāt abhibhavāt samānābhihārāc ca // 7 //

[Something may be imperceptible] due to: remoteness, closeness, sensory impairment, instability of mind, subtlety, obscuration, suppression, similarity with something else.

8 सौक्ष्म्यात्तदनुपलब्धिर्नाभावात् कार्यतस्तदुपलब्धेः ।
महदादि तच्च कार्यं प्रकृतिसरूपं विरूपं च ॥ ८ ॥

saukṣmyāt tad anupalabdhir nābhāvāt kāryatas tad upalabdheḥ /
mahad ādi tac ca kāryaṃ prakṛtisarūpaṃ virūpaṃ ca // 8 //

The non-apprehension of that [i.e. *prakṛti*] is due to subtlety, not non-existence; it is apprehended by means of its effects. Its effects – *mahat* and the others – are both with and without the nature (*rūpa*) of *prakṛti*.

9 असदकरणादुपादानग्रहणात् सर्वसंभवाभावात् ।
शक्तस्य शक्यकरणात् कारणभावाच्च सत् कार्यम् ॥ ९ ॥

asad akaraṇād upādānagrahaṇāt sarvasaṃbhavābhāvāt /
śaktasya śakyakaraṇāt kāraṇabhāvāc ca sat kāryam // 9 //

The [formally] existent [is] an effect due to:[3] the non-causation of non-being; the apprehension of a material cause; the non-production of everything [from everything]; the possibility of causation [only] from that which is capable; and the nature of the cause.

10 हेतुमदनित्यमव्यापि सक्रियमनेकमाश्रितं लिङ्गम् ।
सावयवं परतन्त्रं व्यक्तं विपरीतमव्यक्तम् ॥ १० ॥

hetumad anityam avyāpi sakriyam anekam āśritaṃ liṅgam /
sāvayavaṃ paratantraṃ vyaktaṃ viparītam avyaktam // 10 //

The manifest is caused, temporal, spatially limited, active, non-singular, dependent, a cipher, composite, conditioned; the unmanifest is the opposite.

11 त्रिगुणमविवेकि विषयः सामान्यमचेतनम्प्रसवधर्मि ।
व्यक्तं तथा प्रधानम् तद्विपरीतस्तथा च पुमान् ॥ ११ ॥

triguṇam aviveki viṣayaḥ sāmānyam acetanam prasavadharmi /
vyaktaṃ tathā pradhānam tad viparītas tathā ca pumān // 11 //

The manifest as well as *pradhāna* (i.e. the unmanifest) are tripartite, undiscriminated, objectual, universal, non-conscious, productive; and *pumān* (i.e. *puruṣa*) is the opposite of these.

12 प्रीत्यप्रीतिविषादात्मकाः प्रकाशप्रवृत्तिनियमार्थाः ।
अन्योन्याभिभवाश्रयजननमिथुनवृत्तयश्च गुणाः ॥ १२ ॥

prītyaprītiviṣādātmakāḥ prakāśapravṛttiniyamārthāḥ /
anyonyābhibhavāśrayajananamithunavṛttayaś ca guṇāḥ // 12 //

Of the nature of gladness, perturbation and stupefaction; serving to illuminate, activate and restrain; the strands (*guṇa*s) subjugate, support, generate and combine with one another.

13 सत्त्वं लघु प्रकाशकमिष्टमुपष्टम्भकं चलं च रजः ।
गुरु वरणकमेव तमः प्रदीपवच्चार्थतो वृत्तिः ॥ १३ ॥

sattvaṃ laghu prakāśakam iṣṭam upaṣṭambhakaṃ calaṃ ca rajaḥ /
guru varaṇakam eva tamaḥ pradīpavac cārthato vṛttiḥ // 13 //

Sattva is light and illuminating; *rajas* is impelling and moving; *tamas* is heavy and delimiting; and their purpose is to function like a lamp.

14 अविवेक्यादेः सिद्धिस्त्रैगुण्यात्तद्विपर्ययाभावात् ।
कारणगुणात्मकत्वात्कार्यस्याव्यक्तमपि सिद्धम् ॥ १४ ॥

avivekyādeḥ siddhis[4] *traiguṇyāt tad viparyayābhāvāt /*
kāraṇaguṇātmakatvāt kāryasyāvyaktam api siddham // 14 //

Undiscriminatedness and the other [qualities] are established due to the tripartition, and to the non-existence [of the three *guṇa*s] in the opposite of that. The unmanifest is established [as having the same nature as the manifest] due to the *guṇa*-nature of the effect being also that of the cause.

15 भेदानां परिमाणात् समन्वयात् शक्तितः प्रवृत्तेश्च ।
कारणकार्यविभागादविभागाद्वैश्वरूप्यस्य ॥ १५ ॥

bhedānāṃ parimāṇāt samanvayāt śaktitaḥ[5] *pravṛtteś ca /*
kāraṇakāryavibhāgād avibhāgād vaiśvarūpyasya // 15 //

Due to: the finitude of differentiated [objects], homogeneity, the procession from potency, the distinction between cause and effect, and the undivided form of the world –[6]

16 कारणमस्त्यव्यक्तम् प्रवर्तते त्रिगुणतः समुदयाच्च ।
परिणामतः सलिलवत् प्रतिप्रतिगुणाश्रयविशेषात् ॥ १६ ॥

kāraṇam asty avyaktam pravartate triguṇataḥ samudayāc ca /
pariṇāmataḥ salilavat pratipratiguṇāśrayaviśeṣāt // 16 //

– the unmanifest is the cause, productive due to the combination of the three *guṇa*s, and transformable fluidly in accordance with the specific abode [character?] of each of the *guṇa*s.

17 संघातपरार्थत्वात् त्रिगुणादिविपर्ययादधिष्ठानात् ।
पुरुषो ऽस्ति भोक्तृभावात्कैवल्यार्थं प्रवृत्तेश्च ॥ १७ ॥

saṃghātaparārthatvāt triguṇādiviparyayād adiṣṭhānāt /
puruṣo'sti bhoktṛbhāvāt kaivalyārthaṃ pravṛtteś ca // 17 //

Puruṣa exists due to:[7] composites [being] for another's sake, the opposite of the three *guṇa*s etc., [the need for] a controller, [the need for] an enjoyer, and the process [being] for the purpose of aloneness.

18 जननमरणकरणानां प्रतिनियमादयुगपत्प्रवृत्तेश्च ।
पुरुषबहुत्वं सिद्धं त्रैगुण्यविपर्ययाच्चैव ॥ १८ ॥

jananamaraṇakaraṇānāṃ pratiniyamād ayugapat pravṛtteś ca /
puruṣabahutvaṃ siddhaṃ traiguṇyaviparyayāc caiva // 18 //

Due to various patterns of birth, death, and capacities, and to the disjunction of activities, *puruṣa*'s multiplicity is established; and also due to contrariety of the three *guṇa*s.

19 तस्माच्च विपर्यासात्सिद्धं साक्षित्वमस्य पुरुषस्य ।
कैवल्यम्माध्यस्थ्यं द्रष्टृत्वमकर्तृभावश्च ॥ १९ ॥

tasmāc ca viparyāsāt siddhaṃ sākṣitvam asya puruṣasya /
kaivalyam mādhyasthyaṃ draṣṭṛtvam akartṛbhāvaś ca // 19 //

And thus, due to [its being] the opposite [of *prakṛti*], the witnessing, aloneness, equanimity, awareness and inactivity of *puruṣa* is established.

20 तस्मात्तत्संयोगादचेतनं चेतनावदिव लिङ्गम् ।
गुणकर्तृत्वे च तथा कर्तेव भवत्युदासीनः ॥ २० ॥

tasmāt tat saṃyogād acetanaṃ cetanāvad iva liṅgam /
guṇakartṛtve ca tathā karteva bhavaty udāsīnaḥ // 20 //

Due to the conjunction of those [two, i.e. *puruṣa* and *prakṛti*] the non-conscious *liṅga* appears as though conscious, and similarly, owing to the activity of the *guṇa*s, the non-engaged appears as though active.

21 पुरुषस्य दर्शनार्थं कैवल्यार्थं तथा प्रधानस्य ।
पङ्ग्वन्धवदुभयोरपि संयोगस्तत्कृतः सर्गः ॥ २१ ॥

puruṣasya darśanārthaṃ kaivalyārthaṃ tathā pradhānasya /
paṅgvandhavad ubhayor api saṃyogas tatkṛtaḥ sargaḥ // 21 //

For the purpose of perceiving *pradhāna*, and for the purpose of *puruṣa*'s aloneness, the two [come together] like the blind and the lame; that conjunction is creation, emergence.[8]

22 प्रकृतेर्महांस्ततो ऽहङ्कारस्तस्माद्गणश्च षोडशकः ।
तस्मादपि षोडशकात्पञ्चभ्यः पञ्च भूतानि ॥ २२ ॥

prakṛter mahāṃs tato'haṅkāras tasmād gaṇaś ca ṣoḍaśakaḥ /
tasmād api ṣoḍaśakāt pañcabhyaḥ pañca bhūtāni // 22 //

From *prakṛti* [comes[9]] the great; from that, egoity; and from that, the group of sixteen; again, from five of those sixteen, [come] the five elements.

23 अध्यवसायो बुद्धिर्धर्मो ज्ञानं विराग ऐश्वर्यम्।
सात्त्विकमेतद्रूपं तामसमस्माद्विपर्यस्तम् ॥ २३॥

adhyavasāyo buddhir dharmo jñānaṃ virāga aiśvaryam /
sāttvikam etad rūpaṃ tāmasam asmād viparyastam // 23 //

Buddhi is discernment, its lucid (*sāttvika*) form [comprising] *dharma*, knowledge, non-attachment, [and] masterfulness, and its darkened (*tāmasa*) form [comprising] the opposite.

24 अभिमानो ऽहङ्कारस्तस्माद्द्विविधः प्रवर्तते सर्गः।
एकादशकश्च गणस्तन्मात्रपञ्चकश्चैव ॥ २४॥

abhimāno'haṅkāras tasmād dvividhaḥ pravartate sargaḥ /
ekādaśakaś ca gaṇas tanmātrapañcakaś caiva // 24 //

The thought of self is egoity; from that, a twofold emergence proceeds, namely the group of eleven and the five *tanmātras*.

25 सात्त्विक एकादशकः प्रवर्तते वैकृतादहङ्कारात।
भूतादेस्तन्मात्रः स तामसः तैजसादुभयम् ॥ २५॥

sāttvika ekādaśakaḥ pravartate vaikṛtād ahaṅkārāt /
bhūtādes tanmātraḥ sa tāmasaḥ taijasād ubhayam // 25 //

The lucid (*sāttvika*) eleven proceed from the modified egoity; from the source of the elements,[10] which is opaque (*tāmasa*), the *tanmātra*s [proceed]; from the fiery (*taijasa*), both [proceed].

26 बुद्धीन्द्रियाणि चक्षुःश्रोत्रघ्राणरसनत्वगाख्यानि।
वाक्पाणिपादपायूपस्थान् कर्मेन्द्रियाण्याहु ॥ २६॥

buddhīndriyāṇi cakṣuḥ śrotraghrāṇarasanatvagākhyāni /
vākpāṇipādapāyūpasthān karmendriyāṇyāhu // 26 //

Sense-capacities is the term for seeing, hearing, smelling, tasting and touching; voice, hand, foot, anus and underparts are called action-capacities.

27 उभयात्मकमत्र मनः सङ्कल्पकमिन्द्रियं च साधर्म्यात्।
गुणपरिणामविशेषान्नानात्वं बाह्यभेदाश्च ॥ २७॥

ubhayātmakam atra manaḥ saṅkalpakam indriyaṃ ca sādharmyāt /
guṇapariṇāmaviśeṣān nānātvaṃ bāhyabhedāś ca // 27 //

In this regard, of the essence of both is mind (*manas*), which is synthesis and is, due to its similarity, a capacity. Variousness and external differences are due to the specific modifications of the *guṇa*s.

28 शब्दादिषु पञ्चानामालोचनमात्रमिष्यते वृत्तिः ।
वचनादानविहरणोत्सर्गानन्दाश्च पञ्चानाम् ॥ २८ ॥

śabdādiṣu pañcānām ālocanamātram iṣyate vṛttiḥ /
vacanādānaviharaṇotsargānandāś ca pañcānām // 28 //

The operation (*vṛtti*) of the five [sense-capacities] is held to be bare awareness of sound and so forth; speaking, grasping, walking, excreting and [sexual] pleasure are [the operations of] the five [action-capacities].

29 स्वालक्षण्यं वृत्तिस्त्रयस्य सैषा भवत्यसामान्या ।
सामान्यकरणवृत्तिः प्राणाद्या वायवः पञ्च ॥ २९ ॥

svālakṣaṇyaṃ vṛttis trayasya saiṣā bhavaty asāmānyā /
sāmānyakaraṇavṛttiḥ prāṇdyā vāyavaḥ pañca // 29 //

Each of the three[11] is distinguished by its own operation, which manifests differently [from those of the other two]. Their common operation consists in the five vital currents, [namely] *prāṇa* and the others.[12]

30 युगपच्चतुष्टयस्य तु वृत्तिः क्रमशश्च तस्य निर्दिष्टा ।
दृष्टे तथाप्यदृष्टे त्रयस्य तत्पूर्विका वृत्तिः ॥ ३० ॥

yugapac catuṣṭayasya tu vṛttiḥ kramaśaś ca tasya nirdiṣṭā /
dṛṣṭe tathāpy adṛṣṭe trayasya tatpūrvikā vṛttiḥ // 30 //

The operation of the four[13] with regard to what is present to perception is both instantaneous and progressive; while in the case of what is imperceptible, the operation of the three is preceded by that [i.e. by the perception of a present object].

31 स्वां स्वां प्रतिपद्यन्ते परस्पराकूतहेतुकां वृत्तिम् ।
पुरुषार्थ एव हेतुर्न केनचित्कार्यते करणम् ॥ ३१ ॥

svāṃ svāṃ pratipadyante parasparākūtahetukāṃ vṛttim /
puruṣārtha eva hetur na kenacit kāryate karaṇam // 31 //

The respective operations are performed in co-operation with one another from a common impulse, the sole end being that of *puruṣa*; nothing else activates the instrument.

32 करणं त्रयोदशविधम् तदाहरणधारणप्रकाशकरम् ।
कार्यं च तस्य दशधाहार्यं धार्यं प्रकाश्यं च ॥ ३२ ॥

karaṇaṃ trayodaśavidham tadāharaṇadhāraṇaprakāśakaram /
kāryaṃ ca tasya daśadhāhāryaṃ dhāryaṃ prakāśyaṃ ca // 32 //

The instrument, comprising thirteen parts,[14] is grasping, holding and illuminating; and its object (*kārya*), which is tenfold,[15] is grasped, held and illuminated.

33 अन्तःकरणं त्रिविधम् दशधा बाह्यं त्रयस्य विषयाख्यम् ।
साम्प्रतकालं बाह्यं त्रिकालमाभ्यन्तरं करणम् ॥ ३३ ॥

antaḥkaraṇaṃ trividham daśadhā bāhyaṃ trayasya viṣayākhyam /
sāmpratakālaṃ bāhyaṃ trikālam ābhyantaraṃ karaṇam // 33 //

The inner instrument is threefold, the outer is tenfold [and] is held to be the domain of the three;[16] the outer [operates in] the present moment [alone], the [inner] instrument in all three times.[17]

34 बुद्धीन्द्रियाणि तेषां पञ्च विशेषाविशेषविषयाणि ।
वाग्भवति शब्दविषया शेषाणि तु पञ्चविषयाणि ॥ ३४ ॥

buddhīndriyāṇi teṣāṃ pañca viśeṣāviśeviṣayāṇi /
vāgbhavati śabdaviṣayā śeṣāṇi tu pañcaviṣayāṇi // 34 //

Of these, the five sense-capacities have specific and non-specific objects;[18] the voice manifests sound-phenomena whereas the other remaining [action-capacities] have [all] five modes of phenomena.[19]

35 सान्तःकरणा बुद्धिः सर्वं विषयमवगाहते यस्मात् ।
तस्मात् त्रिविधं करणं द्वारि द्वाराणि शेषाणि ॥ ३५ ॥

sāntaḥkaraṇā buddhiḥ sarvaṃ viṣayam avagāhate yasmāt /
tasmāt trividhaṃ karaṇaṃ dvāri dvārāṇi śeṣāṇi // 35 //

Because *buddhi* along with the other inner instruments is immersed in all objects, the threefold instrument is the chamber, the rest being the doorways.

36 एते प्रदीपकल्पाः परस्परविलक्षणा गुणविशेषाः ।
कृत्स्नं पुरुषस्यार्थं प्रकाश्य बुद्धौ प्रयच्छन्ति ॥ ३६ ॥

ete pradīpakalpāḥ parasparavilakṣaṇā guṇaviśeṣāḥ /
kṛtsnaṃ puruṣasyārthaṃ prakāśya buddhau prayacchanti // 36 //

These specifications of the *guṇa*s, distinct from one another, present the whole [world] to *buddhi*, illuminating it like a lamp for the sake of *puruṣa*.

37 सर्वं प्रत्युपभोगं यस्मात्पुरुषस्य साधयति बुद्धिः ।
सैव च विशिनष्टि पुनः प्रधानपुरुषान्तरं सूक्ष्मम् ॥ ३७ ॥

sarvaṃ praty upabhogaṃ yasmāt puruṣasya sādhayati buddhiḥ /
saiva ca viśinaṣṭi punaḥ pradhānapuruṣāntaraṃ sūkṣmam // 37 //

[This is] because *buddhi* gives rise to every particular enjoyment of the *puruṣa* and, furthermore, discloses the subtle [difference] between *pradhāna* and *puruṣa*.

38 तन्मात्राण्यविशेषाः तेभ्यो भूतानि पञ्च पञ्चभ्यः ।
एते स्मृता विशेषाः शान्ता घोराश्च मूढाश्च ॥ ३८ ॥

tanmātrāṇy aviśeṣāḥ tebhyo bhūtāni pañca pañcabhyaḥ /
ete smṛtā viśeṣāḥ śāntā ghorāś ca mūḍhāś ca // 38 //

The modes of sensory content (*tanmātra*s) are non-specific; from these five [come] the five elements; these are regarded as specific, and as tranquil, disturbing and delusive.

39 सूक्ष्मा मातापितृजाः सहप्रभूतैस्त्रिधा विशेषाः स्युः ।
सूक्ष्मास्तेषां नियताः मातापितृजा निवर्तन्ते ॥ ३९ ॥

sūkṣmā mātāpitṛjāḥ saha prabhūtais tridhā viśeṣāḥ syuḥ /
sūkṣmās teṣāṃ niyatāḥ mātāpitṛjā nivartante // 39 //

Subtle, born of mother and father, and elemental are the three specific types; of these, the subtle are permanent, [whereas those] born of mother and father are corruptible.[20]

40 पूर्वोत्पन्नमसक्तं नियतं महदादिसूक्ष्मपर्यन्तम् ।
संसरति निरुपभोगं भावैरधिवासितं लिङ्गम् ॥ ४० ॥

pūrvotpannam asaktaṃ niyataṃ mahadādisūkṣmaparyantam /
saṃsarati nirupabhogaṃ bhāvair adhivāsitaṃ liṅgam // 40 //

The *liṅga* is already existent, unrestricted, permanent, comprising 'the great' and the rest, down to the subtle;[21] wandering without enjoyment, endowed with dispositions (*bhāva*s).

41 चित्रं यथाश्रयमृते स्थाण्वादिभ्यो विना यथा छाया ।
तद्वद्विना विशेषैर्न तिष्ठति निराश्रयं लिङ्गम् ॥ ४१ ॥

citraṃ yathāśrayam ṛte sthāṇvādibhyo vinā yathā chāyā /
tadvad vinā viśeṣair na tiṣṭhati nirāśrayaṃ liṅgam // 41 //

Just as there is no picture without a support and no shadow without a post or suchlike, so the *liṅga* does not exist without the support of the specific.

42 पुरुषार्थहेतुकमिदं निमित्तनैमित्तिकप्रसङ्गेन ।
प्रकृतेर्विभुत्वयोगान्नटवद्व्यवतिष्ठते लिङ्गम् ॥ ४२ ॥

puruṣārthahetukam idaṃ nimittanaimittikaprasaṅgena /
prakṛter vibhutvayogān naṭavad vyavatiṣṭhate liṅgam // 42 //

This *liṅga*, motivated for the sake of *puruṣa*, by means of the association of causes and effects, and due to its connection with the manifestness of *prakṛti*, performs like a dancer.

43 सांसिद्धिकाश्च भावाः प्राकृतिका वैकृताश्च धर्माद्याः ।
दृष्टाः करणाश्रयिणः कार्याश्रयिणश्च कललाद्याः ॥ ४३ ॥

sāṃsiddhikāś ca bhāvāḥ prākṛtikā vaikṛtāś ca dharmādyāḥ /
dṛṣṭāḥ karaṇāśrayinaḥ kāryāśrayiṅaś ca kalalādyāḥ // 43 //

The dispositions, [namely] *dharma* and the rest, both natural and acquired, are perceived to abide in the instrument, and the embryo and so forth abide in the object (or effect, *kārya*).

44 धर्मेण गमनमूर्ध्वं गमनमधस्ताद्भवत्यधर्मेण ।
ज्ञानेन चापवर्गो विपर्ययादिष्यते बन्धः ॥ ४४ ॥

dharmeṇa gamanam ūrdhvaṃ gamanam adhastād bhavaty adharmeṇa /
jñānena cāpavargo viparyayād iṣyate bandhaḥ // 44 //

By means of virtue (*dharma*) there is movement upwards, by means of non-virtue (*adharma*) there is movement downwards; by means of knowledge liberation is attained, and bondage is due to the opposite.

45 वैराग्यात् प्रकृतिलयः संसारो भवति राजसाद्रागात् ।
ऐश्वर्यादविघातो विपर्ययात्तद्विपर्यासः ॥ ४५ ॥

vairāgyāt prakṛtilayaḥ saṃsāro bhavati rājasād rāgāt /
aiśvaryād avighāto viparyayāt tadviparyāsaḥ // 45 //

Prakṛti's dissolution occurs as a result of non-attachment, wandering[22] is due to attachment, which is impulsive; removal of obstructions is due to masterfulness, the reverse of that is due to the opposite.

46 एष प्रत्ययसर्गो विपर्ययाशक्तितुष्टिसिद्ध्याख्यः ।
गुणवैषम्यविमर्दात् तस्य च भेदास्तु पञ्चाशत् ॥ ४६ ॥

eṣa pratyayasargo viparyayāśaktituṣṭisiddhyākhyaḥ /
guṇavaiṣamyavimardāt tasya ca bhedās tu pañcāśat // 46 //

This is the emergence of mental phenomena (*pratyaya*), comprising delusion, weakness, contentment and excellence; and these are divided into fifty kinds according to the respective imbalance of the *guṇa*s.

47 पञ्च विपर्ययभेदा भवन्त्यशक्तिश्च करणवैकल्यात् ।
अष्टाविंशतिभेदा तुष्टिर्नवधाष्टधा सिद्धिः ॥ ४७ ॥

pañca viparyayabhedā bhavanty aśaktiś ca karaṇavaikalyāt /
aṣṭāviṃśatibhedā tuṣṭir navadhāṣṭadhā siddhiḥ // 47 //

There are five kinds of delusion, and twenty-eight kinds of weakness due to defects in the instrument; contentment is ninefold, excellence eightfold.

48 भेदस्तमसो ऽष्टविधो मोहस्य च दशविधो महामोहः ।
तामिस्रो ऽष्टादशधा तथा भवत्यन्धतामिस्रः ॥ ४८ ॥

bhedas tamaso 'ṣṭavidho mohasya ca daśavidho mahāmohaḥ /
tāmisro 'ṣṭādaśadhā tathā bhavaty andhatāmisraḥ // 48 //

There are eight kinds of dullness, and also of perplexity, ten kinds of great perplexity; depression is eighteenfold, as is intense depression.

49 एकादशेन्द्रियवधाः सह बुद्धिवधैरशक्तिरुद्दिष्टा ।
सप्तदश वधा बुद्धेर्विपर्ययात्तुष्टिसिद्धीनाम् ॥ ४९ ॥

ekādaśendriyavadhāḥ saha buddhivadhair aśaktir uddiṣṭā /
saptadaśa vadhā buddher viparyayāt tuṣṭisiddhīnām // 49 //

Impairments to the eleven capacities[23] along with *buddhi* are said to constitute weakness; impairments to *buddhi* are seventeen, due to the opposites of contentment and excellence.

50 आध्यात्मिकाश्चतस्रः प्रकृत्युपादानकालभाग्याख्याः ।
बाह्या विषयोपरमात् पञ्च नव तुष्टयो ऽभिमताः ॥ ५० ॥

ādhyātmikāś catasraḥ prakṛty upādānakālabhāgyākhyāḥ /
bāhyā viṣayoparamāt pañca nava tuṣṭayo 'bhimatāḥ // 50 //

Nine modes of contentment are distinguished; four are internal, concerning respectively disposition (or natural constitution, *prakṛti*), acquisition, time and fortune; five are external, due to abstinence from [sensory] objects.

51 ऊहः शब्दो ऽध्ययनं दुःखविघातास्त्रयः सुहृत्प्राप्तिः ।
दानं च सिद्धयो ऽष्टौ सिद्धेः पूर्वो ऽङ्कुशस्त्रिविधः ॥ ५१ ॥

ūhaḥ śabdo 'dhyayanaṃ duḥkhavighātās trayaḥ suhṛtprāptiḥ /
dānaṃ ca siddhayo 'ṣṭau siddheḥ pūrvo 'ṅkuśas trividhaḥ // 51 //

The eight ways of attaining excellence are: reasoning, [reception of] verbal instruction, study, eradication of the threefold distress, friendliness, and generosity; the previous three[24] are hindrances to excellence.

52 न विना भावैर्लिङ्गं न विना लिङ्गेन भावनिर्वृत्तिः ।
लिङ्गाख्यो भावाख्यस्तस्माद्द्विविधः प्रवर्तते सर्गः ॥ ५२ ॥

na vinā bhāvair liṅgaṃ na vinā liṅgena bhāvanir vṛttiḥ /
liṅgākhyo bhāvākhyas tasmād dvividhaḥ pravartate sargaḥ // 52 //

Without the dispositions (*bhāva*s) the *liṅga* cannot operate, and without the *liṅga* the dispositions cannot operate; therefore a dual emergence proceeds, distinguishable as *liṅga* and disposition.

53 अष्टविकल्पो दैवस्तैर्यग्योनश्च पञ्चधा भवति ।
मानुषकश्चैकविधः समासतो भौतिकः सर्गः ॥ ५३ ॥

aṣṭavikalpo daivas tairyagyonaś ca pañcadhā bhavati /
mānuṣakaś caikavidhaḥ samāsato bhautikaḥ sargaḥ // 53 //

There are eight varieties of divine beings and five of [non-human] natural beings; mankind is singular; such, in brief, is the elemental realm (*sarga*).

54 ऊर्ध्वं सत्त्वविशालस्तमोविशालश्च मूलतः सर्गः ।
मध्ये रजोविशालो ब्रह्मादिस्तम्बपर्यन्तः ॥ ५४ ॥

ūrdhvaṃ sattvaviśālas tamoviśālaś ca mūlataḥ sargaḥ /
madhye rajoviśālo brahmādistambaparyantaḥ // 54 //

The upper realm is pervaded by luminosity (*sattva*), and the base is pervaded by opacity (*tamas*); the middle is pervaded by activity (*rajas*); [such is the case] from Brahmā down to a blade of grass.

55 तत्र जरामरणकृतं दुःखं प्राप्नोति चेतनः पुरुषः ।
लिङ्गस्याविनिवृत्तेस्तस्माद्दुःखं स्वभावेन ॥ ५५ ॥

tatra jarāmaraṇakṛtaṃ duḥkhaṃ prāpnoti cetanaḥ puruṣaḥ /
liṅgasyāvinivṛttes tasmād duḥkhaṃ svabhāvena // 55 //

Puruṣa, consciousness, acquires there the suffering created by decay and death until its deliverance from the *liṅga*; hence one's own nature is associated with distress.

56 इत्येष प्रकृतिकृतो महदादिविशेषभूतपर्यन्तः ।
प्रतिपुरुषविमोक्षार्थं स्वार्थ इव परार्थ आरम्भः ॥ ५६ ॥

ity eṣa prakṛtikṛto mahadādiviśeṣabhūtaparyantaḥ /
pratipuruṣavimokṣārthaṃ svārtha iva parārtha ārambhaḥ // 56 //

This *prakṛti*-creation, from the great down to the specific elements, is for the sake of the liberation of each *puruṣa*, for the other's benefit as though for its own.

57 वत्सविवृद्धिनिमित्तं क्षीरस्य यथा प्रवृत्तिरज्ञस्य ।
पुरुषविमोक्षनिमित्तं तथा प्रवृत्तिः प्रधानस्य ॥५७॥

vatsavivṛddhinimittaṃ kṣīrasya yathā pravṛttir ajñasya /
puruṣavimokṣanimittaṃ tathā pravṛttiḥ pradhānasya // 57 //

Just as the profusion of unknowing (*ajña*) milk brings about the nourishment of the calf, so the profusion of *pradhāna* brings about the liberation of *puruṣa*.

58 औत्सुक्यनिवृत्त्यर्थं यथा क्रियासु प्रवर्तते लोकः ।
पुरुषस्य विमोक्षार्थं प्रवर्तते तद्वदव्यक्तम् ॥५८॥

autsukyanivṛttyartham yathā kriyāsu pravartate lokaḥ /
puruṣasya vimokṣārthaṃ pravartate tadvad avyaktam // 58 //

Just as [in] the world actions are performed for the purpose of removing [i.e. fulfilling] a desire, so does the unmanifest perform for the purpose of the liberation of *puruṣa*.

59 रङ्गस्य दर्शयित्वा निवर्तते नर्तकी यथा नृत्यात् ।
पुरुषस्य तथात्मानं प्रकाश्य विनिवर्तते प्रकृतिः॥५९॥

raṅgasya darśayitvā nivartate nartakī yathā nṛtyāt /
puruṣasya tathātmānaṃ prakāśya vinivartate prakṛtiḥ // 59 //

Just as, having displayed herself before the gaze of the audience, the dancer desists from dancing, so *prakṛti* desists, having manifested herself to *puruṣa*.

60 नानाविधैरुपायैरुपकारिण्यनुपकारिणः पुंसः।
गुणवत्यगुणस्य सतस्तस्यार्थमपार्थकं चरति ॥६०॥

nānāvidhair upāyair upakāriṅy anupakāriṇaḥ puṃsaḥ /
guṇavatya guṇasya satas tasyārtham apārthakaṃ carati // 60 //

She, being endowed with the *guṇas*, moves without any benefit [to herself] for the sake of *puṃs* (i.e. *puruṣa*), who, being without *guṇas*, does not reciprocate.

61 प्रकृतेः सुकुमारतरं न किञ्चिदस्तीति मे मतिर्भवति ।
या दृष्टास्मीति पुनर्न दर्शनमुपैति पुरुषस्य ॥६१॥

prakṛteḥ sukumārataraṃ na kiñcid astīti me matir bhavati /
yā dṛṣṭāsmīti punar na darśanam upaiti puruṣasya // 61 //

In my view there is no one more tender than *prakṛti*, who, saying 'I have been seen,' never again comes into *puruṣa*'s sight.

62 तस्मान्न बध्यते ऽद्धा न मुच्यते नापि संसरति कश्चित् ।
संसरति बध्यते मुच्यते च नानाश्रया प्रकृतिः॥ ६२॥

tasmān na badhyate 'ddhā na mucyate nāpi saṃsarati kaścit /
saṃsarati badhyate mucyate ca nānāśrayā prakṛtiḥ // 62 //

No one, then, is bound, nor released, nor wanders; it is *prakṛti*, in its various abodes (*āśrayā*), that wanders, and is bound and released.

63 रूपैः सप्तभिरेव तु बध्नात्यात्मानमात्मना प्रकृतिः ।
सैव च पुरुषार्थं प्रति विमोचयत्येकरूपेण ॥ ६३॥

rūpaiḥ saptabhir eva tu badhnāty ātmānam ātmanā prakṛtiḥ /
saiva ca puruṣārthaṃ prati vimocayaty ekarūpeṇa // 63 //

Prakṛti binds herself by herself with the use of seven forms; and, for the sake of each *puruṣa*, liberates herself by means of one form.[25]

64 एवं तत्त्वाभ्यासान्नास्मि न मे नाहमित्यपरिशेषम् ।
अविपर्ययाद्विशुद्धं केवलमुत्पद्यते ज्ञानम् ॥ ६४॥

evaṃ tattvābhyāsān nāsmi na me nāham ity apariśeṣam /
aviparyayād viśuddhaṃ kevalam utpadyate jñānam // 64 //

Thus, from the assiduous practice of that-ness, the knowledge arises that 'I am not,' 'not mine,' 'not I'; which [knowledge], being free of delusion, is complete, pure, and singular.

65 तेन निवृत्तप्रसवामर्थवशात् सप्तरूपविनिवृत्ताम् ।
प्रकृतिं पश्यति पुरुषः प्रेक्षकवदवस्थितः स्वच्छः॥ ६५॥

tena nivṛttaprasavām arthavaśāt saptarūpavinivṛttām /
prakṛtiṃ paśyati puruṣaḥ prekṣakavad avasthitaḥ svacchaḥ[26] // 65 //

Then *puruṣa*, abiding [in itself] like a spectator, sees *prakṛti*, who has returned to inactivity and retreated from the seven forms due to her purpose being complete.

66 दृष्टा मयेत्युपेक्षक एको दृष्टाहमित्युपरमत्यन्या ।
सति संयोगे ऽपि तयोः प्रयोजनं नास्ति सर्गस्य ॥ ६६॥

dṛṣṭā mayety upekṣaka eko dṛṣṭāhamity uparamaty anyā /
sati saṃyoge'pi tayoḥ prayojanaṃ nāsti sargasya // 66 //

'I have seen her,' says the spectating one; 'I have been seen,' says the other, desisting; although the two remain in conjunction, there is no initiation of [further] emergence.

67 सम्यग्ज्ञानाधिगमाद् धर्मादीनामकारणप्राप्तौ ।
तिष्ठति संस्कारवशात् चक्रभ्रमिवद्धृतशरीरः॥ ६७॥

samyagjñānādhigamād dharmādīnāmakāraṇaprāptau /
tiṣṭati saṃskāravaśāt cakrabhramivad dhṛtaśarīraḥ // 67 //

Due to the attainment of perfect knowledge, virtue (*dharma*) and the rest have no impelling cause; [nevertheless,] the endowed body persists owing to the momentum of impressions, like a potter's wheel.

68 प्राप्ते शरीरभेदे चरितार्थत्वात् प्रधानविनिवृत्तौ ।
ऐकान्तिकमात्यन्तिकमुभयं कैवल्यमाप्नोति ॥ ६८॥

prāpte śarīrabhede caritārthatvāt pradhānavinivṛttau /
aikāntikam ātyantikam ubhayaṃ kaivalyam āpnoti // 68 //

Pradhāna being inactive, her purpose having been fulfilled, [*puruṣa*], upon separating from the body, attains aloneness (*kaivalya*), which is both singular and conclusive.

69 पुरुषार्थज्ञानमिदं गुह्यं परमर्षिणा समाख्यातम् ।
स्थित्युत्पत्तिप्रलयाश्चिन्त्यन्ते यत्र भूतानाम् ॥ ६९॥

puruṣārthajñānam idaṃ guhyaṃ paramarṣiṇā samākhyātam /
sthityutpattipralayāś cintyante yatra bhūtānām // 69 //

This esoteric knowledge of *puruṣa*'s goal, examining the existence, arising and dissolution of entities, has been expounded by the highest sage.

70 एतत् पवित्रमग्र्यं मुनिरासुरये ऽनुकम्पया प्रददौ ।
आसुरिरपि पञ्चशिखाय तेन च बहुधा कृतं तन्त्रम् ॥ ७०॥

etat pavitram agryaṃ munir āsuraye 'nukampayā pradadau /
āsurir api pañcaśikhāya tena ca bahudhā kṛtaṃ tantram // 70 //

The quiet monk first passed on this supreme means of purification, compassionately, to Āsuri; Āsuri, again, to Pañcaśikha, and by him the teaching was widely distributed.

71 शिष्यपरम्परयागतमीश्वरकृष्णेन चैतदार्याभिः ।
संक्षिप्तमार्यमतिना सम्यग्विज्ञाय सिद्धान्तम् ॥ ७१ ॥

śiṣyaparamparayāgatam īśvarakṛṣṇena caitad āryābhiḥ /
saṃkṣiptam āryamatinā samyag vijñāya siddhāntam // 71 //

Communicated along a lineage of disciples, this has been thoroughly expounded in *āryā* metre by the noble-minded Īśvarakṛṣṇa, attainer of ultimate knowledge.

72 सप्तत्यां किल ये ऽर्थास्ते ऽर्थाः कृत्स्नस्य षष्टितन्त्रस्य ।
आख्यायिकाविरहिताः परवादविवर्जिताश्चापि ॥ ७२ ॥

saptatyāṃ kila ye 'rthās te 'rthāḥ kṛtsnasya ṣaṣṭitantrasya /
ākhyāyikāvirahitāḥ paravādavivarjitāś cāpi // 72 //

The topics of the seventy [verses] are indeed those of the entire 'sixty doctrines' (*ṣaṣṭitantra*), though excluding illustrative stories and the consideration of opposing views.[27]

APPENDIX B

Diagrammatic representation of classical Sāṃkhya's metaphysical schema

NB: Arrows indicate direction of conditionality. 2 plus the presence of 1 is the necessary condition for all the manifest principles (i.e. 3–25). 3 is the necessary condition for 4, which is in turn the necessary condition for 5–20. 16–20 together constitute the necessary condition for 21–25.

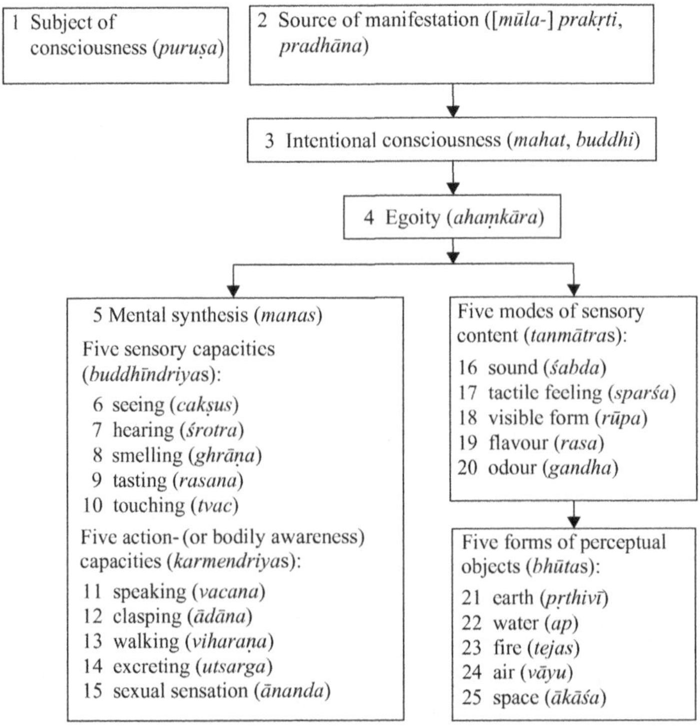

GLOSSARY OF KEY SANSKRIT TERMS

(In English alphabetical order)

abhāva	non-being, non-existent; unmanifest (cf. *asat*)
abhimāna	the thought of (being a) self (cf. *ahaṃkāra*)
abhyāsa	sustained practice, applying oneself to a task
adhyavasāya	discernment, ascertainment (syn. *buddhi*)
advaita	non-dual, non-dualism
ahaṃkāra	'I-maker', egoity (cf. *abhimāna*)
aiśvarya	(possessing the qualities) of īśvara; masterfulness
ajñāna	non-knowledge, ignorance (cf. *avidyā*, *viparyaya*)
ākāśa	space
aliṅga	unmarked, unmanifest (syn. *avyakta*)
anādi	beginningless
ānanda	intense pleasure, bliss
ananta	unending, infinite, eternal (syn. *nitya*)
anātman	not-self; inessential
anitya	non-eternal, temporal
antaḥkaraṇa	inner instrument, comprising buddhi, ahaṃkāra and manas
anugraha	'pulling up'; grace; providence
anuśāsana	exposition
ānvīkṣikī	philosophical inquiry
ap/āpas	water; liquidity
aparigraha	'not grasping around', non-covetousness
apavarga	liberation, fulfilment (syn. *kaivalya*, *mokṣa*)
āraṇyaka	'of the forest'; teachings composed by/for forest-dwelling ascetics (third part of śruti)
artha	end, meaning, purpose, sake; object
asaṃprajñāta	supra-cognitive
asat	formally non-existent; unmanifest (cf. *abhāva*)
aṣṭāṅga	eight-limbed, eightfold
āstika	orthodox

ātman	self, essence, essential nature
avidyā	misperception; false knowledge (cf. *ajñāna*, *viparyaya*)
avikṛti	uncreated, unmanifested
aviśeṣa	non-specific, unparticularized
avyakta	unmanifest (syn. *aliṅga*; cf. *mūlaprakṛti*)
bāhya(-karaṇa)	outer instrument, comprising the ten indriyas
bhakti	devotion
bhāṣya	commentary, exegesis
bhāva	being, existent; disposition, psychological characteristic
bheda	piercing, splitting, separation
bhoga	experience, enjoyment
bhoktṛ	enjoyer, experient
bhūta	being, element
bīja	seed (of mental processes and patterns of behaviour; syn. *saṃskāra*); monosyllabic mantra
brahman	ultimate ground, absolute principle
brāhmaṇa	ritual ceremony; instructive text for the performance of rituals (second part of śruti); person who performs rituals
buddhi	awareness-of, discernment, intentional consciousness (syn. *adhyavasāya*, *mahat*)
buddhīndriya	sense-capacity; sensation
cakra	wheel; energy centre where two or more nāḍīs conjoin or intersect
cetas, cetana	consciousness
cit, citi	consciousness, awareness
citiśakti	consciousness-power
citta	mind; thinking
cittamātra	mind-only, consciousness-only (associated with Yogācāra Buddhism) (syn. *vijñānavāda*)
darśana	vision, viewpoint, seeing; philosophical system (cf. *śāstra*, *tantra*)
dhāraṇā	holding, fixing; concentration
dharma	order; righteousness, virtue
dhyāna	meditation, intense contemplation
diś	space; place
draṣṭṛ	seer
draṣṭṛtva	'seer-ness', consciousness, awareness
dṛśi	seeing
dṛśimātra	seeing alone, mere seeing; awareness
dṛśya	the seen, seeable
duḥkha	distress, dissatisfactoriness

guṇa	strand, quality, constituent
guru	heavy; spiritual preceptor
haṭha	forceful, strong, vigorous
hiraṇyagarbha	golden germ/seed
indriya	capacity, power
īśa, īśvara	lord, master, deity (cf. *aiśvarya*)
jña	knower (syn. *puruṣa*)
jñāna	knowledge, cognition
kaivalya	aloneness, solitariness, absoluteness (cf. *apavarga, kevala*)
kāla	time
karaṇa	instrument, capacity; the antaḥ- and bāhya-karaṇa combined
kārikā	distich, stanza
karman	action, work, deed
karmendriya	action-capacity; capacity for sensation of bodily activity
karuṇā	compassion
kārya	effect; manifestation
kevala	alone, absolute, singular (cf. *kaivalya*)
kleśa	affliction; mental defect
kriyā	activity
kumbhaka	retention (of breath, prāṇa) (syn. *prāṇāyāma*)
kuṇḍalī, kuṇḍalinī(-śakti)	'she-who-is-coiled'; serpent power
laghu	light (not heavy)
liṅga	cipher, sign; composite of the manifest principles from buddhi to the tanmātras (i.e. excluding only the five bhūtas)
liṅgamātra	mere mark (syn.? *mahat*)
mahat	great one, the great (syn. *buddhi*)
manas	mentation; synthesizing aspect of mind
mantra	sacred sound or thought, recited (audibly or inaudibly) as an object of meditation
māyā	creative power; illusion, magic power
mokṣa, mukti, vimokṣa	release, liberation (syn. *apavarga, kaivalya*)
mūla	root, foundation, base
mūlaprakṛti	fundamental producer/productivity (cf. *avyakta*)
nāḍī	channel, flow; conduit of prāṇa
nirbīja	without seed (i.e. without saṃskāras)
nirguṇa	without qualities, unmanifest
nirodha	cessation
nitya	eternal (ambiguously: everlasting *or* atemporal) (syn. *ananta*)
niyama	restraint

pāda	chapter, part (lit. foot, leg)
pariṇāma	'bending around'; transformation, modification
pradhāna	primordial source (syn. *prakṛti*)
prajñā	insight, knowledge
prakāśa	shining forth, illumination
prakṛti	creative source, producer; cf. Latin *prōcreātrix* ('mother') (syn. *pradhāna*)
prakṛtilaya	dissolution of (or into) prakṛti
prāṇa	breath; vital energy
prāṇāyāma	extended retention of prāṇa; breath-holding (syn. *kumbhaka*)
pratiprasava	return to the source or original state
pratyaya	mental content, phenomenon, representation
pravacana	pronouncement, verbal presentation
pravṛtti	engagement, activity
pṛthivī	earth
puruṣa	self; person
rajas	activity, energy
rūpa	form; nature; appearance
sa-	[prefix] with
śabda	word, language, speech, sound
sākṣin	witness
śakti	power, energy; feminine pole of the supreme principle, esp. as conceived in Tantrism
samādhi, samāpatti	mental absorption
saṃhitā	collection (of teachings or mantras); first part of śruti
saṃkalpa	resolve, determination, idea
saṃkhyā	number
sāṃkhya	counting, enumeration; philosophical system
saṃnyāsa	renunciation
saṃprajñāta	cognitive, 'with cognition'
saṃskāra	unconscious or preconscious mental content (such as a memory); cause of habit-patterns (cf. *bīja*, *vāsanā*)
saṃyoga	confusion; conjunction (esp. of puruṣa and prakṛti)
sarga	emergence, surgence, effusion; manifestation
śarīra	body
ṣaṣṭitantra	'sixty doctrines'; name of an ancient Sāṃkhya text (or of several such texts)
śāstra	doctrine; system of philosophy (syn. *tantra*; cf. *darśana*)
sat	real, formally existent, manifest
satkārya	'a formally-existent [entity] is an effect'

sattva	being-ness, existence; capacity to manifest (in the *YS*, syn. *buddhi*)
sāttvika	possessing the quality of sattva
śīla	nature, character
sphoṭa	spurt, burst, erupt
sphoṭavāda	theory that the meaning of a word 'bursts forth' in the mind (rather than being conveyed *via* its linguistic correlate)
śruti	'that which is heard', revealed doctrine; traditionally divided into four categories: Saṃhitā, Brāhmaṇa, Āraṇyaka, and Upaniṣad
sthiti	steadiness, stability
sthūla	gross, coarse; perceptible
sūkṣma	subtle; imperceptible
śūnya	devoid of manifest content, empty
sūtra	thread; apothegm
sva	one's own, oneself
svāmin	self-possessor, owner
tamas	darkness; limitation
tāmasa	possessing the quality of tamas
tanmātra	'that-alone'; sense-content
tantra	doctrine (syn. *śāstra*); text (lit. warp, loom)
tarka	reflection, inquiry
tattva	'that-ness', existence; principle
tejas	fire; heat, light
traiguṇya	three-stranded (cf. *guṇa*)
triguṇa	three strands (cf. *guṇa*)
upaniṣad	'sitting near to'; esoteric text; fourth part of śruti
vāc	voice, speech
vaidika	Vedic (i.e. belonging to, or in conformity with, the Vedas)
vairāgya, virāga	non-attachment, dispassion
vāsanā	memory trace (cf. *saṃskāra*)
vastu	object; entity (cf. *artha*, *viṣaya*)
vāyu	air, wind; gaseousness
veda	knowledge, vision; sometimes used synonymously with *śruti*, while at other times denoting merely the Saṃhitā portion
vedānta	'end of the Veda'; collective term for the Upaniṣads; philosophical systematization of Upaniṣadic teachings
vijñāna/vijñapti	awareness, consciousness; special knowledge, discernment

vijñānavāda	consciousness(-only) view, associated with Yogācāra Buddhism (syn. *cittamātra*, *vijñaptimātratā*)
vikalpa	intuition without an objective basis; imaginative conception
vikṛti	created, manifested
vimokṣa	(see *mokṣa*)
viparyaya	opposite, inversion; misapprehension, delusion (cf. *ajñāna*, *avidyā*)
viṣaya	object, phenomenon, manifest entity (cf. *artha*, *vastu*); domain
viśeṣa	special, specific, differentiated
vitarka	special reflection
viveka	discrimination, discernment
vivekakhyāti	discriminating vision
vivekin	discerning one
vṛtti	whirl, turning; activity; mental activity; subcommentary
vyakta	manifest
yantra	device; symbolic diagram
yoga	union; soteric discipline
yogin	experienced practitioner of yoga

NOTES

INTRODUCTION

1 The practice of chanting the *Yogasūtra* was revived in the twentieth century by the scholar and yoga teacher Tirumalai Krishnamacharya, who died in 1989 at the age of 101. During a stay in Chennai (Tamil Nadu) in 1999 I learnt to recite the *Yogasūtra*'s first chapter (*Samādhi-pāda*) from E. R. Gopalakrishnan, who had been one of Krishnamacharya's disciples.
2 In particular it echoes the title of H. J. Paton's *Kant's Metaphysic of Experience* (1936).
3 See Larson 1979: 196, and Radhakrishnan 1927, II: 274. These passages are both discussed further in Chapter 6 (pp. 108–10, 129 ff.).
4 A list of the editions and translations of these texts that I have consulted is included in the Bibliography (Primary Sources A).
5 See, for example, Larson and Bhattacharya (1987: 227): 'most of the older historical and philosophical treatments of Sāṃkhya are now outdated and require extensive revision.'
6 I am not alone in regarding Kantian and phenomenological philosophy as relevant to the understanding of Sāṃkhya and Yoga. J. N. Mohanty, for one, has remarked that: 'an Indian philosopher... may turn to western philosophy in order to make sense of some obscure doctrine in Indian thought. For example, one may make sense of the Sāmkhya order of evolution by invoking some parts of Kantian epistemology' (2001: 86–87).
7 In most cases I use 'Yoga' (with an uppercase 'Y') to indicate the classical system, in both its practical and theoretical aspects, and 'yoga' (with a lowercase 'y') to indicate the generic category of religious and therapeutic regimens that fall under this head. I freely admit that there will be certain cases where it is not obvious which of these two lexical options should be taken.

1 AN HISTORICAL OVERVIEW OF SĀṂKHYA AND YOGA

1 These include: Dasgupta 1922: ch. 7; Frauwallner 1973, I: ch. 6; and Radhakrishnan 1927, II: chs 4 and 5.
2 Most commonly in such studies it is Sāṃkhya that is treated as the primary subject, with Yoga taking a subordinate place. See, for example, Chakravarti 1975; Gopal 2000; Johnston 1937; Keith 1949.
3 'Of the different systems of philosophical thought that evolved in ancient India, the Sāṃkhya is perhaps the most important and the oldest one' (Mainkar 1972: 1). 'The Sāṃkhya–Yoga philosophy is perhaps the oldest philosophical thought and discipline that has come down to us as a sacred heritage. There may be differences of opinion among scholars regarding the source of the Sāṃkhya–Yoga philosophy but its antiquity is never disputed' (Sen Gupta 1982: ix).

4 An exception is John Davies, who considers the *Sāṃkhyakārikā* itself to contain not merely the most ancient *Indian* system but 'the first recorded system of philosophy' (1894: 101).
5 The dating of the Upaniṣads has become bound up with the whole 'Āryan invasion' imbroglio, and is thus an area of intense historical and political controversy (which I do not wish to enter into here). Those who deny that the Vedas were composed by a people who had migrated to India from the north sometime around 1500 BCE tend to suggest that the first Upaniṣads are earlier than 900 BCE. See, for example, Feuerstein, Kak and Frawley (1995: 96): 'The *Aranyakas* and the *Upanishads*, by [our] reckoning, should belong to the second millennium B.C.'
6 Chakravarti (1975: 34) uses precisely this metaphor.
7 See van Buitenen 1957a, esp.: 19–21. Cf. also pp. 115–16 below.
8 Cf. *YS* 1.2: 'Yoga is the cessation of mental activities'; and 3.1: 'Concentration (*dhāraṇā*) is the binding of the mind (*citta*) to a [single] place.'
9 The term *brahman* has many senses. The one that is invoked here is not to be confused with that in which *brahman* stands for the principle of absolute being.
10 Cf. *YS* 1.24: 'The lord (*īśvara*) is a special self (*puruṣa-viśeṣa*)'; and 2.45: 'By contemplating the lord (*īśvara-praṇidhāna*), spiritual absorption (*samādhi*) is attained.'
11 Cf. *SK* 55: '*cetanaḥ puruṣaḥ*'.
12 Cf. *SK* 37: '... buddhi brings about the enjoyment of puruṣa...'; *YS* 2.18: 'The seen (*dṛśya*), being of the character of illumination, activity and stability... is for the sake of enjoyment and liberation.'
13 The six limbs named at *Maitr*. 6.18 are: control of vital breath (*prāṇāyāma*), withdrawal of [attention from] sensation (*pratyāhāra*), meditation (*dhyāna*), fixing of attention (*dhāraṇā*), reflection (*tarka*) and absorption (*samādhi*). The last five limbs of the classical eight-limbed system are: *prāṇāyāma, pratyāhāra, dhāraṇā, dhyāna* and *samādhi* (*YS* 2.29). Although *tarka* does not feature in this latter list, it should be noted that *vitarka* ('special reflection') is among the four forms of cognitive absorption given at *YS* 1.17, and *savitarka* ('with special reflection') is cited as a stage of meditative 'confluence' (*samāpatti*) at *YS* 1.42.
14 Cf. for example, *Haṭhayogapradīpikā* 4.69 ff.
15 For a survey of the Purāṇas on this matter, see Dasgupta 1940: 496–511. (Because the dates of the Purāṇas are in most cases unknown, it is often difficult to say whether the parts of their content that relate to Sāṃkhya and Yoga should be regarded as 'pre-' or 'post-classical'.)
16 More comprehensive treatments, in addition to the piece by Dasgupta mentioned in the previous note, include: Chakravarti 1975: 42–64; Edgerton 1944, II: ch. 8; Johnston 1937; Keith 1949: ch. 3, and *passim*.
17 Instances of *brahman*'s being used as a synonym of *prakṛti* include the commentaries of Gauḍapāda, Māṭhara and Paramārtha on *SK* 22. Alternatively, under *SK* 1, Māṭhara describes Sāṃkhya as 'presenting the knowledge of brahman', thereby implying that brahman is identical to the self (*puruṣa*). Furthermore, in its commentary on *SK* 22, the *YD* treats *brahman* synonymously with both *mahat* and *īśvara*.
18 See, for example, *MBh* XII.218.14, in which, as Chakravarti notes (1975: 26), 'Āsuri in the assembly of the followers of Kapila is found to explain *brahman*, who is one and immutable and seen in diverse forms.'
19 I have in mind here Daya Krishna's 1968 article 'Is Īśvarakṛṣṇa's *Sāṃkhya-Kārikā* Really Sāṃkhyan?'.
20 A virtually identical statement is made by Yājñavalkya at *MBh* XII.304.2 (cf. Edgerton 1965: 325).
21 The following remark of Edgerton's makes a similar point with regard to the *MBh* more generally and to the Upaniṣads: 'It appears, then, that Sāṃkhya means in the Upaniṣads

and the Epic simply the way of salvation by knowledge, and does not imply any system of metaphysical truth whatever' (1924: 32). Edgerton is, I think, right to associate *sāṃkhya* with salvific knowledge, but he fails to give due emphasis to its sense as 'renunciation', and this failure is especially noticeable in his translation of the *Gītā*, where he consistently (but, in my view, inappropriately) renders *sāṃkhya* as 'reason-method' (see Edgerton 1944, I: 33, 53).

22 Cf. Radhakrishnan and Moore (1957: 227): 'The doctrine [of Cārvāka] is called Lokāyata, as it holds that only this world (*loka*) exists and there is no beyond.'

23 Cf. Cowell and Gough (1882: 2 n. 1): 'Lokáyata may be etymologically analysed as "prevalent in the world" (*loka* and *áyata*).'

24 Vācaspati includes a list of the sixty doctrines (see Jhâ 1896: 113–14).

25 Cf. for example, *Viṣṇu-purāṇa* I.2.18 ff. (Upreti 1986); and *Nāradīya-purāṇa* 1.3.

26 At both *Śvet.* 4.12 and 5.2 the ruling deity is said to behold a first-born. In the former of the two verses the first-born is named as *hiraṇya-garbha* ('golden seed'), and in the latter, he is named *kapila* ('tawny', 'reddish brown').

27 These features include such things as the use of the term 'limb' (*aṅga*) to denote a component of the system of practice, and the classification of types of meditation according to whether they are performed with or without an 'external object' (*bahirtattva*).

28 A concise summary of the scholarly debate on this matter is provided by Larson in *EIP*4: 167–69.

29 Cf. Chakravarti 1975: 158; *EIP*4: 13, 15, 149.

30 This alternative etymology of 'Vārṣagaṇya' derives from a work by Kuei-chi, a direct disciple of Hsüan-tsang (seventh century CE). It is discussed by Takakusu (1933) and under 'Vārṣagaṇya' in *EIP*4: 132 f.

31 Cf. *EIP*4: 134 f.

32 Suryanarayana Sastri's position is reported by Mainkar (1972: 33) and in *EIP*4: 151.

33 See the respective introductions to the entries on *Sāṃkhyasaptativṛtti* and *Māṭharavṛtti* in *EIP*4.

34 Ramakrishna Kavi (1927) alternatively proposes that the composer of the *Jayamaṅgalā* was a certain (non-Buddhist) named Śaṅkara-ārya, who lived in the fourteenth century and was also the author of the *Yogasūtrabhāṣyavivaraṇa*, which several other scholars (e.g. Hacker 1968 and Mayeda 1979) have attributed to the renowned Vedāntin Śaṅkarācārya (cf. discussion in Halbfass 1991: ch. 6). There is little, however, to support Kavi's claims, and therefore Chakravarti's appears to be the most sober and plausible assessment of the available evidence. (Incidentally, the author of the introduction to the entry on *Jayamaṅgalā* in *EIP*4 (p. 271), who I presume to be R. S. Bhattacharya (since the summary of the text that follows the introductory passage is by him), mistakenly identifies Ramakrishna Kavi with Gopinath Kaviraj, thereby giving the impression that the latter put forward two radically conflicting theories.)

35 A selection of legends traditionally associated with Patañjali was brought together by Rāmabhadradīkṣita in his *Patañjalicarita*, which, according to Śrīvatsa Rāmaswāmī (2000: 28), was composed 'over three hundred years ago' (i.e. 1700 CE or earlier), but which others have placed as 'not... earlier than the eighteenth century' (Dasgupta 1922: 230). Rāmaswāmī provides a summary of the legends in ch. 2.

36 See Woods 1914: xv ff. My own view on whether the *YS* contains an anti-idealist polemic will be presented in Chapter 4.

37 Those which appear exclusively in the fourth chapter include: *buddhi* (4.21, 22), *citi* (4.22), *citiśakti* (4.34), *dharmamegha* (4.29) and *vāsanā* (4.8, 24). *Prakṛti* occurs twice there (4.2, 3), while its only other appearance is as part of the conjunct expression *prakṛtilaya* ('dissolution in [or of] prakṛti') at 1.19. Also *vastu* is particularly prevalent in a series of sūtras in the fourth chapter (4.14–17), whereas it appears only once elsewhere (1.9), its sense of 'object', 'thing', or 'entity' more often being conveyed by *artha*.

38 For an attempt to analyse the *Yogasūtra* into its constituent parts, see Hauer 1958.
39 Cf. for example: *Brahmasūtra* I.1.1; *Pūrvamīmāṃsāsūtra* I.1.1; *Vaiśeṣikasūtra* I.1.1. Cf. also Śaṅkara's *BSBh* I.1.1: 'although its meaning may differ, the word *atha* nevertheless serves the purpose of auspiciousness (*maṅgala*) merely by being heard'.
40 I am here placing in question Dasgupta's assertion that '*unlike any other work*' the *Mahābhāṣya* and *Yogasūtra* both begin 'in a similar manner' (1922: 232, emphasis added).
41 Feuerstein (1980: 119), somewhat uncharitably, holds Vācaspati to be entirely to 'blame for this whole confusion'.
42 Cf. *YS* 1.42, where *savitarka-samāpatti* is defined as a mental state in which śabda, artha and jñāna remain intermixed (*saṃkīrṇa*). Here *jñāna* can be regarded as serving the same semantic function as *pratyaya* in *YS* 3.17, that is, to mean 'representation' (or 'intuition' in the Kantian sense), although it is terminological inconsistencies such as this that ought to alert us to the likelihood of the *YS*'s being a composite text.
43 A concise summary of the views of various scholars on the *YS*'s date is provided by Whicher (1998: 42).
44 Feuerstein (1979: 25) approvingly quotes Hauer to this effect, and reiterates the view in the Preface to his own major work on classical Yoga (1980: ix–x).
45 The difficulty pertaining to Vācaspati's dates has been outlined above.
46 So loose is the translation that Dasgupta (1922: 233) suspects that it must be based on a non-standard version of the *YS*. A useful summary of the Al-Bīrūnī work is provided by Gopal (2000: App. 3).
47 Cf. note 34 above, and also Rukmani (1992: *passim*) and Leggett (1990: 39).
48 David White takes this view (1996: 20) and quotes Filliozat's remark that 'the Samkhyan concepts, like those of Āyurveda, are part and parcel of the intellectual baggage common to all Indian thinkers'.
49 Abhinavagupta, *Parātrīśikālaghuvṛtti*, comment on verse 1 (Muller-Ortega 1989: 87, 253 n. 19).
50 Cf. ibid., comments on verses 9 and 1 (Muller–Ortega 1989: 88, 254 n. 21; 87, 253 n. 19).
51 The *Śivasaṃhitā* (2.1–4), for example, instructs us to picture 'Mount Meru within the body, surrounded by seven islands; there are rivers, seas, mountains, fields and also guardians of the fields [etc.]'.
52 'While the vital breath (*prāṇa*) remains in the body, death is vanquished. The full containment of the air (*vāyu*) is kevala-kumbhaka' (*Gheraṇḍasaṃhitā* 5.89; cf. Vasu 1976: 113; the same verse appears as 5.84 in Digambarji and Gharote 1997: 140). Cf. *Haṭhayogapradīpikā* 2.71 ff.
53 Such works are too numerous to mention individually here. A fairly comprehensive list of known Sāṃkhya texts is given in *EIP*4: 14–18. It is worth remarking that a significant proportion of the commentaries composed since the beginning of the twentieth century have been subcommentaries upon, or attempts to paraphrase, Vācaspati's *TK*.

2 THE RELATION BETWEEN THE TWO DARŚANAS

1 Garbe's position concerning the non-Brahmanic origin of Sāṃkhya is presented in various places. See, for example, 1917: 5 f., 54–59. Critical treatments of his position are provided by Keith (1949: 53, 58–59) and Gopal (2000: 47–48).
2 The existence of overlapping and disputed portions of the three later categories (i.e. Brāhmaṇas, Āraṇyakas and Upaniṣads) obliges us to regard the fourfold division as merely approximate rather than as an exact reflection of the textual reality.
3 Cosmogonism, Deussen tells us, is the view that the self (*ātman*) produces the universe from out of itself and then 'enters into it as soul' (Deussen 1919: 238).

4 Deussen would presumably have regarded the distinction between deism and theism in a similar light to Kant, who notes that 'the deist represents this being [i.e. God] merely as a *cause of the world* (whether by the necessity of its nature or through freedom, remains undecided), the theist as the *Author of the world* [who can be conceived as "a supreme intelligence"]' (*CPR* A631/B659–60; original emphasis, my square brackets).

5 Cf. Zimmer (1953: 280): 'These two are regarded in India as twins, the two aspects of a single discipline. Sāṇkhya provides a basic theoretical exposition of human nature, enumerating and defining its elements, analyzing their manner of co-operation in the state of bondage (*bandha*), and describing their state of disentanglement or separation in release (*mokṣa*), while Yoga treats specifically of the dynamics of the process of disentanglement, and outlines practical techniques for the gaining of release, or "isolation" (*kaivalya*).'

6 Some scholars (e.g. Frauwallner and Chakravarti) have speculated that 'Pātañjala-Sāṃkhya' might be a continuation of the school associated with Vārṣagaṇya and Vindhyavāsin (cf. *EIP*4: 12–13). It is unlikely that, on the basis of the evidence currently available, such speculations could be either validated or disproven.

7 One of those who concurs with it is Macdonell, who states that, 'In order to make his system more acceptable, Patanjali introduced into it the doctrine of a personal god, but in so loose a way as not to affect the system as a whole' (1900: 396–97).

8 *Die Sāṃkhya-Philosophie: Eine Darstellung des indischen Rationalismus* (Leipzig: Haessel, 1894; 2nd edn 1917).

9 The term *sāṃkhya* is commonly taken to mean 'enumeration'. Radhakrishnan assumes it, therefore, to imply mathematical reasoning. The derivation of *sāṃkhya* from *saṃkhyā* ('number') has been challenged by Gopal (2000: 38–39), who proposes that it is instead derived from *khyā*, the root of *khyāti* (which Gopal says means exposition). In my view relatively little flows from these etymological disputes.

10 *vyakta-avyakta-jña-vijñāna.*

11 The relevant sūtras are *YS* 2.26, 28; 3.52, 54; 4.26, 29.

12 Whicher's interpretation of Yoga's goal will receive further attention in Chapter 7.

13 The terms *vitarka* and *vicāra* at *YS* 1.17, and *savitarka* at *YS* 1.42, are commonly assumed to denote the presence of conceptual (and hence in a very general sense, rational) thought in early stages of meditative absorption (*saṃprajñāta*, *samāpatti*).

14 *kleśa-karma-vipāka-āśayair aparāmṛṣṭaḥ puruṣa-viśeṣa īśvaraḥ* (*YS* 1.23).

15 See, for example, *YS* 2.18, where the purpose of 'the seeable' (*dṛśya*) is said to be 'experience and liberation' (*bhoga-apavarga*); and *SK* 55–60, where prakṛti is portrayed as bringing forth the profusion of manifest categories (which together produce experience) for the sole purpose of liberating each puruṣa.

16 *tatra niratiśayaṃ sarva-jña-bījam* (*YS* 1.24).

17 See, for example, *YS* 2.20: 'The seer, [that is] seeing-alone, though pure, perceives the mental content' (*draṣṭā dṛśimātraḥ śuddho'pi pratyayānupaśyaḥ*).

18 *sa eṣa pūrveṣām api guruḥ kālena-anavacchedāt* (*YS* 1.25).

19 For an attempt to interpret Īśvara's guiding role in terms of mere passive presence, see, for example, Oberhammer (1964).

20 See esp.: *YS* 2.18; *SK* 12, 13.

21 See, for example, *SK* 21: 'that conjunction [gives rise to] the creative surge' (*saṃyogas tatkṛtaḥ sargaḥ*); *YS* 4.2: 'Transformation into another mode of existence (*jāti*) is due to the overflow (*āpūra*) of prakṛti'.

22 At *YS* 4.25–34 an account is given of the dissolution of phenomena and their conditions that ensues upon the dawning of awareness of the distinction between seer and seeable. Cf. *SK* 65, where prakṛti 'returns to inactivity' (*nivṛtta-prasava*), having been seen by puruṣa and hence having completed her purpose.

23 *YS* 2.21: 'The essence of the seeable is, indeed, [to serve] the purpose of that [seer]' (*tad artha eva dṛśyasya-ātma*); *SK* 60: 'She [prakṛti] moves without any benefit [to herself] for the purpose of *puṃs* [i.e. puruṣa].'
24 *Tanmātra* does not translate easily into English. A literal rendering would be 'a measure of that' or 'merely that'. The standard translation within the context of Sāṃkhya is 'subtle element', which (for reasons I shall explain in Chapter 6) I find unsatisfactory. What *tanmātra* seems to denote in Sāṃkhya is one or other of the five *modes of sensory content* (i.e. the visual content of a seeing episode, the sound of a hearing episode, the flavour of a tasting episode, and so on) and hence I shall in most instances use constructions such as this to translate the term.
25 Vyāsa in fact calls it *asmitā* ('I-am-ness') rather than *ahaṃkāra* (lit. 'I-maker'), but this is merely a terminological nuance.
26 *SK* 3 is discussed more fully in Chapter 5.

3 ANALYSING EXPERIENCE: KANTIAN AND PHENOMENOLOGICAL PHILOSOPHY

1 I am here using the standard method of referring to Kant's *Prolegomena to Any Future Metaphysics* by giving the volume and page numbers as they appear in the edition of Kant's complete works edited by Benno Erdmann (1911).
2 See, for example, *CPR* A108–9: 'Appearances are the only objects that can be given to us immediately.'
3 Aristotle 1987: 5 ff.; cf. Ross 1995: 22 ff.
4 Schopenhauer writes in the Preface to his magnum opus: 'Kant's philosophy is . . . the only one with which a thorough acquaintance is positively assumed in what is to be here discussed. But if in addition to this the reader has dwelt for a while in the school of the divine Plato, . . . [and] has also already received and assimilated the divine inspiration of ancient Indian wisdom, then he is best of all prepared to hear what I have to say' (1969, I: xv).
5 Schopenhauer was preceded by, for example, G. E. Schulze in his *Aenesidemus* (acknowledged by Schopenhauer at 1969, I: 436; cf. Gardner 1999: 330).
6 Albeit with certain modifications to the Kantian position. Crucially, Schopenhauer regards the functioning of the understanding as non-conceptual, and to consist in the 'referring' of sensations to their cause or respective causes. What is more, Schopenhauer thinks, at least on the face of it, that this referring function, alongside the forms of space and time, is all that is needed for an explanation of representational experience (cf. for example, Schopenhauer 1969, I: 444–45).
7 Kant borrowed the term 'phenomenology' from J. H. Lambert (1988 [1764]), and uses it in, for example, the *Metaphysical Foundations of Natural Science* (2004 [1786]), the fourth chapter of which is entitled 'Metaphysical Foundations of Phenomenology'.
8 I am talking here about Husserl's *The Crisis of European Sciences and Transcendental Phenomenology* (1970b), only a small part of which was published during his lifetime (see Husserl 1936).
9 Spiegelberg, for example, refers to Brentano as 'Forerunner of the Phenomenological Movement' (Spiegelberg 1969, I: 27).
10 Cf. Bell (1990: 8–9): 'There is . . . a pronounced solipsistic tendency in Brentano's early thought, a tendency which . . . exercised a profound influence on Husserl's philosophy, both early and late.'
11 Brentano's *Psychology from an Empirical Standpoint* was first published in 1874. Husserl is generally held to have formulated the phenomenological reduction or *epoché* in or around 1905 (cf. Mohanty 1995: 74).

12 Cf. Brentano (1973: 30): 'Indeed, turning one's attention to physical phenomena in our imagination is, if not the only source of our knowledge of laws governing the mind, at least the immediate and principal source.'

13 It has been argued, for example by Twardowski (1977 [1894]), that a weakness of Brentano's theory is his conflation of the *content* with the *object* of an intentional act. Although I accept the validity of this further distinction, for my present purposes it is not necessary to dwell upon it.

14 Husserl discusses this issue at some length at §15 of his Fifth Investigation (1970a: 569–76).

15 See, for example, Husserl (1970a: 574 n. 1): 'I identify the pain-sensation with its "content", since I do not recognize peculiar sensing acts. Naturally I reject Brentano's doctrine that presentive acts, in the term of acts of feeling-sensation, underlie acts of feeling.'

16 Somewhat confusingly, vol. 1 of the English edition of *Logical Investigations* contains vol. 1 *plus* the Introduction and first two Investigations of vol. 2 of the German edition.

17 Cf. Chisholm (1981: 1): 'Despite Brentano's general repudiation of the Kantian philosophy, his views about what he calls "external perception" are very similar to Kant's.' Brentano, however, leans further towards scientific realism than does Kant, since he thinks that physics can tell us something, albeit not very much, about the nature of mind-transcendent reality: 'We can say that there exists something which, under certain conditions, causes this or that sensation. We can probably also prove that there must be relations among these realities similar to those which are manifested by spatial phenomena... But this is as far as we can go' (Brentano 1973: 19).

18 'Phenomenological transcendental idealism has presented itself as a *monadology*, which, despite all our deliberate suggestions of Leibniz's metaphysics, draws its content purely from phenomenological explication of the transcendental experience laid open by transcendental reduction' (Husserl 1977: 150). It should be noted that Husserl's use of the term 'transcendental' is not in accordance with Kant's. From a Kantian perspective, a phrase such as 'transcendental experience', for example, is an oxymoron. There remains no concensus, but much speculation, on precisely what Husserl did mean by the term.

19 More will be said about both the *sat-kārya-vāda* ('existent effect theory') and the *guṇa*s in Chapter 5.

4 THE IMPUTATION OF REALISM

1 Cf. Crispin Wright's description of realism as 'a syndrome, a loose weave of separable presuppositions and attitudes' (1993: 3–4).

2 The following quotations exemplify this line of interpretation: 'It should be noted... that *puruṣa* is not a direct cause of the appearance of the manifest world. The *puruṣa* is simply present, and this presence functions as a kind of <u>catalyst</u> in releasing the casual [*sic*] process of transformation in the *mūlaprakṛti*' (Larson 1979: 173, cf. 191; Larson 1987: 49). '*Prakṛti* is dynamic, self-efficient, and self-contained, but it is not self-sufficient since it acts only when <u>catalyzed</u> by the presence of *puruṣa*' (Organ 1975: 211). '[T]he development of *prakriti* can occur only through the <u>excitation</u> of *purusha*' (Reese 1996: 675). 'It is the transcendental influence of *puruṣa* that <u>rouses</u> *prakṛti* from her slumber at the advent of a new cycle of creation' (Chakravarti 1975: 229). [My underlining in all quotations.]

3 'By *substance* we can understand nothing other than a thing which exists in such a way as to depend on no other thing for its existence. And there is only one substance which can be understood to depend on no other thing whatsoever, namely God' (Descartes 1985, I: 210).

4 The following passage from Schopenhauer vents an opinion widely endorsed by materialists: '[Substance] is an exceedingly superfluous concept, because its only true content already lies in the concept of matter, beside which it contains only a great void. This void can be filled up by nothing except the surreptitiously introduced secondary species *immaterial substance*; and that concept was formed solely to take up this secondary species. Strictly speaking, therefore, the concept of substance must be entirely rejected, and that of matter be everywhere put in its place' (Schopenhauer 1969, I: 491).

5 It should be noted, however, that Radhakrishnan denies that prakṛti is to be regarded as straightforwardly 'material' (ibid.: 261–62, 274).

6 See, for example, Eliade (1969: 19): '[Patañjali] assumes a knowledge of the analysis of Substance, laboriously pursued by Sāṃkhya authors.' Cf. Larson (1987: 71): 'For Sāṃkhya the apparent subject (namely, internal awareness in terms of *buddhi*, *ahaṃkāra*, *manas*, and so forth) is really substance (*mūlaprakṛti* as *triguṇa*).'

7 Some philosophers have distinguished between materialism and physicalism on the grounds that, whereas the former stands for material monism, the latter admits scientific entities that are not strictly 'material', such as energy and natural laws (see e.g. A. D. Smith 1993: 225–26). I am not convinced by this distinction, and nor, it would seem, are most materialists and physicalists, who tend to use the terms interchangeably and view their position as monist. (Whether it *is* strictly monist is a question that cannot be pursued here.)

8 '[A] thought comes when "it" wants, not when "I" want; so that it is a *falsification* of the facts to say: the subject "I" is the condition of the predicate "think"' (Nietzsche 1990: 17).

9 See, for example, the following description of a self by E. J. Lowe: 'a self is conceived to be a subject of consciousness, a being capable of thought and experience and able to engage in deliberative action. More crucially, a self must have a capacity for *self-consciousness*' (entry under 'self' in Honderich 1995: 816). Cf. Thomas Reid (1941: 203): 'Whatever this self may be, it is something which thinks, and deliberates, and resolves, and acts, and suffers.'

10 The crucial term in this connection is *adhyavasāya*, with which buddhi is identified at *SK* 23, and which constitutes part of the definition of 'perception' (*dṛṣṭa*) at *SK* 5. *Adhyavasāya* may be translated as 'ascertainment' or 'determination'. Zimmer defines it more broadly: 'buddhi is the faculty of what is known as *adhyavasāya*, that is, "determination, resolution, mental effort; awareness, feeling, opinion, belief, knowledge, discrimination, and decision"' (1953: 320).

11 See, for example: Conze 1967: 78, 121; Murti 1960: 316 ff.; C. D. Sharma 1964; Chatterjee 1975: 45.

12 'There are indeed passages in the Yogācāra literature which apparently support an idealistic monism. But I maintain that the entire system, when understood in terms of realistic pluralism, makes better sense and that, therefore, even those passages which apparently support idealistic monism have to be interpreted in accordance with realistic pluralism' (Kochumuttom 1982: 1; punctuation slightly amended).

13 See Lusthaus 2002. Although Lusthaus gives his book on Yogācāra the title *Buddhist Phenomenology*, and claims throughout to be challenging the metaphysical idealist interpretation of this system, what he in fact seems to be doing is trying to replace the monistic reading with one according to which perceptual objects, but not pre-conceptual sensations, are viewed as mental constructions. In his concluding remarks, for example, he states that, for Yogācāra, 'While [physical] objects are admissible as conventionalisms, in more precise terms there are no chairs, trees, etc. These are *merely words and concepts* by which we gather and interpret discrete sensations that arise moment by moment in a causal flux. These words and concepts are mental projections' (p. 540, my emphasis).

14 Keith, for example, asserts that 'the *Yoga Sūtra* seems to attack the doctrine of the Vijñānavādins, and... therefore it is probably not older than the third century A.D., and probably is younger' (Keith 1949: 66).
15 That is, a mere appearance, and hence not genuine knowledge at all.
16 *pratyupasthitam idaṃ svamāhātmyena vastu.*
17 See, for example, Berkeley 1962: 66–68; cf. 109. More sophisticated versions of the doctrine have been developed by recent idealists, such as Timothy Sprigge (see esp. Sprigge 1983: 113 ff.).
18 Trans. Gambhirananda 1965: 16. The Sanskrit reads: *na vastuyāthātmyajñānaṃ puruṣabuddhyapekṣam / kiṃ tarhi vastutantram eva tat /*
19 Trans. *idem*: 419. Sanskrit: *na copalabhyamānasyaivābhāvo bhavitumarhati.*
20 Cf. Feuerstein (1989a: 134): 'Patañjali's position is that consciousness and objective reality belong to different levels of existence. He points out that the same object is experienced by many consciousnesses...' [It should be remembered that Feuerstein uses 'consciousness' to translate *citta*, not *puruṣa*.]
21 Woods, for example, has 'levels-of-existence' (1914: 323); Feuerstein, similarly, has 'levels [of existence]' (1989a: 134, Feuerstein's brackets); and Prasāda has 'ways-of-being' (1912: 290). Chapple and Viraj stick with 'path' (1990: 113), as does Taimni (1961: 410), although Taimni also lists 'way of being' as an alternative translation. Leggett's 'categories' (1992: 389) is somewhat different, but not inappropriate.
22 At *YS* 2.19 the levels are listed in ascending order, and hence the 'first' is, ontologically speaking, the most dependent whereas the fourth is the least.

5 THE NATURE OF PRAKṚTI

1 Schopenhauer, for example, writes that 'A peculiar feature of pedantry and narrowness in the Samkhya is the system of numbers, the summation and enumeration of qualities and attributes.' But adds: 'This, however, appears to be customary in India, for the very same thing is done in the Buddhist scriptures' (1974b, II: 400).
2 For examples of the 'catalyst' analogy, see p. 193 n. 2 above. The terms 'vitalized' and 'intelligized' are used mainly by Sen Gupta, who seems to think that they are equivalent, as is evident from the following passage: '*puruṣa* is intelligising *Prakṛti* by its mere sannidhi so as to make Nature fit for the creation of this world. *Puruṣa* is not therefore becoming an agent: *puruṣa* is the principle of consciousness that vitalizes *Prakṛti* by its mere existence' (1982: 84; punctuation slightly amended, underlining added; cf. pp. 76, 132, 140). Larson refers to buddhi's being ' "intelligized" by consciousness' in a discussion of Vācaspati's reflection (*pratibimba*) theory (Larson 1987: 82).
3 H. T. Colebrooke was probably the first to notice the resemblance (1873 [1st edn, 1837] I: 244), and it has subsequently been referred to by, for example, Schopenhauer (1974b, I: 64), Radhakrishnan (1927, II: 274 n. 1), and Larson (1987: 635–6 n. 47).
4 Trans. from the Latin by Myra Uhlfelder.
5 This passage is part of an explanation of *satkāryavāda* in an 'Explanation of Technical Terms' (Āraṇya 1977: 27). The passage was probably written by Āraṇya's translator and editor, Jajneswar Ghosh, although based on Āraṇya's own views.
6 This reading of the opposite of *anitya* as 'atemporal' (rather than, say, 'everlasting'), and of the opposite of *avyāpin* as 'non-spatial' (rather than 'pervasive'), is not especially controversial, although certain interpreters prefer to qualify it by saying, for example, that unmanifest prakṛti is 'outside of *ordinary* space and time' (Larson 1987: 49, emphasis added).
7 See note 6 above.

8 *Rūpa* can also be translated as 'form'. However, this would have to be understood very loosely when applied to unmanifest prakṛti, since something that is unmanifest cannot, strictly speaking, have a form. 'Nature' is therefore a preferable translation in the present context.

9 As Dasgupta puts it: 'Causation as Satkāryavāda (the theory that the effect potentially exists before it is generated by the movement of the cause)...' (1922: 257). Cf. Larson (1987: 43): '...the theory that the effect preexists in the cause in a potential state (*satkāryavāda*).'

10 'The effect is in the material cause in a latent form' (Organ 1975: 212).

11 Cf. Lusthaus (1998: 463): '[*Prakṛti*] is often mistranslated as "matter" or "nature" – in non-Sāṅkhyan usage it does mean "essential nature" – but that detracts from the heavy Sāṅkhyan stress on *prakṛti*'s cognitive, mental, psychological and sensorial activities.'

12 'Perhaps it is not too far-fetched to compare the *guṇas* with the atoms of modern nuclear physics, which are described as localisations of fields' (Feuerstein 1980: 35). 'The sattva, rajas, and tamas guṇas of this ancient system of thought [i.e. Sāṃkhya–Yoga] are *essentially similar* to the current concepts of the proton, electron, and neutron' (Catalina 1968: 127; square brackets and emphasis added).

13 *SPBh* 1.61: 'Sattva and the others [i.e. rajas and tamas] are substances, not specific qualities, for they combine and separate, and [themselves possess] levity, mobility, heaviness and other such qualities' (*sattvādīni dravyāṇi na vaiśeṣikā guṇāḥ saṃyogavibhāgavattvāt laghutvacalatvagurutvādidharmakatvāc ca*). Cf. *YV* 2.18.

14 Cf. Jacobsen (1999: 258): 'One should not confuse the material principle in Sāṃkhya and Yoga texts with the most common modern Western idea of nature by which nature means the beings and things that exist in the natural world.'

15 B. K. Matilal expresses a similar point when he observes that, 'If we have a clear understanding of the meaning of the philosophic term we are trying to translate, then it is expected that we shall be able to find a suitable term in the second language which will "retain" the original sense, provided, of course, such a term is available in the latter. But if the suggested term in the second language has certain shades of meaning that are not compatible with those of the original term, we should not recommend such a translation. For such an incautious translation is likely to generate confusion in the minds of those who are unacquainted with the first language' (1985: 320).

16 Cf. Peters (1967: 88): '*Hyle*, a purely Aristotelian term, does not have its origins in a directly perceived reality... but emerges from an analysis of change.'

17 Aristotle 1941: 235 (*Physics* 192a 31), trans. R. P. Hardie and R. K. Gaye.

18 I therefore reject the claim made by S. K. Maitra that 'The Sāṃkhya theory of experience... answers more nearly to the Aristotelian theory of a monistic becoming of an original primal matter than to the Kantian dualism of appearance and unknowable things-in-themselves' (quoted in Larson 1987: 641 n. 83, my ellipsis). While both the Aristotelian and Kantian theories can provide valid resources for comparison, it is the Kantian notion of the role of *a priori* forms in giving structure to formless content (and thereby making appearances possible), that seems especially fruitful when applied to the Sāṃkhyan categories.

19 Jacobsen may also be taking *SK* 10 into consideration, which, as I noted earlier in this chapter, can be interpreted as including the characterization of unmanifest prakṛti as 'non-spatial'.

20 The ambiguities in Kant's characterization of sensation as the matter of appearances are well discussed by Aquila (1982). One of Kant's most problematic statements on this issue is at A20/B34, where he says: 'I call that in the appearance which corresponds to sensation its *matter*...'. This leaves it unclear whether matter *is* sensation or merely something that *corresponds* to sensation.

21 Cf. p. 32 of the same work, where Feuerstein notes that the guṇas 'invite comparison with the "quantum packets" of modern nuclear physics'.

22 Digambarji *et al.* (1989: 38) elaborate this point as follows: 'Just as oil, a container, a wick, and a flame are brought together in such a way that a light is produced, lasts for some time and illumines objects, in the same way the three *Guṇa*s combine in such a manner that they prove useful for *Puruṣas*.'

23 Cf. Heidegger (1993: 76): 'Kant uses the term "appearance" in this twofold way. On the one hand, appearances are for him the "objects of empirical intuition," what shows itself in intuition. This self-showing (phenomenon in the genuine, original sense) is, on the other hand, "appearance" as the emanation of something that makes itself known but *conceals* itself in the appearance.'

24 *kālaḥ pacati bhūtāni kālaḥ saṃharate jagat / kālaḥ supteṣu jāgarthi kālo hi duratikramaḥ // vyaktāvyaktapuruṣāḥ trayaḥ padārthāḥ tena kālo'ntarbhūto'sti / sa hi vyaktaḥ /*

25 *nityau yau dikkālau tāvākāśaprakṛtibhūtau prakṛter guṇaviśeṣāveva*

26 *śabdajñānānupātī vastuśūnyo vikalpaḥ //*

27 Sanat Kumar Sen begs to differ on this point: 'the mere idea of alteration or transformation need not necessarily include the concept of time' (1968: 410–11). If he had bothered to explain how change can be considered to occur independently of time then there might be some grounds for taking this assertion seriously, but as no such explanation is given, the assertion looks to me very shaky indeed.

28 On this latter point see, for example, Patricia Kitcher (1990: 140): 'The various activities that are described in the [Transcendental] Deduction's account of how the mind influences (or might influence) what we know can only be understood temporally. They are processes and so take time. According to the [Transcendental] Aesthetic, however, the mind's activities *produce* time. So they cannot take place in time.'

6 THE EMERGENCE OF THE MANIFEST PRINCIPLES

1 By referring to the *Sāṃkhyakārikā* as 'esoteric' I mean merely that it was composed primarily for the purposes of instructing initiated disciples and is therefore likely to present interpretive difficulties for uninitiated readers.

2 Van Buitenen's vertical–horizontal model has subsequently been adopted by other interpreters. Cf. for example, Larson (1979: 179): 'The emergence or evolution of the sixteen [i.e. the ten indriyas plus manas, and the five tanmātras]... is not "vertical." It is, rather, "horizontal" – i.e., *ahaṃkāra* becomes or is transformed into mind, senses, subtle elements, etc.'

3 Cf. Suryanarayana Sastri 1948: 45 (and Larson 1979: 262): 'from this (association) creation proceeds'.

4 Cf. Radhakrishnan, who invokes the energy-conservation law to back up his claim that prakṛti cannot be a material substance: 'In spite of the things to which prakṛti gives rise, its substance is in no way diminished. The source of becoming is not exhausted by the things produced. No material thing can act without exhausting some of its latent energy. It is thus difficult to regard prakṛti as purely material in nature' (1927, II: 274). For my own part, I am doubtful about the legitimacy of basing a claim about a metaphysical theory upon a working hypothesis from theoretical physics.

5 Christian Lassen – whose Latin translation of the *Sāṃkhyakārikā* was first published at Bonn in 1832 – shows good judgement, I think, in rendering *adhyavasāya* (by which term *buddhi* is defined) as *intentio* (cited in Davies 1894: 56).

6 Davies exemplifies the standard view when he asserts that, 'In the system of Kapila [i.e. Sāṃkhya], everything connected in function with sensuous objects is as material as the objects themselves, being equally an emanation from Prakṛti' (1894: 18).

7 To me, the intelligibility of Jacobsen's full statement appears highly questionable: 'Sāṃkhya and Yoga are, one could say, materialistic on the top (but not in the ordinary

sense), and bottom, i.e., the ultimate material principle and gross material things such as water and air are non-conscious, and mental in the middle, i.e., *buddhi* and *ahaṃkāra* are mental material principles.'

8 'The ordinary sense of both words (i.e., *abhimāna* and *ahaṁkāra*) is *pride* and the technical import is the pride or conceit of individuality' (Colebrooke, in Colebrooke and Wilson 1837: 91, quoted in Chennakesavan 1980: 24).

9 This point, or one very similar to it, was persuasively made, before Kant and long before Schopenhauer, by Rousseau, who, as Safranski has noted, 'compared the "sensation of self" and the "perception" of the external world, and arrived at the conclusion that an individual could "have" a sensation only if he entered into the sensation of self; and since perceptions brought home what existed outside, while at the same time existing only in the medium of the sensation of the self, it followed that without a sensation of self there was no existence. Or the other way about: the sensation of self produced existence' (Safranski 1989: 110; cf. Rousseau 1995: bk 4). Cf. Schopenhauer: 'the necessity or need of *knowledge in general* arises from the plurality and *separate* existence of beings, from individuation' (1969, II: 274; original emphasis).

10 Cf. for example, Davies (1894: 61), Jhâ (1896: 66), Suryanarayana Sastri (1948: 51), and Larson (1979: 264). Larson later adopted the more act-oriented terms ('seeing', etc.) that I have used in my rendering of the verse; however, both editions of his translation of the *Sāṃkhyakārikā* contain the organ-terms.

11 It is noteworthy that the function of the genitals is represented as sexual pleasure, for interpreters still tend to assume that *procreation* is what these organs primarily stand for in the Sāṃkhya system (e.g. Larson 1987: 49).

12 Cf. Sheets-Johnstone (1998): 'Proprioception refers generally to a sense of movement and position. It thus includes an awareness of movement and position through tactility as well as kinesthesia, that is, through surface as well as internal events, including also a sense of gravitational orientation through vestibular sensory organs. Kinesthesia refers specifically to a sense of movement through muscular effort' (quoted in Gallagher 2005: 7, n. 3).

13 Radhakrishnan speaks of manas as 'suggesting alternative courses of action and carrying out the decrees of the will through the organs of action', but does not identify it with the will itself (1927, II: 269–70). Davies, meanwhile, denies that Sāṃkhya 'attributed volition to any form of matter [i.e. any form of prakṛti]' (1894: 56; my square brackets).

14 Cf. MW: 1126 (under 'Saṃ-kalpa'): 'conception or idea or notion formed in the mind or heart, (esp.) will, volition, desire, purpose, definite intention or determination or decision or wish for'.

15 Cf. for example, *GBh, TK*, and *YD* on *SK* 33.

16 Cf. Davies (1894: 19): 'From Ahaṅkāra . . . proceed the five subtle elements (*tanmātra*) which are the primary forms or essences of gross material things.'

17 Cf. p. 102 of the same work: 'Evolutionary passage, according to the Sāṁkhya-school, is simply the passage from the subtle to the gross. After the emergence of the gross elements, the process of evalution [*sic*] stops in the sense that the *pāñcabhautic* changes are simply changes from gross to more gross.' Balbir Singh adopts a similar continuum model to that of Sen Gupta, but without such a saturating application of the term 'subtle': 'At every stage the evolutes display their continuity with those of the preceding stage, so that there is no break, discontinuity, or gap' (1976: 132).

18 The expression 'subtle matter' does not actually occur in this passage (i.e. *Principles of Philosophy* III.52), but Descartes notes elsewhere (1985, I: 322 [*Description of the Human Body and of All its Functions* IV]) that what the description applies to can be called 'subtle matter'.

19 Monier-Williams considers the most likely verbal root of *sūkṣma* to be *siv*, 'to sew' (see entries under '*sūkshma*' and 'Sūci' in MW: 1240 and 1241), which indicates a close semantic and possibly etymological parallel with the Latin *subtīlis*.

20 At *YS* 1.44, 45; 2.10, 50; 3.25, 44; and 4.13.

21 Hence Whicher's neologism 'sattvification' (1998: 122, and passim). Cf. Chapple's 'subtilization' (1996: 122–23).

22 Vyāsa counts the tanmātras, ahaṃkāra, liṅgamātra, and aliṅga among the subtle objects, thereby apparently excluding manas, the ten indriyas, and the five bhūtas (*YBh* 1.45). Exclusion of the bhūtas is understandable, since it is generally in opposition to them (*qua* 'gross' or *sthūla*) that 'subtle' objects are defined; but why manas and the indriyas should also be left out is unclear.

23 '[The tanmātras] are... subtle, material essences or presuppositions with which perceptual and motor functioning correlate and through which certain aspects of the material world become differentiated' (Larson 1987: 50).

24 Cf. for example, MW (p. 434): 'a rudimentary or subtle element'; Woods (1914: 91, 148–49, and *passim*): 'fine element'; Eliade (1969: 21): 'the five "subtle" (potential) elements, the genetic seeds of the physical world'.

25 '[T]hese *tanmātras* give rise to atoms (*paramāṇu*) and molecules (*sthūlabhūtāni*; literally, "dense material particle"), which in turn give birth to vegetable organisms (*vrikṣa*) and animal organisms (*śarīra*). Thus man's body, as well as his "states of consciousness" and even his "intelligence," are all creations of one and the same substance' (Eliade 1969: 21).

26 It is again the traditional commentaries on *SK* 38 that are to be looked to for lists of the five bhūtas.

27 'Ākāśa corresponds in some respects to the ether of the physicists and in others to what may be called proto-atom (protyle)' (B. N. Seal, quoted in Dasgupta 1922: 253 n. 1).

28 Dasgupta explicitly rejects this line of interpretation, insisting that 'solidity, liquidity and gaseousness represent only an impermanent aspect of matter' (whereas the bhūtas are the constituents of matter *per se*) (1924: 166). Having assumed Sāṃkhya to be staunchly realist, however, he could only consider solidity, etc., in terms of mind-independent states of physical entities, and thus was not in a position to comment upon the kind of phenomenologically-oriented interpretation that I am proposing.

29 Guenther cites the following traditional Buddhist works: Buddhaghoṣa's *Aṭṭhasālinī* 4.3; Vasubandhu's *Abhidharmakośa* 1.12; and Asaṅga's *Abhidharmasamuccaya*, p. 3 (no bibliographical details given).

30 Cf. Gethin (1986: 36): 'What is clear... is the extent to which the early Buddhist account of rūpa [the collective term for the mahābhūtas] focusses on the physical world as experienced by a sentient being – the terms of reference are decidedly body-endowed-with-consciousness (*saviññānaka kāya*)' (my square brackets).

31 Larson supposes that 'tenfold' is here 'relating to the five senses and five actions' (1979: 266), which supposition presumably derives from a mistaken conflation on Larson's part between this tenfold set and the tenfold outer instrument mentioned in the following verse (*SK* 33).

32 Cf. Zimmer (1953: 320): 'Buddhi comprises the totality of our emotional and intellectual possibilities'; and also K. C. Bhattacharyya (1956, I: 274): 'buddhi is the manifest as such'.

33 See, for example, Bradley 1969: 465. Cf. William James's early notion of 'a single pulse of subjectivity' (1950, I: 278).

34 What Kant actually says is that the '*I think*... is the vehicle of all concepts' (*CPR* A341/B399). However, since on Kant's view concepts are in turn necessary for experience, the Sāṃkhya position on this point (as I interpret it) amounts to the same thing.

35 Cf. Suryanarayana Sastri (1948: 63–64): 'speech has sound (alone) for its object'.

36 *tatra śabdatanmātrād ākāśam / sparśatanmātrād vāyuḥ / rūpatanmātrāt tejaḥ / rasatanmātrād āpaḥ / gandhatanmātrāt pṛthivī* / In the *YD* the verses of the *SK* are broken down into short propositions, similar to sūtras. The passage quoted here is from the third part of the commentary on *SK* 38, hence the reference to '38c'. I have, in this respect, followed the critical edition of Wezler and Motegi (1998, I: 225). It should be noted that the *YD* has a complicated interpretation of the tanmātras, considering each of them to possess the 'quality' (*guṇa*) of each of the preceding ones. Thus tactility is held to possess the qualities both of itself and of sound, visual appearance to possess the qualities of visual appearance plus tactility and sound, and so on. I cannot, however, see any reason for attributing this theory to the *SK*.

37 Two main schemata of meditative absorption are presented in the *YS*. The first (at *YS* 1.17–18) distinguishes between cognitive (*saṃprajñāta-*) samādhi and the 'other' (*anya*) type, which is generally (following Vyāsa) taken to be 'supra-cognitive' (*asaṃprajñāta-*) samādhi. Cognitive samādhi is subdivided into four modes: (1) 'reflective' (*vitarka*); (2) 'refined reflective' (*vicāra*); (3) 'blissful' (*ānanda*); and (4) 'egoic' (*asmitā*, literally 'I-am-ness'). The second schema refers to samādhi 'with seed' (*sabīja* [*YS* 1.46]) and 'without seed' (*nirbīja* [*YS* 1.51]), the former type being subdivided (at *YS* 1.42–44) into: (1) 'absorption with reflection' (*savitarka-samāpatti*), (2) '~ without reflection' (*nirvitarka-samāpatti*), (3) 'with refined reflection' (*savicāra-samāpatti*), and (4) '~ without refined reflection' (*nirvicāra-samāpatti*). The two schemata, though differing in certain respects, share the basic structure of a system of gradual progression.

38 See, for example, *Bṛhad.* II.3.6, III.9.26, IV.2.4.

39 Another crucial verse in this regard is *SK* 37, where it is said that, due to buddhi's being responsible for 'bringing about' (*sādhayati*) all experience, it is thus also buddhi that 'discloses (*viśinaṣṭi*) the subtle [difference] between pradhāna and puruṣa'. Larson translates *viśinaṣṭi* as 'distinguishes' (1979: 267), thereby implying that buddhi is the subject of knowledge. Davies, similarly, renders it as 'discriminates' (1894: 72). Other possible translations, however, such as 'exposes' (Jhâ 1896: 77), 'reveals' (Suryanarayana Sastri 1948: 68), and my 'discloses' may be taken to represent buddhi merely as the medium of knowledge, not its possessor.

7 FREEDOM FROM EXPERIENCE

1 'To confuse (as many interpretations of yoga have unfortunately done) the underlining purificatory processes involved in the cessation of ignorance/afflicted identity as being the same thing as (or as necessitating the need for) a radical elimination of our psychophysical being – the prakṛtic vehicle through which consciousness discloses itself – is, I suggest, to misunderstand the intent of the *Yoga Sūtra* itself' (Whicher 2003: 62).

2 The quoted passage is from Āraṇya 1963: 123.

3 Cf. Larson (1999: 186): 'To be sure, "misidentification" is one important component in understanding the meaning of the term "*nirodha*," but the overwhelming textual evidence in all of its interpretive varieties and nuances is that Yoga, finally, is also a radical elimination of ordinary worldly awareness.'

4 Personal correspondence with the author, via e-mail, 25 April 2002. Compare Whicher's published remark that, 'If Patañjali's perception of the world of forms and differences had been destroyed or discarded, how could he have had such insight into Yoga and the intricacies and subtle nuances of the unenlightened state?' (1998: 291).

5 The classic illustration of the Buddha's anti-metaphysical approach occurs at *Majjhimanikāya* 1.483–88, the passage dealing with the 'inexpressibles' (Pali: *avyākata*). See, for example, Warren 1915: 123–28. For further references see Murti 1960: 36 n. 2.

6 The application of the terms *māyā* and *avidyā* in the Advaita Vedānta tradition is not consistent. In some instances the two terms appear to be used interchangeably, whereas in others *māyā* may be taken to denote empirical reality as perceived *under the influence of avidyā*. Even within the works commonly attributed to Śaṅkara there is a lack of consistency on this point (cf. Potter 1981: 79).

7 Potter, paraphrasing the view of Sacchidanandendra Sarasvati, notes that '*avidyā* in Śaṃkara is superimposition, whereas *māyā* is equivalent to *prakṛti* or *nāmarūpa*' (Potter 1981: 79).

8 See, for example, *GBh* 22: '*prakṛti, pradhāna, brahman, avyakta, bahudhātmaka*, and *māyā* are synonyms (*paryāyas*)'.

9 *anityāśuciduḥkhānātmasu nityaśucisukhātmakhyātir avidyā* //

10 I say 'implicitly cited' because the tāmasa modes of buddhi are not named directly, but are said to be the 'opposite' of the sāttvika modes, these latter being 'virtue (*dharma*), knowledge (*jñāna*), non-attachment (*virāga*), and masterfulness (*aiśvarya*)'.

11 That *viparyaya* can stand for precisely the sort of misperception that *avidyā* elsewhere denotes is illustrated by Ghosh in his summary of Āraṇya's *Sāṁkhyatattvāloka*, verse 34 (in Āraṇya 1977: xii): '*Viparyaya* is the reproduction in consciousness of a thing as other than what it is. To assume that the mind, sense-organs and the body constitute the Self is the fundamental *viparyaya*.'

12 Cf. Matilal (1985: 321): 'My main objection against both "nescience" and "ignorance" [as translations of *avidyā*] is that they express a predominantly negative meaning: "lack of knowledge" or "absence of knowledge".'

13 One among many examples of this tendency occurs in a passage from Ghosh (1977: 36), where 'the wise among us' are said to seek 'freedom from the excrescence of a limited personality' and 'the Divinity in them, the *Puruṣa*, who as the ultimate revealer of all appearance is certainly beyond the appearances called pleasure and pain'. The identity of 'the wise' becomes even more uncertain when Ghosh notes that, 'since His [i.e. puruṣa's] conjunction with *Prakṛti*, which results in transitory shows, is maintained by confusion between Him and the empirical ego, they cultivate clearness of insight (*samprajñāna*) that they may attain an effective knowledge of the difference between the two (*vivekakhyāti*)'. I would add simply that, if 'the wise among us' are not really 'empirical ego[s]', then they must be puruṣas, and hence their discovery of 'the Divinity in them' is nothing other than puruṣa's self-discovery (which fact remains unstated in Ghosh's ambiguous account).

14 Feuerstein's declaration that he is 'inclined to read this *sūtra* in the spirit of the preclassical tradition where *kṛta-artha* also denotes the person who has become the Self' (1980: 23) misses the point. Despite his choice of the expression '*become* the Self' – as opposed to, say, 'realized one's true nature *as* the Self' – I doubt whether Feuerstein would demur that the person concerned was in fact *already* the 'Self', and had simply not yet realized it. The situation is therefore equivalent to the 'many puruṣas' view, for if the Self can be realized by one person without such an event initiating the immediate realization of all other persons, *and yet those other persons are all equally 'the Self'*, then that Self must be admitted to be *multiple*.

15 Cf. Deussen (1919: 245): 'What philosophical mind can admit this thought [i.e. the multiple puruṣas doctrine]? The knowing subject is in me (*ahaṃ brahma asmi*) and nowhere else, for everything beside me is object, and for this very reason not subject.'

16 The duck–rabbit is a famous example of an image that can be viewed as two distinct things, but not simultaneously. Wittgenstein attributes it to Jastrow's *Fact and Fable in Psychology*, and includes it in his *Philosophical Investigations* (2001 [1953]: 165–66).

17 See, for example, Steven Katz (1978: 33): 'these images, beliefs, symbols, and rituals define, *in advance*, what the experience [the mystic] *wants to have*, and which he then does have, will be like' (original emphasis); '[t]he notion of unmediated experience seems, if not self-contradictory, at best empty' (ibid.: 26).

18 Forman probably derives the 'knowledge by acquaintance'–'knowledge about' distinction from William James's treatment of it (1950 [1890]: 221 f.), although James himself disclaims any originality on his own part, noting that 'Most languages express the distinction' (p. 221). Roughly the same distinction was advocated by Bertrand Russell in his essay 'Knowledge by Acquaintance and Knowledge by Description' (1917).

19 'The knowledge that I am aware… is not a matter of language, nor does it stand on the back of prior experiences. I *just know* directly and without complex reasoning that I am and have been aware. And I know it simply by virtue of being aware' (1998: 22, Forman's italics, my underlining).

20 At one place Katz suggests that the relation between 'experience' and 'beliefs' is reflexive – that is, that 'beliefs shape experience, just as experience shapes belief' (1978: 30) – but elsewhere he tends to exclusively prioritize the causal role of beliefs (concepts, expectations, etc.). See, for example, p. 46 of the same article: 'mystical experience is "over-determined" by its socio-religious milieu: as a result of his process of intellectual acculturation in its broadest sense, the mystic brings to his experience a world of concepts, images, symbols, and values which shape as well as colour the experience he eventually and actually has'.

21 When, for example, Katz says that 'in order to understand mysticism it is *not* just a question of studying the reports of the mystic after the experiential event but of acknowledging that the experience itself as well as the form in which it is reported is shaped by concepts' (1978: 26), the acknowledgement concerned has no philosophical basis beyond Katz's repeated assertion of epistemological constructivism; and an assertion, no matter how many times or with what degree of dogmatic fervour it is repeated, does not amount to an argument.

22 A vast quantity of research data already exist on this topic. A useful summary and assessment of them are provided by Shear and Jevning (1999).

23 Katz's credentials for interpreting the claims of Sāṃkhya and Yoga are placed in doubt by his statement that the former of these two systems 'understands the goal to be the perfection of the soul which does not lead to any form of *unio mystica* but rather to a splendid self-identity which, like God's perfection, is self-contained and isolated' (1978: 57–58, my underlining). An endnote to this statement invites the reader to 'see R. C. Zaehner, *Hinduism* (New York, 1962; Oxford, 1966), pp. 94 ff.', which suggests that Katz is not familiar with the primary Sāṃkhya material. Giving a terse description of Sāṃkhya's goal is no easy task, but 'perfection of the soul' is less helpful than most.

24 See, for example, the famous First Sermon, where the third enobling truth concerns the 'cessation of *dukkha*' rather than the attainment of something positive (*Saṃyuttanikāya* 5.420, in e.g. Thomas 1927: 87–88).

25 I am far from alone in taking this view, as the following remarks illustrate: 'all we can assert of it [i.e. the liberated self] is that it is contentless consciousness, not consciousness of itself or of object' (K. C. Bhattacharyya 1956, I: 196); 'The ultimate mystical experience in Sāṃkhya–Yoga results from the final elimination of all concepts, all thinking, all words, all feeling, all memory, and all perception. What is left, properly termed *innate*, is consciousness. It is not self-conscious and not symbolically conscious – just consciousness itself' (Pflueger 1998: 69–70).

26 I say '*almost* invariably' because *SK* 18 (discussed earlier in this chapter) constitutes an important exception.

8 CONCLUSION

1 See, for example, Balbir Singh (1976: 140): 'Sāṁkhya… believes the mere presence of *puruṣa* (*saṁnidhyamātra*) to be enough for *prakṛti* to start its evolutionary process. This… shows that all Indian systems are directly or indirectly committed to idealism,

despite the appearance, in some cases, to the contrary. In very unequivocal terms it means that the world exists because the spirit exists, and depends on it for both its evolution and its dissolution.' Although I concur with Singh's point about Sāṃkhya here, I would demur at the suggestion that we can draw conclusions about 'all Indian systems' from a fact about Sāṃkhya metaphysics alone.

2 The expression '*esse* is *percipi*' ('to exist is [merely] to be perceived') was used as a defining slogan of his idealist philosophy by the Irish philosopher George Berkeley (see e.g. Berkeley 1962: 66–68, 109).

3 See, for example, Deussen, who claims that 'monism is the natural standpoint of philosophy, and wherever dualism has appeared in its history it has always been the consequence of antecedent stress and difficulty, and as it were a symptom of the wane of the philosophising spirit', and that 'the dualism of... Sâṅkhya' is 'to be conceived as the consequence of a natural disintegration of the doctrine of the Upanishads' (1919: 244–45).

4 The phrase 'neutral monism' is due to Bertrand Russell, although he borrowed the concept from William James. 'The stuff of which the world of our pure experience is composed is, in my belief, neither mind nor matter, but something more primitive than either. Both mind and matter seem to be composite, and the stuff of which they are compounded lies in a sense between the two, and in a sense above them both like a common ancestor' (Russell, quoted in Bird 1986: 95). As a description of prakṛti, this would be fairly acceptable. But it still leaves the conscious *subject* entirely unaccounted for.

5 The 'unintelligib[ility]' of non-dualism has been noted by Frits Staal (1975: 4): 'there are certain metaphysical theories that can be said to be unintelligible in the sense that they try to point at what cannot be understood. Understanding requires duality, for example, if not multiplicity. Accordingly, in such philosophies as the Advaita Vedānta, according to which reality is non-dual, reality cannot be understood'.

APPENDIX A

1 The editions of Suryanarayana Sastri and Larson include a seventy-third kārikā, even though, since it appears only in the commentary of Māṭhara, it is likely to have been added by Māṭhara himself. I have, in any case, included this extra kārikā in Note 27.

2 Some editions have *prasiddhir* in place of *pratītir*. Both terms can have the sense of 'ascertaining' or 'accomplishing'.

3 The use of the ablative case can be ambiguous: its meaning can be either that (*a*) the *existence* of the proposition's subject is *due to* (or *caused by*, etc.) such-and-such factors, or (*b*) *due to* such-and-such factors we must *infer* that the subject exists. The first of these senses is ontological, whereas the second is epistemological. It is my view that this epistemological sense is to be regarded as primary also in subsequent kārikās, such as 15–19, although I have in most instances retained at least a degree of ambiguity in the translation in order to better reflect the original text.

4 Some editions read *avivekyādiḥ siddhas*; cf. Suryanarayana Sastri 1948: 33.

5 Jhâ's edition (1896: 33) has *kāryataḥ* ('effectiveness') in place of *śaktitaḥ* ('potency').

6 This kārikā does not stand on its own but must be read in conjunction with the following one.

7 Or: 'must be supposed to exist'.

8 *Sarga*, being etymologically close to 'surge' and 'surgence', often has the sense of flowing, spewing forth, emerging and so on. It can also, however, have the sense of a realm of existence (cf. *SK* 53, 54).

9 The fact that *prakṛti* is in the ablative case indicates that 'the great' (*mahat*) is in a relation of dependence upon it, although the nature of the dependence is not made explicit. Therefore, the interpolated 'comes' should not, in my view, be necessarily

assumed to denote material causation. The same applies to the relations between the other 'productive' and 'produced' manifest principles.

10 It would appear that 'source of the elements' (*bhūtādi*) is either an epithet of *ahaṃkāra* or an aspect thereof.

11 It is almost certainly the three members of the 'inner instrument' (*antaḥkaraṇa*) that are being referred to here (cf. *SK* 33), namely *buddhi*, *ahaṃkāra*, and *manas*. Larson thinks that 'the three' denotes 'the *buddhi*, *ahaṃkāra* and senses' (1979: 265), but I can see no basis for this view.

12 According to classical Indian physiology there are five main currents or winds which service different regions of the body. These are usually called, respectively: *prāṇa*, *apāna*, *samāna*, *udāna*, *vyāna*.

13 'The four' here is generally agreed to stand for 'the three' of the preceding kārikā plus any one of the sense-capacities.

14 The thirteen parts are 'the three' mentioned at *SK* 29 and 30 plus the sense-capacities and action-capacities (cf. *SK* 33).

15 That is, the five *tanmātra*s plus the five *bhūta*s. Larson asserts that 'tenfold' is here 'relating to the five senses and the five actions' (1979: 266), which assertion is presumably based on the fact that, in the following kārikā, the tenfold 'outer instrument' appears to comprise the sense- and action-capacities. Larson's view is untenable, however, since the sense- and action-capacities have already been included within the thirteenfold instrument, with which the tenfold object is here being contrasted.

16 I have given here a fairly literal translation of the phrase *trayasya viṣayākhyam*. Some other translators (e.g. Suryanarayana Sastri and Jhâ) try to make better sense of it by taking it to mean that the outer instrument makes objects known to the inner instrument. This may be a correct interpretation, but it requires some manipulation of the original text.

17 What seems to be meant here is that sensations are always present occurrences whereas 'inner' mental phenomena can concern the past (in remembering and retrospection) and the future (in anticipation and prospection) as well.

18 The 'specific' objects are the *bhūta*s and the 'non-specific' are the *tanmātra*s (cf. *K* 38).

19 In other words, the other four action-capacities involve the manifestation or production of all five modes of sensory content (*tanmātra*s).

20 It would appear that what is being referred to in this kārikā are three aspects of a person: the 'subtle' (or mental), the physical body, and the 'elemental' (or the forms of perceptual objects).

21 In this instance 'the subtle' would seem to denote the *tanmātra*s.

22 'Wandering' is a fairly literal translation of *saṃsāra*. It should be understood to mean 'wandering through life, and from one lifetime to another'. It implies rebirth.

23 That is, the five *buddhīndriya*s, five *karmendriya*s, plus *manas*.

24 That is, delusion (*viparyaya*), weakness (*aśakti*) and contentment (*tuṣṭi*).

25 The eight 'forms' (*rūpa*s) here are usually assumed to be 'dispositions' (*bhāva*s). It is at least equally likely, however, that they are the modes of *prakṛti* divided into the following categories: (1) *avyakta* (the unmanifest); (2) *buddhi*; (3) *ahaṃkāra*; (4) *manas*; (5) *buddhīndriya*s; (6) *karmendriya*s; (7) *tanmātra*s; and (8) *bhūta*s. It is when forms (2)–(8) dissolve into (1) that liberation occurs. This interpretation would also make more sense of *SK* 65.

26 There is considerable disagreement among the early commentaries over what the final word in this kārikā should be. *GBh* and *Jayamaṅgalā* read *svasthaḥ* ('self-abiding') whereas *STV* has *susthaḥ* ('well-placed'). I have here followed the *TK* and *YD* with *svacchaḥ*.

27 An extra kārikā that appears in Māṭhara's commentary reads: 'Thus the content of this condensed exposition (*śāstra*) is not deficient, and is like an image of the great body of teachings (*tantra*) reflected in a mirror' (*tasmāt samāsadṛṣṭaṃ śāstram idaṃ nārthataś ca parihīnam / tantrasya ca bṛhanmūrter darpaṇasaṃkrāntam iva bimbam // 73 //*).

BIBLIOGRAPHY

Primary sources

(A) Editions and translations of the Sāṃkhyākarikā *and* Yogasūtra *and their respective commentaries*

Sāṃkhyakārikā *and its commentaries*

Colebrooke, H. T. (trans.) and Wilson, H. H. (ed. and trans.) (1837) *The Sānkhya Kārikā by Īsvara Krishna with the Bhāshya or Commentary of Gaurapāda* [*sic*], Oxford: Valpy.

Davies, J. (1894) *Hindū Philosophy: The Sānkhya Kārikā of Īśwara Kṛishṇa*, 2nd edn, London: Kegan Paul, Trench, Trübner.

Jhâ, G. (trans.) (1896) *Tattva-kaumudī of Vâcaspati Miśra*, Bombay: Tookaram Tatya.

Kumar, S. and Bhargava, D. N. (trans.) (1990) *Yuktidīpikā*, 2 vols, Delhi: Eastern Book Linkers.

Larson, G. J. (trans.) (1979) 'The *Sāmkhyakārikā* of Īśvarakṛṣṇa', in *Classical Sāṃkhya: An Interpretation of its History and Meaning*, 2nd edn, Delhi: Motilal Banarsidass, Appendix B, pp. 255–77.

Mainkar, T. G. (trans.) (1972) *Sāṁkhyakārikā of Īśvarakṛṣṇa, with the Commentary of Gauḍapāda*, 2nd edn, Poona: Oriental Book Agency.

Pandeya, R. C. (ed.) (1967) *Yuktidīpikā: An Ancient Commentary on the Sāṃkhya-Kārikās of Īśvarakṛṣṇa*, Delhi: Motilal Banarsidass.

Śarmā, H. (ed.) (1926) *Jayamaṅgalā: Śrīśaṅkarācāryaviracitā jayamaṅgalā nāma sāṃkhyasaptatiṭīkā*, Calcutta: Law.

Solomon, E. A. (ed.) (1973a) *Sāṃkhya-Saptati-Vṛtti*, Ahmedabad: Gujarat University.

—— (ed.) (1973b) *Sāṃkhya-Vṛtti*, Ahmedabad: Gujarat University.

Srinivasan, S. A. (ed.) (1967) *Vācaspatimiśra's Tattvakaumudī*, Hamburg: Cram, De Gruyter and Co.

Suryanarayana Sastri, S. S. (ed. and trans.) (1948) *The Sāṅkhyakārikā of Īśvara Kṛṣṇa*, 3rd edn, Chennai: University of Madras.

Vaṅgīya, Śrī S. (ed.) (1970) *Sāṃkhyakārikā of Śrimad Īśvarakṛṣṇa with the Māṭharavṛtti of Māṭharācārya and the Jayamaṅgalā of Śrī Śaṅkara*, Varanasi: Chowkhamba.

Wetzler, A. and Motegi, S. (eds) (1998) *Yuktidīpikā: The Most Significant Commentary on the Sāṃkhyakārikā*, critical edn, vol. 1, Stuttgart: Steiner.

Yogasūtra *and its commentaries*

Āraṇya, Swāmī H. (1963) *Yoga Philosophy of Patañjali*, trans. P. N. Mukerji, Calcutta: Calcutta University Press.

Arya, Pandit U. [see also Bhāratī, Swāmī V.] (trans.) (1986) *Yoga-sūtras of Patañjali, with the Exposition of Vyāsa: A Translation and Commentary*, vol. 1: 'Samādhi-pāda', Honesdale, PA: Himalayan Institute.

Baba, B. (trans.) (1976) *Yogasūtra of Patañjali, with the Commentary of Vyāsa*, Delhi: Motilal Banarsidass.

Bhāratī, Swāmī V. [see also Arya, Pandit U.] (trans.). 2001. *Yoga Sūtras of Patañjali, with the Exposition of Vyāsa: A Translation and Commentary*, vol. 2: 'Sādhana-pāda', Delhi: Motilal Banarsidass.

Bhattacharya, R. S. (ed.) (1963) *Pātañjalayogadarśana, with the Tattvavaiśāradī and the Commentary of Vyāsa*, Varanasi: Prakāśan.

Chapple, C. and Viraj, Y. A. (trans.) (1990) *The Yoga Sūtras of Patañjali: An Analysis of the Sanskrit with Accompanying English Translation*, Delhi: Sri Satguru.

Feuerstein, G. (trans.) (1989a) *The Yoga-Sūtra of Patañjali: A New Translation and Commentary*, Rochester, VT: Inner Traditions India.

Leggett, T. (trans.) (1992) *Śaṅkara on the Yoga Sūtras: A Full Translation of the Newly Discovered Text*, Delhi: Motilal Banarsidass.

Prasāda, R. (trans.) (1912) *Pātañjali's* [*sic*] *Yoga Sūtras, with the Commentary of Vyāsa and the Gloss of Vāchaspati Miśra*, Allahabad: Panini Office.

Shastri, Dhundiraja (ed.) (1930) *Pātañjalayogadarśana, with the Rājamārtaṇḍa of Bhojarāja, Pradīpikā of Bhāvāgaṇeśa, Vṛtti of Nāgojībhaṭṭa, Maṇiprabhā of Rāmānanda Yati, Padacandrikā of Anantadeva Pandit, and Yogasudhākara of Sadāśivendra Sarasvatī*, Varanasi: Chowkhamba.

Taimni, I. K. (trans.) (1961) *The Science of Yoga: The Yoga-sutras of Patanjali*, Adyar, Chennai: Theosophical Publishing House.

Woods, J. H. (trans.) (1914) *The Yoga System of Patañjali*, Cambridge, MA: Harvard University Press.

(B) Editions and translations of other Sanskrit works

Ahirbudhnyasaṃhitā

Ramanujacharya, M. D. (ed.) (1966) *Ahirbudhnya Saṃhitā*, 2nd edn, revised by V. Krishnamacharya, Adyar, Chennai: Adyar Library and Research Centre.

Arthaśāstra *of Kauṭilya*

Venkatanathacharya, N. S. (ed.) (1960) *Kauṭalīyārthaśāstra of Śrī Viṣṇugupta*, Mysore: Oriental Research Institute.

Aṣṭādhyāyī *of Pāṇini*

Shastri, D. D. and Shukla, K. P. (eds) (1965–67) *Aśṭādhyāyī of Pāṇini with Kāśikā and Padamañjarī of Haradatta*, 6 vols, Varanasi: P. Bharati.

Bhagavadgītā

Edgerton, F. (trans.) (1944) *The Bhagavad Gītā*, 2 vols, Cambridge, MA: Harvard University Press.

Van Buitenen, J. A. B. (ed. and trans.) (1981) *The Bhagavadgītā in the Mahābhārata*, Chicago, IL: University of Chicago Press.

Brahmasūtra *of Bādarāyaṇa and* Brahmasūtrabhāṣya *of Śaṅkara*

http://203.200.95.164/brahmasutra/bsutravav.php3 (accessed several times between November and December 2003).

Gambhirananda, Swami (trans.) (1965) *Brahma-Sūtra-Bhāṣya of Śrī Śaṅkarācārya*, Calcutta: Advaita Ashrama.

Brahmasūtrabhāṣya *of Śaṅkara (see under* Brahmasūtra *above)*

Buddhacarita *of Aśvaghoṣa*

Johnston, E. H. (ed. and trans.) (1972) [1936] *The Buddhacarita, or Acts of the Buddha*, Delhi: Oriental Reprint Corporation.

Carakasaṃhitā

Sharma, R. K. and Dash, V. B. (eds and trans.) (1976) *Agniveśa's Caraka Saṃhitā: Text with English Translation and Critical Exposition Based on Cakrapāṇi Datta's Āyurveda Dīpikā*, 3 vols, Varanasi: Chowkhamba.

Gheraṇḍasaṃhitā

Digambarji, Swami and Gharote, M. L. (eds and trans.) (1997) *Gheraṇḍa Saṁhitā*, 2nd edn, Lonavala, Mumbai: Kaivalyadhama.

Vasu, Śrīś C. (trans.) (1976) *The Gheraṇḍa Saṁhitā*, 3rd edn, London: Theosophical Publishing House.

Haṭhayogapradīpikā *of Svātmārāma*

Iyangar, S. (trans.) (1972) *The Haṭhayogapradīpikā with the Commentary Jyotsnā of Brahmānanda and English Translation*, revised trans. R. Burnier and A. A. Ramanathan, Adyar, Chennai: Adyar Library and Research Centre.

Mahābhārata

Roy, P. C. (trans.) (1972) *The Mahabharata of Krishna-Dwaipayana Vyasa*, 3rd edn, 12 vols, New Delhi: Munshiram Manoharlal.

Smith, John: http://bombay.oriental.cam.ac.uk/john/mahabharata/statement.html (accessed several times during November 2003).

Sukthankar, V. S., Belvalkar, S. K. and Vaidya, P. L. (eds) (1933–72) *The Mahābhārata*, critical edn, 19 vols, Poona: Bhandarkar Oriental Research Institute.

Mahābhāṣya *of Patañjali* (*see* Vyākaraṇamahābhāṣya)

Manusmṛti

Doniger, W. and Smith, B. K. (trans.) (1991) *The Laws of Manu, with an Introduction and Notes*, New York: Penguin.

Shastri, J. L. (ed.) (1983) *Manusmṛti, with the Sanskrit Commentary Manvartha-Muktāvalī of Kullūka Bhaṭṭa*, Delhi: Motilal Banarsidass.

Purāṇas

Dimmitt, C. and Van Buitenen, J. A. B. (eds and trans.) (1978) *Classical Hindu Mythology: A Reader in the Sanskrit Purāṇas*, Philadelphia: Temple University Press.

Gupta, A. S. (ed.) (1972) *Kūrma Purāṇa*, trans. A. Bhattacharya *et al.*, Varanasi: All India Kashi Raj Trust.

Pargiter, F. E. (trans.) (1969) [1904] *Mārkaṇḍeya Purāṇa*, Delhi: Indological Bookhouse.

Tagore, G. V. (trans.) (1987–88) *Vāyu Purāṇa*, 2 vols, Delhi: Motilal Banarsidass.

Upreti, T. C. (ed.) (1986) *Viṣṇupurāṇa, with Sanskrit Commentary of Śrīdharācārya*, 2 vols, Delhi: Parimal.

Pūrvamīmāṃsāsūtra *of Jaimini*

Jhâ, G. (trans.) (1933–36) *Śabara-Bhāṣya*, 3 vols, Baroda: Oriental Institute.

Sāṃkhyasūtra *of Kapila and its commentaries*

Ballantyne, J. R. (trans.) (1885) *The Sánkhya Aphorisms of Kapila, with Illustrative Extracts from the Commentaries*, ed. F. E. Hall, 3rd edn, London: Trübner & Co.

Garbe, R. (ed. and trans.) (1888) *The Sāṃkhya Sūtra Vṛtti, or Aniruddha's Commentary and the Original Parts of Vedāntin Mahādeva's Commentary to the Sāṃkhya Sūtras*, Calcutta: Thomas.

—— (ed.) (1895) *The Sāṃkhya-pravacana-bhāṣya, or Commentary on the Exposition of the Sāṃkhya Philosophy by Vijñānabhikṣu*, Cambridge, MA: Harvard University Press.

Sāṃkhyasūtra *of Pañcaśikha*

Āraṇya, Swāmī H. (1977) *The Sāṁkhya-sūtras of Pañcaśikha and the Sāṁkhyatattvāloka*, ed. and trans. J. Ghosh, Delhi: Motilal Banarsidass.

Sarvadarśanasaṃgraha

Cowell, E. B. and Gough, A. E. (trans.) (1882) *The Sarva-Darśana-Saṃgraha, or: Review of the Different Systems of Hindu Philosophy, by Mádhava Áchárya*, London: Trübner.

Śivasaṃhitā

Vasu, R. B. S. C. (trans.) (1996) *The Siva Samhita*, New Delhi: Munshiram Manoharlal.

Sphoṭavāda *of Nāgeśabhaṭṭa*

Krishnamacharya, V. V. (ed.) (1956) *Sphoṭavāda of Nāgeśa Bhaṭṭa*, Chennai: Theosophical Society.

Suśrutasaṃhitā

Bhishagratna, K. K. (ed. and trans.) (1963) *The Sushruta Samhita*, 3 vols, Varanasi: Chowkhamba.

Tattvārthādhigamasūtra

Umāsvāti Ācārya, Śrī (1920) *Tattvārthādhigama Sūtra*, trans. J. L. Jaini, Arrah, Bihar, India: Central Jaina Publishing House.

Tattvasamāsasūtra *and its commentaries*

Arya, Pandit U. (trans.) (1986) *Tattvasamāsasūtra*, in *Yoga-sūtras of Patañjali, with the Exposition of Vyāsa: A Translation and Commentary*, vol. 1: 'Samādhi-pāda', Honesdale, PA: Himalayan Institute, pp. 41–47.
Dvivedi, V. P. (ed.) (1969) *Sāṃkhyasaṅgraha*, Varanasi: Chowkhamba.

Upaniṣads

Nikhilānanda, Swāmī (trans.) (1944) *The Māṇḍūkyopanishad, with Gauḍapāda's Kārikā and Śankara's Commentary*, 2nd edn, Mysore: Śri Rāmakrishna Āśrama.
Radhakrishnan, S. (trans.) (1978) *The Principal Upaniṣads*, London: George Allen & Unwin.

Vaiśeṣikasūtra *of Kaṇāda*

Sinha, N. (trans.) (1923) *The Vaiśeṣika Sūtras of Kaṇāda*, 2nd edn, Allahabad: Panini Office.

Vyākaraṇamahābhāṣya *of Patañjali*

Joshi, S. D. (ed.) (1968) *Vyākaraṇa-Mahābhāṣya of Patañjali*, Poona: University of Poona.

Secondary sources

Allison, H. (1983) *Kant's Transcendental Idealism: An Interpretation and Defense*, New Haven, CT: Yale University Press.
—— (1996) *Idealism and Freedom*, Cambridge: Cambridge University Press.

Alston, W. P. (2002) 'Introduction', in W. P. Alston (ed.) *Realism and Antirealism*, Ithaca, NY: Cornell University Press, pp. 1–9.

Āquila, R. E. (1982) 'Is Sensation the Matter of Appearances?', in M. S. Gram (ed.) *Interpreting Kant*, Iowa City, IO: University of Iowa Press, pp. 11–29.

Āraṇya, Swāmī H. (1977) 'Introduction', in Ghosh, J. (ed.) *The Sāṁkhya-sūtras of Pañcaśikha and the Sāṁkhyatattvāloka*, Delhi: Motilal Banarsidass, pp. 1–86.

Aristotle (1941) *The Basic Works of Aristotle*, ed. R. McKeon, New York: Random House.

—— (1987) *A New Aristotle Reader*, ed. J. L. Ackrill, Oxford: Clarendon Press.

Bell, David (1990) *Husserl, The Arguments of the Philosophers Series*, London: Routledge.

Berkeley, G. (1962) *'The Principles of Human Knowledge' and 'Three Dialogues Between Hylas and Philonous'*, ed. G. J. Warnock, Glasgow: Fontana.

Bernard, T. (1989) *Hindu Philosophy*, Mumbai: Jaico.

Bharati, A. (1965) *The Tantric Tradition*, London: Rider.

Bhattacharyya, K. C. (1956) *Studies in Philosophy*, ed. G. Bhattacharyya, 2 vols, Calcutta: Progressive Publishers.

Bird, G. (1986) *William James*, London: Routledge & Kegan Paul.

Block, N. (1995) 'Functionalism', in J. Kim and E. Sosa (eds) *A Companion to Metaphysics*, Oxford: Blackwell, pp. 188–94.

Bradley, F. H. (1914) *Essays on Truth and Reality*, Oxford: Clarendon Press.

—— (1969) *Appearance and Reality: A Metaphysical Essay*, 2nd edn, London: Oxford University Press.

Brentano, F. (1973) [1874] *Psychology from an Empirical Standpoint*, ed. O. Kraus, Eng. edn, ed. L. L. McAlister, trans. A. C. Rancurello, D. B. Terrell and L. L. McAlister, London: Routledge & Kegan Paul.

Brockington, J. (2003) 'Yoga in the *Mahābhārata*', in I. Whicher and D. Carpenter (eds) *Yoga: The Indian Tradition*, London: RoutledgeCurzon, pp. 13–24.

Burley, M. (2000) *Haṭha-Yoga: Its Context, Theory and Practice*, Delhi: Motilal Banarsidass.

—— (2004) ' "Aloneness" and the Problem of Realism in Classical Sāṃkhya and Yoga', *Asian Philosophy*, 14(3): 223–38.

Catalina, F. V. (1968) *A Study of the Self Concept of Sāṅkhya–Yoga Philosophy*, Delhi: Munshiram Manoharlal.

Chakravarti, P. (1975) *Origin and Development of the Sāṃkhya System of Thought*, 2nd edn, New Delhi: Oriental Books Reprint Corporation.

Chapple, C. (1996) 'Living Liberation in Sāṃkhya and Yoga', in A. O. Fort and P. Y. Mumme (eds) *Living Liberation in Hindu Thought*, Albany, NY: State University of New York Press, pp. 115–34.

Chatterjee, A. K. (1975) *The Yogācāra Idealism*, 2nd edn, Delhi: Motilal Banarsidass.

Chattopadhyaya, D. (1968) *Lokāyata: A Study in Ancient Indian Materialism*, 2nd edn, New Delhi: People's Publishing House.

Chennakesavan, S. (1980) *The Concept of Mind in Indian Philosophy*, Delhi: Motilal Banarsidass.

Chisholm, R. M. (1981) 'Introduction to the Theory of Categories', in F. Brentano, *The Theory of Categories*, trans. R. M. Chisholm and N. Guterman, The Hague: Nijhoff, pp. 1–11.

Colebrooke, H. T. (1873) [1837] *Miscellaneous Essays*, 3 vols, London: Trübner.

Conze, E. (1967) *Thirty Years of Buddhist Studies*, Oxford: Cassirer.

Dasgupta, S. (1920) *A Study of Patañjali*, Calcutta: Calcutta University Press.
—— (1922) *A History of Indian Philosophy*, vol. 1, Cambridge: Cambridge University Press.
—— (1924) *Yoga as Philosophy and Religion*, London: Kegan Paul, Trench, Trübner & Co.
—— (1930) *Yoga Philosophy in Relation to Other Systems of Indian Thought*, Calcutta: Calcutta University Press.
—— (1940) *A History of Indian Philosophy*, vol. 3, Cambridge: Cambridge University Press.
Dennett, D. C. (1991) *Consciousness Explained*, London: Penguin.
Descartes, R. (1970) *Meditations on First Philosophy*, in *Descartes: Philosophical Writings*, ed. and trans. E. Anscombe and P. Geach, London: Nelson's University Paperbacks, pp. 59–124.
—— (1985) *The Philosophical Writings of Descartes*, trans. J. Cottingham, Robert Stoothoff, and Dugald Murdoch, 2 vols, Cambridge: Cambridge University Press.
Deussen, P. (1919) *The Philosophy of the Upanishads*, trans. A. S. Geden, London: Clark.
Dewey, J. (1886) *Psychology*, 3rd edn, New York: Harper.
Digambarji, Swami, Sahai, M. and Gharote, M. L. (1989) *Glossary of the Sāṅkhyakārikā*, Lonavala, Mumbai: Kaivalyadhama.
Edgerton, F. (1924) 'The Meaning of Sānkhya and Yoga', *American Journal of Philology*, 45(1): 1–46.
—— (ed. and trans.) (1965) *The Beginnings of Indian Philosophy: Selections from the Rig Veda, Atharva Veda, Upaniṣads, and Mahābhārata*, London: George Allen & Unwin.
Edie, J. M. (1987) *Edmund Husserl's Phenomenology: A Critical Commentary*, Bloomington, IN: Indiana University Press.
Eliade, M. (1969) *Yoga: Immortality and Freedom*, trans. W. R. Trask, Princeton, NJ: Princeton University Press.
Eriugena, J. S. (1976) *Periphyseon: On the Division of Nature*, ed. and trans. M. L. Uhlfelder, with summaries by J. A. Potter, Indianapolis, IN: Bobbs-Merrill.
Feuerstein, G. (1974) *The Essence of Yoga: A Contribution to the Psychohistory of Indian Civilisation*, London: Rider.
—— (1979) *The Yoga-Sūtra of Patañjali: An Exercise in the Methodology of Textual Analysis*, New Delhi: Arnold-Heinemann.
—— (1980) *The Philosophy of Classical Yoga*, New York: St Martin's Press.
—— (1989b) *Yoga: The Technology of Ecstasy*, Los Angeles, CA: Tarcher.
—— (1998) *The Yoga Tradition: Its History, Literature, Philosophy and Practice*, Prescott, AZ: Hohm Press.
—— (2001) 'Foreword', in Swāmī V. Bhāratī (trans.) *Yoga Sūtras of Patañjali, with the Exposition of Vyāsa: A Translation and Commentary*, vol. 2: 'Sādhana-pāda', Delhi: Motilal Banarsidass, pp. xi–xvii.
Feuerstein, G., Kak, S. and Frawley, D. (1995) *In Search of the Cradle of Civilization: New Light on Ancient India*, Wheaton, IL: Quest Books.
Fichte, J. G. (1970) *Fichte: 'Science of Knowledge (Wissenschaftslehre)', with the First and Second Introductions*, ed. and. trans. P. Heath and J. Lachs, New York: Meredith Corporation.
Forman, R. K. C. (1990) 'Introduction: Mysticism, Constructivism, and Forgetting', in R. K. C. Forman (ed.) *The Problem of Pure Consciousness*, Oxford: Oxford University Press, pp. 3–49.

Forman, R. K. C. (1998) 'Introduction: Mystical Consciousness, the Innate Capacity, and the Perennial Psychology', in R. K. C. Forman (ed.) *The Innate Capacity: Mysticism, Psychology, and Philosophy*, Oxford: Oxford University Press, pp. 3–41.

Frauwallner, E. (1973) *History of Indian Philosophy*, trans. V. M. Bedekar, 2 vols, Delhi: Motilal Banarsidass.

Gallagher, S. (2005) *How the Body Shapes the Mind*, Oxford: Clarendon Press.

Garbe, R. (1899) *The Philosophy of Ancient India*, 2nd edn, Chicago, IL: Open Court.

—— (1917) *Die Sāṃkhya-Philosophie: Eine Darstellung des indischen Rationalismus*, 2nd edn, Leipzig: Haessel.

Gardner, S. (1999) *Kant and the 'Critique of Pure Reason'*, London: Routledge.

Gethin, R. M. (1986) 'The Five *Khandhas*: Their Treatment in the *Nikāyas* and Early Abhidhamma', *Journal of Indian Philosophy*, 14(1): 35–53.

Ghosh, J. (1930) *Sāṃkhya and Modern Thought*, Calcutta: Mitra.

Gopal, L. (2000) *Retrieving Sāṁkhya History: An Ascent from Dawn to Meridian*, New Delhi: DK Printworld.

Guenther, H. V. (1974) *Philosophy and Psychology in the Abhidharma*, 2nd edn, Berkeley, CA: Shambhala.

Guyer, P. (1989) 'The Rehabilitation of Transcendental Idealism?', in E. Schaper and W. Vossenkuhl (eds) *Reading Kant: New Perspectives on Transcendental Arguments and Critical Philosophy*, Oxford: Blackwell, pp. 147–67.

Hacker, P. (1968) 'Śaṅkara der Yogin und Śaṅkara der Advaitin, einige Beobachtungen', *Wiener Zeitschrift für die Kunde Süd- und Ostasiens und Archiv für indische Philosophie*, 12–13: 119–48.

Halbfass, W. (1991) *Tradition and Reflection: Explorations in Indian Thought*, Albany, NY: State University of New York Press.

—— (1992) *On Being and What There Is: Classical Vaiśeṣika and the History of Indian Ontology*, Albany, NY: State University of New York Press.

Hauer, J. W. (1958) *Der Yoga*, Stuttgart: Kohlhammer.

Hegel, G. W. F. (1975) *Hegel's Logic, Being Part One of the 'Encyclopaedia of the Philosophical Sciences'* (1830), trans. W. Wallace, 3rd edn, Oxford: Clarendon Press.

Heidegger, M. (1961) *An Introduction to Metaphysics*, trans. R. Manheim, Garden City, NY: Doubleday-Anchor.

—— (1993) 'Being and Time: Introduction', trans. J. Stambaugh in collaboration with J. G. Gray and D. F. Krell, in D. F. Krell (ed.) *Martin Heidegger: Basic Writings*, revised edn, London: Routledge.

Honderich, T. (ed.) (1995) *The Oxford Companion to Philosophy*, Oxford: Oxford University Press.

Husserl, E. (1931) [1913] *Ideas: General Introduction to Pure Phenomenology*, trans. W. R. Boyce Gibson, London: George Allen & Unwin.

—— (1936) 'Die Krisis der europäischen Wissenschaften und die transzendentale Phänomenologie: Eine Einleitung in die phänomenologische Philosophie', *Philosophia*, 1: 77–176; reprinted 1954, ed. W. Biemel, The Hague: Nijhoff.

—— (1970a) [1900–01] *Logical Investigations*, trans. J. N. Findlay, 2 vols, London: Routledge & Kegan Paul.

—— (1970b) *The Crisis of European Sciences and Transcendental Phenomenology: An Introduction to Phenomenological Philosophy*, trans. D. Carr, Evanston: Northwestern University Press.

—— (1977) [1931] *Cartesian Meditations*, trans. D. Cairns, The Hague: Nijhoff.

—— (1981) ' "Phenomenology," Edmund Husserl's Article for the *Encyclopaedia Britannica* (1927)', rev. trans. R. E. Palmer, in *Husserl: Shorter Works*, P. McCormick and F. A. Elliston (eds) Notre Dame, IN: University of Notre Dame Press, pp. 21–35.

Jacobsen, K. A. (1999) *Prakṛti in Sāṃkhya–Yoga: Material Principle, Religious Experience, Ethical Implications*, New York: Lang.

James, W. (1950) [1890] *The Principles of Psychology*, vol. 1, New York: Dover.

Janaway, C. (1989) *Self and World in Schopenhauer's Philosophy*, Oxford: Clarendon Press.

Johnston, E. H. (1930) 'Some Sāṁkhya and Yoga Conceptions of the *Śvetāśvatara Upaniṣad*', *Journal of the Royal Asiatic Society*, October 1930: 855–78.

—— (1937) *Early Sāṁkhya*, London: Royal Asiatic Society.

Kant, I. (1911) *Kant's gesammelte Schriften*, ed. B. Erdmann, Königlich Preußischen Akademie der Wissenschaften, Band 4, Berlin: Reimer.

—— (1967) *Philosophical Correspondence*, ed. and trans. A. Zweig, Chicago, IL: Chicago University Press.

—— (1992) *The Jäsche Logic*, in *Lectures on Logic*, ed. and trans. J. M. Young, Cambridge: Cambridge University Press, pp. 517–640.

—— (1997) [1783] *'Prolegomena to Any Future Metaphysics', with Selections from the 'Critique of Pure Reason'*, ed. and trans. G. Hatfield, Cambridge: Cambridge University Press.

—— (1998) [1781/87] *The Critique of Pure Reason*, trans. P. Guyer and A. W. Wood, Cambridge: Cambridge University Press.

—— (2004) [1786] *Metaphysical Foundations of Natural Science*, ed. and trans. M. Friedman, Cambridge: Cambridge University Press.

Katz, S. T. (1978) 'Language, Epistemology, and Mysticism', in S. T. Katz (ed.) *Mysticism and Philosophical Analysis*, London: Sheldon Press, pp. 22–74.

Kavi, R. (1927) 'Literary Gleanings: Jayamaṅgalā', *Quarterly Journal of the Andhra Historical Research Society*, October 1927: 133–36.

Kaviraj, G. (1926) 'Introduction', in H. Śarmā (ed.) *Jayamaṅgalā: Śrīśaṅkarācāryaviracitā jayamaṅgalā nāma sāṃkhyasaptatiṭīkā*, Calcutta: Law.

Keith, A. B. (1949) *The Sāṁkhya System: A History of the Sāṁkhya Philosophy*, 2nd edn, Calcutta: YMCA Publishing House.

Killingley, D. (1997) *Beginning Sanskrit: A Practical Course Based on Graded Reading and Exercises*, vol. 2, revised by Dermot Killingley and Siew-Yue Killingley, München: Lincom Europa.

Kim, J. (1984) 'Concepts of Supervenience', *Philosophy and Phenomenological Research*, 45: 153–76.

King, R. (1999) *Indian Philosophy: An Introduction to Hindu and Buddhist Thought*, Edinburgh: Edinburgh University Press.

Kitcher, Patricia (1990) *Kant's Transcendental Psychology*, New York: Oxford University Press.

Kochumuttom, T. A. (1982) *A Buddhist Doctrine of Experience: A New Translation and Interpretation of the Works of Vasubandhu the Yogācārin*, Delhi: Motilal Banarsidass.

Kockelmans, J. J. (1967) *A First Introduction to Husserl's Phenomenology*, Louvain: Duquesne University Press.

Krishna, Daya (1968) 'Is Īśvarakṛṣṇa's *Sāṁkhya-Kārikā* Really Sāṁkhyan?', *Philosophy East and West*, 18(3): 194–204; republished in D. Krishna (1991) *Indian Philosophy: A Counter Perspective*, New Delhi: Oxford University Press, ch. 7.

Lambert, J. H. (1988) *Texte zur Systematologie und zur Theorie der wissenschaftlichen Erkenntnis*, hsg. G. Siegwart, Hamburg: Verlag.

Larson, G. J. (1969) 'Classical Sāṃkhya and the Phenomenological Ontology of Jean-Paul Sartre', *Philosophy East and West*, 19(1): 45–58.

—— (1979) *Classical Sāṃkhya: An Interpretation of its History and Meaning*, 2nd edn, Delhi: Motilal Banarsidass.

—— (1980) 'Karma as a "Sociology of Knowledge" or "Social Psychology" of Process/Praxis', in W. Doniger O'Flaherty (ed.) *Karma and Rebirth in Classical Indian Traditions*, Berkeley, CA: University of California Press, pp. 303–16.

—— (1987) 'Introduction to the Philosophy of Sāṃkhya', in Larson and Bhattacharya (eds) *Sāṃkhya: A Dualist Tradition in Indian Philosophy*, Delhi: Motilal Banarsidass, pp. 1–103.

—— (1999) 'On *The Integrity of the Yoga Darśana*: A Review', *International Journal of Hindu Studies*, 3(2): 183–86.

Larson, G. J. and Bhattacharya, R. (eds) (1987) *Sāṃkhya: A Dualist Tradition in Indian Philosophy*, Encyclopedia of Indian Philosophies, vol. 4, Delhi: Motilal Banarsidass.

Lipner, J. (1994) *Hindus: Their Religious Beliefs and Practices*, London: Routledge.

Locke, J. (1975) [1690] *An Essay Concerning Human Understanding*, ed. P. H. Nidditch, Oxford: Clarendon Press.

Lusthaus, D. (1998) 'Sāṅkhya', in E. Craig (ed.) *Routledge Encyclopedia of Philosophy*, 10 vols, London: Routledge, vol. 8: 461–67.

—— (2002) *Buddhist Phenomenology: A Philosophical Investigation of Yogācāra Buddhism and the 'Ch'eng Wei-shih lun'*, London: Routledge.

Macdonnell, A. A. (1900) *A History of Sanskrit Literature*, London: Heinemann.

McKeon, R. (ed.) (1941) *The Basic Works of Aristotle*, New York: Random House.

McMullin, E. (ed.) (1963) *The Concept of Matter in Greek and Medieval Philosophy*, Notre Dame, IN: University of Notre Dame Press.

Maitra S. K. (1963) 'Sāṃkhya Realism: A Comparative and Critical Study', in K. Bhattacharyya (ed.) *Recent Indian Philosophy*, Calcutta: Progressive Publishers, pp. 130–43.

Matilal, B. K. (1985) *Logic, Language and Reality: An Introduction to Indian Philosophical Studies*, Delhi: Motilal Banarsidass.

Mayeda, S. (1979) *A Thousand Teachings*, Tokyo: Tokyo University Press.

Mohanty, J. N. (1993) *Essays on Indian Philosophy, Traditional and Modern*, ed. P. Bilimoria, Delhi: Oxford University Press.

—— (1995) 'The Development of Husserl's Thought', in B. Smith and D. Woodruff Smith (eds) *The Cambridge Companion to Husserl*, Cambridge: Cambridge University Press, pp. 45–77.

—— (2001) *Explorations in Philosophy*, vol. 1: 'Indian Philosophy', ed. B. Gupta, Oxford: Oxford University Press.

Monier-Williams, M. (1963) *A Sanskrit–English Dictionary*, Delhi: Motilal Banarsidass. [Originally published by Oxford University Press, 1899.]

Moran, D. (1989) *The Philosophy of John Scottus Eriugena: A Study of Idealism in the Middle Ages*, Cambridge: Cambridge University Press.

Muller-Ortega, P. E. (1989) *The Triadic Heart of Śiva: Kaula Tantricism of Abhinavagupta in the Non-Dual Shaivism of Kashmir*, Albany, NY: State University of New York Press.

Murti, T. R. V. (1960) *The Central Philosophy of Buddhism: A Study of the Mādhyamika System*, 2nd edn, London: George Allen & Unwin.

—— (1975) 'Foreword', in A. K. Chatterjee, *The Yogācāra Idealism*, 2nd edn, Delhi: Motilal Banarsidass, pp. vii–viii.

Nietzsche, F. (1990) *Beyond Good and Evil*, trans. R. J. Hollingdale, London: Penguin.

Oberhammer, G. (1964) 'Gott, Urbild der emanzipierten Existenz im Yoga des Patañjali', *Zeitschrift für Katholische Theologie*, 86: 197–207.

Organ, T. W. (1975) *Western Approaches to Eastern Philosophy*, Athens, OH: Ohio University Press.

Partridge, E. (1966) *Origins: A Short Etymological Dictionary of Modern English*, 4th edn, London: Routledge.

Paton, H. J. (1936) *Kant's Metaphysic of Experience: A Commentary on the First Half of the 'Kritik der reinen Vernunft'*, 2 vols, London: George Allen & Unwin.

Pflueger, L. W. (1998) 'Discriminating the Innate Capacity: Salvation Mysticism of Classical Sāṃkhya–Yoga', in R. K. C. Forman (ed.) *The Innate Capacity: Mysticism, Psychology, and Philosophy*, Oxford: Oxford University Press, pp. 45–81.

Potter, K. H. (ed.) (1981) 'Introduction to the Philosophy of Advaita Vedānta', in K. H. Potter (ed.) *Advaita Vedānta up to Śaṃkara and His Pupils*, Encyclopedia of Indian Philosophies, vol. 3, Princeton, NJ: Princeton University Press, pp. 1–100.

Quine, W. V. O. (1969) 'Reply to Chomsky', in D. Davidson and J. Hintikka (eds) *Words and Objections: Essays on the Work of W. V. O. Quine*, Dordrecht: Reidel.

Radhakrishnan, S. (1927) *Indian Philosophy*, 2 vols, London: George Allen & Unwin.

Radhakrishnan, S. and C. A. Moore (eds) (1957) *A Sourcebook in Indian Philosophy*, Princeton, NJ: Princeton University Press.

Rāmaswāmī, Śrīvatsa (2000) *Yoga for the Three Stages of Life*, Rochester, VT: Inner Traditions.

Reese, W. L. (1996) 'Sankhya', in *Dictionary of Philosophy and Religion: Eastern and Western Thought*, 2nd edn, Atlantic Highlands, NJ: Humanities Press.

Reid, T. (1941) [1785] *Essays on the Intellectual Powers of Man*, ed. A. D. Woozley, London: Macmillan.

Rorty, R. (1982) *Consequences of Pragmatism*, Minneapolis, MN: University of Minnesota Press.

Ross, D. (1995) *Aristotle*, 6th edn, London: Routledge.

Rousseau, J.-J. (1995) [1763] *Emilius, or: An Essay on Education*, trans. T. Nugent, 2 vols, Bristol: Thoemmes Press.

Rukmani, T. S. (1992) 'The Problem of the Authorship of the *Yogasūtrabhāṣyavivaraṇam*', *Journal of Indian Philosophy*, 20(4): 419–23.

Russell, B. (1917) 'Knowledge by Acquaintance and Knowledge by Description', in *Mysticism and Logic*, London: Allen & Unwin, pp. 152–67.

Safranski, R. (1989) *Schopenhauer and the Wild Years of Philosophy*, trans. E. Osers, London: Weidenfeld and Nicolson.

Sartre, J.-P. (1957) [1937] *The Transcendence of the Ego: An Existentialist Theory of Consciousness*, trans. F. Williams and R. Kirkpatrick, New York: Farrar, Straus and Giroux.

Schopenhauer, A. (1969) [1818] *The World as Will and Representaion*, trans. E. F. J. Payne, 2 vols, New York: Dover.

Schopenhauer, A. (1974a) [1813] *On the Fourfold Root of the Principle of Sufficient Reason*, trans. E. F. J. Payne, La Salle, IL: Open Court.

—— (1974b) [1851] *Parerga and Paralipomena: Short Philosophical Essays*, trans. E. F. J. Payne, 2 vols, Oxford: Clarendon Press.

Searle, J. R. (1983) *Intentionality: An Essay in the Philosophy of Mind*, Cambridge: Cambridge University Press.

Sen, S. K. (1968) 'Time in Sāṁkhya-Yoga', *Indian Philosophical Quarterly*, 8: 407–26.

Sen Gupta, A. (1959) *The Evolution of the Sāṁkhya School of Thought*, Lucknow: Pioneer Press.

—— (1982) *Classical Sāṁkhya: A Critical Study*, 2nd edn, New Delhi: Munshiram Manoharlal.

Sharma, C. D. (1964) *A Critical Survey of Indian Philosophy*, Delhi: Motilal Banarsidass.

Shear, J. and Jevning, R. (1999) 'Pure Consciousness: Scientific Exploration of Meditation Techniques', *Journal of Consciousness Studies*, 6(2–3): 189–209.

Sheets-Johnstone, M. (1998) 'Consciousness: A Natural History', *Journal of Consciousness Studies*, 5(3): 260–94.

Singh, B. (1976) *The Conceptual Framework of Indian Philosophy*, Delhi: Macmillan.

Sinha, B. M. (1983) *Time and Temporality in Sāṁkhya–Yoga and Abhidharma Buddhism*, New Delhi: Munshiram Manoharlal.

Sinha, J. (1958) *Indian Psychology*, vol. 1: 'Cognition', Calcutta: Sinha Publishing House.

Smith, A. D. (1993) 'Non-Reductive Physicalism?', in H. Robinson (ed.) *Objections to Physicalism*, Oxford: Clarendon Press, pp. 225–50.

—— (2003) *Husserl and the 'Cartesian Meditations'*, London: Routledge.

Solomon, E. A. (1974) *The Commentaries of the Sāṃkhya Kārikā: A Study*, Ahmedabad: Gujarat University.

Spiegelberg, H. (1960) *The Phenomenological Movement: A Historical Introduction*, 2 vols, The Hague: Nijhoff.

Sprigge, T. L. S. (1983) *The Vindication of Absolute Idealism*, Edinburgh: Edinburgh University Press.

Staal, F. (1975) *Exploring Mysticism: A Methodological Essay*, Berkeley, CA: University of California Press.

Takakuso, M. J. (1933) [1904] *The Sāṃkhya Kārikā Studied in the Light of its Chinese Version*, trans. (from the French) S. S. Suryanarayana Sastri, Chennai: Diocesan Press.

Twardowski, Kazimierz (1977) [1894] *On the Content and Object of Presentations*, trans. R. Grossmann, The Hague: Nijhoff.

Van Buitenen, J. A. B. (1956) 'Studies in Sāṃkhya (I)', *Journal of the American Oriental Society*, 76: 153–57.

—— (1957a) 'Studies in Sāṃkhya (II)', *Journal of the American Oriental Society*, 77: 15–25.

—— (1957b) 'Studies in Sāṃkhya (III)', *Journal of the American Oriental Society*, 77: 88–107.

—— (1988) *Studies in Indian Literature and Philosophy: Collected Articles of J. A. B. van Buitenen*, ed. L. Rocher, Delhi: Motilal Banarsidass.

Wallace, B. A. (1998) *The Bridge of Quiescence: Experiencing Tibetan Buddhist Meditation*, Chicago, IL: Open Court.

Warren, H. C. (1915) *Buddhism in Translations: Passages Selected from the Buddhist Sacred Books and Translated from the Original Pāli into English*, Cambridge, MA: Harvard University Press.

Webster's Third New International Dictionary of the English Language (1971) 16th edn, 3 vols, Chicago, IL: Hemingway Benton.

Whicher, I. (1995) 'Cessation and Integration in Classical Yoga', *Asian Philosophy*, 5(1): 47–58; also in B. Carr (ed.) (1996) *Morals and Society in Asian Philosophy*, Richmond: Curzon Press, pp. 92–108.

—— (1997) 'Nirodha, Yoga Praxis and the Transformation of the Mind', *Journal of Indian Philosophy*, 25(1): 1–67.

—— (1998) *The Integrity of the Yoga Darśana: A Reconsideration of Classical Yoga*, Albany, NY: State University of New York Press.

—— (2003) 'The Integration of Spirit (*puruṣa*) and Matter (*prakṛti*) in the *Yoga Sūtra*', in I. Whicher and D. Carpenter (eds) *Yoga: The Indian Tradition*, London: RoutledgeCurzon, pp. 51–69.

Whicher, I. and Carpenter, D. (eds) (2003) *Yoga: The Indian Tradition*, London: RoutledgeCurzon.

White, D. G. (1996) *The Alchemical Body: Siddha Traditions in Medieval India*, Chicago, IL: University of Chicago Press.

Wittgenstein, L. (1974) [1921] *Tractatus Logico-Philosophicus*, trans. D. F. Pears and B. F. McGuinness, London: Routledge.

—— (2001) [1953] *Philosophical Investigations*, trans. G. E. M. Anscombe, 3rd edn, Oxford: Blackwell.

Wood, T. E. (1991) *Mind Only: A Philosophical and Doctrinal Analysis of the Vijñānavāda*, Honolulu, HI: University of Hawaii Press.

Wright, C. (1993) *Realism, Meaning and Truth*, 2nd edn, Oxford: Blackwell.

Zimmer, H. R. (1953) *Philosophies of India*, ed. J. Campbell, Princeton, NJ: Princeton University Press.

INDEX

abhāva (non-being) 93, 142, 145
Abhidharma *see* Buddhism
abhimāna 70, 115, 198; *see also ahaṃkāra*
Abhinavagupta 32
abhyāsa (practice) 13, 20, 47, 131, 161
action, activity *see karman*; *kriyā*
adhyavasāya (discernment) 114, 194, 197; *see also buddhi*
Ādiśeṣa 26
advaita (nonduality) 32, 35, 147; *see also* monism; Vedānta, Advaita
ahaṃkāra (egoity) 16–17, 24, 53–54, 70, 81, 84, 89, 91, 92, 99, 108–09, 111–12, 115–16, 118–19, 122, 125–28, 129, 157, 180, 192, 194, 198, 199, 204
Ahirbudhnya-saṃhitā 21–22, 27–28
aiśvarya (masterfulness) 20, 114, 201; *see also abhyāsa*; *īśvara*
ajñāna (ignorance) 145; *see also avidyā*; *viparyaya*
ākāśa (space) 70, 100, 104, 123–24, 180, 199; *see also diś*; space
Al-Bīrūnī 30, 190
aliṅga (unmarked) 53–54, 89, 121, 137, 199
aloneness *see kaivalya*
anādi (beginningless) 161
ānanda (intense pleasure) 116, 180, 200
ananta (unending) 26
Anantadeva 31
anātman (not-self) 131
Aniruddha 34, 35, 104–05
anitya (non-eternal) 94, 105, 195; *see also* time
antaḥkaraṇa (inner instrument) 53, 89, 114, 118, 204
antirealism 72, 76, 77; *see also* idealism
anugraha (grace) 32–33
ānvīkṣikī (philosophical inquiry) 20; *see also darśana*(s)
ap, *āpas* (water, liquidity) 16, 123–24, 128, 180
apavarga (liberation) 78, 101, 142, 191; *see also kaivalya*; *mokṣa*
apperception, unity of 61, 70
Aquila, Richard 196
Āraṇya, Swāmī Hariharānanda 10, 31, 140, 195, 201
Āraṇyakas (forest texts) 38, 188, 190
Aristotle, Aristotelianism 60, 99–100, 196
artha: as meaning 28, 49, 190; object 17, 84, 189; purpose/sake 51, 52, 133, 134, 142
arthamātra 130
Arthaśāstra (Kauṭilya) 20–21
Arya, Pandit Usharbudh *see* Bhāratī, Swāmī Veda
asat (unreal) 80
asceticism *see* renunciation
asmitā (I-am-ness) 70, 192, 200; *see also ahaṃkāra*
Aṣṭādhyāyī (Pāṇini) 26
aṣṭāṅga (eight-limbed) 18, 33
āstika (orthodox) 2
Āsuri 36, 51, 178, 188
atheism 39, 41, 51
ātmāmahat (great self) 17
ātman: essence 83; *śānta-* 17; self 2, 147–48, 153, 190
avibhāga (non-difference) 33
avidyā (misperception) 50, 125, 140, 142, 144–46, 201
avikṛti (uncreated) 92
aviśeṣa (non-specific) 53–54, 89, 127
avyakta (unmanifest) 17, 53, 74, 94, 104, 112, 141, 204; *see also prakṛti*
avyāpin (non-pervasive) 94, 105, 195
Āyurveda 20, 26, 34, 190

bāhya(*-karaṇa*) (outer instrument) 118
Baladevamiśra 31
Bell, David 192
Berkeley, George 85, 203
Bhagavadgītā 3, 17, 18, 19–20, 31, 34, 153, 189
Bhāgavata *see* Pāñcarātra
bhakti (devotion) 30

Made in the USA
Coppell, TX
31 October 2020

40549252R10136